John R. Boatright

MEANING AND ARGUMENT: ELEMENTS OF LOGIC

Other books by Robert G. Olson:

AN INTRODUCTION TO EXISTENTIALISM
THE MORALITY OF SELF-INTEREST
A SHORT INTRODUCTION TO PHILOSOPHY

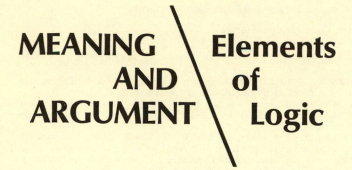

MEANING AND ARGUMENT

Elements of Logic

ROBERT G. OLSON

University College of Rutgers University

 Harcourt, Brace & World, Inc.

New York / Chicago / San Francisco / Atlanta

Library of Congress Catalog Card Number: 71–79483

Printed in the United States of America

ACKNOWLEDGMENTS

GEORGE ALLEN & UNWIN LTD.—For excerpts from R. S. Peters, *Ethics and Education*. Reprinted by permission of George Allen & Unwin Ltd.

ATHENEUM PUBLISHERS—For excerpts from *African Genesis*, by Robert Ardrey. Copyright © 1961 by Literat S.A. Reprinted by permission of Atheneum Publishers.

GEOFFREY BLES LTD.—For excerpts from C. S. Lewis, *Mere Christianity*.

BRANDT & BRANDT—For excerpts from Neil Staebler and Douglas Ross, *How to Argue with a Conservative*. Reprinted by permission of Brandt & Brandt; originally published by Grossman Publishers, Inc.

BRILL TESTAMENTARY TRUST—For excerpt from *Psychoanalysis: Its Theories and Practical Application*, 2nd ed., rev. 1918 by A.A. Brill, M.D. Copyright 1914 by W.B. Saunders Co. Copyright renewed 1942 by A.A. Brill. Reprinted by permission of Gioia Bernheim and Edmund Brill.

CAMBRIDGE UNIVERSITY PRESS—For excerpt from Sir Arthur Eddington, *The Nature of the Physical World*, and for excerpt from Robert H. Thouless, *An Introduction to the Psychology of Religion*.

JONATHAN CAPE LTD.—For excerpts from C. A. R. Crosland, *The Future of Socialism*. Reprinted by permission of Jonathan Cape Ltd.

COLLINS, PUBLISHERS—For excerpts from Robert Ardrey, *African Genesis*. Reprinted by permission of Collins, Publishers.

COWARD-MCCANN, INC.—For excerpts from Gay Gaer Luce and Julius Segal, *Sleep*. Reprinted by permission of Coward-McCann, Inc. Copyright © 1966 by Gay Gaer Luce and Julius Segal.

GROSSMAN PUBLISHERS, INC.—For excerpts from Neil Staebler and Douglas Ross, *How to Argue with a Conservative*. Originally published by Grossman Publishers, Inc., and reprinted with their permission.

HARCOURT, BRACE & WORLD, INC.—For excerpts from Harry M. Johnson, *Sociology: A Systematic Introduction*, © 1960 by Harcourt, Brace & World, Inc., and reprinted with their permission.

WILLIAM HEINEMANN LTD.—For excerpts from Gay Gaer Luce and Julius Segal, *Sleep*. Reprinted by permission of William Heinemann Ltd.

HOUGHTON MIFFLIN COMPANY—For excerpts from Harold A. Larrabee, *Reliable Knowledge: Scientific Methods in the Social Studies*.

THE MACMILLAN COMPANY—For excerpts from C. S. Lewis, *Mere Christianity*.

THE NEW REPUBLIC—For excerpt from Rudolph Von Abele, "Napalm." Reprinted by permission of *The New Republic*, © 1967, Harrison-Blaine of New Jersey, Inc.

NEW YORK POST—For excerpt from Seymour Posner, Letter to the Editor, *New York Post*. Reprinted by permission of Seymour Posner, Assemblyman, State of New York, and the *New York Post*; © 1967, New York Post Corporation. For excerpt from James Wechsler, "In Birchland." Reprinted by permission of the *New York Post*, © 1965, New York Post Corporation.

THE NEW YORK REVIEW OF BOOKS—For excerpt from C. H. Waddington, "That's Life." Reprinted with permission from *The New York Review of Books*. Copyright © 1968, The New York Review.

(*Acknowledgments continue on p. 382*)

Preface

Meaning and Argument: Elements of Logic was written in the conviction that the purpose of an elementary logic course is to give students maximum possible help in understanding and evaluating the kinds of arguments they most commonly encounter in ordinary discourse. In deciding what topics should be included and how they should be treated my final criterion was always practical relevance to the student. The result is a book which, though generally standard in its presentation of symbolic logic, differs significantly from other logic texts. The chief differences are as follows:

1. The first half of the book, "Meaning," is devoted to language, definition, and symbolization, for the problems students confront in analyzing arguments are due at least as often to linguistic confusion as to errors of inference.

2. The second half of the book, "Argument," stresses criteria for evaluating the soundness, as opposed to merely the formal validity, of arguments. This emphasis is dictated by the fact that most arguments in ordinary discourse are nondeductive, and even when an argument is deductive practical problems of evaluation are likely to center on questions other than its validity.

3. Most of the exercises, as well as the illustrations in the text itself, deal with controversial issues of contemporary interest, since arguments generally arise in the context of controversy or interest us primarily because of their controversial implications. Moreover, I have found that students work far harder in analyzing

arguments that raise issues of genuine human concern than in analyzing arguments that are without practical relevance.

Some instructors may find that there is more material in *Meaning and Argument* than they wish to cover in a single semester. If so, I suggest one of the following plans: (1) Assign Chapters I, VIII, XV, and XVI, which are relatively undemanding, for independent reading. (2) Omit all or most of Chapters X and XI. The omission of these chapters will not impair the students' grasp of the material in later chapters.

This book has greatly benefited from the generosity and critical acumen of the following persons, who read all or part of the manuscript versions: Raziel Abelson, William P. Alston, Gail Belaief, Albert E. Blumberg, Justus Buchler, Gertrude Ezorsky, David Lilien, and Rudolph H. Weingartner. Their many suggestions, like those of two anonymous readers for the publisher, were invaluable in preparing the final draft. I have not, however, always followed their advice and must personally assume full responsibility for all errors and inadequacies.

I should also like to express my gratitude to W. K. Frankena and the late Paul Henle, whose *Exercises in Elementary Logic* was a useful reference in selecting a number of excerpts appearing in this book.

ROBERT G. OLSON

Contents

Part One · M E A N I N G

Part Two · A R G U M E N T

General Introduction

The purpose of *Meaning and Argument: Elements of Logic* is to provide practical help in understanding and evaluating arguments. It must be understood, however, that in logic the word 'argument' does not mean, as it sometimes does in ordinary discourse, a disagreement or a debate.* In logic an *argument* refers to a group of statements consisting of a *conclusion*, the statement the argument is alleged to establish, and one or more *premises*, statements the arguer offers as evidence for the conclusion. If, for example, someone says "Jones must earn a good income because he is a doctor and all doctors earn good incomes," he is arguing. The conclusion is 'Jones earns a good income,' since this is clearly the statement the arguer wishes to establish. The premises are 'Jones is a doctor' and 'All doctors earn good incomes,' since these are clearly offered as evidence for the conclusion.

A good, or acceptable, argument must satisfy three conditions: (1) Its components must be clearly expressed. (2) Its premises must give evidence for its conclusion. (3) There must be reason to believe that its premises are true. If at first sight an argument

---

*When a word or other linguistic expression appears in single quotes, we are referring to the expression itself rather than to that for which it ordinarily stands (for example: 'Cat' is a three-letter word). Double quotes are used to enclose citations, imaginary dialogue (for example: Suppose somebody says "Close the door, please"), and expressions used in an unusual or questionable way (for example: He made every effort to tell it "like it was").

1

appears to satisfy these three requirements, it is called *plausible*. If an argument, whether initially plausible or not, actually does satisfy these requirements, it is called *sound*.

Although a sound argument must satisfy all three requirements, logicians are primarily concerned with determining whether the premises do in fact give evidence for the conclusion. Why logicians do not stress questions relating to the truth of the premises will be explained in Chapter Nine. It should be noted here, however, that since we can not decide whether the premises of an argument give evidence for the conclusion unless we understand the meaning of the argument's components, the need for clarity of expression has always received considerable attention from logicians. And in the twentieth century the importance of questions relating to meaning has become increasingly apparent. Accordingly, this text is divided into two roughly equal parts, of which Part One, entitled "Meaning," is essentially a preparation for Part Two, entitled "Argument."

Part

One

MEANING

Introduction to Part One

In the *Meno*, one of Plato's most intriguing dialogues, Socrates
and Meno are inquiring into the nature of virtue.[1] At one point
Meno raises an objection that Socrates summarizes in the following way: "You argue," he says, "that a man cannot inquire
either about that which he knows, or about that which he does
not know; for if he knows, he has no need to inquire; and if not,
he cannot; for he does not know the very subject about which he
is to inquire." [2] This argument, known as Meno's dilemma, arose
in the course of a discussion about virtue, but it could arise
during almost any inquiry. One might say, for instance, that
either you know what a swan is or you do not. If you know what
a swan is, there is no need to inquire. If you do not know what
a swan is, you can not inquire since you are unable to identify
the subject of inquiry.

Meno's dilemma fails to convince. If the argument were sound,
it would be impossible to inquire with profit into anything whatsoever. And it is evident that useful inquiries do often take place.
Nonetheless, the argument is not easy to refute. If the reader
thinks otherwise, let him pause here and try. Even Socrates did
not succeed in giving Meno a satisfactory answer. In fact,

---

[1] Socrates is the first of the great philosophers in the Western tradition.
Plato was his foremost disciple and the author of many dialogues in which
Socrates is the principal character. Socrates was executed by his fellow
Athenians in 399 B.C.

[2] *Plato's Meno*, The Liberal Arts Press, N.Y., 1949, p. 36.

Socrates' answer impresses us today as pure fantasy. It goes like this: The souls that presently inhabit our bodies existed before birth, at which time they saw "all things that are"—particularly the models or patterns after which God created what we see here on earth. Knowing what a swan truly is, therefore, is a matter of recalling the pattern or model after which swans were made—something akin to remembering the temporarily forgotten name of an acquaintance.

Fortunately, philosophy has made progress since Plato's day, and it is no longer necessary to believe in the pre-existence of the soul in order to solve Meno's dilemma. Progress has not been easy, however, and if the reader has attempted to solve Meno's dilemma on his own, he will probably see why. Few of us, unless we have had some training in logic, are equipped to deal with it. The reason is that few of us have taken the trouble to be clear about the meaning of 'to know.' It is a fact worth marking that the terms that give us the greatest difficulty are not technical expressions, but expressions used almost daily by all of us. It is said of persons that familiarity breeds contempt; it may be said of words that familiarity breeds neglect. When an expression has become thoroughly familiar to us, we are lulled into believing that we fully understand it, and we relax our vigilance. It runs away from us, and when we finally catch up with it, if ever we do, we find that it has acquired a dense tangle of meanings which we can succeed in unraveling only by painstaking analysis.

The problem posed by Meno's dilemma is, of course, a theoretical problem, not an urgent practical problem. Also, the conclusion is so patently false that nobody would accept it. Meno's dilemma should, however, alert us to the fact that no argument may be properly assessed if we have not understood the meaning of the terms used to express it.

I • PRELIMINARY REMARKS ABOUT AMBIGUITY AND VAGUENESS

It was said that Meno's dilemma often defeats efforts at rebuttal because of unsuspected difficulties with the verb 'to know.'

knowing how/ that
kennen / wissen

Specifically, the verb 'to know' is *ambiguous*—that is, it has more
than one meaning. In fact, the term has many different meanings.
To illustrate the danger of ambiguity, however, it will suffice to
mention two of these meanings that are particularly relevant to
the analysis of Meno's dilemma. On the one hand, when we say
that we know what something is, we frequently mean merely that
we would be able to recognize it if we saw it. As a rule, this is all
that most of us would mean if we said that we know what a swan
is. On the other hand, we often feel justified in saying that we
know what a thing is only if we can give a formal definition of
the word used to refer to it, enumerating explicitly a set of
properties that belongs to all objects of this kind and that distinguishes them from all others. This would certainly be the case
if we were zoologists or students of zoology and had just been
asked if we knew what a swan is. *This looks more like vagueness?*

Once we are clearly aware of this ambiguity, we will no longer
be willing to accept uncritically the premise in Meno's dilemma
that says we either know or do not know what a thing is. And
once we have seen the ambiguity in this premise, we will reject
the argument. Obviously, if we know what swans are in the sense
of being able to recognize them, we can conduct a useful inquiry.

A second source of confusion, closely related to ambiguity, is
called 'vagueness.' We have just said that an ambiguous term is
one with two or more different meanings. A *vague* term, on the
other hand, refers to a certain range of phenomena without exact
boundaries. Examples are 'bald man' and 'tall man.' In both cases
there are a number of borderline cases to which we do not know
whether the term correctly applies or not. If a man has no hair
at all on his head and if he is six feet three inches in height, we
are clearly justified in calling him 'bald' and 'tall.' But if he has
a hairless pate and a bushy fringe of hair around the sides of his
head and if he is five feet ten or eleven, most of us are unsure
whether the terms 'bald' and 'tall' describe him accurately.

The difference between ambiguity and vagueness can be
highlighted by observing that a statement containing an ambiguous term will often be entirely true if one of that term's
meanings is intended but entirely false if a second is intended.
For example, the statement 'John knows what swans are' may be
entirely true in one sense of 'knows' but completely false in a

second sense. If a statement contains a vague term, however, the interpretation of that term will not ordinarily have so radical a bearing on the truth or falsity of the statement. If John were five feet ten or eleven and someone said of him, "He is tall," we would not ordinarily dismiss the statement as false, but neither would we be wholly satisfied that it is true. We would say rather that the statement is partially true or partially false.

Although ambiguity and vagueness are independent properties of words, many words are both ambiguous and vague. Consider, for instance, the word 'democracy.' The term is no doubt ambiguous, since several clearly distinguishable meanings are currently given to it. For some persons a democracy is a form of government in which the citizens participate directly in the decision-making process; for others a democracy is a form of government in which the citizens have a right to vote for legislators, who alone participate directly in decision making. Again, some persons regard any society in which the people have the right to vote a democracy; whereas others insist that a society is not democratic, even if people have the right to vote, unless any sizeable segment of the population which chooses to do so has the right to form a political party and to run candidates for public office.

In each of these meanings, however, 'democracy' is also vague. If a society is democratic only if citizens directly participate in decision making, to what extent must citizens participate? And if a society is not democratic unless its members have the right to vote for legislators, how many must possess this right? Is a society democratic if only property owners are permitted to vote? If women or minority groups are disenfranchised? If, as in ancient Athens and the United States up to the time of the Civil War, there are many slaves who have been deprived of the right to vote? Again, if the term 'democracy' is used in a sense which requires that any sizeable segment of the population that chooses to do so be permitted to form political parties and to run candidates for political office, how big must that segment of the population be? If a society with a total population of a hundred million refused to permit the formation of a political party upon application from two million petitioners, would it be a democracy?

Still another illustration (many more could be given) is the fact that many persons define a 'democracy' in terms of the rights enjoyed by the individual citizen which the majority, whether directly or through their representatives, can not take away. But what kinds of rights are involved? How many of them must be enjoyed? And to what degree must their exercise be guaranteed? Here as in the case of 'to know' we are confronted by a word constantly on our lips—yet its meaning, partly for that very reason, is far more complex and troublesome than most of us realize.

II • COGNITIVE AND NON-COGNITIVE MEANING

The proper understanding and use of language requires not only an attitude of wariness but also an appreciation of the meaning of 'meaning.' Like the terms 'to know' and 'democracy,' the term 'meaning' is surprisingly ambiguous. In this section we shall consider two of its meanings.

One kind of meaning—which we shall call *non-cognitive meaning*—may be attributed to almost anything. For example, smoke means fire, a rapid pulse means fever, the bombing of Pearl Harbor meant America's entry into World War II. In each of these cases, as in all cases of non-cognitive meaning, that to which meaning is attributed is a *sign* of something else in the sense that it permits us to make a reasonably accurate inference about the nature or existence of some other phenomenon. If we see smoke, we can reasonably infer that somewhere in the neighborhood there is fire. If we know that someone's pulse beat is unusually rapid, we can reasonably infer that he has a fever. When one heard that Pearl Harbor had been bombed, one had reason to infer that the United States would declare war. (Although every sign must give reasonable grounds for some inference, a sign need not conclusively support that inference. Smoke, for example, is not an unfailing indicator of fire, and it was at least logically conceivable that the United States not react to the bombing of Pearl Harbor by declaring war.)

This first sense of 'meaning' is itself ambiguous. We may, for instance, distinguish between the non-cognitive meaning a sign has for us given our actual knowledge and the non-cognitive meaning it would have for us if we were better informed. This distinction is often implicit when someone says that no one will ever know the full meaning of some event. We may also distinguish between the non-cognitive meaning something has for one individual or group given their knowledge and interests, and the non-cognitive meaning it has for a second individual or group whose knowledge and interests are different. This distinction is implicit when someone says that the bombing of Pearl Harbor meant one thing to the Japanese and another to Americans, or that its meaning for the younger generation today is different from what it was for those who were adults in 1941.

Signs are classified as 'natural' or 'artificial.' If a sign (1) is a product or creation of human beings, (2) is used for the purpose of communication, and (3) has acquired its meaning through some kind of convention, agreement, or understanding among its users, it is an *artificial* sign. All other signs—such as smoke or a rapid pulse beat—are *natural* signs. Artificial signs in turn are classified as 'linguistic' or 'non-linguistic.' Words, phrases, and sentences are *linguistic* signs. Maps, traffic signals, and nods of assent are *non-linguistic* signs.

By definition all signs—whether natural or artificial and whether linguistic or non-linguistic—permit us to make inferences. If we see a red light at an intersection we know that there is danger of collision or arrest if we do not stop. If somebody nods in assent, we may reasonably infer that he agrees with something just said. If somebody says "Ouch!" we may infer that he is in pain. If somebody says "Please close the door," we may conclude that he desires the door to be closed. If somebody says "The door is closed," we may infer that he believes the door to be closed. If somebody says simply "door," we may infer that he is alive, that he has vocal cords, that he knows at least one word of English. Also by definition, every sign has non-cognitive meaning. In fact, to say of something that it has non-cognitive meaning is merely another way of saying that it is a sign and therefore permits inferences.

The second sense of 'meaning' to be discussed in this section is called 'cognitive meaning.' This expression has a much narrower application than the term 'non-cognitive meaning.' As pointed out earlier, almost everything has non-cognitive meaning. *Cognitive meaning*, however, applies exclusively to linguistic signs, and even more narrowly to linguistic signs of the following two sorts: (1) whole sentences, such as 'The door is closed,' used to make assertions that may be qualified as true or false, and (2) words or phrases, such as 'the door' and 'is closed,' that may be used to express the cognitive meaning of sentences. Linguistic signs in this second category are technically called *terms*.

Ordinarily, when we talk about the meaning of linguistic signs, we have in mind their cognitive rather than their non-cognitive meaning. If somebody said "door," this would be, as already pointed out, a sign that the speaker is alive, has vocal cords, and knows at least one word of English. But if asked *the* meaning of this utterance, no one would answer by citing such non-cognitive meanings. It must, however, be borne in mind that whereas all linguistic signs have at least some non-cognitive meaning, many have no cognitive meaning at all. Suppose, for example, that someone says "Ouch!" or "Close the door, please." Neither of these sentences expresses a knowledge claim, or makes an assertion that can be called true or false. If someone uttered either of these sentences, no one would think of saying "What you have just said is true" or "What you have just said is false." Their meanings, like the meanings of all artificial signs, depend upon human convention. Nonetheless, they are not essentially different from the meanings of natural signs. 'Ouch!' means pain and 'Close the door, please' means that the speaker wishes the door to be closed in much the same way that smoke means fire. By contrast, the primary meanings of 'I am in pain' and 'The door is closed' are quite unlike those of natural signs, since we can properly ask whether what they express is true or false.

Although 'cognitive meaning' has a much narrower application than 'non-cognitive meaning,' cognitive meaning is a much more important concept for the student of logic. The reason is that arguments must be expressed through language and that only the cognitive meanings of the sentences and terms used to express arguments are directly relevant to their understanding and evaluation. As a matter of fact, our principal reason for discussing non-cognitive meaning is to help the reader avoid certain common pitfalls in reasoning caused by confusing cognitive and non-cognitive meaning. More will be said about these pitfalls in later chapters. The important point here is that to determine whether any linguistic unit has cognitive meaning one must ask: Is it a whole sentence used to express an assertion that may be called 'true' or 'false'? If not, is it a term that may be used in such a sentence? When the answer to either of these questions is affirmative, the linguistic unit has cognitive meaning and may properly figure in an argument. When the answer to both questions is negative, the linguistic unit does not have cognitive meaning and may not properly figure in an argument.

III • FURTHER AMBIGUITIES OF THE WORD 'MEANING'

An important fact about words is that their meanings are determined by communities of human beings. Men did not decide that the natural sign smoke means fire, and it is not within their power to alter this meaning of smoke. Men did, however, in some sense decide that 'chairs' means chairs, and if we decided to use 'chairs' to refer to tables, the term would come to mean tables. This fact is often expressed by saying that linguistic communities are free to give symbols whatever meanings they like. From this it is sometimes inferred that a single person has the same freedom. That is, if one person chooses to use the word 'chairs' to refer to tables, then it means tables, at least when used by that person. Now, in one sense this inference is perfectly correct. But the power of the individual to confer meanings on words is sharply limited by the fact that language is intended to help human beings communicate with one another. Since this purpose would be wholly defeated if every individual were able to confer any meaning he chose on any linguistic symbol, society has adopted safeguards to limit this power of the individual—safeguards reflected in several common meanings of the word 'meaning.'

In order to clarify this situation we must make a three-fold distinction. First, we shall distinguish between the 'intended meaning' of a symbol and its 'interpreted meaning.' The *intended meaning* of a symbol is the meaning which the speaker or writer attributes to it; the *interpreted meaning* is the meaning the auditor or reader believes the symbol to have. In successful communication the two meanings will, of course, coincide. But since communication is not always successful, the distinction has to be made.

Second, we must distinguish between what logicians call 'verbal tokens' and 'verbal types.' Suppose somebody asks you how many words are printed immediately below:

> chair
> chair
> chair

There are two possible answers: "one" or "three." If you answered "one," you would be identifying a verbal type. If you answered "three," you would be identifying verbal tokens. A verbal token is defined as a member of a verbal type; a verbal type, as a class of verbal tokens. It should be noted, however, that the class of symbols constituting a verbal type includes not only physically similar written tokens (in print, in chalk, in pencil, etc.) but also the spoken sounds that are conventionally regarded as the equivalents of those tokens. It should also be noted that an occurrence of a physical configuration such as 'the' in the word 'their' is not a token of the type 'the.' The terms 'verbal type' and 'verbal token' are not used to refer to parts of words.

Third, we must distinguish between conventional meanings and nonconventional meanings. If many tokens of a given type are used with the same intended meaning, this is a *conventional meaning* of the type, and a token with this intended meaning is being used conventionally. If, however, a token has an intended meaning rarely if ever given to other tokens of the same type, this meaning is a *nonconventional meaning* of the type and the token is being used nonconventionally. The terms 'conventional meaning' and 'nonconventional meaning' are, of course, vague; but their vagueness does not rob them of their utility.

With the aid of these distinctions the individual's power to confer meanings on symbols may be stated with some precision. First, the individual has by definition unlimited and absolute control over the intended meaning of any verbal token he employs. Second, the individual has limited power over the interpreted meanings of the tokens he employs. If a token of an unambiguous type is used in its conventional meaning, the speaker can usually expect to be understood. If a token of an ambiguous type is used in one of its conventional meanings, the speaker can usually expect to be understood if he states which conventional meaning he intends or if the context makes this clear. If, finally, the intended meaning of a given token is nonconventional, the speaker can often expect to be properly interpreted provided that he explicitly states his intended meaning. It not infrequently happens, however, that the person addressed does not know the conventional meaning or meanings of the terms being used, or that the addressee forgets the nonconventional meaning assigned to them, or that the speaker himself is unclear about his intended meaning. In all these cases the individual's power over the interpreted meaning of the terms he uses is sorely limited. Third, a single person has almost no power over the conventional meanings of verbal types. Verbal types are public, not private, property. As the word 'conventional' itself suggests, conventional meanings are determined by groups of human beings, not single persons.

The distinctions just made are also important to an understanding of ambiguity. To say simply, as we did earlier, that a word is ambiguous if it has two or more clearly different meanings is inadequate because 'a word' is itself ambiguous. When we say that a word is ambiguous, we may be referring either to a verbal type or to a verbal token, and our meaning is not the same in the two cases. When we say that a verbal type is ambiguous, we mean that some tokens of that type have a different conventional meaning from other tokens of the same type. One example of an ambiguous verbal type is 'bull.' By convention some tokens of this type refer to a certain animal, other tokens to a papal edict. When, however, as is much more frequently the case, we use the word 'ambiguous' to refer to a verbal token, we mean that we can not infer which of two or more possible intended meanings the speaker has in mind. The important point is that even if a verbal token belongs to an ambiguous verbal type, the token itself will not be ambiguous if we can reasonably infer which meaning the speaker intended.

Our earlier account of ambiguity also failed to take into account the distinction between cognitive and non-cognitive meaning. When we say that a term such as 'bull' is ambiguous, we are referring solely to the fact that it has two or more different cognitive meanings. A term might have any number of different non-cognitive meanings without being ambiguous.

You may feel that some of the distinctions made in this chapter are so obvious that the introduction of technical names for them is superfluous. If so, so much the better. Nonetheless, fix in mind the technical terminology, since further use will be made of it. And beware if in the heat of controversy you find yourself objecting to someone else's use of a term on the grounds that it is not the term's "true" or "real" meaning. To be sure, you will often have good reason for disputing the propriety of the intended meaning of some term or for objecting to the interpretation put upon your own words. But all meanings are equally real or true.

EXERCISES FOR CHAPTER ONE

A. The following quotation from the American philosopher William James has been cited so often in logic texts that it has become a classic. Describe the situation reported, making use of our special vocabulary, and decide whether the disputants who were not satisfied with James' solution to the problem had reason for their dissatisfaction:

> Some years ago, being with a camping party in the mountains, I returned from a solitary ramble to find every one engaged in a ferocious metaphysical dispute. The *corpus* of the dispute was a squirrel—a live squirrel supposed to be clinging to one side of a tree-trunk; while over against the tree's opposite side a human being was imagined to stand. This human witness tries to get sight of the squirrel by moving rapidly round the tree, but

no matter how fast he goes, the squirrel moves as fast in the opposite direction, and always keeps the tree between himself and the man, so that never a glimpse of him is caught. The resultant metaphysical problem is this: *Does the man go round the squirrel or not?* He goes round the tree, sure enough, and the squirrel is on the tree; but does he go round the squirrel? In the unlimited leisure of the wilderness, discussion had been worn threadbare. Everyone had taken sides, and was obstinate; and the numbers on both sides were even. Each side, when I appeared, therefore, appealed to me to make it a majority. Mindful of the scholastic adage that whenever you meet a contradiction you must make a distinction, I immediately sought and found one, as follows: "Which party is right" I said, "depends on what you *practically* mean by 'going round' the squirrel. If you mean passing from the north of him to the east, then to the south, then to the west, and then to the north of him again, obviously the man does go round him, for he occupies these successive positions. But if on the contrary you mean being first in front of him, then on the right of him, then behind him, then on his left, and finally in front again, it is quite obvious that the man fails to go round him, for by the compensating movements the squirrel makes, he keeps his belly turned towards the man all the time, and his back turned away. Make the distinction, and there is no occasion for any further dispute. You are both right and both wrong according as you conceive the verb 'go round' in one practical fashion or the other."

Although one or two of the hotter disputants called my speech a shuffling evasion, saying they wanted no quibbling or scholastic hair-splitting, but meant just plain honest English 'round' the the majority seemed to think that the distinction has assuaged the dispute. (William James, *Pragmatism*)

B. Express in our vocabulary the locution: "That may be what you meant, but it is not what you said."

C. A justice of the United States Supreme Court once said, "The meaning of the U.S. constitution does not change with the ebb and flow of events." In what sense is this true? In what sense is it false?

D. Point out as many ambiguities in the term 'to know' as occur to you.

The Classification and Meaning of Terms

In this and succeeding chapters our concern will be with linguistic signs. Not all linguistic signs, however, have the same kind of meaning, and an analysis appropriate to some will be misleading if applied to others. Sentences have a different kind of meaning from the terms used to construct them. Moreover, both sentences and terms fall into several different, though often overlapping, categories and subcategories. In this chapter we shall discuss only 'categorematic terms.'

Categorematic terms are conventionally grouped under three heads: (1) *Singular names* (for example, 'Fido,' 'George Washington,' and 'Times Square') that have reference to some one individual being. (2) *Property terms* (for example, 'triangular,' 'sang,' and 'two-legged') that refer to traits or activities of individuals. (3) *Class terms* (for example, 'men,' 'revolutions,' and 'telephones') that refer to sets of individuals with some common property or properties. Terms that do not fall into any of these categories (for example, 'all,' 'are,' 'not,' 'the,' 'if,' and 'in') are called *syncategorematic terms* and will be discussed in later chapters.

I • NON-COGNITIVE MEANING

The sign functions, or non-cognitive meanings, of categorematic terms are extremely heterogeneous and have so far defied sys-

17

tematic classification. Categorematic terms do, however, have two widely recognized kinds of non-cognitive meaning that are of special importance to the student of logic: emotive meaning and pictorial meaning.

Emotive Meaning

When we say that a given term-type has *emotive meaning*, we mean that tokens of this type are often signs of the speaker's approval or disapproval of that which the term names or describes. If the inference is that the speaker disapproves, the term is said to have *negative emotive meaning*. If the inference is that the speaker approves, the term is said to have *positive emotive meaning*. If neither inference is reasonable, the term is said to be *emotively neutral*. An example of a term-type whose tokens almost invariably have negative emotive meaning is 'nigger.' 'Democracy' is a term whose tokens almost always have positive emotive meaning. Tokens of the term-type 'table,' by contrast, are emotively neutral.

Allowance must always be made, of course, for nonconventional usage. A token occurrence of an emotive term-type is no more an unfailing sign of approval or disapproval than smoke is an unfailing sign of fire. The Negro comedian Dick Gregory, for instance, has written a book called *Nigger*, but anybody who concludes from this that he disapproves of Negroes would be wholly mistaken.

Moreover, terms with favorable emotive meaning for one group of users may have an unfavorable emotive meaning for a second and little or none for a third. 'Communist,' for example, is a term with negative emotive meaning for most Americans, positive emotive meaning for most citizens of the Soviet Union, and little or no emotive meaning for many persons who are politically uncommitted.

Finally, it should be observed that a term is not emotive merely because the speaker does in fact approve or disapprove of that which it names or describes. Some Negroes now prefer 'Black' to 'Negro,' and some whites, especially in the South of the United States, prefer 'Nigra' to 'Negro.' Those who prefer

'Black' to 'Negro' tend to find 'Negro' pejorative, while those who prefer 'Nigra' to 'Negro' tend to find 'Negro' honorific. For most persons, however, including many violent racists, the term 'Negro' is emotively neutral. A speaker's use of the word 'Negro' is emotive only if we have reason to believe that he is a member of a class of users who conventionally employ the term to express approval or disapproval.

Pictorial Meaning

The pictorial meaning of a term-type consists of the ideas, images, or mental pictures that it tends to evoke in the minds of its users or interpreters. In general, the best technique for determining the pictorial meaning of a given term is free association.

Most terms with strong emotive meaning are also rich in pictorial meaning. For many persons 'nigger' evokes an image of some popular stereotype of Negroes. For many of us 'anti-Semite' evokes the image of a sadistic guard in a Nazi concentration camp. Pictorial meaning is not, however, restricted to emotive terms. Almost all categorematic terms have at least some pictorial meaning. 'Smoke,' for example, suggests an image of fire. And a mental diagram of a miniature solar system is a part of the pictorial meaning of 'atom.'

Our principal basis for determining the pictorial meaning of a given term-token is any knowledge we may have about the pictorial meaning of its type. Since, however, pictorial meaning is more variable than emotive meaning, even greater allowance must be made for individual cases. Often the pictorial meaning of a term-token for a given speaker or interpreter can be determined only from a knowledge of his personal history or psychological set. The fact that 'anti-Semite' suggests a sadistic Nazi guard to many of us does not guarantee that it evokes the same idea in others. Often, too, the pictorial meaning of a token depends upon the speaker's beliefs. For a devout Christian 'the history of mankind' calls to mind the story of Adam and Eve and the Last Judgment. For an ardent Communist, however, 'the history of mankind' suggests a division between the oppressed and the oppressors and revolutionary upheaval. The variability of pictorial meaning from person to person or group to group must not, however, be exaggerated. The success of poets and other literary artists in creating certain effects that depend on pictorial meaning testifies not only to their skill but also to the relative stability of pictorial meaning.

II • COGNITIVE MEANING

As indicated at the beginning of this chapter, categorematic terms fall into three categories: singular names, property terms, and class terms. These categories of terms correspond to the common-sense concepts of individual beings, traits or activities of individual beings, and sets of beings who share some common traits or activities. All of us readily recognize the difference between an individual such as Socrates, the property of being a philosopher, and the class of individuals who practice philosophy. This three-fold distinction is an important part of our Western intellectual heritage and is deeply embedded not only in our thought habits but also in our language. The distinction between properties and classes, however, is somewhat artificial and tenuous, since every property defines a class—namely, the set of individuals possessing that property—whereas every class is a class simply by virtue of the fact that its members have common defining properties.[1] And for many purposes the distinction is dispensable. For example, the term 'human' is a property term whereas the term 'men' is a class term; but it matters little whether we say 'Greeks are human' or 'Greeks are men,' since both sentences have the same cognitive meaning. Nonetheless, the distinction is not wholly artificial. Despite their identity of cognitive meaning, 'Greeks are human' and 'Greeks are men' are different sentences, and their differences can not be fully explained without distinguishing between properties and classes. In this

[1] The statement that every property defines a class is not true without qualification. There are certain properties—for example, the properties of being or not being a member of itself—for which we can not posit a corresponding class without self-contradiction. Although these exceptions are of great theoretical interest, the practical purposes this book is designed to serve do not require that we take them into account.

discussion, therefore, we shall observe the traditional three-fold distinction. It will be convenient to begin by discussing property terms.

Property Terms

Property terms, like almost all terms, are of little or no use for purposes of communication except as components of sentences. Within sentences, however, they may serve two roles. Sometimes they are used to identify a subject of discourse. The property terms 'triangularity' and 'walking' in the sentences below serve this function:

> Triangularity is a property of some plane figures.
> Walking is good exercise.

When so used property terms are called *property names*. Other examples of property names are 'laughter,' 'being a widow,' and 'hardness.' When not used to identify a subject of discourse, property terms are used to say something about an identified subject of discourse. This is the case with 'blue' and 'under thirty years of age' in

> The sky is blue.
> John is under thirty years of age.

Used in this way property terms are called *attributive property terms*. Other examples of attributive property terms are 'hard,' 'sang,' and 'suffers from a head cold.'

Most property term-types in English function exclusively as names or exclusively as attributive terms. A few property term-types, however, function as names in some token occurrences and as attributive terms in others. Thus, we say both 'Walking is good exercise' and 'He is walking'; 'Blue is a color' and 'The sky is blue.' It should also be noted that all complete predicates are property terms. For example, in the sentences

> The sky is blue.
> John is under thirty years of age.

the terms 'is blue' and 'is under thirty years of age' are as much property terms as 'blue' and 'under thirty years of age.' This rule holds even when a complete predicate contains no property terms. Take, for example, these sentences:

The Nazis were racists.
Men are sinners.

'Were racists' and 'are sinners' are property terms, even though the components of these terms are all class terms or syncategorematic terms. For purposes of logical analysis the sentences cited are interpreted as asserting respectively that Nazis have the defining properties of racists and men the defining properties of sinners.

The property referred to by a property term is called its *designatum,* and for all practical purposes the cognitive meaning of a property term may be equated with the property it designates. A good understanding of the cognitive meaning of property terms requires, however, that we be aware of some of the ways in which they are classified.

One classification involves a distinction among *one-place terms, two-place terms, three-place terms,* and so forth. The use of these terms is easier to illustrate than to explain. Speaking loosely, however, we may say that this classification is based on the number of entities we are obliged to bear in mind in order to understand sentences in which a given property term occurs. Since, for example, 'Socrates is snub-nosed,' which identifies a single individual, and 'Men have lungs,' which identifies a single class, are fully intelligible, 'is snub-nosed' and 'have lungs' are both one-place terms. The terms 'is taller than' and 'is later than,' on the other hand, are two-place terms, since sentences in which they occur are intelligible only if they take the forms 'X is taller than Y' and 'X is later than Y.' Similarly, since sentences containing the terms 'lies between' and 'gave' are intelligible only if they have the forms 'X lies between Y and Z' and 'X gave Y to Z,' these terms are three-place terms. Property terms with more than one place are called *relational terms;* the properties designated by relational terms are called *relations;* and the entities related are called *relata.*

Note that in determining the status of a property term according to this principle of classification entities identified by the property term itself are not counted. For example, 'has a population in excess of eight million' is not an eight-million-plus property term. Since this term can be intelligibly attributed to a single entity (as in 'New York has a population in excess of eight million'), it is a one-place term.

Note also that in determining the status of a given property term it is not enough simply to count the number of entities explicitly identified by any sentence in which the term occurs. For, any term that designates a relation is a relational term, but the rules of English usage often permit us to employ relational terms without identifying all of the relata. For example, the two-place relational term 'is married' occurs not only in sentences of the form 'X is married to Y' but also in sentences of the form 'X is married.' To determine the status of a property term we must ask not "How many entities are explicitly mentioned by sentences in which it occurs?" but rather "How many entities must we assume or presuppose in order to understand these sentences?" If a sentence such as 'John is married,' contains a relational term but does not explicitly identify all of the relata, the term is said to be *implicitly relational*. Other examples of implicitly relational terms are 'are tall' in 'Skyscrapers are tall' and 'is important' in 'Money is important.' Since sentences of the form 'X is tall' make no sense unless we tacitly presuppose some standard of comparison, 'is tall' is a two-place term. And since nothing can be important except to some person and for some purpose, 'is important' is a three-place term.

Relational terms are classified as 'symmetrical,' 'asymmetrical,' or 'non-symmetrical.' A relational term is *symmetrical* if the knowledge that it may be correctly attributed to one of the relata permits us to infer that it may also be attributed to the others. 'Being married' is symmetrical, since if X is married to Y then Y is obviously married to X. A relational term is *asymmetrical* if the knowledge that it may be correctly attributed to one of the relata permits us to infer that it can not be attributed to the others. An example is 'being a wife'; for if we know that X is the wife of Y, it follows that Y is not the wife of X. Finally, a relational term is *non-symmetrical* if neither sort of inference can be made. For example, if we know that X is the brother of Y, we can not infer whether Y is or is not the brother of X. Y may be X's brother or Y may be X's sister. 'Is a brother' is thus non-symmetrical.

Relational terms are also classified as 'transitive,' 'intransitive,' and 'non-transitive.' A relational term is *transitive* if when we know that X is related to Y and that Y is related to Z by virtue of the property designated, we may infer that X stands in the same relationship to Z. For example, if X is older than Y, and Y is older than Z, it follows that X is older than Z. A relational term is *intransitive* if when we know that X is related to Y and Y to Z by virtue of the same property, we can infer that X does not stand in the same relation to Z. If, for instance, X is the mother of Y and Y is the mother of Z, it follows that X is not the mother of Z. Finally, a relational term is *non-transitive* when neither sort of inference can be made. The relational term 'loving' is, unfortunately, non-transitive. If X loves Y and Y loves Z, it does not follow that X loves Z. X may or may not. Sad to say, the property of loving is not even symmetrical; if X loves Y it does not follow that Y loves X.

Class Terms

For our purposes in this text a *class term* is defined as any token occurrence of a word type or phrase type that refers to a set of things or events with one or more common properties. Plural common nouns (for example, 'dogs,' 'tables,' 'wars') as well as certain noun phrases (such as 'dogs with long ears,' 'persons suffering from cancer,' 'the first three Presidents of the United States') are class terms. And so are many tokens of singular common nouns. For example, since the sentence 'Man is mortal' is equivalent in cognitive meaning to 'Men are mortal,' the term 'man' obviously has the same function in the first that 'men' has in the second and must also be classified as a class term. In the sentence 'The man I met this morning was very aggressive,' however, 'man' is not a class name, since it is not being used to refer to a set of individuals.

If a token of a class term is used in a sentence to name a subject of discourse, it is called a *class name;* if used to say something about a subject already named, an *attributive class term.* It should be noted, however, that class terms have the same grammatical form regardless of which role they assume. Thus we say both 'All mammals are animals' (where 'mammals' is used as a class name), and 'All men are mammals' (where 'mammals' is used as an attributive class term).

If a class term refers to a definitely assignable number of individual things or events, it is said to stand for a *closed class.* Examples are 'the first three Presidents of the United States,' 'all of the persons present at Carnegie Hall on February 8, 1966,' and 'the living members of the English royal family.' If it is impossible to enumerate all the individuals referred to by a class term, it is said to stand for an *open class.* Examples are 'men,' 'tables,' 'revolutions.'

Denotation or Extension

One kind of meaning of class terms is technically called *denotation* or *extension.* These expressions are used synonymously to refer to the entire set of individuals that a given class term stands for. With terms for closed classes, the members of their denotations or extensions can be exhaustively enumerated. The extension of 'the first three Presidents of the United States,' for instance, includes no one but Washington, Adams, and Jefferson. With terms for open classes, however, the members of their denotations or extensions can not be exhaustively enumerated. The extension of 'men,' for instance, includes not only persons of whom we have knowledge, such as Washington, Madison, and Jefferson, but also all those persons of whose existence no historical record exists and, in addition, all those men of whom we have no knowledge because they are yet to be born.

Problems arise with terms like 'centaur,' 'Lilliputians' and 'elves.' All authorities agree that these are class terms. There is, however, disagreement about the best way to analyze them. According to some philosophers, these terms differ from those like 'dog' and 'revolutions' only in that they denote classes of beings who are imaginary, mythical, or fictional. Within their proper domains of discourse, these terms denote in the same way as other class names. According to a second group of philosophers, however, these terms do not denote at all. And according to still a third group of philosophers these terms denote what is called a *null set* or an *empty class*. For our purposes it is not necessary to examine the relative merits of these different analyses. In this text, however, the third analysis will be adopted and class terms that denote no real member will be said to denote a null set, or an empty class.

Connotation or Intension

A second kind of meaning of class terms is called technically *connotation* or *intension*. These terms differ from 'denotation' and 'extension' in that they refer not to the individuals a class term stands for but rather to properties shared by these individuals. It should be observed at the outset, however, that the properties in the intensions of class terms fall into three distinct categories, each of which defines a special kind of intension. When, therefore, we have occasion to refer to all of the properties in a term's intension, we shall use the expression *total intension*.

DEFINING PROPERTIES AND STRICT INTENSION

A defining property of a class term is one that any object must possess to be included in the term's extension. Being human, being male, being adult, and being unmarried, for example, are all defining properties of the class term 'bachelor,' since any being who fails to possess even one of these four properties is automatically excluded from its denotation. Similarly, the property of being half horse and half man is a defining property of 'centaur,' since it is the fact that no real individual possesses this property which justifies our saying that 'centaur' denotes an empty class. The set of defining properties of any class term is called its *strict intension*.

It follows from this definition of 'defining property' that every defining property of a term will belong to every individual in its denotation. But it does not follow that every property belonging to every individual in a term's denotation will be a defining property. The property of being less than ten feet tall, for instance, most certainly belongs to every member of the past and present denotation of 'bachelor,' and there is good reason to believe that all future members of the term's denotation will also possess this property. Yet if a being should turn up who had all the defining properties of a bachelor and was more than ten feet tall, we would not for that reason alone refuse to call him a 'bachelor.'

MEANING CRITERIA AND LOOSE INTENSION

The *meaning criteria* of any given class term are properties we invoke, as we do defining properties, to determine whether a given object belongs to the class term's extension. Defining properties, however, are tests that all candidates for inclusion in a term's extension absolutely must pass, whereas meaning criteria are less decisive tests. If a candidate for inclusion in the denotation of a term possesses one of these latter properties, this is counted as a reason, but not a conclusive reason, for including it. Similarly, if a candidate fails to have one of these properties, this is counted as a reason, but not a conclusive one, for excluding it. The meaning criteria for a given term constitute that term's *loose intension.*

Consider the class term 'poem.' To determine whether a group of words is a poem we ask ourselves such questions as: Does it rhyme? Is it in meter? Does it contain metaphors and similes? Is it rich in emotive and pictorial meaning? If the answer to all such questions is affirmative, we will ordinarily be satisfied that this group of words is a poem; and if the answer to all such questions is negative, we will be satisfied that it is not a poem. The fact that any one answer is affirmative or negative, however, is far from decisive. Many prose works have one or more of these properties. Similarly, a good many poems lack one or more of these properties. Poems in blank verse do not rhyme. Poems in free verse lack meter. Didactic poems are rarely rich in emotive or pictorial meaning, and they often lack metaphors and similes.

Although no meaning criterion is itself a defining property of a term, the complex property designated by assembling expressions for each of the criteria in the loose intension of a term and linking these expressions with the word 'or' is. A poem need not rhyme, nor need it have meter, nor need it be rich in emotive and pictorial meaning, nor need it have metaphors and similes, etc. But since a poem must have at least one of these meaning criteria, the complex property term

> being in rhyme *or* being in verse *or* being rich in emotive and pictorial meaning *or* containing metaphors and similes, etc.

is a defining property of 'poem.' Complex property terms formed by linking their components together with the word 'or' are called *disjunctive property terms.*

CONTINGENT PROPERTIES AND CONTINGENT INTENSION

The third class of properties belonging to the intension of a term are called 'contingent properties'; and the set of such properties with respect to any given term is said to constitute its *contingent intension.* By a *contingent property* we mean any property that belongs to all or nearly all the objects in a term's extension *without* being either a defining property or a meaning criterion. An example is the property of being less than ten feet tall with respect to the class term 'bachelor'; for, although all bachelors are in fact less than ten feet tall, the fact of someone's being over ten feet tall would be altogether irrelevant in determining whether he belongs to the class denoted by 'bachelor.' It would be neither a conclusive reason for excluding him, as it would have to be if it were a defining property, nor a partial test for including or excluding him, as it would have to be if it were a meaning criterion. In other words, though contingent properties are a part of a term's total intension, they are not a part of a term's meaning.

It might be asked, therefore, why the concept of contingent intension is introduced at all in an analysis of meaning. The answer is that although contingent properties are not now part of the meaning of the terms with which they are associated, there is no guarantee that they never will be. The meanings of terms often change with time, and not infrequently what was once merely a contingent property becomes a meaning criterion or even a defining property. For instance, 'gold' was once defined in terms of color, malleability, and other properties easily discoverable by our physical senses. Later, it was learned that all or nearly all gold as originally defined has a specific atomic weight. When this happened, physicists and chemists quickly promoted the property of having this specific atomic weight, which had previously been merely a contingent property, to the status of a defining property.

Connotation and Pictorial Meaning

Although connotation is conceptually distinct from pictorial meaning, the connotation and pictorial meaning of a term are often closely associated. The logical connotation of 'centaur,' for instance, is the property of being half horse and half man, while the picture evoked by the term is one of a being that is half horse and half man. And in nonphilosophical discourse, 'connotation' refers as often to pictorial or even emotive meaning as to connotation in the technical sense just outlined. It is said, for example, that a white bridal gown "connotes" chastity. Certainly, however, chastity is not a part of the intension of 'white bridal gown.'

The importance of keeping connotation and pictorial meaning distinct can easily be seen by scanning the class terms listed below, stopping at each only long enough to jot down for each the first word that comes to mind:

Man
Italian
Pure
Brother
Cigarettes

A typical right-hand column might read from top to bottom: woman, spaghetti, impure, Cain, lung cancer. As these examples show, the ideas or images most readily evoked by a term often have nothing to do with its logical connotation.

As earlier noted, the best technique for discovering the pictorial meaning of a term is free association; the imagination must be given free play. But imagination is only one tool for discovering the intensional meaning of a term, and when used it must at some stage be directed to answer very specific questions. To discover the strict intension of a term we must ask: What are the properties whose absence in an object is a conclusive reason for refusing to use the term to denote it? To discover a term's loose intension we must ask: What are the properties whose absence in an object gives partial grounds for excluding it from the term's denotation and whose presence gives partial grounds for its inclusion? To discover a term's contingent intension we must study the objects it denotes.

Singular Names

Singular names are hereby defined as tokens of a word type or phrase type used to refer to a single individual, either real or imaginary. Some singular names are proper nouns—for example, 'George Washington,' 'the French Revolution,' 'Hamlet,' 'Times Square.' Some are pronouns, such as 'he,' 'she,' 'it.' Some, called *definite descriptions,* consist of a class name preceded by the word 'the' or some other singularizing expression—for example, 'the first President of the United States,' 'the present king of France,' 'my left hand.' Still others are *collective nouns,* that is, common nouns used to refer collectively to a group as a single unit rather than distributively to every member of the group. In the sentence 'Man is a mammal,' the common noun 'man' is a class name used distributively to assert that every man is a mammal. In the sentence 'Man will someday destroy himself,' however, 'man' is a collective noun or singular name, since the obvious intent is to assert that mankind or the human species considered as a single unit will someday destroy itself, not that every man will do so.

Real individuals denoted by singular names are, of course, a part of that name's meaning. The meaning of singular names, however, can not merely be equated with their denotations. First, there are singular names like 'Hamlet,' 'Uncle Sam,' and 'the present king of France' that obviously have no denotation but are nonetheless meaningful. Second, there are singular names, like 'God' and 'Satan,' which have the same meaning for different persons even though these persons disagree about the existence of a denotation for them. Third, there are pairs of singular names which though obviously different in meaning have precisely the same denotation. A classic example is 'the morning star' and 'the evening star,' both of which name the planet Venus.

These facts suggest that singular names have an intension as well as a denotation; and if a singular name is carefully examined, an intension will usually be found for it. Although Hamlet, for example, is a creature of Shakespeare's imagination, he was portrayed so fully that we would have little difficulty specifying the properties any real individual would have to possess if the name 'Hamlet' were to apply. Similarly, although God's existence is a matter of dispute, many people, whether they believe in God or not, would refuse to use the word 'God' for a being who lacked the properties of omnipotence and benevolence. In the case of definite descriptions the intension is usually suggested by the term itself. 'The morning star,' for instance, has in its intension the relational property of appearing to earth-dwellers in the morning, whereas 'the present king of France' includes in its intension the properties of being a king, being alive today, and ruling in France.

EXERCISES FOR CHAPTER TWO

A. Which of the following term-types have emotive meaning as conventionally employed? What is their conventional pictorial meaning, if any?

1. a telephone
2. an anarchist
3. a pinko
4. the administration
5. a politician
6. a statesman
7. a ward heeler
8. a cynic
9. a pessimist
10. a realist

11. a utopian	24. good
12. an optimist	25. morally right
13. an intellectual	26. Black Power
14. a radical	27. a patriot
15. a liberal	28. a chauvinist
16. a conservative	29. a nationalist
17. a reactionary	30. a flag waver
18. an idealist	31. a racist
19. peace loving	32. an anti-Semite
20. a bleeding heart	33. killing
21. a Cassandra	34. murder
22. not quick enough	35. pride
23. too quick	36. humility

B. Which of the following terms are relational? Classify the relational terms as two-place, three-place, etc.:

1. won	6. committed
2. sang	7. fought
3. is friendly	8. means
4. is a mother	9. is essential
5. is useful	10. blue

C. Classify the following relations as symmetrical, asymmetrical, or nonsymmetrical and also as transitive, intransitive, or nontransitive:

1. is a husband of	10. is a godfather of
2. is older than	11. is employed by
3. is east of	12. is a symbol of
4. is included in the class of	13. is excluded from the class of
5. is a friend of	
6. is as old as	14. is hated by
7. is not older than	15. is kind to
8. is a spouse of	16. is a member of
9. is a cousin of	

D. Below is a list of class terms followed by several property terms. Which of the properties designated belong to the term's total intension? Of these, which are defining properties, which meaning criteria, and which contingent properties? In some cases the proper answer to these questions will be "It's hard to say."

1. *A candidate for the Presidency of the United States:* (a) is a citizen of the United States, (b) is male, (c) is Caucasian, (d) is over thirty-five years of age, (e) has two legs, (f) is a hard-working campaigner, (g) is either rich or is backed by others who are rich, (h) was born within United States territory.

2. *A neurotic:* (a) is unhappy, (b) is tortured by feelings of guilt, (c) angers easily, (d) has phobias, (e) has an inferiority complex, (f) believes that others are always persecuting him, (g) finds it difficult to make up his mind, (h) suffered traumas as a child.

3. *An economic depression:* (a) is characterized by a high level of unemployment, (b) is characterized by a reduction in industrial output, (c) is marked by deflation, (d) is marked by political unrest, (e) occurs in cycles, (f) occurs only in capitalist countries.

4. *A human being:* (a) is born of human parents, (b) has no season for sexual intercourse, (c) is capable of tears and laughter, (d) is able to make promises, (e) has a backbone, (f) is a rational being, (g) is an animal, (h) possesses an immortal soul, (i) uses tools, (j) uses language.

5. *A labor union:* (a) is an organization of workers, (b) has the power to strike, (c) negotiates contracts with employers, (d) has democratically elected officials, (e) has political concerns, (f) encourages featherbedding, (g) fails to consider the interests of the public.

6. *An Italian:* (a) is a citizen of Italy, (b) is descended from persons who were citizens of Italy, (c) is either a citizen of Italy or descended from persons who were citizens of Italy, (d) is a great lover, (e) has a swarthy complexion, (f) has a big family.

7. *A university:* (a) has a college of arts and sciences, (b) has a medical school, (c) has at least one professional

school, (d) is an institution of higher learning, (e) has a faculty, (f) has a student body, (g) has fraternities, (h) is a haven for impractical intellectuals, (i) is a hotbed of radicalism, (j) is a community of scholars and students.

8. *A good concert pianist:* (a) practices long hours every day, (b) almost invariably hits the right notes, (c) plays with a unique, personal style, (d) is vain and temperamental, (e) has long fingers, (f) chooses his programs with great care, (g) has long hair, (h) is constantly traveling.

9. *A dogmatist:* (a) has strong opinions, (b) refuses to subject his opinions to the criticism of others, (c) refuses to recognize the logical weight of arguments that oppose his own views, (d) is intolerant of those who hold opposing views, (e) rarely if ever changes his mind, (f) loves to argue.

10. *A nation:* (a) is a group of persons who speak a common language, (b) is a group of persons with a common history or culture, (c) is a group of persons who live under the same government and are subject to the same legal code, (d) is a group of persons united by ties of blood or race, (e) is a group of persons who identify with one another when confronted by a common enemy, (f) is a group of persons with a common religion, (g) is a group of persons with an emotional attachment to certain symbols or emblems such as a flag, (h) is a group of persons who live within the borders of a single territory.

11. *A work force with good morale:* (a) has a high level of productivity, (b) has a low rate of absenteeism, (c) is united by a sense of hostility to management, (d) tends to regard management as a partner in a common enterprise, (e) is very reluctant to strike, (f) is easily persuaded to strike, (g) is characterized by a high degree of cooperativeness among its members, (h) is characterized by a high degree of competitiveness among its members, (i) resists technological innovations, (j) welcomes technological changes.

E. Classify each of the underlined terms in the sentences below under the appropriate rubrics in the chart on the facing page.

Classification of Terms

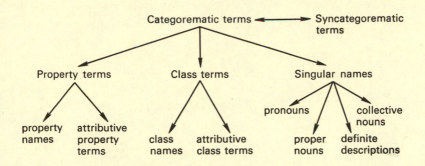

1. Henry is six feet tall.
2. Henry is six feet tall.
3. Death comes to all men.
4. The cat is on the mat.
5. The cat is on the mat.
6. Professors are absent-minded.
7. All nations should disarm.
8. Love is a many-splendored thing.
9. Man is a mammal.
10. Poltergeists are destructive.
11. The present king of France is bald.
12. American universities should not engage in secret research.
13. The team played well.
14. Men are mammals.
15. Prayer is good for the soul.

Some Common Characteristics of Terms

In this chapter we shall discuss in greater detail than in Chapter One the concepts of vagueness and ambiguity. In addition, we shall discuss a number of other expressions, such as 'abstract' and 'concrete,' 'general' and 'specific.' Most of the expressions discussed apply to all categorematic terms. Initially and primarily, however, our analysis will focus on their use in describing class terms. Their applicability to property terms and singular names will be discussed in the last section of the chapter.

In ordinary discourse most of the expressions to be analyzed have fairly strong emotive meaning. For example, 'precise,' 'unambiguous,' 'concrete,' and 'specific' tend to have positive emotive meaning, whereas their opposites tend to have negative emotive meaning. Since excessive vagueness, ambiguity, abstractness, and generality rank among the principal causes of breakdown in communication, this is hardly surprising. As employed by logicians, however, these expressions are emotively neutral. Logicians do not contest the desirability of being able to express oneself with due precision, unambiguity, concreteness, and specificity. Nonetheless, if vague, ambiguous, abstract, and general terms were abandoned, the result would be not a gain but a loss. Our vocabulary would be so impoverished as to render successful thinking and communication impossible. On the practical and human level the interdiction against such terms would be disastrous. No longer could we say "Come to dinner a little

after eight" or "I love you." On the theoretical and scientific
level the interdiction would be equally disastrous. Science and
mathematics are inconceivable without a large vocabulary of
abstract and general terms. What is to be condemned is not
vagueness, ambiguity, abstractness, and generality as such, but a
degree of vagueness, ambiguity, abstractness, or generality that
impedes effective thinking or communication.

I • VAGUENESS

In Chapter One a vague term was said to refer to a range of
phenomena without well-defined boundaries. With the aid of the
distinctions made in Chapter Two we will now be able to refine
this initial definition.

Vague class terms have three features in common. First, although the objects properly denoted by any vague class term
must resemble one another with respect to every defining property, the resemblance with respect to at least one of the term's
defining properties is imperfect or incomplete. Objects in the
extension of a precise class term, on the contrary, completely
resemble one another with respect to all the term's defining properties. Contrast, for example, the vague term 'blue object' and
the precise term 'quadrilateral.' The defining properties of a
'quadrilateral' are being a closed plane figure with four and only
four sides. Every object denoted by this term is exactly like
every other with respect to these defining properties. By contrast, one of the defining properties of 'blue object' is having a
readily visible degree of blue pigment; and since the visibility of
blue pigment is a matter of degree, the resemblance of blue
objects is in this respect imperfect.

Second, because objects denoted by a vague class term do not
perfectly resemble one another with respect to some defining
property, it is possible to rank these objects serially according to
the degree in which that defining property is present. This is
never true of objects denoted by precise class names.

Finally, candidates for inclusion in the denotation of a vague
class term fall into two groups. First, there are *paradigm cases—*

that is, cases which we see almost immediately belong in the term's denotation and about whose inclusion we can easily agree. Second, there are *borderline cases*—that is, cases over which many users hesitate even after deliberation or about whose inclusion they may disagree. Precise terms do not have borderline cases.

Although these three features are common to all vague terms, their presence can be accounted for in one of two different ways. Depending upon which account is appropriate, a term will be said to be characterized either by 'linear vagueness' or by 'vagueness of family resemblance.'

Linear Vagueness

'Blue object' is a paradigm of a term with linear vagueness. Blue objects may be serially ordered according to the visibility of their blue pigment. This serial order is continuous with a more inclusive serial order of objects ranked not according to the degree of visibility of blue pigment but according to the degree to which blue pigment is actually present. Picture a color chart consisting of a hundred patches of color ranked serially by equal degrees from a reddish violet at one end to a greenish turquoise at the other. Since violet is a mixture of red and blue and since turquoise is a mixture of green and blue, all hundred patches will contain some blue pigment. But since the blue pigment is readily visible only in the middle ranges of the chart, not all patches will properly be called 'blue.' Moreover, no rule of usage tells us where to demarcate the less inclusive series of visibly blue objects from the more inclusive series of objects actually containing blue pigment. Thus, to say that a class name exhibits *linear vagueness* is to say (1) that the serial ordering of the objects it denotes is continuous with a more inclusive serial ordering of some related class and (2) that there is no rule of usage which specifies at what point in the continuum the less inclusive series is to be demarcated from the more inclusive series.

Other examples of linear vagueness are 'tall man' and 'bald man.' By definition a 'tall man' is one who exceeds most other men in height, but since the serial order of tall men is continuous with the more inclusive serial order of men arranged according to height and since no rule of usage gives us a precise cut-off point, 'tall man' is vague. In like fashion, a 'bald man' is by definition one with few or no hairs on his head, but since the serial order of bald men is continuous with the serial order of men arranged according to the number of hairs on their head (ranging from zero to hundreds of thousands) and since no practical purpose could be served by specifying the precise number of hairs a man must possess if he is to be excluded from the denotation of 'bald man,' the term is vague.

Vagueness of Family Resemblance

To say that a class term exhibits *vagueness of family resemblance* is to say that (1) at least one of its defining properties is a disjunctive property whose components are meaning criteria, (2) candidates for inclusion in its denotation may be arranged serially according to the number of component meaning criteria they possess, and (3) there is no rule of usage specifying how many of these components must be present.

'Poem' is characterized by vagueness of family resemblance. As we know from the last chapter, the disjunctive property formed by this term's meaning criteria (having rhyme or having meter or having pictorial meaning or having metaphor, etc.) is a defining property of 'poem,' since a group of words that had none of these features would undoubtedly be excluded from its denotation. There is, however, no rule of usage telling us how many of these properties it must have. If it had all of them, it would probably be a paradigm, and we would all readily agree that it is a poem. If, however, it had only two or three, we would probably hesitate and at times even disagree.

Another example is the term 'slum.' The loose intension of this term includes meaning criteria such as overcrowding, inadequate plumbing facilities, inadequate garbage disposal, poor ventilation, and the presence of vermin. The disjunctive property formed by these meaning criteria is clearly a defining property of 'slum.' Since, however, there is no rule of usage specifying how many of these meaning criteria must be present, 'slum' is characterized by vagueness of family resemblance.

In the two examples given, as in practically all other cases of vagueness of family resemblance, there are two additional features that add to the vagueness of the term. First, the individual components of the disjunctive property themselves exhibit linear vagueness. A poem, for example, may be more or less rich in emotive and pictorial meaning and may have a more or less pronounced metrical scheme. Second, the several meaning criteria may be assigned different relative weights. Some persons, for instance, contend that rhyme is more essential to poetry than metaphor, whereas others maintain the converse. Whether a group of words will be included in the denotation of 'poem' will therefore depend not only on how many meaning criteria of 'poem' are present but also on the degree to which they are present and the relative importance we attach to each.

II • AMBIGUITY

In Chapter One we distinguished between type ambiguity and token ambiguity. A type, we said, is ambiguous if it has two different cognitive meanings, whereas a token is ambiguous if it belongs to an ambiguous type and the circumstances of its utterance do not make clear which type-meaning is intended. Given the distinctions introduced in Chapter Two, this initial definition of ambiguity may also be refined.

At this point it is hardly necessary to point out that the term 'meaning' is itself highly ambiguous. It is, however, of the utmost importance to understand that when we say a class name is ambiguous because it has at least two different meanings, the relevant sense of 'meaning' is strict intension. A class name is ambiguous only if it has two different strict intensions.

It must also be observed that expressions of the form 'A means B' are elliptical, since when properly interpreted 'means' is a four-place term. The complete expression would have to take the form 'A means B to C in D,' with 'C' standing for a class of users and 'D' standing for the context or circumstances in which 'A' is uttered. Usually 'C' and 'D' are not made explicit, and often there is no good reason to do so. It would be sheer pedantry for an American high school geometry teacher who has just defined 'triangle' to add that this is the meaning the term has for persons who speak English or that in German one would have to use the word *'Dreieck'* to convey the same meaning. And it would be at best a poor joke if he were to add that the meaning he gave to the term is the one used in geometry classes, but that in a divorce court the term would mean something else. Nonetheless, the meaning of any term is always relative to a class of users and a context of discussion.

This observation is particularly pertinent to an understanding of ambiguity. For, to say that a class term is *ambiguous* is to say either (1) that it may be employed by a single class of users with two or more different strict intensions in different contexts or (2) that it may be employed by different classes of users with two or more different strict intensions in the same context. By contrast, an unambiguous class term is one whose strict intension is the same for all users in all contexts.

'Triangle' is an example of an ambiguous class term in sense 1, since the defining properties of 'triangle' when used in the context of a geometry discussion are not the same as the defining properties of 'triangle' when used in discussions of personal relationships. Another example is the term 'cardinal,' whose strict intension in the context of a discussion on birds is different from its strict intension in a discussion about members of ecclesiastical hierarchies. An example of ambiguity in sense 2 is the word 'subway.' As defined by Americans the term stands for an underground mode of transportation. As defined by Britishers it stands for a pedestrian underpass. To mark the distinction between these two kinds of ambiguity we shall use the expressions *contextual ambiguity* and *user ambiguity*.

Often a single term is characterized both by user ambiguity and by contextual ambiguity. This point is well illustrated by 'democracy.' This term is unquestionably characterized by contextual ambiguity. Almost all users of this term agree that a small group such as a New England township would not be a democracy unless every citizen had the right to participate directly in decision-making, whereas a large industrial society may be a 'democracy' even though this is not the case. The term is no less obviously characterized by user ambiguity. If challenged to give definitions of 'democracy' appropriate to a discussion of large industrial societies, citizens of the Soviet Union and citizens of the United States would no doubt cite different defining properties. For example, most Russians would list complete equality of educational opportunity at all levels and a constitutionally guaranteed right of every citizen to gainful employment as defining properties, whereas most Americans would not. On the other hand, most Americans would list the existence of at least one opposition political party and a high degree of freedom in political discussion as defining properties, whereas most Russians would not.

For any class of tokens of a given term-type as employed in a specific context or by a specific group of users we shall use the expression *subtype*. Thus, the class of tokens used to refer to certain birds and the class of tokens used to refer to certain members of an ecclesiastical hierarchy are subtypes of 'cardinal.' Similarly, the tokens of 'subway' used by Americans constitute one subtype of 'subway' while the tokens used by Britishers constitute another.

(Care must be taken to avoid confusing subtypes with subclasses. If someone claimed that the class term 'man' is ambiguous because it is used to refer to Caucasians, Negroes, Indians, and Orientals, he would be guilty of this confusion. It is true, of course, that the class of men can be subdivided into these four subclasses; but for this to be a sound reason for declaring the class term 'man' ambiguous, it would be necessary to show that a specific skin pigmentation is a defining property of 'man' for some class of users or in some context. In fact, however, a specific skin pigmentation is not a defining property of man in any context or for any users in any conventional use of 'man.' If a being should turn up who was like a man in every respect except that his skin was bright green, we would not refuse to call him a 'man.' The fact that a class has subclasses is no more a reason for supposing the class term is ambiguous than the fact that a class has more than one member.)

III • LABILITY

When we use the expression *labile* to refer to a class term, we mean that there is some class of users who are confused or un-

decided about the status of one or more properties in its total
intension. For example, having the atomic weight of 197.0 is a
part of the total intension of 'gold,' and for contemporary
physicists and chemists it is almost always a defining property of
'gold.' Yet, there was a time immediately after this property was
discovered when scientists vacillated in their use of 'gold,' not
knowing whether to classify the specific atomic weight of gold
as a contingent property, a meaning criterion, or a defining
property. Even today, for beginning chemistry students the term
is usually labile, since for them its status is almost always unclear. If asked to say whether they would refuse to call an
element 'gold' unless it had an atomic weight of 197.0 or whether
having this atomic weight is simply a fact about gold—'gold'
being definable without reference to atomic weight—they would
as a rule not be able to answer with assurance. On the one
hand, knowing that in the table of chemical elements gold is
listed as having this atomic weight, they would hesitate to call
any element 'gold' if it did not possess this weight. On the other
hand, when told that gold has this weight they do not feel that
they are being instructed in the use of a word, but rather that
they have been given information about gold itself. In the first
case, they are tempted to classify the sentence 'Gold has an
atomic weight of 197.0' with sentences such as 'Bachelors are
unmarried.' In the second, they are tempted to classify it with
sentences such as 'Bachelors are under ten feet tall.'

Another example of a labile term is 'God.' Many persons in our
society would flatly refuse to call a being 'God' if they did not
believe this being to be omnipotent. Usage is far from firm,
however. Some persons, especially those called "believers in a
finite God," exclude omnipotence not only from the strict intension of the term but even from its loose and contingent intension. Still other users are highly confused. If asked whether
omnipotence is a defining property of the word 'God' or a fact
about God, they would not know how to answer. For them the
term is labile with respect to the property of omnipotence.

Most terms characterized by user ambiguity are also labile to
some degree; for whenever in any society there are two classes
of users who employ a given term with different strict intensions, there is likely to be a third class of users who vacillate in

their own usage or who cannot make up their minds. So, too, most terms characterized by vagueness of family resemblance in their conventional use tend toward some measure of lability; for we are often torn between an impatience with vagueness and a respect for conventional usage despite its vagueness. To the extent that our impatience gets the better of us, we will be tempted to promote certain meaning criteria to the status of defining properties while demoting the rest to the status of contingent properties. The person who says "Of course it's a poem: it's in rhyme and meter," or who says, "You can't call that a poem: it has neither rhyme nor meter," has obviously yielded to that temptation. But to the extent that our respect for conventional usage prevails, we will restrain our impatience and accept the term in all its conventional vagueness.

IV • GENERALITY

When in ordinary discourse a term is said to be 'vague' or 'ambiguous' it is often difficult to know which of the three characteristics of terms so far discussed in this chapter the speaker intends to attribute to it. Few of us are fully aware of the differences among vagueness, ambiguity, and lability; and ordinary language even lacks a term for lability. Common usage is still less clear with regard to the three pairs of terms we are about to discuss: 'general' and 'specific,' 'theoretical' and 'observational,' 'abstract' and 'concrete.'

Perhaps the most broadly and loosely used of these terms are 'abstract' and 'concrete.' Suppose that an instructor in an English composition class tells you to be less 'abstract' or more 'concrete.' What does he mean? He might mean several things: (1) If you are describing something with the help of common nouns or class terms, use the most descriptive expression possible. Do not, for example, say that so-and-so is 'a baseball player' if he can be more fully described as 'a Yankee pitcher.' (2) If you are giving a report of some event—say, a student convention—in which you participated, tell more about what you actually experienced and less about what you think explains your experience. In other words, tell it "as it was"; do not get bogged down in lengthy explanations. (3) If you are discussing some complex state of affairs, do not overuse adjectives. Use more nouns, especially proper nouns. If, for example, you are recounting your experiences as a worker in some political campaign, do not say simply that you met lots of interesting people. Name them and describe what kinds of things they did and said.

Of these three popular meanings of 'concrete,' 3 is closest to the technical meaning of the term. The advice implicit in 1 would be better expressed technically by saying: "Be more specific," or "Be less general." The advice implicit in 2 would be better expressed technically by saying: "Be less theoretical" or "Use more observational terms." Let us analyze these expressions.

The terms 'general' and 'specific' derive from the Latin words *genus* and *species*. Zoologists use these terms in classifying living creatures. There is an important difference, however, between their use in zoology and their use in logic. In zoology the meaning of these terms is ordinarily absolute or fixed. The fact that mammals are a subclass of vertebrates does not justify saying that mammals are a species of vertebrates; nor does the fact that Caucasians are a subclass of man justify regarding man as a genus. In logic, however, 'genus' and 'species' are strictly relative terms. Any more inclusive class is a genus with respect to its subclasses, and any subclass is a species of any more inclusive class comprehending it. In logic mammals *are* a species of the genus vertebrates, and Caucasians *are* a species of the genus man.

When, therefore, we say that one class term is more specific than a second, it is usually the case that the first denotes a species, or subclass, of a larger class denoted by the second term. The term 'mammals,' for instance, is more specific than the term 'vertebrates,' because the class of mammals is smaller than the class of vertebrates. Similarly, the term 'Caucasian' is more specific than the term 'man,' since the class of Caucasians is smaller than the class of men. However, because the terms 'general' and 'specific' also apply to class terms denoting null sets, a definition of generality and specificity in terms of class size would not be satisfactory. The term 'gremlins' is more specific than the term 'imaginary beings,' but since both denote empty classes, we can not say that one denotes a smaller class than the other.

Accordingly, we offer the following definition. One term is *specific* relative to a second if its strict intension includes all the properties found in the strict intension of the second and in addition a property or set of properties not found in the strict intension of the second. Thus 'mammals' is specific relative to 'vertebrates,' because mammals, being vertebrates, have all of the defining properties of 'vertebrates' and in addition, certain defining properties, called *specific differences*, that set off the class of mammals from all other subclasses of vertebrates. Conversely, of course, the term 'vertebrates' is general relative to 'mammals,' since the strict intension of 'vertebrates' lacks the specific differences of 'mammals.'

Frequently it is possible to list groups of terms in order of increasing specificity. For example: 'vertebrates,' 'mammals,' 'men,' 'Caucasians.' And it should be noted that in such rankings the more specific term is always more descriptive than its predecessor. If we say that some being is a mammal, we are giving more information than if we say it is a vertebrate. If we say that it is a man, we are giving more information than if we say it is a mammal. And so forth. It should also be noted, however, that no class term ever includes in its intension all the properties of any real individual. Almost all class terms are introduced into language because of a need to refer to a group of individuals who have been observed to possess common properties, and they describe these individuals entirely in terms of these common properties. Only rarely does a class term denote a class with a single member; and even in these unusual cases it does not give an exhaustive description of this single member in its uniqueness as an individual. For example, the only member of the denotation of the class term 'a natural satellite of the earth' (which is not to be confused with the definite description 'the natural satellite of the earth') is the moon; but obviously the moon has many properties in addition to that of being a natural satellite of the earth.

V • THEORETICALITY

A *theoretical term* is any term standing for something that is not immediately or directly experienced itself but is believed to be useful in explaining things that are immediately or directly experienced. An *observational term,* on the other hand, stands for something that can be immediately or directly experienced. Since the expression 'immediately or directly experienced' is vague, and like many vague terms relative as well, the expressions 'observational terms' and 'theoretical terms' are also vague and relative. In the context of scientific inquiry, for instance, terms standing for physical objects that may be touched or seen are normally considered observational terms. Some philosophers, however, have argued that no physical object is ever directly experienced. One of the defining properties of a 'physical object,' they say, is that of continuing to exist when unperceived; but obviously there can be no direct experience of something existing when unperceived. They also argue that every physical object is by definition three-dimensional and that we can never directly experience all three dimensions. When we look at a table we can not observe both the sides facing us and the sides hidden from our view. According to these philosophers, all that can be immediately or directly experienced are the elements of physical objects out of which physical objects themselves are constructed by inference. Thus, all terms standing for physical objects are theoretical terms.

Even if one waives these difficulties, there are still other problems with the notion of direct experience. Are terms for bacteria, which can only be observed through a microscope, observational or theoretical? What about 'stars'? Do we directly experience stars many thousands of light-years away from the earth? What about 'God'? Some persons claim that God totally transcends human experience; others, that God is for them an immediate living presence.

Notwithstanding these difficulties, paradigm cases can be found to illustrate the distinction between theoretical and observational terms. 'Atoms' and 'genes' are certainly theoretical terms.

'Twinges of pain' and 'blue sensation' (which denotes the experience a person with normal vision has when he observes a blue
object in ordinary light rather than a blue object itself) are
no less certainly observational terms. Moreover, the scientist's
designation of terms for physical objects as 'observational' is
perfectly harmless within the context of his inquiry. Without
question these terms are less theoretical than 'atoms' and 'genes,'
and there is no reason at all why the scientist should share the
philosopher's preoccupations.

Also, despite its vagueness the distinction between theoretical
and observational terms has the great merit of directing our attention to independent properties of terms all too often confused
with abstractness or generality.

VI • ABSTRACTNESS

Speaking loosely, we may say that a word or phrase is 'concrete' if it is used in a sentence to refer to some individual or
group of individuals; and 'abstract' if used to refer not to individuals or groups themselves but to their properties. More
specifically and accurately, a term is *concrete* if it is used to refer
to a thing or event conceived as having an independent existence
in a space-time continuum or to a class of things or events whose
members are so conceived; *abstract,* if it is used to refer to a trait
or activity of individuals so conceived. Thus, in the sentence
'George Washington was under six feet tall,' the name 'George
Washington' is a concrete term, since George Washington had a
unique and independent existence in space and time. But the
attributive property term 'under six feet tall' is abstract, since the
trait of being under six feet tall can not be conceived as having
an independent existence in space and time; it is rather a property
of individuals so conceived. Similarly, in the sentence 'All men
have sinned,' the class name 'men' is concrete, since each member
of its denotation is a separate individual, but the attributive property term 'have sinned' is abstract, since the property of having
sinned has no unique and definitely locatable niche in a space-
time continuum. Again, in the sentence 'Hamlet was melancholy,'

'Hamlet' is a concrete term, for although Hamlet did not exist he must nonetheless be thought of as having existed at a definite place and time; whereas 'melancholy' is abstract, since melancholy is not conceived as having a definite spatial or temporal location.

All property terms are by definition abstract. Class terms, however, may be either abstract or concrete, depending upon whether they are used as names or attributions. In the sentence, 'All men are sinners,' for instance, both 'men' and 'sinners' are class terms, but whereas 'men' is concrete, 'sinners' is abstract. This is not to deny, of course, either that sinners are individuals or that the term-type 'sinners' may denote a set of individuals. But in the sentence cited, 'sinners' is used not to name individuals but to attribute a property to individuals already named. Its logical function is no different from that of the attributive property term 'have sinned.' This may be seen by comparing the sentences 'All men have sinned' and 'All men are sinners.' The cognitive meaning of the two sentences is identical. The temptation to equate the distinction between abstract and concrete terms with the distinction between property terms and class terms must therefore be resisted.

So too we must resist the temptation to equate the distinction between concrete and abstract terms with the distinction between names and attributions. For although all attributive terms are by definition abstract, not all names are concrete. Property names (for example, 'blueness' and 'triangularity') are always abstract. In ordinary English grammar they are, in fact, known as 'abstract nouns.'

VII • PROPERTY TERMS AND SINGULAR NAMES

Of the terms discussed above used to characterize class terms, all but 'concrete' may be applied to property terms as well. That is, property terms are invariably abstract rather than concrete; but they may be either vague or precise, ambiguous or unambiguous, labile or non-labile, general or specific, theoretical or observational. Since, however, the definitions of these expressions in the preceding sections are framed in terms of intension and extension, these definitions do not apply directly to property terms, which have neither intension nor extension. Nonetheless, the definitions can be applied indirectly. Since every property defines a class—namely, the class of beings who possess this property—it is always possible to find or construct a class term corresponding to any property term: triangular, triangle; blue, blue thing; widowed, widowed person; is a man, man, etc. Thus, to determine the status of a given property term, one need simply translate it into its corresponding class term and inquire into the latter's status. If the corresponding class term is vague, ambiguous, labile, etc., so is the property term itself.

The characterization of singular names is a somewhat more complex matter. For obvious reasons 'general' and 'specific' do not apply. On the other hand, the expressions 'theoretical' and 'observational,' 'ambiguous' and 'unambiguous,' 'labile' and 'non-labile' do apply, and in exactly the same sense as when applied to class terms or property terms. 'God,' for example, is a relatively theoretical term; it is also, as noted earlier, ambiguous and labile. 'Vague' and 'precise' are also applicable; but not in exactly the same meaning as when applied to class terms or property terms. For example, 'the Renaissance' and 'the Industrial Revolution' are both vague terms, but only in the sense that they refer to vast, complex entities whose spatio-temporal span can not be precisely delimited and many of whose components can not be readily determined.

That leaves us with 'abstract' and 'concrete.' According to some philosophers a defining property of any 'individual' is that it have its own niche in a space-time continuum. Given this definition, all singular names are necessarily concrete. Some philosophers, however, object to this definition, arguing that many individuals do not have this property. It has been argued, for example, that although God is an individual he is outside both space and time. It has also been argued, to take another example, that the numerals '1,' '2,' '3' denote what are called 'natural numbers'—which though obviously not locatable in a space-time continuum are nonetheless individuals. There can be no doubt, however, that the vast majority of individuals do exist in space and time and consequently that the vast majority of singular names are concrete. Moreover, the existence and nature of alleged individuals such as God and natural numbers are controversial matters.

In conclusion we note once again the importance of not being misled by the fact that many of the terms discussed in this chapter have negative emotive meaning in popular discourse. Few logicians would care to justify token ambiguity. Type ambiguity, however, can be perfectly harmless; and vague, general, theoretical, and abstract terms are indispensable in any even moderately adequate language.

EXERCISES FOR CHAPTER THREE

A. Which of the following terms as conventionally employed are vague, ambiguous, or labile? (Remember that many of these terms will have more than one of these properties.) If vague, is their vagueness linear or a matter of family resemblance? If ambiguous, are they instances of contextual ambiguity or user ambiguity?

1. a science	10. a quadrilateral
2. a social science	11. a desirable political system
3. a physical science	12. a labor union
4. a sick man	13. an Italian
5. a friend	14. a neurotic
6. a brother	15. a fish
7. an economic depression	16. a tragedy
8. a mental illness	17. a holiday
9. an intelligent man	

B. If the terms 'vague,' 'ambiguous,' and 'labile' were used strictly in accord with the definitions given in this text, which, if any, would themselves be vague, ambiguous, or labile?

C. Which, if either, of the following terms in the pairs listed below is more general than the other?

1. a science, a physical science
2. a property term, a property name
3. a spinster, a woman
4. a stallion, a horse
5. a democracy, a representative democracy
6. a lawyer, a professional
7. a sister, a sibling
8. a relative, a cousin
9. a relative, a brother
10. a brother, a cousin

D. Which, if either, of the following terms in the pairs listed below is more theoretical than the other?

1. love, a physical embrace
2. the Empire State Building, the Thirty-Fourth Street side of the Empire State Building
3. a straight stick half submerged in water, a bent stick half submerged in water
4. two good friends, two persons often in one another's company
5. a weightless body, a ten-pound body
6. a flag waver, a patriot
7. pleasure, happiness
8. the blinking reflex, the gambling instinct
9. an element, an atom
10. the pioneer spirit, self-reliance

E. Which of the underlined terms in the sentences below are concrete and which abstract?

1. George Washington slept here.
2. Horses have four legs.
3. Blue is a color.
4. Horses are quadrupeds.
5. Ponies are horses.
6. Death comes to us all.
7. There will be a Third World War.

F. If the terms 'abstract,' 'general,' and 'theoretical' were used consistently as defined in this text, which of the terms defined in this chapter would be applicable to them and under what conditions?

G. Which of the terms in the right-hand column would ordinarily apply to the terms in the left-hand column?

<table>
<tr><td>1. the present king of France</td><td>a. vague</td></tr>
<tr><td>2. blueness</td><td>b. ambiguous</td></tr>
<tr><td>3. friendship</td><td>c. labile</td></tr>
<tr><td>4. George Washington</td><td>d. general</td></tr>
<tr><td>5. my inferiority complex</td><td>e. abstract</td></tr>
<tr><td>6. my index finger</td><td>f. theoretical</td></tr>
<tr><td>7. the solar system</td><td></td></tr>
<tr><td>8. mankind</td><td></td></tr>
<tr><td>9. Renaissance painting</td><td></td></tr>
<tr><td>10. Santa Claus</td><td></td></tr>
</table>

Classifying and Symbolizing Sentences

Sentences, like terms, have two kinds of meaning. Insofar as a sentence is a sign of the existence or nature of something other than itself, it has non-cognitive meaning. Insofar as it is used to make an assertion that is either true or false, it has cognitive meaning. Several kinds of cognitive and non-cognitive meanings of sentences will be discussed in the following chapter. First, however, it will be necessary to indicate various ways in which sentences, particularly sentences with cognitive meaning, are classified and symbolized.

The technical term for the cognitive meaning, or assertive content, of a sentence is *proposition;* and although in ordinary discourse the terms 'proposition' and 'sentence' are often used interchangeably, this practice can be misleading. First, although every proposition must be either true or false, sentences as such are neither true nor false. Sentences are physical realities (ink marks, pencil marks, chalk marks, sounds produced in the human throat, etc.) and are no more true or false than mountains and table tops. Second, two or more sentence-tokens of a given type may express different propositions. For example, each token of 'He is in California' in which 'he' denotes a different individual expresses a different proposition even though each is a token of the same type. Conversely, a single proposition can be expressed in many different sentence-types. For example, 'Socrates is human' and 'Socrates is a man' express the same proposition even though they are tokens of different sentence-types.

55

The fact that almost any proposition may be given a number of different linguistic expressions has long disturbed logicians. Consider for example, the following sentences:

(1) John went home and Mary stayed.
(2) Even though John went home, Mary stayed.

These sentences express exactly the same proposition, since there is no difference between them that must be taken into account to determine the truth or falsity of what they are used to assert. However, sentence 2, unlike sentence 1, is a sign of some surprise or interest on the part of the speaker that Mary should have stayed; and since we are not always quick to disentangle non-cognitive meaning from cognitive meaning, we may easily be led to believe that these two sentences express different propositions. Consider also:

(1) All men are mortal.
(2) It is not the case that any man is immortal.

These sentences also express a single proposition. But once again the difference in linguistic expression can easily obscure the identity of meaning. In this case, however, possible misunderstanding is due not to misleading non-cognitive meanings but rather to differences in grammatical form.

Logicians have devised two techniques for reducing these possible confusions and thereby simplifying the task of analyzing propositions. The older and more traditional technique was devised by Aristotle in the fourth century B.C. It consists of specifying certain rules for expressing propositions in a relatively small set of sentences. Propositions expressed according to these rules are said to be in *standard sentence form*. And when we wish to interpret or evaluate an argument whose component propositions are not expressed in standard sentence forms, we first restate the argument using none but standard sentence forms. The advantages of this technique may be seen by comparing the two arguments below.

1. All men are mortal.	1. It is not the case that any man is immortal.
2. All Greeks are men.	2. All Greeks are men.
All Greeks are mortal.	All Greeks are mortal.

The argument on the left, whose components are all expressed in standard sentence forms, is obviously easier to evaluate than the argument on the right, whose components are not all in standard sentence forms.

The second technique was devised by many nineteenth- and twentieth-century philosophers. This technique also involves a specification of standard sentence forms and rules for rewriting sentences not already in standard form. However, it carries us two steps further. First, it provides us with a relatively small set of artificial symbols, each standing for a distinctive logical feature of sentences. Second, it provides rules for translating sentences into this artificial language.

In section I of this chapter we shall classify standard sentence forms. In section II we shall show how sentences can be translated into the artificial language of modern symbolic logic.

Before we proceed to the main business of this chapter, however, a further word should be said about propositions. Since the meaning of a sentence does not exist in space and time and since it can not be directly observed, 'proposition' is a theoretical term. And the existential status of propositions—like that of God and the natural numbers presumably denoted by the numerals '1,' '2,' '3,' etc.—is a matter of debate. The standard philosophical interpretations of 'proposition' or 'cognitive sentence meaning' are difficult to understand, and some appear to contradict one another. Fortunately, it is not necessary to resolve these problems to acquire a working knowledge of the rules of logic. The nature of propositions constitutes a chapter in the theory rather than the practice of logic. It must be emphasized, however, that since propositions can not be directly observed, most of the expressions used to describe them are defined indirectly by specifying features of sentences used to express them. For example, when we say that certain propositions are 'universal,' we mean that they may be properly expressed in standard sentence forms beginning with the words 'all' or 'no.' For most practical purposes, therefore, the classification and symbolization of propositions is a classification and symbolization of the sentences used to express them, and most of the vocabulary introduced in this chapter is used to describe both propositions and sentences.

I • CLASSIFYING SENTENCES

Sentences that contain other sentences as components are called *compound sentences*. For example, the sentence 'John went home and Mary went home' contains two component sentences: 'John went home' and 'Mary went home.' Similarly, the sentence 'If Socrates is a man, then Socrates is mortal' contains the component sentences 'Socrates is a man' and 'Socrates is mortal.' Sentences like 'Socrates is mortal' and 'All men are mortal,' which do not contain other sentences as components, are called *noncompound sentences*.

Compound Sentences

The *truth value*, that is, the truth or falsity, of the propositions expressed by many compound sentences may be inferred if we know the truth value of the propositions expressed by their component or components. When this is the case, both the sentences and the propositions expressed by these sentences are said to be *truth-functional compounds*. 'John went home and Mary stayed' is a truth-functional compound, since if either or both of the propositions expressed by its components ('John went home' and 'Mary stayed') are false, the whole is false, whereas if the propositions expressed by both components are true, the whole is true. Similarly, 'It is not the case that resident aliens are subject to the draft' is truth-functional, since if the proposition expressed by its component ('Resident aliens are subject to the draft') is true, the whole is false, whereas if the component is false, the whole is true.

By contrast, 'Jim said that John went home' and 'I hope that resident aliens are not subject to the draft' are not truth-functional, since the truth value of the compound propositions so expressed can not be determined from a knowledge of the truth values of their component propositions. Compounds that are not truth-functional will be omitted from this discussion.

Truth-functional compounds are conventionally given a five-fold classification. One category, called *conjunctions,* have two or more components, called *conjuncts,* which when in standard sentence form are connected by the word 'and.' 'John went home and Mary stayed' is a conjunction in standard form. Its conjuncts are 'John went home' and 'Mary stayed.' The syncategorematic term 'and' that links the conjuncts is called a *logical operator.* The following sentences (among many others) express the same proposition in ordinary English:

Although John went home, Mary stayed.
Although Mary stayed, John went home.
John went home, but Mary stayed.
John went home; even so, Mary stayed.
John went home; however, Mary stayed.

None of these, however, is in standard sentence form, since none contains the standard logical operator 'and.'

Another example of a conjunction in standard form is 'John went home and Mary went home.' This standard sentence form is more awkward than the more common and cognitively equivalent English formulation 'John and Mary went home.' The grammatical simplicity of the latter sentence, however, tends to conceal its logical complexity. The rule is that each separate proposition must be fully expressed. Still another example of a conjunction in standard form is 'John went home and Mary went home and Bill went home.' Here, there are three conjuncts rather than two, and it should be noted that there is no logical limit to the number of a conjunction's components.

No matter how many components it has, a conjunction itself is true if every conjunct is true, and false if one or more conjuncts are false.

The second group of truth-functional compounds are known as *disjunctions.* These have two or more components, called *dis-*

juncts, which when in standard form are connected by the syn-categorematic term 'or.' 'Or,' like 'and,' is called a 'logical opera-tor.' 'John went home or Mary went home' is a disjunction. Dis-junctions, like conjunctions, may have any number of com-ponents. But in this case the compound itself is true if any one of its disjuncts is true, and false if all its disjuncts are false.

Sometimes an English sentence formed with the aid of the operator 'or' is used to assert that one disjunct is true and the other false, thereby denying the possibility of both being true. If, for example, a wife asks her husband to buy two new house-hold items, and he refuses, saying "No, it's going to be one or the other," he is using 'or' in this way. Disjunctions with this meaning are called *exclusive disjunctions,* whereas disjunctions allowing for the possibility of all disjuncts being true are called *inclusive disjunctions.* Exclusive disjunctions, however, are very rare. In this text, therefore, the word 'disjunction,' when used without prefix, refers to inclusive disjunctions, and all standard sentence forms containing the operator 'or' are to be interpreted as inclusive disjunctions.

The third group of truth-functional compounds are called *negations.* The standard logical operator for negations is either 'It is not the case that,' as in 'It is not the case that resident aliens are subject to the draft,' or 'not,' as in 'Resident aliens are not subject to the draft.' The operator 'It is not the case that' has the advantage of more clearly exhibiting the truth-functional character of the sentence in which it occurs. But since it is some-what cumbersome, the shorter operator 'not' is also allowed.

The fourth group of truth-functional compounds are called *conditionals.* 'If Socrates is a man, then Socrates is mortal' is a conditional in standard sentence form. Some alternative but non-standard formulations are: 'Socrates is mortal, if Socrates is a man,' 'The fact that Socrates is human implies that he is mortal,' and 'Either Socrates is not a man, or he is mortal.' The com-ponent of a conditional in standard form that immediately follows the operator 'if' is called the *antecedent;* the component following the operator 'then' is called the *consequent.*

Conditionals are the most puzzling of truth-functional com-pounds. In fact, most conditionals would not ordinarily be re-garded as fully truth-functional. We would all, of course, say that if the antecedent of a conditional is true and its consequent false, then the conditional as such is false. If, for instance, it were shown that Socrates, though a man, is nonetheless immortal, we would deny the truth of the proposition expressed by 'If Socrates is human, then Socrates is mortal.' But given any other truth values for the components, most of us would make no inference at all about the conditional itself. If, for instance, Socrates were known not to be human, we would ordinarily say that the truth of the conditional as a whole must be determined by considerations other than the truth or falsity of its components. More will be said about this in Part Two. Until then, it need only be noted that in accordance with standard logical practice, we shall here treat all conditionals as fully truth-functional—a conditional being false if its antecedent is true and its consequent false, but true for any other combination of truth values of its components. Thus, if the antecedent of a conditional is false, the conditional as a whole is true regardless of the truth value of the consequent. Similarly, if the consequent of a conditional is true, the conditional as a whole is true regardless of the truth value of the antecedent.

Finally, there are truth-functional compounds called *biconditionals*. To understand biconditionals, it must be carefully noted that every conditional proposition has what is known as a *converse*, formed by interchanging its antecedent and consequent. For example, the converse of 'If Socrates is human, then Socrates is mortal' is 'If Socrates is mortal, then Socrates is human.' It must also be carefully noted that when we assert the truth of a conditional, we are *not* asserting the truth of its converse. When, for example, we assert "If Socrates is human, then Socrates is mortal," we are not also asserting "If Socrates is mortal, then Socrates is human." Sometimes, however, we do wish to assert that both a conditional and its converse are true. An assertion of this kind is a biconditional, and when expressed in standard form a biconditional will contain the logical operator 'if and only if'—for example, 'He will come if and only if he feels like it,' or 'The triangle on the blackboard is equilateral if and only if it is equiangular.' A biconditional, then, asserts that its component propositions are either both true or both false, and the biconditional as a whole is true whenever this is the case. If one component is true and the other false, the biconditional itself is false. The components of biconditionals are called *right-hand components* and *left-hand components*.

In the examples of truth-functional compounds given above, each component is a non-compound proposition. However, components themselves can be compound. For instance, 'If all men are mortal and Socrates is a man, then Socrates is mortal' is a conditional whose antecedent is a conjunction. Again, 'It is not the case that he caught the train, or the train is very late' is a disjunction whose first disjunct is a negation. In such cases we speak of 'first-order components,' 'second-order components,' 'third-order components,' and so on. *First-order components* are those whose truth value is directly relevant to the determination of the truth value of the proposition as a whole; *second-order components,* those whose truth value is directly relevant to a determination of the truth value of a first-order component; *third-order components,* those whose truth value is directly relevant to that of a second-order component, and so on. In the proposition 'If all men are mortal and Socrates is a man, then Socrates is mortal,' the antecedent 'All men are mortal and Socrates is a man' is a first-order component, since it is directly relevant to the truth value of the proposition as a whole. 'All men are mortal' and 'Socrates is a man,' however, are second-order components, since their truth values are directly relevant to the truth value of the antecedent, which is a first-order component, but only indirectly relevant to the truth value of the proposition as a whole.

Non-Compound Sentences

In traditional Aristotelian logic propositions expressed by non-compound sentences were given a four-fold classification. Although this traditional classification will be expanded later, our analysis in this section will be restricted to these four categories of propositions.

Propositions of this kind, as well as the sentences used to express them, are called *categorical*. Their standard sentence forms each contain one class name and one attributive term. Two separate principles underlie their classification. The first is known as the *principle of quantity*. If a proposition says that all individuals in the denotation of the relevant class name possess or lack the property designated by the attributive term, it is said to be a *universal proposition* and its standard English sentence form will begin with the words 'all' or 'no.' Thus, 'All men are mortal' and 'No men are angels' are standard sentence forms of their respective universal propositions. If, however, a proposition says only that some of the individuals in the denotation of the class name possess or lack the property designated by the attributive term, it is said to be a *particular proposition* and its standard sentence form will begin with the word 'some.' 'Some men are heroes' and 'Some men are not heroes' are standard sentence forms of their respective particular propositions.

The second principle of classification is the *principle of quality*. If a proposition affirms that all or some of the individuals in the denotation of the class name possess the property designated by the attributive term, it is an *affirmative proposition*. If, however, a proposition denies that the property designated by the attributive term belongs to all or some of the individuals denoted by the class name, it is a *negative proposition*. Thus, 'All men are mortal' and 'Some men are heroes' both express affirmative propositions, whereas 'No men are angels' and 'Some men are not heroes' express negative propositions. The standard sentence form of all universal negative propositions begins with the word 'no.' Where a particular negative proposition is expressed in standard form, the word 'not' immediately precedes the attributive term.

Thus we have four categories in all: *universal affirmative* (for example, 'All men are mortal'); *universal negative* ('No men are dogs'); *particular affirmative* ('Some dogs are white'); and *particular negative* ('Some dogs are not white').

If we use the letter 'N' in place of class names and the letter 'A' in place of attributive terms, the respective standard sentence forms may be schematically represented in the chart below:

	AFFIRMATIVE	NEGATIVE
UNIVERSAL	All N are A	No N are A
PARTICULAR	Some N are A	Some N are not A

Categorical propositions often appear in non-standard sentence forms. For instance, 'All men are mortal' is equivalent to 'Men are mortal,' 'Man is mortal,' 'Any being who is human is mortal,' 'If a being is human, then it is mortal,' and so on. Some non-standard formulations of the universal negative 'No men are dogs' are 'Men are not dogs,' 'If any being is a man, then it is not a dog,' and 'Human beings are not dogs.' Among the non-standard English equivalents of the particular affirmative 'Some dogs are white,' we find 'Dogs are sometimes white,' 'There are dogs that are white,' and 'White dogs are one kind of dog.' Among the non-standard English equivalents of the particular negative 'Some dogs are not white,' must be included 'Not all dogs are white,' 'There are dogs that are not white,' and 'White dogs are only one kind of dog.'

The syncategorematic terms 'all,' 'some,' 'no,' 'not,' and 'are' serve functions similar to 'and,' 'or,' 'if . . . then,' etc., and, like the latter, are called 'logical operators.' Their logical uses generally correspond to their uses in ordinary English discourse and pose no special problems. 'Some,' however, is a significant exception. In ordinary discourse 'some' usually signifies more than one and less than all. Particular propositions when expressed in standard form, however, are interpreted as true if the attributive term applies to only one of the individuals in the extension of its class name and no less true if it applies to all. Thus, when used as a standard operator, 'some' has the precise meaning: at least one. Accordingly, the non-standard sentence form 'One doctor is in attendance' will be written in standard form as 'Some doctor is in attendance.' In like manner, propositions asserting that most, or half, or twenty percent, or a few members of a certain class have a certain property are all put into standard form with the word 'some.' This convention makes it impossible to preserve the full cognitive meaning of many particular propositions. It does, however, preserve a good part of the cognitive meaning of a very large and important class of logically similar propositions.

Although in this traditional four-fold classification universal negative and particular negative propositions appear as non-compound propositions, they may also be symbolized in the manner indicated earlier as truth-functional compounds. For example, the proposition expressed by 'No resident aliens are subject to the draft,' which is in standard non-compound sentence form, may also be expressed by 'It is not the case that some resident aliens are subject to the draft,' which is in standard compound form. Both formulations of this proposition are perfectly correct. The choice of formulation in a particular case will depend on what logical features of the proposition in question we need to exhibit in order to evaluate the argument in which the proposition occurs.

II • SYMBOLIZING SENTENCES

The goals of clarifying propositions and evaluating their role in arguments are obviously promoted by rewriting English sentences in standard form, but these ends are even better achieved by modern symbolic techniques. There are two principal reasons for this. First, most English sentences, even in standard form, have distracting non-cognitive meanings that can best be eliminated by the use of artificial symbols. Second, many English sentences that can not be satisfactorily expressed in standard sentence form can be satisfactorily symbolized.

Truth-Functional Compounds

In symbolizing truth-functional compounds we use three kinds of symbols. First, each of the five standard English operators is assigned a logical symbol:

It is not the case that . . .	−
. . . or . . .	v
. . . and . . .	.
If . . . then . . .	→
. . . if and only if . . .	↔

Second, we use the capital letters of the alphabet 'A' through 'W' as abbreviations for the component propositions. The letter we use to represent a given component is largely a matter of arbitrary choice, although it is customary and helpful to use the first letter of some key term in the component sentence. If, for example, we wanted to symbolize 'John went home,' it would be better to use 'J' or 'W' than 'C' or 'D.' It is important to observe, however, that in a given context each different component must be assigned a different letter and that if the same component occurs more than once in a given context, the same letter must be used in symbolizing each occurrence.

These symbols for logical operators and component propositions allow us to symbolize a large number of truth-functional compounds. For example,

It is not the case that resident aliens are subject to the draft: $-R$

John went home or Mary stayed: $J \lor M$

John went home and Mary stayed: $J \cdot M$

If Socrates is human, then Socrates is mortal: $H \to M$

This is an equilateral triangle if and only if it is an equiangular triangle: $L \leftrightarrow A$

If Socrates is human, then Socrates is human: $H \to H$

John went home and Mary went home and Albert went home: $J \cdot M \cdot A$

John went home or Mary went home or Albert went home: $J \lor M \lor A$

Finally, in symbolizing truth-functional compounds we shall often need parentheses to serve as punctuation marks. Consider for example, the following formula:

$$J \cdot M \to A$$

where 'J' stands for 'John went home,' 'M' for 'Mary went home,' and 'A' for 'Albert went home.' This formula as it stands might be interpreted in two ways:

(1) If John went home and Mary went home, then Albert went home.

(2) John went home; and if Mary went home, then Albert went home.

To eliminate this confusion, propositions 1 and 2 are symbolized as follows:

(1) $(J \cdot M) \to A$
(2) $J \cdot (M \to A)$

The general rule governing the use of the parentheses is that every component that is itself compound must be enclosed in parentheses. Thus, in proposition 1, the component 'J · M,' which is itself compound, is enclosed in parentheses, while the component 'A,' which is not compound, is not enclosed in parentheses. To take a more complex illustration, suppose we are given a conditional proposition whose antecedent is a conjunction whose first conjunct is a disjunction. If we used 'A,' 'B,' 'C,' and 'D' to stand for the component propositions, the symbolization would be:

$$((A \lor B) \cdot C) \to D$$

In this case the outer set of parentheses—around '(A ∨ B) · C'—encloses a compound first-order component, while the inner set of parentheses—around 'A ∨ B'—encloses a compound second-order component.

There is, however, one exception to the general rule. This exception follows from a convention whereby the negation sign applies to the smallest component to which it could conceivably apply. Thus, if we are given a disjunction whose first disjunct is a negation and we use the symbols 'A' and 'B' for the components, this proposition would *not* be symbolized

$$(-A) \lor B$$

but rather

$$-A \lor B$$

Since the negation sign can conceivably apply to 'A' alone, convention decrees that it must and does.

The logical operators and the parentheses are called *logical constants*. The signs for the component propositions are called *propositional constants*. And the formulas that result when a sentence expressing a proposition has been symbolized by logical constants and propositional constants are called *propositional abbreviations.*

Although no symbols other than those already introduced are needed to symbolize truth-functional compound propositions, for purposes of logical analysis we are often not interested in a given proposition as such but merely in what is called its *logical form*— that is, its logical features. And to symbolize the logical form of a proposition, as opposed to the proposition itself, a fourth group of symbols is required. These symbols, the lower-case letters of the alphabet 'p' through 'w,' are called *propositional variables* and are used in the place of propositional constants to stand for any proposition whatsoever. Any propositional variable may be used in place of any propositional constant provided that (1) each different constant in a given context is symbolized by a different variable and (2) any constant that occurs more than once in a given context is symbolized by the same variable in each occurrence. Thus to symbolize the logical form of a proposition abbreviated to '$(A \cdot J) \rightarrow J$' we write '$(p \cdot q) \rightarrow q$.' This latter formula, obtained by replacing constants with variables, is called a *propositional form.* And it should be noted that '$(p \cdot q) \rightarrow q$' symbolizes the form not only of the single proposition '$(A \cdot J) \rightarrow J$' but also of any other proposition with the same logical features.

Non-Compound Sentences

The four categories of non-compound propositions discussed earlier, for which tradition has specified standard sentence forms, by no means exhaust the class of non-compound propositions, and one of the great advantages of modern symbolic logic is that it can be used to symbolize a wide assortment of other propositions. Let us begin, however, by showing how the traditional standard sentence forms are symbolized.

Standard Categorical Sentences

In abbreviating standard categorical sentences we need several symbols in addition to those already introduced:

(x): called the *universal quantifier* and used to replace the standard English operators 'all' and 'no'

(∃x): called the *existential quantifier* and used to replace the standard English operator 'some'

x: called an *individual variable* and used to stand for any individual being whatsoever—a piece of chalk, a chair, a dog, the French Revolution, the solar system, or what have you

The capital letters of the alphabet 'A' through 'W': called *property constants* and used to replace categorematic terms

With the help of these symbols the universal affirmative proposition expressed by 'All human beings are mortal' can be symbolized as follows:

$$(x)(Hx \to Mx)$$

This formula is read: for any x, if x is human, then x is mortal.

To symbolize the universal negative proposition expressed by 'No men are angels' we may write:

$$(x)(Mx \to -Ax)$$

This formula is read: for any x, if x is a man, then x is not an angel.

To symbolize the particular affirmative and the particular negative propositions expressed by 'Some men are heroes' and 'Some men are not heroes' we write respectively:

$$(1) \quad (\exists x)(Mx \cdot Hx)$$
$$(2) \quad (\exists x)(Mx \cdot -Hx)$$

These formulas are read: (1) there is at least one x such that x is a man and x is a hero, and (2) there is at least one x such that x is a man and x is not a hero.

Since all standard-form categorical sentences contain at least one class term, it might be asked how a formula that contains no symbols for class terms can adequately symbolize these sentences. How can we use property constants to stand for all categorematic terms, even when they are class terms? To answer this question, it must be observed that just as every property term has at least one corresponding class term, so every class term has at least one corresponding property term. Since a class is merely a set of individuals sharing one or more properties, for every class term there is (or we may construct) a property term that designates the shared property or properties. The class term 'man,' for example, has the corresponding property terms 'humanity,' 'human,' 'being a man,' 'is a man.' Thus, although the proposition 'All human beings are mortal' was traditionally interpreted as asserting that all individuals included in the class of men are also included in the class of mortals, it is equally correct to interpret this proposition as asserting that all individuals having the property of being human also have the property of mortality. And in modern symbolic logic this latter interpretation has been adopted.

The adequacy of the formulas given above might be questioned on other grounds. Consider again 'All human beings are mortal.' It might be argued that the proposition so expressed asserts the existence of human beings, in which case its symbolic formulation

$$(x)(Hx \to Mx)$$

is inadequate, since the symbolic formula asserts simply that *if* there is an individual who is human, then it is mortal. To meet this objection we must once again recall the distinction between cognitive and non-cognitive meaning. For, although in most contexts the utterance 'All human beings are mortal' does give grounds for inferring the existence of human beings, this is not a part of the cognitive meaning, or the propositional content, of the sentence. In other words, the person who says "All human beings are mortal" may presuppose the existence of human beings; but this presupposition is not actually asserted.

It must be noted, however, that *particular* propositions do assert the existence of at least one individual and that this assertion is part of their cognitive meaning. In technical language, particular propositions have *existential import*. If we say that some men are heroes, we are not merely giving grounds for in-

ferring that men who are heroes exist; we are actually asserting
that at least one man who is a hero does exist. This is immediately
apparent in the English reading of abbreviations for particular
propositions. Thus, '$(\exists x)(Mx \cdot Hx)$,' where 'M' stands for the
property of being a man and 'H' for the property of being a hero,
reads: There is at least one x such that x is a man and x is a hero.

If we use the Greek letters 'ϕ' and 'ψ' (*phi* and *psi*) as *property
variables*, the logical forms of categorical propositions can be
represented as follows:

	AFFIRMATIVE	NEGATIVE
UNIVERSAL	$(x)(\phi x \rightarrow \psi x)$	$(x)(\phi x \rightarrow -\psi x)$
PARTICULAR	$(\exists x)(\phi x \cdot \psi x)$	$(\exists x)(\phi x \cdot -\psi x)$

Other Non-Compound Sentences

Non-compound propositions not falling into one of the traditional molds are an extremely heterogeneous lot, and many are
too complex for treatment in an elementary logic text. Three
types, however, are of special importance, and should be mentioned here.

EXISTENTIAL

The term *existential proposition* has two meanings. Sometimes,
it is used widely to denote any proposition with existential import. At other times it is used narrowly to denote any proposition that functions exclusively as an assertion of existence. In its
wider meaning all particular propositions are existential, but in
its narrower meaning no particular proposition is existential.
Here we shall use the term in its narrower meaning.

Consider the sentence 'Human beings exist.' Beginning logic
students often erroneously symbolize such a sentence as a universal proposition. The error arises because 'exist' is a *grammatical* predicate and most grammatical predicates are attributive terms. 'Exist' is not, however, a *logical* predicate. The impossibility of treating 'exist' as a logical predicate or an attributive term can perhaps best be seen in the following way: 'Human

beings exist' is obviously equivalent in cognitive meaning to
'There are human beings.' It follows that 'exist' does the same
job in the first sentence as 'There are' does in the second. And
since 'There are' obviously does not function as an attributive
term, 'exist' does not function as one either.

The propositional form of existential propositions, therefore,
is *not* '(x)(ϕx $\rightarrow$ ψx)' but rather '($\exists$x)(ϕx).' And if we wish to
symbolize 'Human beings exist,' we must do so with the abbrevia-
tion '($\exists$x)(Hx),' *not* with the abbreviation '(x)(Hx $\rightarrow$ Ex).' To
symbolize negative existential propositions we merely place a
negation sign before the quantifier. Thus, 'There are no gremlins'
becomes '$-$($\exists$x)(Gx).'

SINGULAR

All non-compound sentences whose subjects are singular names
are singular sentences. In abbreviating them symbolically we use
the symbols already introduced and, in addition, the lower-case
letters of the alphabet 'a' through 'w' as *individual constants*.
Thus, to abbreviate 'George Washington slept here' we write
'Sw.' This may be read back into English: There is an individual
w who possesses the property S.

Since sentences abbreviated with the aid of individual constants
have existential import, these constants should not be used to
symbolize singular names standing for entities that do not exist
or whose existence is in doubt. Such sentences are best symbolized as universals. Thus, 'Pegasus has wings' and 'God is
omnipotent' should be abbreviated as '(x)(Px $\rightarrow$ Wx)' and
'(x)(Gx $\rightarrow$ Ox),' respectively.

RELATIONAL

Any sentence, and any proposition thereby expressed, is relational if the sentence contains a two-place term, a three-place
term, a four-place term, etc. For some purposes relationality can
be ignored and a relational proposition symbolized as though
the relational term were a simple one-place term. For example,
in symbolizing the proposition expressed by 'John is taller than
Bill,' we might allow 'T' to stand for 'is taller than Bill' and write
simply 'Tj.' It is clear, however, that this symbolization does not

do justice to the logical complexity of the proposition and that it could be more fully symbolized as 'Tjb,' where 'T' stands for 'is taller than.'

In symbolizing relational propositions we often need quantifiers in addition to '(x)' and '(∃x).' For this purpose '(y),' '(z),' '(∃y),' '(∃z)' have been reserved. Thus, to symbolize 'All Quakers hate war,' we might write

$$(x)(y)((Qx \cdot Wy) \rightarrow Hxy)$$

This is read: for any x and for any y, if x is a Quaker and y is a war, then x hates y. To symbolize 'A few Quakers have committed acts of violence' we might write

$$(\exists x)(\exists y)(Qx \cdot Vy \cdot Cxy)$$

This is read: there is an x and there is a y such that x is a Quaker and y is an act of violence, and x has committed y.

The symbols introduced here are not adequate to deal with all relational propositions. Moreover, there are no strict rules for symbolizing even those propositions for which our symbolic vocabulary is adequate. When we have to symbolize three-place or four-place terms, our ingenuity is often sorely taxed, and even two-place terms can pose serious problems. For example, 'There is a man for every woman' does not make the relational property fully explicit and in addition has a grammatical structure that leads us to suppose erroneously that its logical formulation would begin as follows: (∃x)(Mx . . .). Actually, its correct symbolization must begin: (x)(Wx . . .). When completely symbolized, the abbreviation reads:

$$(x)(Wx \rightarrow (\exists y)(My \cdot Syx))$$

This is read: for any x, if x is a woman, then there is a y such that y is a man and y is suitable for x.

In view of these difficulties a full discussion of relational sentences is properly the subject matter of an advanced course in logic. It is important, however, to realize that language is an extremely complex and subtle instrument and that the difficulties in symbolizing these sentences are due not to artificial complexities invented by logicians but to the nature of language itself.

EXERCISES FOR CHAPTER FOUR

A. The sentence 'If he comes, then he will be seen and he will be heard' expresses a conditional proposition whose consequent is a conjunction. Describe in similar fashion the propositions expressed by the following sentences:

1. We will eat and we will drink and we will be merry.
2. If it is not the case that he will work, then it is not the case that he will eat.
3. If it is not the case that he will come, then it is not the case that he will be seen and it is not the case that he will be heard.
4. If he is not rich or if he will not work, then he will starve.
5. If he is rich, then he will not starve; and if he works, then he will not starve.
6. If he is a United States citizen, then he was born on United States territory or he was born abroad of parents who are United States citizens or he has acquired United States citizenship by naturalization.
7. If he is poor and it is not the case that he will work, then he will starve.
8. If all mammals have wings and all men are mammals, then all men have wings.
9. If the antecedent of a conditional is false, then the conditional itself is true; and if the consequent of a conditional is true, then the conditional itself is true.
10. If the antecedent of a conditional is false or the consequent is true, then the conditional itself is true.
11. If the antecedent of a conditional is true and the consequent false, then the conditional itself is false.

12. A biconditional is true if and only if its first-order components are both true or its first-order components are both false.
13. If a biconditional is true, then if one of its first-order components is true the other is true, and if one of its first-order components is false the other is false.

B. If 'A,' 'B,' and 'C' stand for true propositions and 'R,' 'S,' and 'T' for false propositions, which of the truth-functional compounds below are true and which are false:

1. $(A \vee B) \cdot C$ 7. $R \to ((A \vee B) \cdot (R \vee S))$
2. $(A \cdot B \cdot R)$ 8. $R \leftrightarrow S$
3. $(A \vee R \vee S)$ 9. $((A \to B) \vee (B \to A)) \to A$
4. $A \leftrightarrow R$ 10. $-R \to ((A \to B) \vee (B \to A))$
5. $A \to R$ 11. $-(R \vee S) \to C$
6. $A \to B$ 12. $((A \to B) \vee (B \to A)) \to -R$

C. Rewrite the following sentences in standard compound sentence form.

1. No man is a law unto himself.
2. John is not a law unto himself.
3. Neither John nor Bill is a law unto himself.
4. He will come despite the bad weather.
5. There is always political unrest when large numbers of persons are unemployed.
6. When there is serious unemployment and political unrest, the result is a weakening of the nation's moral fiber.
7. Serious unemployment means political unrest.
8. John will come only if the weather is good.
9. Political unrest is a consequence of serious unemployment.
10. If he will eat he must work.

D. Put the following sentences into standard sentence form, if they are not already in standard form. Classify each as universal affirmative, universal negative, particular affirmative, or particular negative.

1. No man is a law unto himself.
2. Every man has his price.
3. Some men are not corruptible.
4. All men are not corruptible.
5. Some men are incorruptible.
6. There are many dishonest men.
7. It is not possible to be a politician and to be honest.
8. Ladies are present.
9. Gentlemen prefer blondes.
10. If any man is a radical then he is a bad diplomat.
11. Only the rich are truly free.
12. There are honest politicians.
13. None but the rich are free.
14. God helps those who help themselves.
15. Heavy storms sometimes cause great damage.

E. Symbolize the truth-functional compound sentences in Exercise A, page 74, using propositional abbreviations.

F. Symbolize the sentences in Exercise C, page 75, using propositional abbreviations.

G. Symbolize the sentences below:

1. Lincoln and McKinley were both assassinated.
2. There are no centaurs.
3. Uncle Sam wears a tall hat.
4. George Washington had false teeth.
5. There is a father and a mother for every child.
6. A sailor has a girl in every port.
7. Every sibling has either a brother or a sister.
8. Every man has been charmed by some woman.
9. Spinach and kale are nutritious.
10. John is some man.

The Meaning of Sentences

We have noted that the cognitive meaning of sentences is especially important to the student of logic, since cognitive meaning alone is directly relevant to the evaluation of arguments. Because the cognitive and non-cognitive meanings of sentences may be easily confused, however, both kinds of meaning will be discussed in this chapter.

I • COGNITIVE MEANING

Depending on what we must do to determine the truth or falsity of the propositions they express, sentences fall into three distinct categories, each of which represents one kind of cognitive meaning. A sentence is *formal* if the truth or falsity of the proposition it expresses can be fully determined through an understanding of its logical form alone. A sentence is *definitional* if the truth or falsity of the proposition it expresses can be fully determined only if we understand (1) its logical form and (2) the cognitive meaning of its categorematic terms. Finally, a sentence is *material* if to determine the truth or falsity of the proposition it expresses we must (1) understand its logical form, (2) understand the meaning of its categorematic terms, and (3) have some additional knowledge about whatever is denoted or designated by its categorematic terms.

Thus, 'Lincoln was assassinated or Lincoln was not assassinated' is a formal sentence, since it has the form 'p v —p' and all propositions having this form are true by virtue of their form alone. 'All bachelors are unmarried' and 'All men are less than ten feet tall,' however, are *not* formal sentences, since the form of the propositions they express—namely, '(x)(ϕx → ψx),'—does not suffice to guarantee their truth or falsity. The sample propositions of this second form happen to be true, but many propositions of the same form (for example, the proposition expressed by 'All men are over ten feet tall') are false.

Despite their identity of logical form, 'All bachelors are unmarried' and 'All men are less than ten feet tall' have different kinds of meanings. Anybody who recognizes the logical form of the sentence 'All bachelors are unmarried' and who, in addition, knows the meanings of 'bachelors' and 'unmarried' can see at a glance that the proposition it expresses is true. But still more is required to determine the truth of the proposition expressed by 'All men are less than ten feet tall.' In this case we must not only recognize its logical form and understand the meanings of its categorematic terms, we must also observe men and see whether they are in fact under ten feet tall. Thus, whereas 'All bachelors are unmarried' is definitional, 'All men are less than ten feet tall' is material.

Formal Meaning

The formal sentence 'Lincoln was assassinated or Lincoln was not assassinated' expresses a true compound proposition. Formal propositions may, however, be either true or false and either compound or non-compound. For example, 'Lincoln was assassinated and Lincoln was not assassinated' expresses a false compound proposition. 'All unmarried men are unmarried' expresses a true non-compound proposition. 'All unmarried men are married' expresses a false non-compound proposition. When a formal proposition—compound or non-compound—is true, it is a *tautology*. When a formal proposition—compound or non-compound—is false, it is a *self-contradiction*. Thus, 'Lincoln was assassinated or Lincoln was not assassinated' and 'All unmarried men are unmarried' both express tautologies, whereas 'Lincoln was assassinated and Lincoln was not assassinated' and 'All unmarried men are married' both express self-contradictions.

As with all formal propositions, the truth or falsity of these examples can be determined simply by inspecting their logical forms. Any sentence or proposition whose form is 'p v −p' expresses a tautology, regardless of what sentence or proposition replaces 'p.' Thus all the propositions expressed below are tautologies:

> Lincoln was assassinated or Lincoln was not assassinated.
> Washington was assassinated or Washington was not assassinated.
> John is in the library or John is not in the library.
> The moon is made of blue cheese or the moon is not made of blue cheese.

Similarly, all sentences whose form is '$(x)((\phi x \cdot \psi x) \to \phi x)$,' such as 'All unmarried men are unmarried,' express tautologies. For example,

> All single men are single.
> All unmarried women are unmarried.
> All wild animals are wild.
> All blue objects are blue.
> All old houses are old.

Although we defined a 'formal proposition' by saying that its truth value depends wholly on its logical form, we could define a 'formal proposition' alternatively by saying that its truth value is wholly determined by the meaning of the logical operators used to express it. If, for example, someone were to say "It is false that all unmarried men are unmarried," we would not claim that he had misunderstood the use of the categorematic terms 'unmarried' and 'men,' since the truth of the proposition expressed by this sentence does not depend on the meaning of these terms. We would say, rather, that the person does not understand the rules of usage for the syncategorematic terms 'all' and 'are.' Similarly, if someone were to say "It is true that Lincoln was assassinated and that Lincoln was not assassinated," we would not assume that he had misunderstood the meaning of 'Lincoln was assassinated,' but rather that he failed to recognize the conventional usage of the syncategorematic terms 'and' and 'not.'

Tautologous and self-contradictory non-compound propositions are almost always intuitively recognizable when expressed in standard sentence form. Tautologous and self-contradictory truth-functional compounds, however, are not always easy to recognize even when in standard sentence form. In such cases we employ diagrams called 'truth tables' to determine their status. However, since these diagrams are also useful for the purpose of defining the logical operators and since tautologies and self-contradictions acquire their status through the way in which their operators are being used, it will be helpful to explain first how these diagrams are employed to define the logical operators.

Truth-Table Definitions of Logical Operators

When in the last chapter we defined the logical operators used in expressing truth-functional compounds, what we did was to state informally the combinations of truth values of the first-order components of a negation, a conjunction, a disjunction, etc. that would make a negation, a conjunction, a disjunction, etc. true or false. Truth tables do the same thing diagrammatically. In constructing truth tables for this purpose, we first make an exhaustive list of every possible combination of truth values for the first-order components linked by the given operator. We then indicate the truth values for any compound proposition whose components are so linked, given each possible combination of truth values.

Since negations have only one first-order component and consequently only two possible truth values, the simplest truth table is one for the negation sign. In constructing this table (as in constructing any truth table) we begin by writing the symbol for the first-order component (or components) at the head of a column to the left and the symbol for the truth-functional compound itself at the head of a column to the right. Thus,

$$p \quad -p$$

In the left-hand column, called a *guide column* (or *guide columns*), we give an exhaustive enumeration of the possible truth values for the first-order component (or components), and in the right-hand column, the truth value of the compound itself, given the truth value of the component (or components) indicated at the left in the same row. Thus, the truth table for a negation is:

	p	-p
(1)	T	F
(2)	F	T

Row 1 of this table specifies that if the proposition symbolized by 'p' is true, then '—p' is false. Row 2 specifies that if the proposition symbolized by 'p' is false then the proposition symbolized by '—p' is true. Since these specifications follow from the way we have chosen to use the symbol '—,' this truth table defines the negation symbol.

Since conditionals consist of two first-order components, an antecedent and a consequent, a truth table defining the conditional symbol '→' will have two guide columns, one for the antecedent and one for the consequent. In addition, there will be a column for the conditional itself. And since a proposition with two components has four possible combinations of truth values, there will be four rows. Thus, to define '→' we need the following table:

	p	q	p → q
(1)	T	T	T
(2)	T	F	F
(3)	F	T	T
(4)	F	F	T

By reading this table we see that any proposition properly symbolized by 'p → q' is true if both the antecedent and the consequent are true (row 1), if the antecedent is false and the consequent true (row 3), and if both antecedent and consequent are false (row 4). The conditional is false if and only if the antecedent is true and the consequent false (row 2).[1]

The truth table for the biconditional symbol '↔' is as follows:

	p	q	p ↔ q
(1)	T	T	T
(2)	T	F	F
(3)	F	T	F
(4)	F	F	T

As the truth table indicates, a biconditional is true whenever both components are true (row 1) or whenever both components are false (row 4). It is false whenever one component is true and the other false (rows 2 and 3).

Since disjunctions can have any number of first-order components, it is impossible to give a complete definition of the disjunction sign in a single truth table. It is possible, however, to define this symbol by stating general rules to be observed in constructing a truth table for any disjunction. First, one counts the number of first-order components and writes down a heading for each. Second, one determines the number of rows that are required to show every possible combination of truth values for the component first-order propositions. If there are two components, four rows are required; if there are three components, eight rows are required; if four, sixteen rows. The rule is that for each additional first-order component the number of rows required will double. Third, one fills in the guide columns. To be sure that every possible combination of truth values for the components is represented, it is customary to split the first column into half 'T's' and half 'F's,' beginning with 'T's.' The second column is divided into quarters, beginning with 'T's.' The third

[1] As noted in Chapter Four, although all propositions whose standard sentence form requires the use of the English operator 'If . . . then . . . .' are symbolized with the aid of '→,' this symbol does not always have the same meaning as 'If . . . then . . . .' The meaning of '→' is defined by the truth table. Why '→' does not preserve the meaning of the corresponding standard English operator will be discussed in a later chapter. At this point it is enough to note that there is a disparity.

column is divided into eighths, beginning with 'T's.' And so forth. If this procedure is properly followed, the last guide column will consist of an alternation of single 'T's' and 'F's.' Assume, for example, that we wish to determine the meaning of 'v' in sentences whose form is 'p v q v r.' Since there are three components, we need eight rows. If we follow the third rule, the result will be

	p	q	r	p v q v r
(1)	T	T	T	
(2)	T	T	F	
(3)	T	F	T	
(4)	T	F	F	
(5)	F	T	T	
(6)	F	T	F	
(7)	F	F	T	
(8)	F	F	F	

To complete the construction of the table we write a 'T' in a column immediately to the right of the heading for the disjunction itself in every row where one or more 'T's' appear in the guide column and an 'F' for every row in which only 'F's' occur in the guide columns. Thus the complete truth table for 'p v q v r' is as follows:

	p	q	r	p v q v r
(1)	T	T	T	T
(2)	T	T	F	T
(3)	T	F	T	T
(4)	T	F	F	T
(5)	F	T	T	T
(6)	F	T	F	T
(7)	F	F	T	T
(8)	F	F	F	F

As this table clearly indicates, propositions having the form 'p v q v r' are true for every possible combination of truth values of their components except that indicated by row 8, where all components are false.

Note that in constructing truth tables for negations, conditionals, and biconditionals, the column indicating the truth value of the compound proposition as a whole is placed directly under the logical operator. And if we were symbolizing a disjunction or a conjunction with only two first-order components, the same procedure would be followed. Thus, the truth table for 'p v q' would be written

	p	q	p v q
(1)	T	T	T
(2)	T	F	T
(3)	F	T	T
(4)	F	F	F

This symbolization is convenient and appropriate, since with fewer than three first-order components, there is only one occurrence of the logical operator and the meaning of that operator is defined by the column directly below it. If, however, there are three or more first-order components, there will be at least two occurrences of the operator, and what must be defined is their joint occurrence. To place the column indicating the truth value of the proposition as a whole under one occurrence of the operator rather than another would therefore be inappropriate.

In constructing truth tables for conjunctions, the initial steps are the same as in constructing truth tables for disjunctions. But since a conjunction is true if and only if all its components are true, the column indicating the truth value of the compound itself will have to be filled in accordingly. Thus, the truth table for propositions having the form 'p · q · r' is

	p	q	r	p · q · r
(1)	T	T	T	T
(2)	T	T	F	F
(3)	T	F	T	F
(4)	T	F	F	F
(5)	F	T	T	F
(6)	F	T	F	F
(7)	F	F	T	F
(8)	F	F	F	F

Using Truth Tables to Classify Propositions

Once we understand the use of truth tables to define logical operators, it is a relatively easy matter to construct truth tables to determine whether a given truth-functional compound is a tautology or a self-contradiction.

In constructing truth tables for this purpose, we assign a different symbol to each component proposition—not merely to each different first-order component, but to every different component—and of course we use the same symbol for all token occurrences of the same component proposition. The number of guide columns will be determined by the number of different components, and the number of rows by the number of guide columns, in the manner already indicated. The abbreviated proposition will be written to the right of the headings for the guide columns. Thus, to determine the status of the obvious tautology 'If there is rain and the crops grow, then the crops grow' one begins as follows:

	R	C	$(R \cdot C) \to C$
(1)	T	T	
(2)	T	F	
(3)	F	T	
(4)	F	F	

To complete this relatively simple truth table one must determine the truth value of the proposition as a whole, given each possible combination of truth values indicated in the guide columns for the components. Since our sample proposition is conditional, and since the truth value of a conditional as a whole depends on the truth value of its first-order components—in this case the antecedent '$(R \cdot C)$' and the consequent 'C'—we must first determine the truth value of these components in each row. Determining the truth value for each row of the simple component 'C' is easy, since the values are already given in the guide column headed 'C.' To determine the truth value for each row of the compound component '$(R \cdot C)$,' however, we must refer back to both guide columns while bearing in mind the meaning of the conjunction symbol. Thus, we begin to fill in the truth table by writing the appropriate symbol, 'T' or 'F,' under the first-order components of the abbreviated proposition, as follows:

	R	C	(R · C)	→ C
(1)	T	T	T	T
(2)	T	F	F	F
(3)	F	T	F	T
(4)	F	F	F	F

We can now determine the truth value of the proposition as a whole by referring to the truth values of the first-order components and by bearing in mind the meaning of the logical operator that connects them. Thus, the complete truth table of the sample proposition is:

	R	C	(R · C)	→	C
(1)	T	T	T	T	T
(2)	T	F	F	T	F
(3)	F	T	F	T	T
(4)	F	F	F	T	F

To set up truth tables for more complex propositions we use the same basic procedure. First we fill in the columns for the lowest-order, or smallest, components, referring back to the initial guide columns. Then we fill in the columns for the next lowest-order components, referring back to their components. This procedure is repeated step by step until we have filled in the column for the proposition as a whole. The one exception to this procedure is that columns under the very lowest-order components may be omitted, since the lowest-order components are obviously non-compound components whose truth value is already given in the guide columns. Thus, in the above truth table, we did not duplicate the separate guide columns for 'R' and 'C' under the antecedent 'R · C,' and we need not have duplicated the guide column for the consequent 'C.'

Since '(R · C) → C' is a conditional with only two first-order components the column for the proposition as a whole was written under the conditional sign. Where there are more than two first-order components, however, the column for the proposition as a whole is written immediately to the right of the abbreviated proposition. Consider, for example, the self-contradictory proposition '—A · B · (B → A) · (A → C).' Its truth table will be written as follows:

	A	B	C		—A · B · (B → A) · (A → C)				
(1)	T	T	T		F	T	T	T	F
(2)	T	T	F		F	T	T	F	F
(3)	T	F	T		F	F	T	T	F
(4)	T	F	F		F	F	T	F	F
(5)	F	T	T		T	T	F	T	F
(6)	F	T	F		T	T	F	T	F
(7)	F	F	T		T	F	T	T	F
(8)	F	F	F		T	F	T	T	F

Once we construct a truth table for a given proposition, we may go on to determine whether that proposition is a tautology or a self-contradiction. If the column for the proposition as a whole contains only 'T's,' then the proposition is true for all possible combinations of its components' truth values and it is a tautology. If the column for the proposition as a whole contains only 'F's,' then the proposition is false for all possible combinations of its components' truth values and is a self-contradiction. Since even the truth or falsity of their component propositions is irrelevant to the truth or falsity of a tautology or self-contradiction as a whole, obviously the meaning of their component propositions is also irrelevant. The truth value of both tautologies and self-contradictions depends entirely on the meaning of the logical operators used to express them.

Propositions whose truth or falsity does not depend entirely upon the meaning of their logical operators are called *factual propositions*. All factual propositions are either definitional propositions or material propositions.

Definitional Meaning

A definitional sentence, we noted earlier, is one that expresses a proposition whose truth or falsity can be fully determined by examining its logical form and the cognitive meaning of its categorematic terms. If a definitional proposition is true, it is said to be a *definitional truth;* if false, a *definitional falsehood.* The propositions expressed by 'All bachelors are unmarried men' and 'Every triangle has three sides' are definitional truths. The propositions expressed by 'Some bachelors are married men' and 'Some triangles do not have three sides' are definitional falsehoods.

Definitional propositions are related to formal propositions and can usually be reduced to the latter. For example, by substituting 'unmarried men' for 'bachelors' the proposition expressed by 'All bachelors are unmarried men' may be reduced to the proposition expressed by 'All unmarried men are unmarried men.' Moreover, since 'bachelors' and 'unmarried men' are synonyms, there is a sense in which the two sentences 'All bachelors are unmarried men' and 'All unmarried men are unmarried men' may be said to express the same proposition.

It would be a serious mistake, however, to suppose that because definitional propositions may be reduced to formal propositions, they do not differ significantly from the latter. In the first place, the truth or falsity of formal propositions does not depend in any way upon the meaning of categorematic terms used to express them, whereas the truth or falsity of definitional propositions obviously does. Indeed, if we did not know the meaning of 'bachelors' we could not even reduce the proposition expressed by 'All bachelors are unmarried men' to a formal proposition. In the second place, definitional propositions are factual, or informative. More specifically, they tell us how words are actually used. The intended meaning of 'All bachelors are unmarried,' for example, is

> The word 'bachelor' is conventionally employed to denote an unmarried man.

and the proposition is true because the word 'bachelor' is in fact so used. Formal propositions, however, are completely uninformative. The person who says "All unmarried men are unmarried men," for example, does not purport to state a fact or to give us any information. The truth of the proposition follows, not from the accuracy with which it describes some actual state of affairs, but quite simply from the meaning of its logical operators.

Definitional propositions are also related to material propositions insofar as both are factual. Here too, however, care must be taken not to confuse the two types of propositions. For although both definitional and material propositions are factual, or informative, the former have to do with linguistic facts, whereas the latter have to do with non-linguistic facts. For example, whereas 'All bachelors are unmarried men' gives us information about the word type 'bachelor,' 'All bachelors are under ten feet tall' gives us information about bachelors. In technical language, the subject term of the definitional proposition 'All bachelors are unmarried men' is being *mentioned*—that is to say, it refers to a term-type rather than to that which the term-type ordinarily denotes. The subject term of the material proposition 'All bachelors are under ten feet tall,' on the other hand, is being *used*—that is to say, it refers to bachelors rather than to 'bachelors.'

If we agree to use single quotes around the property constant that symbolizes a term being mentioned, the difference between the sentences

All bachelors are unmarried.
All men are under ten feet tall.

can be unambiguously represented as follows:

$$(x)('B'x \rightarrow Ux)$$
$$(x)(Mx \rightarrow Tx)$$

The first formula above may be read: for any x, if x is called 'B' then x is U.

Material Meaning

A material sentence, as we have noted, is any sentence that expresses a proposition whose truth or falsity can be determined only by understanding (1) its formal meaning, (2) the cognitive meaning of its categorematic terms, and (3) facts about whatever its categorematic terms denote or designate. Some material sentences are 'All men are under six feet tall,' 'Most bachelors are irascible,' 'Smokers contract lung cancer,' 'Chicago is west of New York,' and 'Atoms have a complex internal structure.' If the proposition expressed by a material sentence is true, it is *materially true;* if false, *materially false.*

That the sample sentences do not express tautologies or self-contradictions is intuitively obvious and can easily be demonstrated by noting that propositions of the same form are sometimes true and sometimes false. The proposition expressed by 'Most bachelors are irascible,' for instance, has the form $(\exists x)(\phi x \cdot \psi x)$.' But so does the false proposition expressed by 'Most Quakers believe in violence' and the true proposition expressed by 'Most women marry.' That they are not definitional propositions is equally obvious and as readily demonstrated. No one would refuse to call a man 'a bachelor' because he is sweet-tempered, or deny that someone is a smoker because he has lived to a ripe old age without contracting lung cancer. Clearly the logical form and cognitive meanings of the various categorematic terms used in these sentences do not guarantee either the truth or the falsity of the propositions these sentences express. To determine their truth or falsity an understanding of logical form and knowledge of linguistic facts are not enough. We must also have knowledge of non-linguistic facts—more specifically, knowledge of facts about whatever is denoted or designated by their logical subjects.

Sentence Lability

Sentences may be characterized by any of the expressions used to characterize cognitive terms: vague, ambiguous, general, abstract, etc. The general rule is that these expressions apply to a sentence if and only if they apply to one or more of the categorematic terms in the sentence. This general rule, however, has exceptions. Take sentence ambiguity, for example: a sentence may be ambiguous not only if, as the rule states, one or more of its cognitive terms is ambiguous, but also if the grammatical construction of the sentence permits two different interpretations. This latter kind of ambiguity is known as *amphiboly*. A classic example is a prophecy made by the Delphic oracle to King Croesus of Lydia. The oracle, when asked whether the King should wage a war with Cyrus of Persia, prophesied that if Croesus went to war with Cyrus, he would destroy a mighty kingdom. When Croesus lost the war, the priests at Delphi contended that they had spoken the truth, for Croesus had destroyed a mighty kingdom—his own. There are also exceptions to the rule that a sentence is vague, ambiguous, abstract, etc., if it does contain a categorematic term with one of these features. 'The Pope issued a bull' contains the ambiguous term-type 'bull' but the context eliminates all ambiguity. Except for lability, however, exceptions to the general rule are fairly obvious and do not require separate discussion.

In the vocabulary of this book a sentence will be said to be *labile* if there is indecision or confusion about whether it should be classified as definitional or material. Sentence lability is often caused by carelessness, abetted by the fact that the rules of English grammar permit us to express definitional and material propositions in sentences having the same grammatical form. Often, however, lability results simply because there is no practical need to make the distinctions necessary to eliminate it. Indeed, there may be practical advantages in not making these distinctions. The proposition expressed by 'Gold has an atomic weight of 197.0,' for example, is true on either interpretation of the sentence. If, for example, having this specific atomic weight is a defining property of 'gold,' the proposition is true by definition. If, on the other hand, 'gold' is defined exclusively in terms of other properties, such as malleability and melting temperature, the proposition is materially true. An urgent, practical need to eliminate the lability of the term 'gold' with respect to the property of having this specific atomic weight would arise only if we discovered a substance otherwise like gold, but with an atomic weight more or less than 197.0. And since this is something that may never happen or that may happen only in the distant future, a decision at this time could be premature. Possibly other properties of the substance commonly called 'gold' may be discovered in the future that are even more suitable for purposes of definition than any yet known.

Nonetheless, the fact that lability is sometimes harmless or even desirable should not blind us to its dangers, for every labile term is a potential source of confusion. For example, the worker who is not aware that the term 'labor union' is labile with respect to the property of possessing the legal right to strike might erroneously assume that a conservative politician who declared himself "for" labor unions favored their right to strike, when in fact he vigorously opposed this right. Similarly, since the term 'free enterprise system' is labile with respect to the number and kind of permissible government controls over the economy, the liberal who declares himself "for" free enterprise might erroneously give the impression that he favors abolishing or reducing government controls that now exist.

Lability is particularly dangerous in extended arguments. For instance, somebody might say that all politicians are dishonest, and then, when confronted with an example of an honest politician, declare that the honest politician is not really a politician but a statesman. Obviously, 'All politicians are dishonest' was originally advanced as a material proposition and subsequently converted into a definitional proposition in order to score a point. Similarly, someone might say that historical Christianity has been a force for good. When, however, his opponents object by citing religious wars, persecutions of heretics and witches, the refusal to credit scientific discoveries, etc., he might answer that these were the consequences of human frailty, not of Christianity. Again, what was at first taken to be a contingent property of Christianity—being a force for good—has probably been elevated to the status of a defining property.

II • NON-COGNITIVE MEANING

The non-cognitive meanings of sentences, like the non-cognitive meanings of terms, have defied systematic and comprehensive classification. Assume that you overheard someone who was unaware of your presence say in a loud and gruff voice "Close the door!" Although this utterance does not express an assertion, it is rich in non-cognitive meaning. One could ordinarily construe it as a sign of many different things and be reasonably confident in making a number of inferences from it: that the door in question is open, that there is a third person within hearing distance who understands English, that the speaker himself knows English, that the speaker wishes the door to be closed, that the speaker is ill-mannered or in a temper, and that the door will soon be closed. In view of the many non-cognitive meanings of this one sentence-token, it is not surprising that the non-cognitive meanings of sentences as a class should resist tidy classification. Nonetheless, logicians have distinguished and labeled some of the more important types of non-cognitive meaning.

If a sentence functions as a sign of the speaker's feelings or attitudes, it has *emotive meaning*. All sentences containing categorematic terms with emotive meaning are, of course, emotive. So are interjections or exclamations such as 'Ouch!' To the extent that a sentence, like most sentences in poetry, arouses feelings in others it has *evocative meaning*. If a sentence signifies a desire on the speaker's part to influence the behavior of others, it has *directive meaning*. Imperatives like 'Close the door' are directive, and so is most demagogic political oratory. If a sentence can be reasonably interpreted as a sign of the speaker's regard for social etiquette or the amenities of human intercourse, it has *ceremonial meaning*. 'It is my privilege to introduce the speaker of the evening,' for instance, whether sincere or insincere, is such a sentence. The ceremonial meaning of a sentence is not unlike that of a bow, a handshake, or any other conventional gesture of politeness. Finally, if a sentence is more conspicuously an instance of doing than of saying, if to understand it one must understand the circumstances in which it is uttered or its impact on the lives of the speaker or other persons, it is said to have *performative meaning*. 'I now pronounce you man and wife' is a classic example.

The different kinds of non-cognitive meaning are not mutually exclusive. Commands, for instance, are principally directive and poems principally evocative, but as a rule both reveal the wishes, desires, or feelings of their author and are thus also emotive.

Similarly, the chief goal of a demagogue is to influence the behavior of his audience, but since this goal is often best achieved by arousing the audience's passions, his language will ordinarily be highly evocative as well as directive.

The emotive meaning of sentences can be particularly deceptive. Often two or more sentences with very similar or even identical cognitive meaning have vastly different emotive meaning, and we mistakenly assume a difference of cognitive meaning as well. The philosopher Bertrand Russell well illustrated this danger with what he called the "conjugation of irregular verbs." One of Russell's illustrations was "I am firm; you are obstinate; he is a pig-headed fool." Another example is "I am candid; you are too outspoken; he can't keep his damn mouth shut."

EXERCISES FOR CHAPTER FIVE

A. Construct truth tables for the following propositional forms. Specify whether they are tautologous, self-contradictory, or factual.

1. p
2. $p \vee q$
3. $p \rightarrow (p \vee p)$
4. $p \rightarrow (p \vee q)$
5. $(p \rightarrow q) \rightarrow (q \rightarrow p)$
6. $(p \rightarrow q) \rightarrow (-q \rightarrow -p)$
7. $-(p \vee q) \rightarrow (-p \cdot -q)$
8. $-(p \vee q) \leftrightarrow (-p \cdot -q)$
9. $p \cdot q \cdot -p$
10. $(p \cdot q) \cdot (p \rightarrow -q)$
11. $(p \cdot q \cdot r) \rightarrow (-r \rightarrow -p)$
12. $(p \vee q \vee r) \rightarrow (r \cdot (p \vee q))$

B. Classify the following sentences as formal, definitional, or material. Which are true? Which are false?

1. If Chicago is north of New Orleans and Ottawa is north of Chicago, then Ottawa is north of New Orleans.
2. The sun will rise tomorrow.
3. Water expands on freezing.
4. Unjustified extremism is always bad.

5. If it is going to happen, it is going to happen.
6. If every good mathematician makes occasional mistakes, then nobody who fails to make occasional mistakes is a good mathematician.
7. Communists are human.
8. Communists are Communists.
9. If all men are mortal and Socrates is a man, then Socrates is mortal.
10. Any person over twenty-one years of age is an adult.
11. If it is impossible to be a politician and honest, then no politician is honest.
12. Triangles are three-sided plane figures.
13. Santa Claus does not exist.
14. A chair is an object used to sit on.
15. Elephants have long lives.
16. Either he is a hero or he is not a hero.
17. Either he is a hero or he is a coward.
18. Every event has a cause.
19. Every effect has a cause.
20. The Empire State Building is in Chicago.
21. Fire burns.
22. My spinster aunt has been married since she was sixteen.
23. There are thirteen inches in a linear foot.
24. If he is neither good nor bad, then he is probably good.
25. Murder is murder.

C. Assuming that the terms in the following passages are being used conventionally, are the passages definitional, material, or labile?

1. No decent woman would wear a topless bathing suit.
2. Persons who wonder whether they are introverts or extroverts are probably introverts.
3. Few of us fall completely into either the category of extroverts or the category of introverts, but most of us have marked tendencies toward one or the other.
4. The extrovert is concerned about what others think; the introvert is more an individualist.
5. Extroverts are easier to influence than introverts.

6. The extrovert is not necessarily braver than the introvert; he just has a greater tolerance for pain.
7. Because the introvert is more sensitive to his own feelings and emotions, he has a greater capacity for happiness as well as unhappiness.
8. Mr. Johnson will always defy simple characterization because he is a complex figure.
9. Nobody who has not lived through a war can possibly understand what war means.
10. Too much order paralyzes change.
11. "We in the United Steelworkers of America learned long ago that achievement of the legislative goals and enforcement of the democratic rights envisioned by our constitution and detailed by our conventions, is inextricably intertwined with the election of liberal legislators and executives. Conversely, we know from experience that election of reactionary officials not only negates chances for forward looking legislation, but poses grave threats to the rights of legitimate activities of the labor movements." (I. W. Abel, Secretary-treasurer of the United Steelworkers of America, Testimony to the United States Senate Special Committee to Investigate Political Activities, Lobbying, and Campaign Contributions. Quoted in Gould and Steele, *People, Power, and Politics*)
12. Every cynic is a covert idealist.
13. The essence of honest democracy is stubborn uniformity in applying the rules.
14. Tigers are natives of India.
15. All men are mortal.
16. Most poems are in rhyme.
17. Some poems are sonnets.
18. All men must die.
19. Educators generally appear to believe that although four years in college could cost $15,000 to $16,000, any young person who really wants a higher education will get it somehow.
20. I would like a good martini, not too dry.
21. "When large numbers of people are out of work, unemployment results." (Calvin Coolidge)

22. Utopians believe that it is possible to create a perfect society.

23. Utopians are excessively optimistic about the possibilities of social progress.

24. A realist is not a utopian.

25. Utopianism is an impractical attempt to effect social change.

26. Utopians believe that the use of force is justified if necessary to achieve desired social goals.

27. "Anarchism is the absence of coercive authority." (Paul Goodman in a radio forum.)

28. "Anarchism is grounded in a rather definite social-psychological hypothesis: that forceful, graceful, and intelligent behavior occurs only when there is an uncoerced and direct response to the physical and social environment; that in most human affairs, more harm than good results from compulsion, top-down direction, bureaucratic planning, pre-ordained curricula, jails, conscriptions, states." (Paul Goodman, *Like a Conquered Province*)

29. "Liberalism finds in every social situation 'problems' to be solved collectively by planned action, almost always government action. Conservatism rejects this 'problem' approach to human affairs. It considers some of these situations natural manifestations of the human condition—not problems to be solved at all; others it recognizes as situations that can and should be improved, but only by time and the working of free human energies, individually or in voluntary association. Above all, it considers the outstanding social and political issues of our time to be the increasing provenance and power of government. Therefore, it regards further increases of that provenance and that power a greater evil than the specific evils against which the liberals call government into action." (Frank S. Meyer, *National Review*, February 7, 1967)

30. The drawback to a completely rational mind is that it is apt to assume that what is flawless in logic is therefore practicable.

31. Science is tentative; ideology is dogmatic.

32. "The frontier spirit is one of daring, of unorthodoxy, of a willingness to reach out into new and unexplored regions and prevail by the vigor and skill of the unfettered individual. The same qualities that brought the pioneers victorious from Atlantic to Pacific could bring Americans today to undreamed-of heights of achievement in the conquest of nature, the advance of technology and the development of new ideas." (H. L. Hunt, *Hunt for Truth*)

33. "The psychopath, like the child, cannot delay the pleasures of gratification; and this trait is one of his underlying, universal characteristics. He cannot wait upon erotic gratification which convention demands should be preceded by the chase before the kill; he must rape. He cannot wait upon the development of prestige in society: his egotistic ambitions lead him to leap into headlines by daring performances. Like a red thread the predominance of this mechanism for immediate satisfaction runs through the history of every psychopath. It explains not only his behavior but also the violent nature of his acts." (Robert Lindner, *Rebel Without a Cause*)

D. What kinds of non-cognitive meaning, if any, do the following passages have?

1. "Life is a tale told by an idiot, full of sound and fury, signifying nothing." (Shakespeare, *Macbeth*)
2. "We have nothing to fear but fear itself." (Franklin D. Roosevelt)
3. We, the jurors, find the defendant guilty.
4. Promise never to leave me.
5. I promised never to leave her.
6. I promise never to leave you.
7. If it please your honor, I should like to speak to this question.
8. He is utterly contemptible.
9. Murder is murder.
10. "I have seen, and heard, much of Cockney impudence before now; but never expected to hear a coxcomb ask two hundred guineas for flinging a pot of paint in the

public's face." (John Ruskin's comment on a painting by Whistler)

11. "A free man thinks of nothing less than of death, and his wisdom is not a meditation upon death but upon life." (Spinoza, *Ethics*)

12. "It is only the man whose intellect is clouded by his sexual impulses that could give the name of 'the fair sex' to that undersized, narrower-shouldered, broad-hipped, and short-legged race; for the whole beauty of the sex is bound up with this impulse." (Schopenhauer, "On Women")

E. Give a few original "conjugations of irregular verbs."

Reportive Definitions

The term 'definition' is one of the least clear in the logician's lexicon, and any simple formula that purports to do justice to its actual usage would be a woefully inadequate introduction to the subject. If a parent points to a dog in the presence of his child and utters the word 'dog' in an attempt to communicate the word's meaning, he is engaged in an act of definition. So too was a former chairman of the House Un-American Activities Committee who declared, "Americanism is conservatism!" And so too the scientist who makes a very precise list of the defining properties of a technical term he has just coined. Though all these activities deal with the meaning of some linguistic unit, they appear to have no other significant feature in common with one another or with other activities conventionally called 'defining.' Despite this difficulty, however, logicians have succeeded in sorting out and labeling various kinds of definitions.

If the purpose of a definition is to acquaint someone with the conventional meaning or meanings of a term, it is a *reportive definition*. The attempt to teach the meaning of 'dog' by pointing to dogs is an instance of reportive definition. If the purpose of a definition is to announce a personal or group resolve to use a word with a certain meaning, it is a *stipulative definition*. The person who lists the defining properties of a term he has just coined is offering a stipulative definition. If the purpose of a definition is to recommend the adoption of a certain meaning for a term, it is a *recommendatory definition*.

Often a given definition is intended to serve more than one of these purposes. The primary purpose of

'Americanism' is conservatism

is undoubtedly to recommend what the speaker regards as a proper use of 'Americanism.' But in making this recommendation the speaker clearly indicates that he has personally resolved to use 'Americanism' as a synonym for 'conservatism,' and in all likelihood the speaker is also suggesting that 'Americanism' does mean roughly the same thing as 'conservatism' in at least one conventional usage of 'Americanism.' His definition, therefore, though primarily recommendatory, is almost certainly stipulative and probably reportive as well.

In this chapter several types of reportive definitions will be discussed. In Chapter VII we shall turn to a discussion of stipulative and recommendatory definitions.

I • DENOTATIVE DEFINITIONS

When a term is defined by acquainting us with instances in its extension, the definition is said to be *denotative*. Pointing to a dog while pronouncing the word 'dog' is an example of denotative definition. Denotative definitions of this kind, which involve pointing, are called *ostensive definitions*.

It often happens, however, that a denotative definition is wholly verbal and does not involve pointing. When this is the case, it is either a *definition by example*, in which a single instance in the denotation of a term is cited, or a *definition by enumeration*, in which more than one individual in the denotation is cited. A definition by enumeration may be either *complete* or *incomplete*, depending upon whether it enumerates all or only some of the individuals in the denotation of the term being defined.

Definitions by example are legion. Every time someone is asked, "What do you mean by X?" and answers by saying, "Well, let me give you an example," he is proposing such a definition.

An example of a complete definition by enumeration is

The 'standard English truth-functional logical operators' are 'It is not the case that . . . ,' 'not,' 'and,' 'or,' 'if . . . then,' and '. . . if and only if . . . .'

An example of an incomplete definition by enumeration is

The 'standard English logical operators' are terms of the following kind: 'all,' 'some,' 'or,' and 'if . . . then . . . .'

Since property terms have no denotation, they can not be defined directly by citing instances in their denotation. They can, however, be defined denotatively in an indirect way. For example, if we tried to teach a child the meaning of the word 'blue' by showing him a variety of blue objects, each time pronouncing the word 'blue,' we would be engaged in ostensive definition. Strictly speaking, however, the term thereby defined is not 'blue' but rather 'blue object.'

Although in common usage the term 'meaning' is applied to both extension and intension, logicians have traditionally argued that the meaning of a term is more properly equated with intension than with extension and have strongly tended to favor connotative definitions. First, they point out, the meaning of a term denoting an empty class, such as 'centaur' or 'elf,' obviously has to be its intension rather than its extension. Second, two terms with clearly distinct meanings sometimes have exactly the same extension. For example, we know that all equilateral triangles are equiangular and also that all equiangular triangles are equilateral. Obviously, therefore, the difference in the meaning of 'equilateral triangle' and 'equiangular triangle' relates to intension rather than to extension. Third, if we know the strict intension of a term, we have in effect a precise rule for determining what does and what does not fall within its extension. Mere familiarity with members of the extension of a term, on the other hand, does not guarantee an understanding of that term's intension. We may know that a term denotes a certain number of individuals without knowing what properties are common to these individuals or which common properties are defining rather than merely contingent properties. The difficulty of determining the intension of a term from mere familiarity with its extension is particularly evident when the term stands for an open class. In a case like this, the number of known or observed members in the term's denotation will necessarily be smaller than the total number of members, and we can never be sure that the properties present in all observed members will also be present in the unobserved members.

These arguments for the superiority of connotative over denotative definitions are impressive, and there is no question that connotative definitions are generally preferable to denotative definitions. There are several important points, however, that must not be overlooked. First, the intensions of many terms, especially the troublesome ones we are most interested in clarifying, are often inadequately understood. In such cases close familiarity with their denotations is often essential to a better understanding of their intensions. Second, knowledge of a term's present intension is not a wholly reliable guide to future usage, since the intension of a term may change as a result of discoveries or changing beliefs relating to the objects in its denotation. Third, connotative definitions are sometimes impractical. For example, it is better to teach children the meanings of words like 'dog' and 'mother' denotatively when they are very young than to wait until they are old enough to understand the strict intensions of these terms.

II • CONNOTATIVE DEFINITIONS

A *connotative definition* is any proposition or set of propositions presumed to give a reasonably full account of the meaning of a class term by acquainting us with certain properties in its strict intension. In discussing these and other definitions, it is customary to use the expressions *definiendum* and *definiens*. The former denotes the term being defined; the latter, the term or terms that do the defining.

Connotative definitions are related to definitional propositions, but not all definitional propositions are definitions. Consider, for example:

(1) A 'quadrilateral' is a closed plane figure.
(2) A 'quadrilateral' is a closed plane figure having four and only four sides.

Both sentences express definitional propositions, since the truth of both propositions can be established solely by analyzing their logical forms and the meanings of the categorematic terms used to express them. No material knowledge about the individuals or properties denoted by the categorematic terms is needed. Only proposition 2, however, is a definition, since proposition 1 does not give a reasonably full account of the strict intension of 'quadrilateral.'

What do we mean by a 'reasonably full account' of the meaning of a term? The answer varies with the case. If a term is precise and unambiguous, a reasonably full account will cite one or more defining properties of the term that permit us to identify any object it denotes and to distinguish such objects from all others. For precise and unambiguous terms, the difference between definitional propositions that are not definitions and definitional propositions that are can be clearly indicated in symbols. For example,

A 'quadrilateral' is a closed plane figure having four and only four sides.

can be symbolized with the biconditional sign as follows:

$$(x)('Q'x \leftrightarrow (Px \cdot Fx))$$

This symbolization is appropriate because anything to which the term 'quadrilateral' applies is a closed plane figure having exactly four sides; and conversely, any closed plane figure having exactly four sides is something to which the term 'quadrilateral' applies. However,

A 'quadrilateral' is a closed plane figure.

cannot be symbolized with the biconditional sign; for although anything to which the term 'quadrilateral' applies is a closed plane figure, not all closed plane figures are quadrilaterals—some are circles, others are triangles, others are pentagons, etc.

If a term is ambiguous, then a reasonably full account will give an adequate account of each of its subtypes. Definitions of ambiguous terms can be symbolized with the aid of the biconditional sign and the sign of disjunction. For example,

> A 'subway' is either a pedestrian underpass or an underground train.

can be symbolized

$$(x)(`S'x \leftrightarrow (Px \vee Tx))$$

If a term is vague, a reasonably full account will specify some property or set of properties that permits us to identify paradigm cases without excluding borderline cases. And if a term is labile, a reasonably full account will specify the term's defining properties and also make explicit the property or properties with respect to which the term is labile. Definitions of vague and labile terms can not, however, be symbolized with the biconditional sign. Assume, for example, that we can give an adequate account of a poem by observing that poems are groups of words having the four meaning criteria 'A,' 'B,' 'C,' and 'D.' The proper symbolization of this definition would be

$$(x)(`P'x \rightarrow (Wx \cdot (Ax \vee Bx \vee Cx \vee Dx)))$$

In this case we must use the simple conditional rather than the biconditional sign, because, although every poem has at least one of these meaning criteria, a group of words that has only one of these criteria is not necessarily a poem. There is simply no rule telling us how many meaning criteria a group of words must have to count as a poem.

Sometimes the strict intension of a term is sufficiently rich to permit more than one reasonably full account of its meaning. We say that such a term has more than one *complete strict intension*. One can, for instance, give a reasonably full account of 'blue object' in terms of color pigment. But one can also give a reasonably full account of 'blue object' in terms of a certain length of reflected light waves. On the other hand, the strict intensions of some terms are not rich enough to permit even one reasonably full account of the objects in their denotations. This appears to be the case with the term 'definition' itself. Terms like these have an *incomplete strict intension.*

A common form of connotative definitions is *definition by genus and specific difference.* In this kind of definition the definiendum is a class name and the definiens is a class name plus a property term. A classic example is

A 'man' is a rational animal.

Here the definiendum is 'man' and the definiens 'rational animal.' 'Man' is a class name denoting the species man, and 'animal' is a class name denoting a genus of which man is a species. 'Rational' is an attributive term designating the specific difference—that is, a property of men that distinguishes them from all other members of their genus. Another example would be

A 'triangle' is a closed plane figure consisting of three and only three straight lines.

In this case 'triangle' names the species, 'closed plane figure' names the genus, and 'consisting of three and only three straight lines' designates the specific difference.

Searching for a genus and a specific difference is often a helpful technique in constructing definitions. From a purely logical point of view, however, definitions by genus and specific difference are highly artificial. As you already know, every class term defines a property and every property term defines a class. Thus, both of the sentences below express the same proposition:

A 'man' is a rational animal.
A 'man' possesses the properties of rationality and animality.

The difference between these two sentences is purely grammatical. Moreover, even grammatically, definitions by genus and difference are somewhat artificial. For example,

A 'man' is a rational being characterized by animality.

is more awkward than

A 'man' is a rational animal.

but both are grammatically correct—even though in the first sentence rationality is taken to be the genus and animality the difference. Thus,

A 'man' is a rational animal.

can be symbolized in either of the following ways:

$$(x)('M'x \leftrightarrow (Rx \cdot Ax))$$
$$(x)('M'x \leftrightarrow (Ax \cdot Rx))$$

In both cases 'A' and 'R' designate properties, and the order in which the defining properties appear in the definiens is of no significance.

Connotative definitions, like denotative definitions, can not be used directly to define property terms. But property terms can be defined indirectly through connotative definitions of their corresponding class terms.

III • SYNONYMOUS DEFINITIONS

Two terms are *synonymous* if both have the same cognitive meaning; and since the success of a connotative definition depends upon the extent to which the definiens accurately reports the cognitive meaning of the definiendum, the definiens and the definiendum in a successful connotative definition will always be synonymous. It is customary, however, to distinguish between connotative definitions and synonymous definitions. The essential difference is that a *synonymous definition* merely tells us *that* the definiendum and the definiens have the same connotation, whereas a successful connotative definition tells us *what* the connotation of the definiendum actually is. In other words, in synonymous definitions such as

The German word *'Dreieck'* means 'triangle.'
$(x)('D'x \leftrightarrow 'T'x)$

'Bashful' means 'shy.'
$(x)('B'x \leftrightarrow 'S'x)$

both the definiendum and the definiens are mentioned, as indicated by the single quotes around both. On the other hand, in connotative definitions such as

A 'man' is a rational animal.
$(x)('M'x \leftrightarrow (Rx \cdot Ax))$

A 'triangle' is a closed plane figure with exactly three sides.
$(x)('T'x \leftrightarrow (Cx \cdot Px \cdot Tx))$

the definiendum is mentioned but the definiens is used to spell out the defining properties of the definiendum. Thus we employ single quotes only for the definiendum.

Since synonymous and connotative definitions in ordinary English often have the same grammatical form, the proper classification of a given definition must sometimes be determined from the context. If the addressee is completely unfamiliar with the meaning of the definiendum (like the ordinary student of German when learning *'Dreieck'*) and if the purpose of the definition is merely to increase his vocabulary, the definition is synonymous. If, however, the addressee is already in some degree familiar with the meaning of the definiendum and the purpose of the definition is to improve or sharpen his understanding of it, the definition is connotative.

Synonymous pairs of terms such as *'Dreieck'* and 'triangle' or 'bashful' and 'shy' used simply to extend someone's vocabulary are called *non-explicative synonyms*. Terms such as 'rational animal' and 'closed plane figure with exactly three sides,' on the other hand, used to improve someone's understanding of another term are called *explicative synonyms*.

IV • CONTEXTUAL DEFINITIONS

A 'contextual definition' analyzes the meaning of a term by showing how it or some closely related term is used in sentences. More specifically, the definiens of a *contextual definition* cites conditions that must be present in order for propositions expressed by a certain class of sentences containing the definiendum to be true. Almost any term susceptible to connotative definition may be defined as well or even better contextually. Contextual definitions are especially useful, however, in defining syncategorematic and relational terms.

The definitions of the logical operators given in Chapters Four and Five illustrate contextual definitions of syncategorematic terms. To illustrate the contextual definition of a relational term, let us consider 'is a grandparent of.' To define this term contextually we must ask, "What is the common cognitive meaning of sentences having the form 'x is a grandparent'?" or "Under what conditions are propositions expressed by sentences of this form true?" The answer in symbols is:

$$(x)('G'x \leftrightarrow (\exists y)(\exists z)((Pxy) \cdot (Pyz)))$$

This is read: for any x, x is a grandparent if and only if there is a y and there is a z such that x is a parent of y and y is a parent of z.

Consider also the term 'blue color sensation,' which denotes a human *experience* of blue rather than a blue object itself. The term 'blue object' can be defined connotatively in the ways already indicated. The term 'blue color sensation,' however, can not be defined connotatively, since the only describable specific difference between a blue color sensation and other color sensations is the property of being blue. Consider, then, a sentence of the form 'x is having a sensation of blue.' The propositions expressed by sentences of this form would be true if x were a person with normal vision viewing a blue object in ordinary light. They would also be true if x were having an experience not occasioned by a blue object but similar in quality to the sensation so occasioned. And a sentence of the form in question can be interpreted as asserting that either of these two complex sets of conditions is present. Unfortunately, the symbolic apparatus at our command does not allow us to symbolize adequately this explication of the meaning of 'x is having a sensation of blue.' Despite its informality the example illustrates an important use of contextual definitions.

A subclass of contextual definitions are known as *operational definitions,* in which a term is defined by specifying certain operations, or tests, that may be performed and certain observable results that must follow if the proposition expressed by a sentence containing this term is true. A classic example is a definition of 'is harder than.' According to this definition every sentence of the form 'x is harder than y' asserts that if x is rubbed against y, y will show a scratch whereas x will not. (Note that this formula defines not only 'x is harder than y' but also 'x is hard.' Since nothing can be meaningfully said to be hard unless some standard of comparison is invoked, a sentence of the form 'x is hard' is no less relational than a sentence of the form 'x is harder than y.' The only difference is that the one is implicitly rather than explicitly relational.)

Another classic operational definition is a definition of 'length' in terms of operations to be performed with measuring rods. The full definition is very complex, but in general we can say that if sentences of the form 'x is two feet long,' 'x is three feet long,' etc. are true, then if a standard measuring rod of, say, one foot were laid horizontally adjacent to one of the ends of x, the two extremities touching, and upended a certain number of times, then after the last operation the other extremity of x would touch an extremity of the measuring rod.

Operational definitions have proved very successful in modern science and are being used with increasing frequency. Their great value was dramatically demonstrated when Einstein and others realized that spatial measures made by rigid rods do not necessarily coincide with spatial measures made by telescopes or other optical instruments. 'Space' is therefore an ambiguous term—and one whose ambiguity can be best exposed through operational definitions.

V • DEFINITIONS BY CLASSIFICATION

An attempt to explain the meaning of a class term by citing subclasses is called a *definition by classification*. For example,

A 'grandparent' means either a grandmother or a grandfather.

If every individual denoted by the definiendum is a member of one of the subclasses cited in the definiens, the definition is *comprehensive*. If, in addition, the subclasses are mutually exclusive—so that no individual belongs to more than one subclass—the definition is *systematic*. Since every grandparent is either a grandmother or a grandfather and since no one is both, the sample definition is both comprehensive and systematic. Another comprehensive and systematic definition by classification is

A 'United States citizen' is a person born in United States territory, or a person born abroad of parents who hold United States citizenship, or a person who has acquired United States citizenship by naturalization.

Systematic definitions by classification may be symbolized with the aid of the special symbol '$\vee$,' known as the symbol of *exclusive disjunction*. Thus,

A 'grandparent' is either a grandmother or a grandfather.

can be symbolized

$$(x)('G'x \leftrightarrow (Mx \vee Fx))$$

Many definitions by classification, however, are neither comprehensive nor systematic. For example, the definition of 'definition' in this and the following chapter is primarily a definition by classification. But it is not comprehensive, since some kinds of definition have been omitted from this discussion. Nor is it systematic. The classification of definitions as reportive, stipulative, and recommendatory, which is based on the definer's purpose or intent, overlaps with their classification as denotative, connotative, synonymous, etc., which is based on the form of the definition itself. Moreover, as already noted, reportive, stipulative, and recommendatory definitions are not mutually exclusive.

Again, some persons have attempted to define 'a morally right act' in terms of conventional moral rules like promise-keeping, truth-telling, generosity, tolerance, etc. The comprehensiveness of such definitions is open to serious question, however, since some morally right acts do not appear to conform to any conventional moral rule. And it is most unlikely that such a definition could be made wholly systematic. An act of tolerance, for example, could often be classified as an act of generosity as well.

When a definition by classification is nonsystematic, it must be symbolized with the sign of inclusive disjunction. And when so symbolized, definitions by classification will have the same formal pattern as connotative definitions specifying meaning criteria. Despite the formal similarity between non-systematic definitions by classification and connotative definitions by meaning criteria, there is a relatively simple test for distinguishing between them. If a question should arise, we can resolve our perplexity by asking whether a paradigm denoted by the definiendum would possess all or nearly all of the properties cited in the definiens. If the answer is "Yes," we have a definition by meaning criteria; otherwise, we have a definition by classification. For example, 'poem,' as we already know, may be defined by citing meaning criteria. In addition, however, 'poem' can be defined by classification, since poems fall into many subclasses—sonnets, epics, odes, ballads, etc. In a definition of 'poem' by meaning criteria, the properties cited in the definiens—having rhyme and meter, being rich in pictorial and emotive meaning, containing many metaphors and similes, etc.—would all or nearly all apply to a paradigm of 'poem.' In a definition of 'poem' by classification, however, the subclasses cited in the definiens would *not* all apply to a paradigm of 'poem.' Obviously, a poem cannot at once be a sonnet, an epic, an ode, and a ballad.

Similarly, 'a morally right act' may be defined by classification in terms of conventional moral rules, as indicated above. However, it may also be defined in terms of such meaning criteria as promoting the well-being of others, eliciting widespread approval, being motivated by sense of duty or benevolence. All or nearly all the criteria in a definition by meaning criteria—promoting the well-being of others, eliciting widespread approval, being motivated by duty or benevolence—would apply to a paradigm of a morally right act. On the other hand, a morally right act would only occasionally conform to more than one conventional moral rule cited in a definition by classification.

VI • GENERAL AND SPECIFIC DEFINITIONS

The distinction between *general* and *specific definitions* is entirely relative: one definition of a given term is more specific than a second if it provides an analysis of the definiens of the second. For example, 'an intelligent being' has sometimes been defined as a being capable of adjusting to its environment. The ability to adjust to the environment, however, is itself a complex faculty involving such things as memory, abstract thought, linguistic skill, problem solving, etc. A definition of 'an intelligent being' that detailed these capacities would therefore be specific relative to the definition in terms of adjustment. Similarly, 'a citizen of the United States'—which was specifically defined above as a person born in United States territory, a person born abroad of parents with United States citizenship, or a person who has acquired United States citizenship through naturalization—could be generally defined as a person who would be recognized as a citizen by American courts. To take a third example, if one believes that all 'morally right acts' have the property of promoting the greatest happiness of the greatest number, a definition in terms of this property would be general relative to a definition of 'a morally right act' by classification in terms of conventional moral rules.

It should be carefully noted, however, that two or more sentences which appear to express general and specific definitions of the same term often pose difficult problems of interpretation. If, for example, somebody said both

(1) A morally right act is one that promotes the greatest happiness of the greatest number.

(2) A morally right act is an act of promise-keeping, or an act of truth-telling, or an act of generosity, etc.

one must not jump to the conclusion that both sentences are offered as definitions. Several other interpretations are also possible. The speaker may intend sentence 1 as a definition and sentence 2 as a material proposition asserting that acts in accordance with the conventional moral rules do in fact promote the greatest happiness of the greatest number. Or he may intend sentence 2 as a definition and sentence 1 as a material proposition asserting that acts conforming to the conventional moral rules do in fact promote the greatest happiness of the greatest number. Or he may intend *both* sentences 1 and 2 as material propositions. If, for example, someone defined 'a morally right act' as one in accordance with the will of God, but believed that in fact God approves both of acts promoting the greatest happiness of the greatest number and of acts in accordance with the conventional moral rules, this interpretation would be appropriate. Finally, it could well be that either or both sentences 1 and 2 are labile.

VII • CONSTRUCTING AND APPRAISING EXPLICATIVE DEFINITIONS

The purpose of synonymous definitions, as noted earlier, is merely to increase someone's vocabulary. Either the addressee has never heard the definiendum before or he has no idea what it means. Most reportive definitions, however, are addressed to persons who do already have some understanding of the definiendum but whose understanding is insufficient to insure fully correct use. In such cases the addressee is said to have a *pre-analytic notion* of the definiendum; and a definition designed to replace this pre-analytic notion with a fuller and more accurate knowledge of the definiendum's meaning is called an *explication* or an *explicative definition*.

Unfortunately, constructing and appraising explicative definitions is largely an art. Our success depends more on general
knowledge and insight than on the mechanical application of
rules. Apart from indicating the forms a definition may assume
and providing a helpful vocabulary, all the logician can do is to
indicate a few general rules for avoiding common mistakes.

Rule 1

A successful definition will be neither too broad nor too narrow.
This rule applies exclusively to unambiguous, precise, and non-
labile terms. A connotative definition satisfies this rule if the
definiens denotes neither more nor fewer objects than the
definiendum. A contextual definition satisfies this rule if it applies to all sentences of the kind being defined and to no others.
'Man is a featherless biped' is a classic example of a definition
that is too broad. This definition, offered by a philosophical
school of antiquity, was refuted by a rival school, one of whose
members plucked a chicken and deposited it on the grounds
of the first. The definition may, however, be remedied by saying
'Man is a featherless biped with broad nails.'

Rule 2

If a term has more than one complete strict intension, a successful definition will designate as many as are needed to insure
successful communication. A good reportive definition of 'blue
object,' for example, should mention at least three complete
strict intensions: one in terms of chemical pigment, another
in terms of aptitude for reflecting light waves of a certain
length, and a third in terms of aptitude for producing a blue
sensation in a person with normal vision who observes it under
standard conditions. Each of these intensional meanings uniquely
identifies paradigm cases of blue objects. None of them alone,
however, fully explicates our pre-analytic notion of 'blue object';
and an appreciation of the richness of this term's strict intension
is often essential to successful communication.

Note, however, that this second rule does not imply that every complete strict intension of a term is equally adequate or that all of them must be included in a good definition. Even if we assume that being a featherless biped with broad nails and being a rational animal are both complete strict intensions of 'man,' we would probably not criticize a definition that failed to mention the former. The reason is that rationality weighs far more heavily in our pre-analytic notion of man. A failure to realize that man is a biped, or featherless, or has broad nails does not seriously impair our understanding of the word 'man,' whereas a failure to realize that man is rational does.

Rule 3

A successful explicative definition will not be *circular*. Specifically, neither the definiendum nor a non-explicative synonym of the definiendum should appear in the definiens. Synonymous definitions are circular by definition, and if a purported connotative or contextual definition violated this rule, it would not be a genuine explication. Suppose, for instance, that someone said,

A 'sleeping potion' is a potion with a dormitive power.

thinking that he was explicating the term 'sleeping potion.' In fact, since 'potion with a dormitive power' is a conventional non-explicative synonym of 'sleeping potion,' he has added nothing to our understanding of the definiendum.

In some definitions the definiendum and a term in the definiens are *correlative*—that is to say, each is defined by reference to the other. If, for example, somebody defined 'a blue object' as an object that produces a blue sensation in a person with normal vision who views it under standard conditions and then in turn defined 'a blue sensation' as a sensation produced by a blue object, 'a blue object' and 'a blue sensation' would be correlative terms. Definitions whose definiens includes a correlative term of the definiendum are closely related to circular definitions, and where possible should be avoided. Obviously, our understanding of 'a blue object' and 'a blue sensation' is much further advanced when at least one is given an independent definition. It must be noted, however, that correlative definitions are sometimes very hard to avoid and are not necessarily worthless. For example, when in Chapter One we defined a 'term-token' as a member of a term-type and a 'term-type' as a class of term-tokens, we were treating 'term-token' and 'term-type' as correlative terms. And, although an independent definition of one of these terms would have been preferable, it is not clear that these terms can be defined independently, nor is the definition actually given useless for the purpose intended.

Rule 4

A successful definition will be positive rather than negative. A few terms are inherently negative, and in such cases this rule does not apply. For example, 'orphan' denotes a child with no parents. The proper genus of such terms for purposes of definition is (1) immediately recognizable and (2) divisible into a few mutually exclusive species. The class of orphans obviously belongs to the genus of children and is exhaustively divisible into two mutually exclusive species: those having parents and those not having parents. When, therefore, we say that an orphan is a child who has no parents, we uniquely identify the individuals denoted by 'orphan' and there is no possibility of misunderstanding.

Most classes, however, can properly be included under a large number of genera whose species are numerous and often not mutually exclusive. Consider, for example, the class of men. For purposes of definition should men be subsumed under the genus animal, the genus mammal, or under still another genus? This question is hard to answer. And even if we assumed that the proper genus for men is mammal, the species of mammals are so numerous that any definition of 'man' that stated the properties man does not share with other mammals would be either very long, in which case it is impractical, or too incomplete to identify man uniquely, in which case it violates our first rule.

Rule 5

The definiens of a successful definition will be neither more vague nor more precise than the definiendum. This rule must not be interpreted to mean that we are never justified in re-defining terms so as to eliminate vagueness. Often this is most desirable. But a definition introduced for this purpose would not be a reportive definition, and it is only reportive definitions that concern us in this chapter.

Rule 6

If the definiendum is an ambiguous term, a successful reportive definition will include in the definiens a separate definition of each of the term's subtypes.

Rule 7

The definiens of a successful definition will not contain terms that the interpreter is unlikely to understand. Since the primary purpose of a reportive definition is to acquaint others with the conventional meaning of a term and thereby facilitate communication, hardly anybody quarrels with this rule in theory. It is remarkable, however, how often it is breached in practice. All too often the primary purpose of reportive definitions is defeated by the definer's intoxication with words or by his desire to impress others with his erudition.

Rule 8

The definiens of a successful definition will not contain figurative or metaphorical language. This rule, like Rule 7, is more of practical than theoretical interest. Its principal violators are persons with a greater interest in literary experiences than in clear thinking. Consider, for example, the definition of 'archi-

tecture' as frozen music. The most that can be said for a definition like this is that it is suggestive. It might possibly start a
train of association that culminates in a genuine definition, but
it is far more likely that such a definition will lead us into still
more peripheral areas of pictorial meaning.

EXERCISES FOR CHAPTER SIX

A. Give a connotative definition of each of the following:

1. A stallion
2. A colt
3. A wife
4. A spinster
5. Masculinity (in its non-biological meaning)
6. Femininity (in its non-biological meaning)
7. A novel
8. A romantic work of art
9. A romantic person
10. A friend

B. Do either of the following expressions have a complete
strict intension: 'total intension,' 'linguistic unit with cognitive
meaning'? If either of these terms does have a complete strict
intension, what is it?

C. Give a general and a specific definition for each of the
following: 'sentence with cognitive meaning' and 'term with
cognitive meaning.'

D. Define the following terms in the manner you think most
suitable.

1. Soluble   3. A twin
2. If and only if   4. An identical twin

5. A fraternal twin
6. Friendly
7. A friend
8. Knowledge
9. A value
10. Generosity
11. A political conservative
12. A political radical
13. A political liberal
14. A science
15. Music
16. A sibling
17. To be
18. A law

E. Which of the following passages are definitions? Classify and appraise those that are. Can you think of better definitions of the same terms?

1. Health is the absence of disease; disease, the absence of health.
2. "High art . . . [is] any art that would attempt to describe or characterize some portion of the profound meaningfulness of human life with any finality or truth." (LeRoi Jones, *Home*)
3. Mental health is achieved if man reaches full maturity in a characteristically human way.
4. Objectivity is the faculty of seeing people and things *as they are*, objectively, and being able to separate this objective picture from a picture which is formed by one's desires and fears.
5. Objectivity means a decent respect for the facts and a readiness to fit interpretations to them.
6. A saint is a person like Francis of Assisi or Joan of Arc.
7. "During slavery a liberal, or a moderate, was a man who didn't want the slaves beaten. But he was not asking that they be freed." (LeRoi Jones, *Home*)
8. Day is the absence of night; night, the absence of day.
9. "Love is pleasure accompanied by the idea of an external cause." (Spinoza, *Ethics*)
10. "*Social femininity*. The tendency to answer questions on a masculinity-femininity test as women do rather than as men do." (Ernest R. Hilgard and Richard C. Atkinson, *Introduction to Psychology*)
11. "Paradox is the poisonous flower of quietism, the iridescent

surface of the rotting mind, the greatest depravity of all."
(Thomas Mann, *The Magic Mountain*)

12. "By religion, then, I understand a propitiation or concilia-
tion of powers superior to man which are believed to direct and control the course of Nature and of human life."
(James George Frazer, *The Golden Bough*)

13. Religion is "the belief in an everliving God, that is, in a
Divine Mind and Will ruling the Universe and holding
moral relations with mankind." (James Martineau, *A
Study of Religion*)

14. "Religion is clearly a state of mind. . . . It seems to me
that it may best be described as an emotion resting on a
conviction of harmony between ourselves and the universe
at large." (John Ellis McTaggart, *Some Dogmas of Religion*)

15. "Perhaps the most that can be done by way of a definition
of religion is to list . . . characteristic features. Here is
such a list . . . :
   1. Beliefs in supernatural beings (gods).
   2. A distinction between sacred and profane objects.
   3. Ritual acts focused around sacred objects.
   4. A moral code believed to be sanctioned by the gods.
   5. Characteristically religious feelings (awe, sense of
      mystery, sense of guilt, adoration, etc.), which tend to
      be aroused in the presence of sacred objects and dur-
      ing the practice of ritual, and which are associated
      with the gods.
   6. Prayer and other forms of communication with gods.
   7. A world view. (By a world view I mean a general
      picture of the world as a whole and the place of the
      individual therein, this picture containing some speci-
      fication of an over-all purpose or point, and an in-
      dication of how the individual fits into this whole.)
   8. A more or less total organization of one's life based on
      the world view.
   9. A social group bound together by the first eight fac-
      tors." (William P. Alston, *Religious Belief and Philo-
      sophical Thought*)

16. There are three kinds of evil: *physical evil*, by which is

meant physical disability and suffering; *moral evil,* by
which is meant imperfection of character and the behavior
resulting from such imperfection; and *intellectual evil,* by
which is meant ignorance and false belief.

17. "That education should be 'democratic' no one in a democracy would seriously dispute. This would be the
equivalent of announcing in the Middle Ages that all education should be Christian. But what such an announcement would commit anyone to is far from clear. This is
partly because of the vagueness which all such general
terms of commendation must have if they are to fulfill their
function of reminding a people of their ultimate valuations.
It is also because of different interpretations which it is
possible to give of the predication of 'democratic' to 'education.'

"This could mean, first of all, that the educational system
of a community should be democratically distributed and
organized, whatever interpretation is given to 'democratic.'
A system, for instance, which neglected the education of
half the population or about whose organization 'the people' had no say would commonly be thought to be 'undemocratic.' Alternatively it might suggest that the organization of schools themselves should be 'democratic.' In
other words a plea might be being made for the rights of the
inmates, staff and pupils alike, to some say in the running
of their institution. . . . Alternatively the announcement
might be drawing attention to the desirability of the content of education being democratic. The school's part in
training citizens in the skills and attitudes appropriate for
membership in a democratic community might be being
stressed." (R. S. Peters, *Ethics and Education*)

18. "*Homosexuality.* (1) In psychoanalytic theory, a normal
stage of psychosexual development in which attachment
is to members of one's own sex. (2) The adoption in adult
life of the cultural role appropriate to a member of the
opposite sex. (3) Engaging in sexual relations with a
member of the same sex." (Ernest R. Hilgard and Richard
C. Atkinson, *Introduction to Psychology*)

19. "Can we define 'life'? I think the answer is No; certainly

there is no single snappy phrase which can be applied to decide unequivocally whether a system is living or not. But we can describe a few major properties which, if possessed by any system, would unhesitatingly determine that the system be called living—though doubts would arise about systems which had only some of them. The properties usually quoted in this connection are metabolism, growth, reproduction, and evolution. These differ in importance. A capacity for growth would surely not be enough in itself to qualify a system for being called living— a cloud, for instance, can grow under suitable atmospheric conditions. Again, simple reproduction, in the sense of increasing numbers, is not enough—a raindrop, condensing out of a cloud, will split into two and 'reproduce' when it reaches a certain upper limit of size.

"The other two qualities, metabolism and evolution, are much more crucial. It is a major characteristic of all things which we commonly consider alive to 'metabolize,' that is, take in simple substances from their surroundings and build these up into more elaborate substances out of which the body is made. Many biologists accept this biochemical ability as the overriding criterion for life. Others argue that the capacity to undergo evolution is even more important, since any system that can evolve will thereby gradually become more complex and will eventually acquire these capacities for metabolism. If one can think of a way by which natural processes produce a system that starts evolving, then it may be permissible to think of such a system as being on an escalator that may take it to any level of biological complexity." (C. H. Waddington, "That's Life," *The New York Review of Books,* February 29, 1968)

20. "The essential thing about marriage is that it is a stable relationship in which a man and a woman are socially permitted, without loss of standing in the community, to have children. In some societies an unmarried girl may give birth to a child without loss of standing provided that she gets married soon afterward; sometimes, in fact, this proof of fertility is necessary before a girl can get a husband. Whether every relationship in which a man and woman are

permitted to become parents is to be called a marriage depends, of course, upon how narrowly one wishes to define 'marriage.' A society may make a distinction between a wife of full status and a concubine while permitting both to have children by the husband.

"The right to have children implies, of course, the right to sexual relations. According to a narrow definition of marriage, two other conditions must be fulfilled; namely, regular or normal cohabitation in the same household, and some degree of economic cooperation. . . . This definition, however, is probably too narrow. At least, in the socialist *kibbutzim* (collective farms) of Israel, although all adults who are able participate in the economy and all share in its fruits, there is virtually no economic cooperation between husband and wife as such. Yet most people would recognize that these *kibbutzim* have the marriage tie, and we should have to admit that their family groups are at least as close-knit as family groups in our own society. The socialist economy is so arranged that fathers, for example, see their children more often, for longer periods, and in more relaxed circumstances than is usually possible in the United States." (Harry M. Johnson, *Sociology: A Systematic Introduction*)

21. "First of all, let us start by noting roughly what is meant by suggestibility. It is a state or trait causing a person to perform certain acts without having any motivation of his own to do so, or even in spite of having a certain degree of motivation to the contrary." [The author then outlines six tests of suggestibility. The first three correlate with one another in the sense that persons who rate high on one tend to rate high on the other two. There is a similar result in the case of the second three tests. There is, however, no relationship at all between the two groups. One of the first three tests is called the Body Sway Test. The subject is told to stand with eyes closed and repeatedly told that he is falling forward, while the experimenter measures the degree of body sway. One of the second three tests is called a Memory Suggestion Test. The subject is told to memorize the details of a picture shown him. When the picture

is taken away, the experimenter will ask questions such as "Was the cat lying on the chair in the right corner or the left corner of the room?" Although there was no cat in the picture, many persons are persuaded by this question that there was. To distinguish between the kinds of suggestibility measured by the first three tests and those measured by the second three tests, the terms 'primary suggestibility' and 'secondary suggestibility' are introduced.]

[The author continues.] "Not only are these two types of suggestibility not related to each other; they behave quite differently in a number of ways. Thus, primary suggestibility is not at all correlated with intelligence; intelligent people are no less suggestible than dull ones. Secondary suggestibility, however, does correlate with intelligence. Here the more intelligent ones are less suggestible and the dull ones are more suggestible. Again, primary suggestibility is closely related to hypnosis; a person who is highly suggestible also tends to be easily hypnotizable. This is not true of secondary suggestibility. A person who is suggestible along the lines defined by this set of tests is neither more easily nor less easily hypnotizable than a person who is non-suggestible. . . .

"Nor are these the only two types of suggestibility. A third variety, which does not seem to correlate with either of the other two, . . . has been called tertiary suggestibility." [Tertiary suggestibility is measured by tests showing the extent to which persons will change their opinions on a variety of political and social issues when told that persons with high prestige hold different opinions.] "Thus, we find that there are at least three types of suggestibility, and probably several more different types quite unrelated to those mentioned so far will be unearthed by future experimentation." (H. J. Eysenck, *Sense and Nonsense in Psychology*)

22. 'Well-being,' like 'progress' is a relative term. To ask how many desirable changes must be made if there is to be progress is like asking how much progress is progress. Similarly, to ask how many or to what degree basic needs or desires must be satisfied to ensure well-being is like

asking how much well-being constitutes well-being. To define 'well-being' is to list the criteria in the light of which comparative estimates may be made. To ask for more is to misunderstand the meaning of the term and the functions it can legitimately serve in human discourse.

If I am correct, the basic and universal human needs or desires whose fulfillment constitutes well-being can be classified under four heads.

(1) The first of these is health (and the absence of physical disability or pain) with all that is required to maintain it—adequate food, shelter, medical care, etc.

(2) The second is warmth, good will, or respect in our dealings with fellow human beings.

(3) The third is a reasonable balance between the individual's aspirations and the objective possibility of moving toward his goals.

(4) Finally, I list pleasures. By 'a pleasure' I here mean any relatively short-lived satisfaction of which we are immediately conscious throughout its duration. I mean to include not only the so-called lower pleasures, such as sexual gratification and the delectations of the palate, but also the so-called higher pleasures, such as aesthetic delight, the joys of creation, and great moments of romantic love or exalted friendship.

23. Scientific knowledge differs from common-sense knowledge in the following respects: (1) Scientific knowledge is more systematic and has greater explanatory power. (2) Scientific knowledge is more precise. (3) Scientific knowledge has a greater measure of logical consistency. (4) Scientific knowledge is based to a much greater extent on experiment or manipulation as opposed to mere passive observation of the environment. (5) Scientific knowledge is less immediately concerned with practical goals or the achievement of human values.

24. The root sense of 'rationality' is the adaptation of means to ends. The term may, however, be more profitably defined in terms of the following practices: (1) Before deciding on matters of any moment, the rational man will seek out whatever relevant data he believes it practically possible to

uncover without undue difficulty. (2) Both in the collec-
lection of data and in the drawing of implications from
this data, the rational man will employ the generally accepted principles of inference. (3) The rational man will
make great efforts to discover and to protect himself against
those innate or acquired dispositions and habits of thought
that warp his judgment. (4) The practice of rationality
requires that one frequently submit one's views to the
criticism of others. (5) The rational man will remain open-
minded with respect to all of those issues that do not
warrant firm conviction.

I believe that the above definition is a faithful explication of the ordinary use of 'rationality.' If, however, the
reader does not agree, let him regard it as a stipulative definition; for I am more interested in defending the practices
enumerated than in defining 'rationality.'

25. "When the soldier is pressed as to why he is in Vietnam,
his answers are couched in a quite individualistic frame of
reference. For example: 'I'm here because my unit was sent
here,' 'I was fool enough to join this man's Army,' 'My
own stupidity for listening to the recruiting sergeant,' or
'I happened to be at the wrong place at the wrong time.'
When asked specifically what the United States is doing
in Vietnam, the soldier will usually say that it is there 'to
stop Communism.' And 'to stop Communism' is the only
ideological slogan that the combat soldier can be brought
to utter.

"When further queried as to what is so bad about Communism that it must be stopped at the risk of his own life,
the combat soldier is often perplexed. After thinking about
it, he will generally express his distaste for Communism by
stressing its authoritarian aspects. Typical descriptions of
Communism are 'That's when you can't do what you want
to do,' and 'Somebody's always telling you what to do.'
As one man wryly put it: 'Communism is something like
the Army.'" (Charles S. Moskos, Jr., "A Sociologist Appraises the G.I.," *The New York Times Magazine,* September 24, 1967)

26. "'Anomie' literally means normlessness. The term can be

and has been applied to the state of mind of individuals regardless of the state of society. . . . We shall use the term, however, to refer solely to a certain condition in a social system, large or small. Quite adequate and less recondite terms already exist to refer to the personality states for which the term 'anomie' has been used. Anomie, then, is a condition in which many persons in a social system have a weakened respect for some social norm or norms, and this loss of legitimacy is traceable in part to something about the social structure itself.

"Anomie is not the same thing as the absence of norms (even though this is the literal meaning of the term). Anomie is not even lack of clarity in norms—vague definition of what behavior is required. If there were no norms at all, we could not speak of deviant behavior; and if the norms were not clear, we should be almost equally embarrassed to call any specific action deviant. In the condition called anomie, norms are present, they are clear enough, and the actors in the social system are to some extent oriented to them. But this orientation, on the part of many, is ambivalent; it either leans toward conformity, but with misgivings, or leans toward deviation, but with misgivings. Furthermore, anomie is not any condition whatever in which there is a high rate of deviation from a social norm or from a system of norms. . . . Anomie . . . is due in part also to some structural factor in the social system." (Harry M. Johnson, *Sociology: A Systematic Introduction*)

Stipulative and Recommendatory Definitions

Unlike reportive definitions, which constitute a special kind of definitional proposition, stipulative and recommendatory definitions are not as such propositions at all and thus can not be characterized as true or false. Stipulative definitions express a resolve or intention to use a linguistic unit in a certain way. Recommendatory definitions are proposals that a certain usage be adopted by others. In the former case we are being directed to interpret the definer's intended meaning in the manner stipulated. In the latter, we are being asked to use the term in the recommended manner ourselves.

As we noted at the beginning of Chapter Six, however, many definitions can be legitimately classified under more than one, or even all three, of these rubrics. In fact, unless the speaker explicitly declares otherwise, reportive definitions are almost invariably stipulative and recommendatory as well. Students would be perplexed if a geometry teacher who had just given a reportive definition of 'triangle' were to use the term with some other meaning. And it would be a perverse student who, having had the conventional meaning of the term explained to him, used it with another meaning, saying, "You told us this is what the term ordinarily means; you did not tell us to use it this way." In this chapter it will be particularly important to remember that a given definition may be intended to serve more than one purpose, for purely stipulative and purely recommendatory definitions are even rarer than purely reportive ones.

I • PERSUASIVE DEFINITIONS

If in proposing a definition we exploit the emotive meaning of the definiendum or the definiens in order to arouse favorable or unfavorable attitudes toward something of which we personally approve or disapprove, our definition is *persuasive*. For example,

> 'Americanism' is conservatism.
> 'Socialism' is economic democracy.

The influence of persuasive definitions on the attitudes of their interpreters has been explained in two ways. According to one view the favorable or unfavorable aura of the emotive terms themselves tends to be transferred by psychological association to whatever these terms are used to denote. The interpreter assumes more or less unconsciously that because a certain term is a good term or bad term, whatever is denoted by it must be good or bad. According to the second explanation persuasive definitions influence attitudes because of the human tendency toward conformity. As a rule, it is easier and pleasanter to agree with others than to disagree, especially when those soliciting our agreement impress us by the weight of their numbers or by their prestige and authority. Thus, when other persons indicate by the use of persuasive definitions that they themselves have certain attitudes, we tend to adopt their attitudes more or less unreflectively.

To be sure, most Americans' attitudes toward socialism are unlikely to be altered because a few choose to define 'socialism' as economic democracy. But persuasive definitions of this kind have undoubtedly played a role in making converts to socialism; and, as the example of the Soviet Union attests, they can be remarkably successful if widely used and completely unchallenged. Similarly, a definition of 'Americanism' as conservatism is unlikely to influence the convinced American liberal; but such a definition, particularly if repeated often enough by enough men in positions of authority, would almost certainly alter the attitudes of the uncommitted and reinforce the attitudes of those who already favor conservatism.

It is one thing, of course, to win favor for socialism or conservatism by persuasive definitions, and another altogether to secure acceptance for the definitions *as* definitions. Even a man who is already persuaded that Americanism and conservatism are both good things might nonetheless refuse to define 'conservatism' as Americanism. Similarly, the man who thinks that socialism and democracy are both good things might well balk at a definition of one in terms of the other. Both men would probably argue that, as conventionally employed, 'Americanism' and 'conservatism' or 'socialism' and 'economic democracy' have different cognitive meanings and that it is unwise to abandon the established cognitive meanings of these terms merely to win adherents to one's own views. In so arguing, these men would find themselves in the company of all respectable logicians. The fact that two terms both refer to things of which we approve or disapprove is not in itself a good logical reason for defining one in terms of the other—not even when the conventional cognitive meanings are closely related.

Nonetheless, persuasive definitions are sometimes accepted as definitions. Our conformist tendencies apparently dispose us to accept recommendations concerning the use of a word, just as they dispose us to accept recommendations about other matters. Moreover, by adopting suitable persuasive definitions we satisfy our natural human desire to flatter ourselves and to insult our enemies. To the extent that 'Americanism' is defined as conservatism, conservatism tends to elicit the same favorable attitudes that Americanism does, and liberals automatically become 'un-American.' Similarly, to the extent that 'socialism' is defined as economic democracy, 'socialism' takes on the favorable emotive meaning of 'democracy,' and the anti-socialist is guilty of 'undemocratic' tendencies.

To achieve these ends, however, we must pay a price—namely, the impoverishment of language as an instrument of communication. Obviously, we could not employ 'Americanism' and 'conservatism' as synonyms and still preserve the difference in cognitive meaning implicit in their current conventional use.

Whether the price is worth paying is an ethical, not a logical, problem; but the fact that many persons do pay the price is one which no student of language can safely ignore.

II · NOMINATIVE DEFINITIONS

A *nominative definition* is one that names or designates something for which the definer finds no adequate label already in existence. Nominative definitions are sometimes occasioned by new discoveries, as when a scientist discovers a new chemical element. At other times they are occasioned by the emergence of some new phenomenon. For example, in early democratic societies such as Athens in the fifth century B.C. all citizens directly participated in the decision-making process. With the emergence of larger communities and nation-states, however, government by elected legislative bodies replaced government by direct participation, and the term 'representative democracy' was introduced for this new form of government. Similarly, in the nineteenth century 'imperialism' designated a process whereby larger, more powerful, and more industrially developed nations conquered smaller, less developed nations by force of arms, maintained military control, and forced the conquered nation to supply the imperial power with raw materials and to buy its manufactured goods. Today, imperialism of this kind is virtually extinct; but it has been replaced by a relationship between industrially developed countries and industrially backward countries, whereby the former attempt to influence the domestic and foreign policies of the latter by granting or withholding military and economic aid. Many persons have introduced the term 'neo-imperialism' to describe this new phenomenon. Finally, nominative definitions are often proposed because existing labels are too vague or too ambiguous.

The definiendum in a nominative definition may be a newly coined term or a term borrowed from another language. Or it may be a term already in general use for which the speaker stipulates or recommends a new meaning. For instance, someone might stipulate at the beginning of a lecture entitled "Democracy" which of this ambiguous term's many subtypes he intends to discuss.

Since a language requires a relatively fixed and stable vocabulary to facilitate communication, nominative definitions often encounter considerable resistance, particularly when they involve a redefinition of terms already in use. It is clear, however, that whatever is worth calling attention to deserves a label and that we cannot legitimately object to the introduction of new terms or the redefinition of old terms simply because this involves a departure from existing linguistic practice. Nominative definitions are legitimately subject to criticism only if (1) they do not label something worth labeling or (2) an available term as conventionally employed serves this purpose equally well. If, for example, someone suggested that the term 'bald man' henceforth be used to refer to men with fewer than 201 hairs on their heads, we would rightly reject the proposal on the grounds that we do not need a label for the class of men so designated, and that if we did, 'men with fewer than 201 hairs on their heads' would serve our purpose much better than 'bald man.'

III • JUDICATIVE DEFINITIONS

A *judicative definition* is a redefinition of a term already in use introduced either to facilitate inquiry or to incorporate the results of inquiry into language. A judicative definition introduced to prepare the way for inquiry is called a *working definition*. A definition introduced to incorporate the results of an inquiry already undertaken is called a *terminal definition*. If a group of economists and sociologists were asked to undertake a study of poverty in America and worked out an initial formula whereby, depending upon the number of persons in the family, a family would count as poor if its annual income ranged from $2200 to $4200, they would be giving a working definition of 'poverty.' The redefinition of 'gold' in terms of atomic weight was a terminal definition. Working definitions may be either stipulative or recommendatory. Terminal definitions are always recommendatory.

The discriminable properties of things do not bear tags announcing their significance or insignificance. Whether a given property is sufficiently important to count as a defining property can only be determined in the light of our needs, interests, aims, or goals. And since these differ from one context to another, satisfactory judicative definitions differ accordingly. A satisfactory working definition of 'poverty' used to determine how available resources should be allocated in combating poverty within the United States would be wholly unsatisfactory if our purpose were to lay the groundwork for a program of international aid to underdeveloped countries. Similarly, a terminal definition of colored objects in terms of light waves, though highly satisfactory to physicists, would be far less satisfactory to artists and paint manufacturers, whose needs dictate a definition in terms of chemical pigment.

Although it is impossible to enumerate all the considerations relevant to understanding and evaluating judicative definitions, many judicative definitions, especially those in the physical and the social sciences, are designed to satisfy one or more of the needs discussed below.

Systematic and Comprehensive Classifications

At one time 'fish' was used to denote living creatures whose natural habitat is water and who are capable of swimming. Later 'fish' was judicatively defined. The defining properties of living in water and being able to swim were retained, but the denotation of the term was narrowed by the addition of further defining properties such as being cold-blooded, breathing through gills, and reproducing by the laying and fertilizing of eggs. Under the new definition, whales, otters, and other creatures formerly called 'fish' were excluded from the denotation of the term. The original definition was the product of a crude threefold classification of living creatures: those that live in water, those that live in the air, and those that live on land. The later definition is the product of a much more refined classification of living creatures that is largely the work of the eighteenth-century Swedish scientist Linnaeus. The wide acceptance of his classification accounts for the modern definition of 'fish.'

Theoretical Understanding

At one time it was widely believed that the difference between a cold and a hot object could best be explained by assuming that hot objects contained a distinct physical element. Although this element could not be observed, its existence was nonetheless theorized: it was called 'phlogiston.' Accordingly, when a scientist of that day was asked to define 'heat,' he answered that heat was phlogiston. The chief objection to the theory underlying this definition was that most bodies lose weight when burned, and it was difficult to understand how the presence of a physical element could cause a body to lose weight. Defenders of the theory suggested that phlogiston was a very special element in that it had a negative weight. Today the concepts of phlogiston and negative weight have been abandoned. A hot body, it is now said, differs from a cold body principally because the molecules of the former are moving at a more rapid pace. Accordingly, 'heat' today is defined in terms of the movement of a body's molecules. Judicative definitions based on considerations like these are frequently called *theoretical definitions.*

Amenability to Experimental Investigation

One of the chief claims made for modern science is that its conclusions are based upon experiments or tests that can be repeated with the same results by any competent investigator. Often, however, a proposed subject for scientific inquiry must be redefined before it becomes directly amenable to experimental manipulation and readily available to all competent observers. Definitions designed for this purpose are called *experimental definitions.*

The problem of constructing experimental definitions has been particularly acute for psychologists, much of whose subject matter is indicated by terms like 'learning,' 'personality trait,' and 'motive.' As conventionally employed, these terms refer to mental phenomena that are neither directly manipulable for experimental purposes nor directly observable by anyone except the agent who experiences them. Accordingly, many psychologists have proposed redefinitions of these lay concepts in terms of publicly observable behavioral responses to publicly observable environmental stimuli that may be experimentally manipulated. Definitions of psychological states in terms of observable stimuli and behavioral response are often called *behavioral definitions* and constitute an important species of experimental definitions.

Mathematical Precision

Another important claim made for modern science is that its conclusions can be stated in precise mathematical terms; and indeed much of the success of modern science can be attributed to its substitution of a quantitative approach for the dominantly qualitative approach that characterized the science of Antiquity and the Middle Ages. As conventionally used, however, many lay terms denoting phenomena that scientists wish to explain are not susceptible to precise quantitative analysis, and scientists have a strong propensity to redefine these terms. The scientific definition of color is an obvious illustration of this propensity. A more recent example from the social sciences is Kinsey's working definition of sexuality in terms of sexual contacts, which may be counted, rather than in terms of sexual feelings or dispositions.

In appraising judicative definitions, the following points should be borne in mind. First, a given judicative definition often serves several purposes at once and may be justified on several grounds. Consider once again the definition of 'gold' as a chemical element with an atomic weight of 197.0. This definition is obviously theoretical, since it has no meaning outside the context of atomic theory. No less obviously, it satisfies the scientist's demand for mathematical exactitude. In addition, it reflects a major advance in the systematic classification of chemical elements, as one can see by comparing an up-to-date table of chemical elements with the four-fold division of elements into air, earth, fire, and water that prevailed well into the early period of modern science.

Second, when an inquiry has more than one purpose, these

purposes may conflict. That is, sometimes a judicative definition which satisfies one purpose of inquiry frustrates a second purpose, and there appears to be no available alternative that satisfies both. Kinsey's definition of sexuality, for instance, satisfies the need for mathematical precision; but it has been widely criticized as detrimental to theoretical understanding on the ground that an adequate understanding of sexuality requires knowledge about what is felt as well as what is done.

Finally, it should be emphasized that the distinction between working and terminal definitions is highly relative. A definition may be terminal in the context of one inquiry and a working definition in the context of a second inquiry. Moreover, to the extent that science is a continuing enterprise whose conclusions are always subject to modification by further discoveries, every terminal definition is at least potentially a working definition. Conversely, since adequate working definitions can be formulated only in the light of already accumulated knowledge, every working definition is in a sense a terminal definition. Insofar as language is used to crystallize and communicate knowledge, it inevitably reflects any tentativeness that accompanies the actual process of inquiry.

IV • LEGAL DEFINITIONS

Can a man who does not believe in God claim exemption from the draft on the grounds that he has 'religious' objections to war? The Supreme Court of the United States has ruled that he can. Is a faculty member who says that he would welcome victory by an enemy in an undeclared war being fought by his country guilty of 'treason' and therefore subject to dismissal? The board of governors of an American university decided that he was not. Is an army officer who publicly opposes participation in an undeclared war fought by his country guilty of 'ungentlemanly conduct?' An army court ruled that he was. Is a housetrailer to be taxed as a 'vehicle' or as a 'dwelling?' Most states have ruled that it be taxed as a dwelling. What kinds of countries are 'democratic?' Since the charter of the United Nations stipulates that only democratic countries be admitted, it has by its admissions policies given that term a very broad meaning. A woman in the eighth month of pregnancy was shot in the stomach during a quarrel. The bullet hit the unborn child, who died shortly afterwards. Was the assailant guilty of 'homicide?' In some states the answer would be affirmative; in others, negative.

Decisions like these, whether accompanied by a written opinion or not, constitute, in effect, a special kind of judicative definition and are usually justified as representing: (1) the intended meaning of whoever framed any laws or rules that may be relevant, (2) the generally accepted meaning of the crucial terms at the time the decision is rendered, and (3) the best interests of all parties concerned.

It is largely agreed in principle that where there are relevant laws or rules, 2 and 3 should be ignored and the decision based entirely on 1. This is especially true in countries such as England and America, where a sharp distinction between legislative and judicial functions is considered highly desirable.

Whatever the merits of this general principle, however, in practice 2 and 3 do play a significant role in decision making even when existing laws or rules are applicable. The principal reason is that those who have authority to frame laws or other official rules are often torn between conflicting purposes. On the one hand, laws and rules should be framed with sufficient precision that those affected will know what is expected of them. On the other hand, it is undesirable that laws constantly be changed and extremely difficult to frame precise laws that will not require constant change to meet new conditions. Thus, legislators are often obliged to strike a delicate balance—to be sufficiently precise that those affected will have a reasonable idea where they stand and yet sufficiently vague to allow for some latitude of judicial interpretation in light of changing circumstances. Had the founding fathers, for instance, been much less precise than they were in framing the Constitution of the United States, American political institutions would have lacked stability and the nation would constantly have been exposed to the threat of anarchy. On the other hand, had the framers been much more precise and allowed considerably less latitude for judicial interpretation, it is most unlikely that the document would still stand as the supreme law of the land.

It should also be noted that in one sense consideration 3 is more fundamental than either of the others; for even those who argue that 1 or 2 should be stressed usually justify their choice as being for the common good or best interests of society. For example, those who stress legislative intent argue that if judges or other interpreters of the law were permitted to invoke considerations other than legislative intent, the result would be intolerable uncertainty on the part of those affected by the law. Similarly, those who stress current usage argue that when the current popular meaning of crucial terms diverges from the intended meaning of the original formulators of the law, the current meaning better reflects the predominant values of society as well as any new knowledge about that which the terms originally denoted.

EXERCISES FOR CHAPTER SEVEN

Which of the following passages are or contain definitions? Classify and appraise the definitions given. Can you think of better definitions of the same terms?

1. Democracy is a political system which seeks to institutionalize freedom.
2. The essence of democracy is the tendency to value the individual more than the state.
3. Man is a naked ape.
4. "What is a primate? It is of all animals the most difficult to define. At various stages of primate evolution various branches of the family have made themselves conspicuous. At one time it was the tree-shrews, at another the tarsiers or the lemurs. Monkeys and apes have for varying periods been those primates best illuminated by evolution's restless spotlight; and for the time being, at least, it is man. . . .

Primates as a group are distinguished by their lack of specialization. One anatomical feature alone have they all developed beyond the common animal lot: the brain. From tree-shrew to man it would seem to be the secret of primate strength that he has combined an extraordinary, oversized brain with a commonplace, undersized body. . . . But so unspecialized are we as a family that when one seeks for a quick means of distinguishing monkey from ape, one can only say that the ape swings from the bough that the monkey runs on; that monkeys have tails, the apes none." (Robert Ardrey, *African Genesis*)

5. "What does the establishment of a 'fair day's work' mean concretely? What is required of a worker? The basic wage contract between the U.S. Steel Corporation and the CIO Steel Workers can be taken as an example. The contract, first negotiated on May 8, 1946, defines a 'fair day's work' as 'that amount of work that can be produced by a qualified employee when working at a normal pace. A normal pace is equivalent to a man walking, without load, on smooth, level ground at a rate of three miles per hour!' " (Daniel Bell, *The End of Ideology*)

6. A woman on relief who wanted to teach school was refused a tuition allowance by her local welfare department. Under the rules of the department cost of tuition can not be given to a relief recipient "except for vocational training." The welfare lawyers argued that the term 'vocational' does not mean a profession such as law or medicine or architecture. It applies primarily to a trade or skill "where one would, say, make use of the hands as a primary means of sustenance."

7. "A rich man told me recently that a liberal is a man who tells other people what to do with their money. I told him that that was right from the side of the telescope he looked through, but that as far as I was concerned a liberal was a man who told other people what to do with their poverty." (LeRoi Jones, *Home*)

8. A liberal is a radical who got married.

9. "Is inflation a one to two percent increase in our cost of living year after year, as measured by the Consumer Price

Index? Or is it three percent? Or four percent? Or more?

". . . I submit that an annual cost of living increase of up to two percent is tolerable in a society as dynamic as ours. It is, modern history indicates, close to the equivalent of price stability.

"Undeniably, this rise erodes the dollar's buying power. Even a mild annual increase of two percent would mean the dollar which buys one hundred cents of goods and services today would buy only eighty-two cents worth ten years from today. But in a growing society, our income gains generally would outrun these price increases.

"Since we've not learned how to control absolute price stability with an expansion powerful enough to absorb our work force, this erosion is a tolerable price to pay for prosperity." (Sylvia Porter, in *The New York Post*, February 24, 1966)

"The rate of desertion—always a wartime problem for the military—has fluctuated considerably during the U.S. military involvements in this century.

"On the basis of current figures . . . Vietnamese war desertions are running below those for the Korean war and World War II. But accurate comparisons are difficult because of changes in the definition of desertion.

"During World War II if a man was absent without leave (A.W.O.L.) for thirty days or more it was considered proof of intent to stay away. In the early 1950's the United States Court of Military Appeals ruled that all aspects of an unauthorized absence had to be considered to prove desertion.

"One veteran Army lawyer notes, however, that after the Military Appeals Court ruling, a number of A.W.O.L. Army men were picked up with frayed old bus or old railroad tickets to their military posts in their possession. 'How could we prove they intended to stay away if, when they were picked up months after going A.W.O.L., they had tickets back to the post in their pockets?' he asks. 'The stockade lawyers had counseled them well.'" ("Deserters: Problem for the Military," *The New York Times*, November 19, 1967)

11. " 'The shortest definition of what a nation is,' says Dr. Gert Scholtz, editor of the Afrikaans newspaper *Die Transvaler,* 'is that it's a spiritual entity. If you don't subscribe to its principles, you belong to another group.' Thus, Dr. Scholtz maintains, there can never be an Afrikaans Communist— by definition. Therefore Bram Fischer, the former barrister whom the security police accuse of having led the banned Communist party, cannot possibly be an Afrikaner, even though he comes from one of the Free State's most distinguished Afrikaans families." (Joseph Lelyveld, "The Afrikaner Feels Lonely in the World," in *The New York Times Magazine,* February 6, 1966)

12. An English law of 1959 declared that a publication is obscene "if its effect is, if taken as a whole, such as to deprave and corrupt persons who are likely, having regard to all circumstances, to read, see, or hear the matter contained or embodied in it."

13. A thirty-two year old midget refused to pay the state sales tax on a coat bought in a department store's children's department because state law exempted children's clothing from the tax. The State Tax Commissioner ruled that 'children's clothing' meant legally "clothing for the express and exclusive use of a child."

14. "Political power, properly so called, is merely the organized power of one class for oppressing another." (Karl Marx and Friedrich Engels, *The Communist Manifesto*)

15. "Political power, then, I take to be a right of making laws with penalties of death, and consequently all lesser penalties, for the regulating and preserving of property, and of employing the force of the community in the execution of such laws, and in defense of the commonwealth from foreign injury." (John Locke, *Essay Concerning Civil Government*)

16. "The difference between political power and any other kind of social 'power,' between a government and any private organization, is the fact that *a government holds a legal monopoly on the use of physical force.* . . .

    "What is economic power? It is the power to produce and to trade what one has produced. . . . Men trade their goods or services by mutual consent to mutual advantage, according to their own independent, uncoerced judgment. . . .

"Now let me define the difference between economic power and political power: economic power is exercised by means of a *positive*, by offering men a reward, an incentive, a payment, a value; political power is exercised by means of a *negative*, by the threat of punishment, injury, imprisonment, destruction. The businessman's tool is *values;* the bureaucrat's tool is *fear*." (Ayn Rand, *Capitalism: The Unknown Ideal*)

17. "*Economic* power . . . is the power to make, or at least predominantly influence, both the major production-decisions (whether, how much, how, what, and where to produce) and distribution-decisions (about the division of the national income between different social groups)." (C. A. R. Crosland, *The Future of Socialism*)

18. "'Socialism' has different meanings for different people. The most useful definition is: production managed and controlled by the government." (Lawrence Abbott, *Economics and the Modern World*)

19. "As the term is understood by students of comparative economic systems and others who do not use it loosely, socialism is identified with extensive nationalization, a dominant public sector, a strong cooperative movement, egalitarian income distribution, a total welfare state and central planning." (Oded I. Remba, letter to the editor, in *The New York Times*, November 1, 1964)

20. "With the exception of the United States, socialism is what the most democratic forces in the West call their dream. And even more basically, the nineteenth-century socialists, for all their failures of prediction, were the first to anticipate the present plight and to attempt to resolve it. They were right when they said that the way in which men produce their worldly goods is becoming more and more social. They were right in asserting that this complex, interdependent technology could not be contained within a system of private decision-making. And if there is to be a humane outcome of the contemporary Western adventure,

they will have to be made right in their faith that the people can freely and democratically take control of their own lives and society.

"And this last idea is the heart of the socialist hope as I define it in this book. From the very beginning, the socialists knew that modern technology could not be made just by dividing it up into tiny parcels of individual ownership. It is of the very nature of that technology to be concentrated and collective. Therefore, the socialists assigned a new and radical meaning to democracy. The people's title to the social means of production would be guaranteed, they said, not through stock certificates, but through votes. The basic economic decisions would be made democratically.

"In this context, the nationalization of industry is a technique of socialism, not its definition. It is one extremely important way of abolishing the political and social power that results from concentrated private ownership. It also facilitates directing economic resources to the satisfaction of human needs. When the people 'own' the state through political democracy, then public corporations are truly theirs, and nationalization is an instrument of freedom. But there are other ways to forward the democratization of economic and social power. Fiscal and monetary policy, a cooperative sector, and taxes are among them.

"In these terms, the one set and undeviating aspect of socialism is its commitment to making the democratic and free choice of the citizens the principle of social and economic life. All other issues—the extent of nationalization, the mode of planning, and the like—have to be empirically tested and measured in the light of how they serve that end. For certainly the old popular definition of socialism as the simple and wholesale nationalization of the economy has not survived the experience of this century, and particularly the Communist experience. At the same time, it has become abundantly clear that the commanding heights of the economy—where decisions affect more of life than most laws of Congresses and Parliaments—cannot be left to private motives.

"But it is better to leave this plane of socialist generality and move to the definition of specific examples." (Michael Harrington, *The Accidental Century*)

21. "The various schools of thought which have called themselves, and been called by others, 'socialist' . . . have differed profoundly over the right means [of achieving their goals.] . . . The one single element common to all the schools of thought has been the basic aspirations, the underlying moral values. It follows that these embody the only logically and historically permissible meaning of the word socialism; and to this meaning we must now revert. . . .

"Perhaps one can list them [basic socialist values] roughly as follows. First, a protest against the material poverty and physical squalor which capitalism produced. Secondly, a wider concern for 'social welfare'—for the interests of those in need, or oppressed, or unfortunate, from whatever cause. Thirdly, a belief in equality and the 'classless society,' and especially a desire to give the worker his 'just' rights and a responsible status at work. Fourthly, a rejection of competitive antagonism, and an ideal of fraternity and cooperation. Fifthly, a protest against the inefficiencies of capitalism as an economic system, and notably its tendency to mass unemployment." (C. A. R. Crosland, *The Future of Socialism*)

22. "Probably the most difficult conservative charge to handle is the accusation that liberalism leads to socialism. This is not because the conservatives have an especially strong case, but because their criticism in this vein is usually vague and hard to define. If the conservative will accept the standard definition of socialism—'government ownership of the means of production'—the liberal can easily point out that federal ownership is very limited and that the government is constantly divesting itself of holdings.

"But most conservatives today talk of modern socialism in terms of federal control of the economy through regulation and planning. Since every set of officeholders in our history has intervened in the economy to one extent or another, the question of socialism becomes one of degree. This is why the conservative claim that 'we're on the road to socialism' is tricky to pin down." (Neil Staebler and Douglas Ross, *How to Argue with a Conservative*)

23. "The word capitalism might reasonably be taken to mean one of two things. First, it might be used in a historical sense to describe the society which developed in nineteenth-century Britain after the Industrial Revolution. . . . What . . . were the salient features of that society . . . ?

(1) . . . the decentralisation of economic decisions . . . and the subordination of these decisions to (mainly) market forces; that is, what is crudely called *laissez-faire*. . . .

(2) At the level of the unit of production, decisions were effectively controlled by a class of private owner-managers, or capitalists, who . . . largely monopolised economic power. . . .

(3) Industrial capital was privately owned, as of course is implied in the previous point. . . .

(4) The distribution of wealth was characteristically unequal. . . .

(5) Capitalism was historically associated with an explicit, assertive, and, in the perspective of history, unusual ideology. Its essential features were, first, the veneration of individualism and competition: secondly, an insistence on the absolute and unconditional rights of private property: thirdly, an intellectual belief that the unfettered exercise of private rights must, by 'the invisible hand' of economic competition, maximise the welfare of the community. . . .

(6) Lastly, capitalism was characterised . . . by an intense class antagonism. . . .

"But it might be objected that the word capitalism has often been used not in the meaning so far assumed, namely as a definition or description of a whole society: but simply to describe one feature of that society which was thought, rightly or wrongly, to be the basic determinant of all other features, namely, the private ownership of large-scale instruments of production. . . .

"Now it is a matter for argument which is the 'proper' definition of capitalism: that is, whether the word has normally been used in this narrow sense, or in the wider sense suggested above. But if the narrower definition is insisted on, we cannot of course prove that it is 'wrong'; we can only ask whether it retains any significance or interest if the assumption behind it turns out to be false; that is, if it appears that ownership is not the fundamental conditioning factor which determines the character of the society." (C. A. R. Crosland, *The Future of Socialism*)

24. "For purposes of this discussion 'democracy,' 'capitalism,' and 'liberalism' are alternative names for the same thing. This is not to deny that there are important differences between the capitalist system as it works with comparatively little adulteration in the United States and the social-democratic Welfare State which has been created in Great Britain. It means only that there are certain describable characteristics concerned with electoral methods, representative government, the rights of the individual in the Courts, the freedom of the Press from Government control, and the virtual absence of Government interference with religious teaching which are found in varying degrees in the United States and Western Europe and which are not found in the U.S.S.R., China, and most of Eastern and Central Europe. . . . Common usage in Western Europe and the United States is the decisive factor. One can say 'capitalist democracies' and 'communist' or 'new democracies,' but this only promotes confusion. Some would further claim that Welfare States on the British model constitute or will soon constitute a new intermediate type, and that our classification should be 'capitalist democracies' and 'socialist democracies' as opposed to 'communist States.' This is purely a matter of convenience. . . ." (T. D. Weldon, *The Vocabulary of Politics*)

25. "The forms of bourgeois states are exceedingly variegated, but their essence is the same: in one way or another, all of these states are in the last analysis inevitably a *dictatorship of the bourgeoisie*. The transition from capitalism to communism will certainly bring a great variety and abundance of political forms, but the essence will inevitably be only one: *the dictatorship of the proletariat*." (Lenin, *State and Revolution*)

26. "The title Conservative was sunk in the latest general elections in Canada, Britain and the U.S. The name Conservative lessens the popularity of a philosophy, however sound it may be. The glowing title Liberal has been, is now and ever will be a popular banner around which its many and varied followers wax warm.

"Conservative suggests Tory, mossback and old guard at its worst, and at its very best safety, reliability, soundness, veracity and other virtues which, however commendable, somehow lack romance. The proven course cannot carry the four-syllable name Conservative and win against sweet-sounding beliefs called Liberal. If the harsher term could be nicknamed something catchy, it might help. Public Opinion polls in 1950 revealed Conservative as a name for a philosophy was 14 percentage points less popular than Republican as a name for a party. In New York City today the difference would be 35 points.

"One philosophy has captured, over the protests of the other, the title Liberal. The other should follow the admonition of George Washington, 'Let us raise a standard to which the wise and honest shall repair,' and choose and use the three-syllable title Constructive. To discredit someone it may be said, 'He is too conservative.' But not: 'He is too constructive.' Someone may ask, 'What's in a name?' The answer can often be, 'The difference.'" (H. L. Hunt, *Hunt for Truth*)

27. "There are now, says the Bureau of Labor Statistics' latest tally, 2,573,000 unemployed Americans. But included in this figure are 68,000 fourteen- and fifteen-year-olds, 80,000 workers who actually have jobs but are looking for other jobs, some 150,000 job trainees under the Manpower Development & Training Act. Should these groups properly be counted as jobless?" (Sylvia Porter, in the New York *Post*, October 26, 1966)

28. "The traditional unemployment measure only counts those individuals who are full-time unemployed and actively seeking work. The sub-employment concept adds the following to 'official' unemployment counts: (1) part-time employed and seeking full-time work, (2) full-time em-

ployment at substandard wages, (3) one-half of the male 'non-participants' in the labor force (individuals not actively seeking work for a variety of reasons, e.g., frustration), and (4) one-half of the estimated male 'undercount' (Jacob S. Siegel of the Census Bureau estimates that 9.5 percent of the male nonwhite population does not get counted)." (Michael Marien, letter to the editor, in *The New Republic*, October 28, 1967)

29. "The draft is clearly unconstitutional. No amount of rationalization, neither by the Supreme Court nor by private individuals, can alter the fact that it represents 'involuntary servitude.'" (Ayn Rand, *Capitalism: The Unknown Ideal*)

30. Capital punishment is unconstitutional, since it is clearly "cruel and unusual punishment."

31. During World War II, the U.S. Office of Price Administration defined 'an antique' as "an object that tended to increase in value because of age, and was purchased primarily because of its age, authenticity, rarity, and style rather than its utility." A minimum age of seventy-five years was set.

32. "*Objective science.* A science whose data are open to observation by any competent observer, as in the physical and biological sciences. Behaviorism sought to eliminate subjectivity from psychology, hence to make it an objective science." (Ernest R. Hilgard and Richard C. Atkinson, *Introduction to Psychology*)

33. "Individuals will only tend to assert their rights as individuals, to take pride in their achievements, to deliberate carefully and choose 'for themselves' what they ought to do, and to develop their own individual style of emotional reaction—in other words they will only tend to manifest all the various properties which we associate with being 'persons'—if they are encouraged to do so." (R. S. Peters, *Ethics and Education*)

Rules for the Informative Use of Language

Language is used informatively whenever the speaker's intent is to communicate information about some identified subject of discourse. The subject may be a linguistic unit, as in reportive definitions, but more often it is a non-linguistic fact. In either case successful communication requires that the interpreters be able to identify the subject of discourse and to understand the attributive terms used in describing it. In view of the complexity of language, misunderstanding is often hard to avoid, and as we have noted before, there is no simple remedy to this situation. There are, however, some general rules worth noting.

I • Avoid Emotive Terms Whenever Possible

It is sometimes difficult, or even impossible, to communicate a specific item of information without using emotive terms. If we want to say that someone is honest, for example, it is not easy to do so without suggesting personal approval. It seems there are no common terms for honesty that are not emotive. Many things, however, can be characterized with equal precision both by emotive and by emotively neutral terms. In such cases there are several reasons for preferring the neutral terms. First, emotive terms tend to have a richer pictorial meaning than their neutral equivalents, and the cognitive meaning of an emotive term often gets drowned in a sea of pictorial meaning. Sec-

153

ond, sentences containing emotive terms tend to be evocative, and strong feelings easily distract us. Third, emotive terms have a high degree of *descriptive spread*—that is, over a period of time they tend to be applied to many more individuals than they did originally. As a result the cognitive meaning of emotive terms is rarely as precise or stable as the cognitive meaning of neutral terms. At one time, for example, the term 'communist' was almost purely cognitive: its sole purpose was to describe someone who espoused the basic views of Marx and Engels. Gradually, however, the term acquired negative emotive meaning in the Western world, especially in America, and there was a growing readiness to apply the term, quite without regard for its original cognitive meaning, to almost anyone whose political views were to the left of the speaker's. The stronger the emotive force of the expression, the greater the descriptive spread. In the Soviet Union, one can trace a similar history for the word 'bourgeois.' Originally this term was relatively neutral and denoted a property-owner whose social behavior and political views were influenced by his property interests. A story told by an American visitor to Moscow illustrates how its unfavorable emotive force for Soviet citizens has influenced its current use. According to the visitor, he witnessed a quarrel between a Russian soldier and a prostitute. It started with a mild exchange of insults, became more and more acrimonious, and terminated only after the soldier came out with the crowning insult and parting shot, "Bourgeoise!" The prostitute was unable to top this and the soldier had the last word.

II • Be as Precise, Concrete, and Specific as Your Purpose Requires

It is unfortunate that the terms 'precise,' 'concrete,' and 'specific' have favorable emotive meaning, whereas their opposites—'vague,' 'abstract,' and 'general'—have negative emotive meaning.[1] In fact, vague, abstract, and general terms are as necessary to the successful communication of information as precise, concrete, and specific terms. What advantage would we gain by

[1] Short, emotively neutral terms with an equivalent cognitive meaning would be highly preferable, but unfortunately they do not exist.

banishing the vague term 'bald' from our language? What advantage would there be in abolishing property terms, all of which are abstract? Would geometry be a more advanced science if geometricians were permitted to use the relatively specific terms 'isosceles triangle,' 'right triangle,' and 'equilateral triangle' but not the more general term 'triangle?' These questions are rhetorical, of course. Such restrictions could only result in a disastrous loss, and we would not even have the means of recording it. Thus, though in stating Rule 2 we deferred to popular prejudice, we could just as well have written: "Be as vague, abstract, and general as your purpose requires."

It is true that we often err on the side of excessive vagueness, abstraction, and generality. For example, when the purpose is to narrate an observed sequence of events or to describe an observed object, the appropriate level of precision, concreteness, and specificity is difficult to attain even by the most accomplished writer. Similarly, when the purpose is to help resolve political or social issues, we are all prone to speak vaguely and in loose generalities or irrelevant abstractions.

On the other hand, when the purpose is to define a troublesome term, we err more often than not on the side of excessive concreteness and specificity, and thus sacrifice precision; for typically we define terms by citing examples instead of constructing precise definitions. Similarly, when the purpose is to explain something, we tend to be too concrete and specific. Almost any adequate explanation requires that the subject of discourse be classified at many levels of generality in terms of abstract properties; and the more adequate the explanation, the more likely it is to include a large number of general and abstract terms. It is remarkable and significant that the highly general and abstract terms of science—despite their remoteness from the concrete things and events in our daily lives—are nonetheless indispensable to a full understanding of daily experiences.

In fact, what ordinarily passes for excessive abstractness and generality is usually not excessive at all, but rather insufficient or inappropriate. After all, to describe something fully is to catalogue its properties; and, since all property terms are abstract, to describe an object well is to invoke a large number of abstractions. The person guilty of "excessive generality and abstraction" is thus one who seizes upon certain traits or properties of individuals to the exclusion of others. He is the person who says, "So-and-so is *just* a Jew (or a Negro or a criminal)," and who thereby blinds himself to the many other characteristics that constitute the person's uniqueness. A better term for "excessive generality and abstraction" is *stereotyped thinking*. Ironically, those who pride themselves most on their specificity and concreteness are usually the ones most guilty of excessively abstract, stereotyped thinking.

III • Do Not Use Ambiguous Verbal Tokens

Type-ambiguity, as pointed out earlier, is not dangerous in itself, since we communicate with tokens rather than types, and the context in which a given token is used will frequently make clear the intended meaning. When the context does not make the intended meaning of a token clear, however, there is a real danger of misunderstanding. Several things can be done to avoid token ambiguity. If there is an unambiguous term with the same intended meaning, we need only substitute the unambiguous term. If no unambiguous term is available, as is often the case, we can stipulate which of the term's subtypes we intend. Unfortunately, most people's memories are short, and in an extended discussion it is very likely that our stipulation will be forgotten not only by the interpreters but even by ourselves. A more desirable method, therefore, is to qualify the term. If, for example, the term is 'democracy,' we can qualify it with the adjectives 'direct' or 'representative,' 'popular' or 'Western,' etc. If the term is 'imperialism,' we can qualify it by saying 'nineteenth-century imperialism' or 'neo-imperialism.'

It is a serious mistake, however, to become entangled in a discussion about the "true" or "real" meaning of an ambiguous term. All subtypes of an ambiguous term are equally real or true. And although one or more of these subtypes may require judicative definition, ambiguous terms as such cannot be judicatively defined. Similarly, although many ambiguous terms such as 'democracy' and 'imperialism' are susceptible to persuasive definition, persuasive definitions have no role to play in informative discourse. Informative language communicates information about an identified subject of discourse. The only information that a persuasive definition might be said to communicate is information about the speaker's attitudes or feelings.

IV • Be Explicit in Your Use of Relational Terms

When the relata of a relational term are explicitly identified, the term is unlikely to give any trouble. But when the relata are not explicitly stated, there will often be great confusion. For example, there is an old rule of logic according to which a good definition must state the essential property or the essence of the definiendum. This rule was based on the supposition that 'essential' is a one-place term and that the essence of a thing could be discovered by simple inspection in the way that we discover a property like being snub-nosed. Recently, however, philosophers have learned that 'essential' is a three-place term, nothing being essential except to some person and for some purpose. Accordingly, logicians no longer say that a good definition must state the essence of the definiendum. A modern version of this rule would say simply that a good definition must cite those properties of the definiendum essential to the purpose of the definer.

The slogan 'We are committed,' frequently heard in support of military escalation in Vietnam, is another instance of how an implicitly relational term can give trouble. By virtue of its pictorial meaning and emotive force, a slogan like this has great propaganda value. But to what did we commit ourselves in Vietnam? And to whom? Was our commitment to supply military hardware and technical advice or to supply armed troops? Did we commit ourselves to the people of South Vietnam or to the government? If to the government, was our commitment to any government that held power or only a legitimate government? Unless 'We are committed' is expanded so as to answer questions like these, it has little or no cognitive meaning, conveys little or no information, and cannot reasonably be evaluated as true or false.

V • Do Not Depart from Established Usage Without Good Reason

As already noted, departures from established usage are warranted if and only if (1) there is no convenient already-existing label for our chosen subject of discourse, or (2) we are engaged in an inquiry whose purpose can best be served by redefining some term already in use. In specific cases, however, there is ample room for debate about the applicability of this general rule. Where redefinitions are concerned, debate often revolves around questions of material fact: What is the precise object of the inquiry? And what is the true nature of the subject of discourse? Often, however, debate will revolve around questions of linguistic fact—the problem being to decide whether existing linguistic resources have been fully exploited. These are the cases that interest us here.

Sometimes new terms are introduced or old ones redefined simply because the speaker is unfamiliar with a perfectly good term already in use that would fully convey his intended meaning. In such cases the rule is violated out of simple ignorance. More often, however, the problem in implementing the rule is one of judgment. In most cases we must balance the advantages and disadvantages of a linguistic revision against the advantages and disadvantages of making do with existing terms. For example, the terms 'vague,' 'precise,' and 'abstract' have the disadvantage of possessing negative emotive meaning but the advantage of being familiar to the reader. If we coined new terms for which we stipulated the same cognitive meanings, the new terms would be free of negative emotive meaning but the reader would have greater difficulty remembering their cognitive meaning. Would we then be justified in coining new terms for these concepts?

Similarly, the concepts expressed by terms such as 'loose intension,' 'linear vagueness,' 'vagueness of family resemblance,' and 'lability' have long been known to logicians, but the terms themselves are not in standard employ. Are these concepts sufficiently important to warrant separate labels? Could other labels have been used that would better convey the intended meanings?

Another illustration from this text is the term 'contingent intension.' As conventionally employed, the term designates only those non-defining properties of a class term that belong to every member of the term's denotation; in this text, however, we have judicatively defined this term to include properties belonging to nearly all of the objects denoted by the term as well. Many logicians would object to this redefinition on the grounds that a precise term has thereby been rendered vague. The counterargument is that the definition in this text, though vaguer, is more useful since it sheds greater light on the way in which terms acquire new meanings.

In all of these cases there is a question of judgment on which reasonable men may disagree.

VI • When Departing from Established Usage Make Your Reasons Clear

This rule is a natural sequel to Rule 5. By explicitly stating our reasons for departing from established usage, we guard against misunderstanding; and we may engage our interpreters in a dialogue leading to the adoption of an alternative and more desirable linguistic revision.

There are times, of course, when it is unnecessary or undesirable to observe this rule. We have sometimes violated it in introducing judicative definitions of technical terms in this text. In a book written for logicians already familiar with these terms, these violations would have been completely unjustifiable. However, since this text is intended for students not already familiar with these terms, there are no established habits of usage to be overcome and no danger that the reader will misunderstand our intended meaning because of previous associations with these terms. Moreover, the practical mastery of a technical vocabulary is difficult enough for beginning students. To detail disagreements among logicians on essentially theoretical issues would be to add a largely gratuitous burden. Remember, however, that even technical terms are subject to redefinition and that not every author employs them with exactly the same meaning.

VII · Be Flexible in Your Use of Language in Controversial Discussions

To discuss a controversial issue profitably two minimal conditions must be met. First, the parties to the dispute must adopt common meanings for crucial terms. Second, the agreed-upon meanings must be such that the parties to the dispute may each state his own views. And to meet these conditions it is often necessary to accept a usage for a term even though one is convinced that a different usage would ordinarily be preferable. For example, one of the parties to a dispute may use a term in a nonconventional or even highly idiosyncratic way. If, however, he can not be persuaded to abandon his special meaning for this term, it is often best to accept his meaning tentatively in order that the discussion may proceed.

This rule is especially relevant when one has defined a crucial term on the basis of a personal position relating to some aspect of the controversy. For example, Hannah Arendt in *Eichmann in Jerusalem* argued that Adolph Eichmann was not a moral monster even though she readily granted that Eichmann's actions were morally monstrous. Some of her critics argued against her by saying that a 'moral monster' is by definition someone with a demonstrated capacity for morally monstrous actions and that consequently Miss Arendt must be wrong. Note, however, that since Miss Arendt's position obviously depends on this definition of a 'moral monster' being wrong, the controversy can not profitably proceed unless (1) the parties to the dispute agree to abandon this controversial term and rephrase the issue or (2) the critics undertake to defend their definition of a 'moral monster' judicatively.

EXERCISES FOR CHAPTER EIGHT

A. Which of the following passages are informative? What rules for the informative use of language, if any, do they violate?

1. All men are born equal.
2. Bertrand Russell's War Crimes Tribunal was thoroughly irresponsible.
3. "Germany is the great menace to world peace. She invaded Belgium in 1914 although she had pledged herself by treaty to respect Belgium's neutrality. Although she robbed France of two million pounds after the war of 1870 she whined to the Allies about the hardships she would suffer from their reparations demands in 1919, which were her just punishment for her guilt in starting the 1914 war. Do not let Germany's pleas for mercy after her defeat in this war deceive you. Nothing but the annihilation of Germany can secure the future peace of the world." (Quoted in Robert H. Thouless, *Straight and Crooked Thinking*)
4. Nine out of ten doctors recommend X.
5. According to Jean-Paul Sartre, men are totally free and each must "invent his own way." A commentator writes: "Sartre calls this quite arbitrarily the 'new humanism,' centered on man in contrast to a God-centered way of life. Such a use of the term 'humanism' is arbitrary because humanism has never believed in an unbridled yielding to instincts and complete detachment from the laws of morality. It believes in the freedom of the individual for the sake of his own moral perfection and that of society. Sartre's freedom is nothing but moral anarchy." (William Hubben, *Dostoevsky, Kierkegaard, Nietzsche, and Kafka*)
6. "Academic freedom does not mean academic license. It is the freedom to do good and not to teach evil." (From a decision by a New York judge who in 1940 declared Bertrand Russell unfit to teach and legally voided his appointment to the College of the City of New York)
7. "But then, that word, *Fascist,* and with it, *Fascism,* has been made obsolete by the words *America,* and *Americanism.*" (LeRoi Jones, *Home*)
8. "Evil, be thou my good." (Satan, in Milton's *Paradise Lost*)
9. Mechanical contraception is unnatural.
10. "I have settled down to the task of writing these lectures and have drawn up my chair to my two tables. Two tables! . . .

". . . One of them has been familiar to me from earliest years. It is a commonplace object of that environment which I call the world. . . . It has extension; it is comparatively permanent; it is coloured; above all it is *substantial.* . . . It is a *thing;* not like space . . . nor like time. . . .

"Table No. 2 is my scientific table. . . . It does not belong to . . . that world which spontaneously appears around me when I open my eyes. . . . It is part of a world which in more devious ways has forced itself on my attention. My scientific table is mostly emptiness. Sparsely scattered in that emptiness are numerous electric charges rushing about with great speed; but their combined bulk amounts to less than a billionth of the bulk of the table itself. . . .

"There is nothing substantial about my second table. It is nearly all empty space—space pervaded, it is true, by fields of force, but these are assigned to the category of 'influence,' not of 'things.' . . .

"It makes all the difference in the world whether the paper before me is poised as it were on a swarm of flies and sustained in shuttlecock fashion by a series of tiny blows from the swarm underneath, or whether it is supported because there is substance below it, it being the intrinsic nature of substance to occupy space to the exclusion of other substance; all the difference in conception at least, but no difference to my practical task of writing on the paper.

"I need not tell you that modern physics has by delicate test and remorseless logic assured me that my second scientific table is the only one which is really there—wherever 'there' may be." (Arthur Eddington, *The Nature of the Physical World*)

11. All men in the last analysis are selfish. Everyone acts for his own interests. Even a parent who sacrifices for his children is acting selfishly, since the protection of his children's welfare is his own strongest desire.

B. The passages below all raise issues concerning the proper use of language. Define the issues as clearly as possible. Give reasons for whichever position on the issue you believe to be best justified.

1. "Much as I dislike having to dissent from Malcolm Muggeridge . . . , I must say that I see nothing wrong with applying the word 'ghetto' to the Negro-Puerto Rican quarters of our cities. It is an entirely proper extension of the term, one that was recognized at least as far back as 1957 by Webster's *New International Dictionary*.

   "Mr. Muggeridge says that by equating Negro slums with a ghetto, white racialism is associated with the additional horrors of Nazi anti-Semitism. Not necessarily; the Nazis did not invent the ghetto.

   "In his next sentence he seems to be complaining that the use of the word casts the wrongs against the Negro 'in terms of pogroms and other distant and remote wickednesses, rather than of nearby and present social and economic inequalities.' It seems to me that the word's effect could be just the reverse: to bring a realization that the ghetto is not distant and remote but something right here in this country at this time.

   "On the linguistic level I do not disagree with Mr. Muggeridge on the need for 'the maintenance of the true meaning and correct usage of words.' But the true meaning of a word is not necessarily its original meaning. If it were, we would not be able to speak of space 'docking' operations or call a dilapidated tenement a 'rookery'; the word 'fruition' would mean gratification derived from possession, 'prevent' would mean to come before, 'nice' would mean ignorant—shall I go on? The true meaning of a word is determined by how it is used by cultivated speakers and writers.

   "One need not be a permissivist to affirm that words take on new meanings to meet new conditions. That is the way in which the language remains vital. The current extension of the word 'ghetto' seems to me to be both legitimate and useful." (Theodore Winner, letter to the editor, in *The New York Times*, May 12, 1968)

2. "It is indeed regrettable that the word 'race' has been so widely adopted by the press as a synonym for political elec-

tion. The public is bombarded with phrases such as 'primary race,' 'gubernatorial race,' 'Presidential race,' etc.

"Used in this sense, 'race' connotes, above all, a sporting event. As the metaphor gains sway over popular imagination, the electorate is subtly transformed into a crowd of spectators whose principal purpose is to cheer the winner. The voter is becoming increasingly afraid of backing a loser. Thus elections are further degraded to the level of mere popularity contests, devoid of significant political debate.

"Responsible newspapers and broadcasters should strive to avoid contributing in this way to the undermining of free democratic elections." (Alfred Soman, letter to the editor, in *The New York Times*, May 12, 1968)

3. "The formula by which the sacrificial animals are to be fooled and tamed is being repeated today with growing insistence and frequency: businessmen, it is said, must regard the government, not as an enemy, but as a 'partner.' The notion of a 'partnership' between a private group and public officials, between business and government, between production and force, is a linguistic corruption . . . typical of a fascist ideology—an ideology that regards force as the basic element and ultimate arbiter in all human relationships.

" 'Partnership' is an indecent euphemism for 'government control.' There can be no partnership between armed bureaucrats and defenseless private citizens who have no choice but to obey. What chance would you have against a 'partner' whose *arbitrary* word is law, . . . who will always have the last word and the legal 'right' to enforce it on you at the point of a gun, holding your property, your work, your future, your life in his power? Is *that* the meaning of 'partnership'?" (Ayn Rand, *Capitalism: The Unknown Ideal*)

4. "The assault on patriots throughout this country, which has been in full swing for several years, shows no signs of abating.

"There are two very striking features about this assault. First is its vehemence. Second is the unwillingness or inability of the attackers to tell anyone clearly and reasonably what it is they are so bitterly against.

"An example of the vehemence of the assault and a key to its meaning is the constant use of the word 'hate.' This is a very strong and ugly word. It creates a climate which makes calm and sensible judgments very difficult. Certainly if the anti-patriots said openly they hated their opponents, their use of this word would turn public opinion against them.

"But they are clever; instead, they pretend it is their opponents, the patriots, who 'hate' them; and they never miss an opportunity to use the word.

"To decide who the real 'haters' are, simply ask yourself how often you have heard that word used as a weapon by a friend of American liberties and national independence.

"But what are these attackers of patriotism really against? They rise up in fury if anyone suggests they are opposed to patriotism itself; they simply say they dislike 'too much' of it. They dislike 'extremists' and prefer 'moderates.'

"These words and ideas have no sensible content. If patriotism is good then a lot of it should be extremely good and who wouldn't want something that is extremely good? The attack seems intended to destroy sound thinking about its targets." (H. L. Hunt, *Hunt for Truth*)

5. "A major symptom of a man's—or a culture's—intellectual and moral disintegration is the shrinking of vision and goals to the concrete-bound range of the immediate moment. This means: the progressive disappearance of abstractions from a man's mental processes or from a society's concerns. The manifestation of a disintegrating consciousness is the inability to think and act in terms of *principles*.

"A principle is 'a fundamental, primary, or general truth, on which other truths depend.' Thus a principle is an abstraction which subsumes a great number of concretes. It is only by means of principles that one can set one's long-range goals and evaluate the concrete alternatives of any given moment. It is only principles that enable a man to plan the future and to achieve it.

"The present state of our culture may be gauged by the

extent to which principles have vanished from public discussion, reducing our cultural atmosphere to the sordid, petty senselessness of a bickering family that haggles over trivial concretes, while betraying all its major values, selling out its future for some spurious advantage of the moment.

". . . There is nothing as impractical as a so-called 'practical' man. His view of practicality can best be illustrated as follows: if you want to drive from New York to Los Angeles, it is 'impractical' and 'idealistic' to consult a map and to select the best way to get there. . . ." (Ayn Rand, *Capitalism: The Unknown Ideal*)

6. "It is a perversion of language to assign any law as the efficient, operative cause of anything. A law presupposes an agent; for it is only the mode according to which an agent proceeds." (William Paley, *Natural Theology*)

7. In my view, conscience is not the voice of a super-empirical authority, nor is it the vision of eternal ideas of right and wrong. It is rather the voice of our more basic desires and the abstract awareness of the full consequences of our acts protesting against the claims of more or less compulsive, lower-level desires with their more immediate appeal. This definition is based on a concrete analysis of specific cases of what we ordinarily call states of 'bad conscience.' Many of my critics will no doubt object, however, that the cases analyzed were not true instances of bad conscience since no one can be troubled by a bad conscience unless he *knows* that his behavior is wrong.

This objection has a superficial plausibility. To meet it, the procedure followed up to this point should be made explicit. At the beginning of this argument cases of conflict between conscience and desire were characterized in terms of states of indecision, distress, and / or regret accompanying the performance or contemplation of acts that are contrary to rules of behavior to which the agent feels committed or which he believes promote his own interests at the expense of others. In effect, this was my working definition of 'bad conscience.' My justification for initially defining a case of bad conscience in this way without men-

tion of right or wrong is twofold. First, it seems clear that
the characteristics cited are alone sufficient to identify all
paradigm cases of what we ordinarily mean to denote when
we speak of conflict between conscience and desire. Second,
if I incorporated into my initial definition a mention of right
and wrong, I would be courting serious confusion by allowing my critics to beg the very question at issue. They say
that the cognitive element in cases of conscience is knowledge of right and wrong imparted by a special faculty of
the soul. I say that the cognitive element involved is ordinary, empirical knowledge of our more basic desires and
the full consequences of our acts. My contention turns on a
point of material fact, and presumably that of my critics
does as well.

8. " 'The John Birch Society is no extremist, ultra-rightist con-
spiracy-minded group on the far-out lunatic fringe. It is
rather a public-spirited organization that really walks a
tight line between the political extremes of the left and
right.'

"So says Thomas J. Davis, regional manager of the Birch
Society's new public relations office at 180 E. Post Road in
White Plains.

" 'Somebody got the idea of calling the John Birch Society an extremist group,' says Mr. Davis, 'but we certainly
didn't.' He went on to define his political directions in this
fashion:

" 'On the 'total left' are the Nazis, Fascists, socialists, and
Communists, all those who believe in 'absolute government.' On the 'extreme right' are the anarchists, those who
want no government. The John Birch Society stands precisely in the middle of those two extremes, believing in the
American constitutional government.'

"If you stick by his definition of the political spectrum—
which defies the conventional system of assigning Fascists
to the reactionary right and Communists to the revolutionary left—then you can locate Birchers in the middle of the
road, he says."   (Martin G. Berck, "A Bircher Defines His
Society's Aims," in the New York *Herald Tribune,* Decem-
ber 27, 1964)

9. "A machine does not act spontaneously, you will say. That is not at all certain. I am told by a man who knows the facts that when the draught-playing machine was about to lose its first game, it cheated. Whenever I tell this story to laymen in the presence of calculator-specialists, the specialist is eager to explain: 'But that, of course, was only a mistake.' Of course it was a mistake, but was so by definition. Whenever the machine does what we have not planned it to do we call it a mistake." (C. F. von Weizsacker, *The Relevance of Science*)

10. "The term *Afro-American*, which I will use or not use, as I please, is in growing usage among Negroes, and . . . it escapes me why you think you should have something to say about the desirability of its use. . . . A great many black people feel that *Afro-American* is an historically and ethnically correct term and that it is preferable to the word *Negro*, which is, after all, an *adjective*. Also, there has never been any clamor raised over other peoples' ethnic hyphenations, e.g., Italian- (or Italo-) Americans, Irish-Americans, etc. Why so much fuss about Negroes wanting to call themselves Afro-Americans?" (LeRoi Jones, *Home*)

11. The Epicureans, who held that pleasure is the highest end in life, were accused of demeaning men and preaching a doctrine worthy only of swine. They answered that not they but their accusers represented human nature in a degrading light, for the accusation makes no sense unless human beings are thought to be incapable of any pleasures other than those which swine enjoy.

12. The reviewer of a textbook in zoology criticized the book for neglecting to give information about the size of various animals. There was, he said, no "more obvious difference" than size.

ARGUMENT

Introduction to Part Two

In logic, the term *argument* denotes any group of propositions consisting of a *conclusion*—the proposition the argument is alleged to establish—and one or more *premises*—propositions offered as evidence for the conclusion. When (1) an argument is clearly expressed, (2) the premises give evidence for the conclusion, and (3) there is good reason to believe that the premises are true, the argument is called *sound.*

For purposes of logical analysis the components of an argument are usually written in a sequence whose last member is the conclusion. Each premise is written on a separate line and given a number. The premises are separated from the conclusion by a solid line. For example,

1. Either cancer is caused by smoking or cancer is caused by air pollution.
2. Cancer is not caused by air pollution.

    Cancer is caused by smoking.

Sometimes, however, it is desirable to put a group of sentences expressing an argument into what is called its *corresponding conditional:* a standard-form conditional sentence whose antecedent is the conjunction of the premises and whose consequent is the conclusion. Thus, the above argument could also be formulated as follows:

If either cancer is caused by smoking or cancer is caused by air pollution and cancer is not caused by air pollution, then cancer is caused by smoking.

Strictly speaking, an argument is a set of propositions, not sentences. Nonetheless, for the sake of convenience we shall hereafter use the term 'argument' to refer to sets of sentences as well as sets of propositions. We shall also on occasion drop the cumbersome phrase 'proposition expressed by' when we use a sentence or other symbol in single quotes to identify a proposition.

The conventional symbols used to represent arguments are the same as those used to represent sentences and propositions. Thus, our sample argument can be abbreviated in either of the following ways:

$$
\begin{array}{ll}
1.\ S \vee A & \\
2.\ \dfrac{-A}{S} & ((S \vee A) \cdot -A) \to S
\end{array}
$$

And the logical form of this argument can be shown in either of the following ways:

$$
\begin{array}{ll}
1.\ p \vee q & \\
2.\ \dfrac{-q}{p} & ((p \vee q) \cdot -q) \to p
\end{array}
$$

No matter how an argument is formulated, it is important to understand that the science of argument is primarily concerned with the logical relationship between premises and conclusion. More specifically, the primary aim of the science of argument is to determine whether the premises of an argument *would* give evidence for the conclusion *if they were true*, regardless of whether they are or are not true.

There are two principal reasons for emphasizing the relationship between premises and conclusion. First, since an argument should and normally does proceed from that which is better known to that which is less well known, the premises are usually less controversial than the conclusion, and it is the truth of the conclusion rather than the truth of the premises which is at issue.

Second, sometimes the truth or falsity of an argument's premises can be established non-argumentatively—for example, by direct observation or by an appeal to authority. When, however, the premises of an argument are themselves controversial, it is almost always the case that they, too, must be supported by argument. And in a case like this the crucial issue is once again the relationship between premises and conclusion—though this time in some second argument whose conclusion is the controversial premise of the first argument.

I • IDENTIFYING ARGUMENTS IN ORDINARY DISCOURSE

Any mental process culminating in the belief that one or more propositions assumed to be true give evidence for, or support, some other proposition is called an *inference*. And language used to express inferences is called *argumentative*. Of course, not all thinking is inferring and not all discourse is argumentative. Thinking includes a broad range of mental activities—not only inferring but remembering, daydreaming, free associating, observing, and countless other mental activities. Similarly, discourse includes not only arguments but narrations, descriptions, commands, exclamations, and so forth.

As a rule argumentative discourse includes terms like 'because,' 'therefore,' 'infer,' 'imply,' 'so,' 'since,' by which the argumentative intent may be recognized. These terms are not unfailing signs of an argumentative intent, however. If, for example, someone says, "Jones is absent because he is ill," it would not be reasonable to assume that he is expressing an inference, or arguing. In almost any context the speaker would have direct knowledge of the truth of both components: 'Jones is absent' and 'He is ill.' The speaker would not, therefore, have inferred one from the other; and the compound sentence 'Jones is absent because he is ill' would be purely informative rather than argumentative. Conversely, arguments are sometimes expressed without the aid of any term conventionally used to indicate argumentative intent. Suppose someone says: "Why do you think Jones is in Paris? When he phoned me yesterday, he said he was in Istanbul." In this case, we must assume not only that the speaker has inferred 'Jones is not in Paris' from the premise 'Jones is in Istanbul' but also that the speaker has inferred 'Jones is in Istanbul' from the premise 'When Jones phoned me yesterday he said he was in Istanbul.'

Often, as in the last example, one or more of the component propositions of an argument is not actually expressed. Sometimes this happens because the unexpressed proposition is obvious to both arguer and interpreter. If, for example, someone said, "John cannot be eligible; he is over twenty," the relevant unexpressed premise is clearly 'No person over twenty is eligible.' In such cases unexpressed components pose no serious problem. But at least as often unexpressed components can lead to serious mis-understanding and confusion—especially when the missing prop-ositions are not fully formulated in the arguer's own mind. No argument, however, can be properly analyzed until all component propositions are made explicit.

On occasion the unexpressed component of an argument is the conclusion. For example, in the argument 'Jones is a Communist, and no good Americans are Communists' the unexpressed propo-sition is the conclusion: 'Jones is not a good American.' Cases like this, however, are relatively rare. Usually our problem is to supply a missing premise, not a missing conclusion. Hereafter, unex-pressed premises will be called *implicit premises.*

In supplying implicit premises we should use any clues pro-vided by the context or by our knowledge of the arguer. In the absence of such clues, it is best to assume that the missing premise is one that would strengthen the argument and that relevant general knowledge indicates to be true. All too often, however, the attempt to supply a missing premise for an in-complete argument leads to a dilemma: we are confronted by a choice between a dubious premise that would considerably strengthen the argument and a premise that is probably true but gives little or no support to the conclusion. For example, in the argument 'Jones must be a Communist, because he supports socialized medicine,' the missing premise could be either 'All persons supporting socialized medicine are Communists,' which is more than dubious but gives conclusive support to the conclusion, or 'Some persons who support socialized medicine are Communists,' which is undeniably true but gives little support to the conclusion.

II • DEDUCTIVE AND NON-DEDUCTIVE ARGUMENTS

Whenever the premises of an argument do in fact give evidence for the conclusion, the premises are said to *imply* the conclusion. The term 'imply,' however, has a stronger and a weaker meaning. In its stronger meaning the premises of an argument 'imply' a conclusion if and only if they give conclusive evidence for it. In its weaker meaning the premises of an argument 'imply' a conclusion if and only if they give reasonably good but less than conclusive evidence in its favor. Sometimes this distinction is expressed by saying that the premises of some arguments *necessarily imply* their conclusions, whereas the premises of other arguments *probably imply* their conclusions.

If the arguer believes that the premises of an argument necessarily imply the conclusion, the argument is *deductive* (or *necessary*). If the arguer believes that the premises of an argument probably imply the conclusion, the argument is *non-deductive* (or *probable*). The following argument is a classic paradigm of deductive arguments:

1. All men are mortal.
2. Socrates is a man.
   _____
   Socrates is mortal.

Since this argument's premises do obviously give conclusive evidence for the conclusion, we must assume that this argument is deductive. A classic paradigm of non-deductive arguments is:

Every swan I ever saw was white.
_____
All swans are white.

In this case the premise clearly does not give conclusive evidence for the conclusion, since what is true of a limited sample of a class is not necessarily true of all members of that class. It would therefore be unreasonable to suppose that any rational person would offer the above argument as an instance of a deductive argument.

In ordinary discourse the terms 'valid argument' and 'invalid argument' are often used as synonyms for 'sound argument' and 'unsound argument.' In logic, however, the terms have a much narrower meaning than in ordinary discourse. They apply only to deductive arguments; non-deductive arguments are neither 'valid' nor 'invalid.' If the claim made on behalf of a deductive argument is true—if the premises do necessarily imply the conclusion—the argument is 'valid.' If the claim made on behalf of a deductive argument is false—if the premises do not necessarily imply the conclusion—the argument is 'invalid.' However, since the term 'necessarily imply' is itself unclear, the terms 'validity' and 'invalidity' are more profitably defined as follows: An argument is *valid* if its logical form is such that it is impossible for the conjunction of the premises to be true and the conclusion false. An argument is *invalid* if it is alleged to be valid but its logical form is such that it is possible for the conjunction of the premises to be true and the conclusion false.

Although the full implications of these definitions will become clear only in Chapters Ten and Eleven, two of them should be noted here. First, when we say that an argument is 'valid,' we are not saying that the premises are true or that the conclusion is true. We are saying rather that by virtue of the argument's logical form the relationship between the premises and the conclusion is such that *if* all the premises are true the conclusion is also true. The validity of an argument, therefore, is compatible with any one of the following three combinations of truth value for the conjunction of the premises and the conclusion:

Premises	Conclusion
True	True
False	False
False	True

Consider, for example, the following three arguments, all of which are valid and which exemplify respectively each of the three possible combinations of truth value indicated above:

1. If Rockefeller is rich, then he has a bank account.
2. Rockefeller is rich.

   Rockefeller has a bank account.

1. If all men have wings, then Socrates has wings.
2. All men have wings.

   Socrates has wings.

1. If Marilyn Monroe had written *War and Peace*, she would have been famous.
2. Marilyn Monroe wrote *War and Peace*.

   Marilyn Monroe was famous.

The only combination of truth values for the conjoined premises and the conclusion with which validity is not compatible is:

Premises	Conclusion
True	False

Second, since an argument is valid by virtue of its logical form alone, we can prove any allegedly valid argument invalid by showing that there is even one argument with the same form whose premises are true and whose conclusion is false. Suppose, for example, that we wish to determine the validity or invalidity of the following argument:

1. If capitalism is a better economic system than socialism, then capitalist countries would have a greater gross national product than socialist countries.
2. Capitalist countries do have a greater gross national product than socialist countries.

   Capitalism is a better economic system than socialism.

If this argument is valid, then no argument with the same form, namely,

1. $p \to q$
2. q
   ___
   p

will have true premises and a false conclusion. Note, however, that the following argument, whose premises are obviously true and whose conclusion is obviously false, does have exactly the same form:

1. If Marilyn Monroe had written *War and Peace*, she would have been famous.
2. Marilyn Monroe was famous.

Marilyn Monroe wrote *War and Peace*.

Consequently, neither this nor the original argument of the same form is valid.

Although the terms 'valid' and 'invalid' apply primarily to arguments, they are also used in characterizing argument forms. If an argument form is such that every argument of that form with true premises also has a true conclusion, the argument form is valid. If an argument form is such that there is even one argument of that form with true premises and a false conclusion, the argument form is invalid.

Because the claim made on behalf of deductive arguments is stronger than that made on behalf of non-deductive arguments, it might be inferred that deductive arguments are superior to non-deductive arguments. This inference is not warranted. In their own way and for their own legitimate purposes, non-deductive arguments can be just as good as deductive arguments. Moreover, it must be clearly understood that validity is not the same thing as soundness and that some valid arguments are thoroughly unsound. Consider, for example, the following argument:

1. Every college student fails every college course.
2. Every course in logic is a college course.

Every college student fails every course in logic.

This argument is perfectly valid, since if the premises were true the conclusion would have to be true. But since the premises are false, the argument is not sound.

As already indicated, the distinction between deductive and non-deductive arguments turns on what claim the arguer wishes to make; but since arguers are rarely explicit about this and often not sure themselves, classification can be difficult. The problem of classification is particularly acute when an argument has weight as a non-deductive argument but at the same time bears some misleading resemblance to a class of valid deductive arguments. Consider, for example, the argument cited earlier on behalf of capitalism. On the one hand, this argument has some weight as a non-deductive argument, insofar as a country's economic system is one factor determining what its gross national product will be, and gross national product is in turn one factor determining the excellence of an economic system. And it may be that the arguer claims only that the premises give probable evidence for the conclusion. On the other hand, we cannot exclude the possibility that the arguer believes that the premises give conclusive evidence for the conclusion. To be sure, the argument is invalid, as we have already seen; but it is not obviously invalid, and many persons have erroneously assumed that it is valid. Unlike the paradigms of deductive and non-deductive arguments cited earlier, therefore, a token of this argument can not reasonably be classified without specific knowledge of the arguer's intent.

III • FALLACIES

The word 'fallacy' has three meanings. (1) A *belief* is a fallacy if it is widely held but false. For example, the beliefs expressed by 'Vagueness is always undesirable' and 'Persons in the upper socio-economic strata suffer more from serious mental illness than persons in the lower socio-economic strata' are fallacies, since each is widely held and each is false. (2) An *inference* is fallacious if the person making that inference mistakenly judges that his premises give either more or less support for the conclusion than is in fact the case. If, for example, someone judged that the premises of the invalid argument cited below give conclusive evidence for the conclusion, he would be guilty of a fallacious inference:

1. If Smith is a Communist, then he supports socialized medicine.
2. Smith supports socialized medicine.

Smith is a Communist.

(3) *Arguments* and *argument forms* are said to be fallacies if they have some feature that tends to encourage fallacious inferences. For example, the form of the argument just cited, namely,

1. $p \rightarrow q$
2. q

p

is a fallacy in this third sense. Because this invalid argument form superficially resembles the valid argument form

1. $p \rightarrow q$
2. p

q

we are often misled into believing that an argument with the first form is also valid.

In this text the term 'fallacy' will be used to characterize inferences or arguments and argument forms. When we characterize an argument form as a fallacy, however, we are not suggesting that every argument of this form is in fact misleading. We are simply saying that the argument form has some feature that *may* cause us to underestimate or overestimate the strength of the relationship between premises and conclusion. In this respect fallacious argument forms are like ambiguous term-types. Just as we need not be misled by a token occurrence of an ambiguous type, so we need not be misled by an argument whose form is fallacious.

Since man has a far greater intellectual capacity than any of the lower animals, he is often called a rational animal. He could, however, with equal justice be called an irrational animal insofar as there are countless ways in which human beings misinterpret the objective value of arguments. In fact, despite persistent efforts dating from antiquity, a systematic classification of fallacies has yet to be worked out. The traditional, standard classification is based on a dichotomy between 'formal fallacies' and 'informal fallacies.' If we mistakenly assume an argument to be valid because its form resembles a valid argument form, we have committed a *formal fallacy*. A fallacy due to any other cause is said to be an *informal fallacy*. This basic classification is useful and comprehensive. But it is not systematic, since a given argument, as we shall see below, may be misleading not only because its form resembles a valid argument form, but for other reasons as well. And the traditional subcategories within each of these basic categories are even less systematic. In this section we shall merely enumerate a few of the more common types of fallacies within each category. Others will be pointed out in later chapters.

Formal Fallacies

As already noted, the argument form

1. $p \rightarrow q$
2. q

p

is a formal fallacy, since its form, though invalid, resembles a valid argument form. This fallacious argument form is called the *fallacy of affirming the consequent*. The valid argument form that it mimics is called *Modus Ponens*:

1. $p \rightarrow q$
2. p

q

A related formal fallacy is known as the *fallacy of denying the antecedent*. An example is

1. If the enemy offers to negotiate, then it wants peace.
2. The enemy has not offered to negotiate.

The enemy does not want peace.

The logical form of this argument is

1. $p \rightarrow q$
2. $-p$

$-q$

The apparent validity of some arguments with this form stems from their similarity to a class of valid arguments, called *Modus Tollens.* For example,

1. If the enemy wants peace, it would offer to negotiate.
2. The enemy has not offered to negotiate.

The enemy does not want peace.

The logical form of these valid arguments is

1. $p \rightarrow q$
2. $-q$

$-p$

A third formal fallacy, known as the *fallacy of false conversion,* has three forms. Each consists of a single premise—either a universal affirmative, a particular negative, or a conditional proposition—and a conclusion consisting of the converse of the premise. If the premise is universal affirmative or particular negative, its converse is formed by interchanging subject and predicate. If the premise is conditional, its converse is formed by interchanging antecedent and consequent. In symbols:

$$\frac{(x)(\phi x \rightarrow \psi x)}{(x)(\psi x \rightarrow \phi x)}$$

$$\frac{(\exists x)(\phi x \cdot -\psi x)}{(\exists x)(\psi x \cdot -\phi x)}$$

$$\frac{p \rightarrow q}{q \rightarrow p}$$

That these argument forms are invalid is clear from the fact that the following arguments, which exemplify respectively each of these forms, have true premises and false conclusions.

All men are animals.
_____
All animals are men.

Some men are not heroes.
_____
Some heroes are not men.

If Marilyn Monroe were the author of *War and Peace,* she would be famous.
_____
If Marilyn Monroe were famous, she would be the author of *War and Peace.*

Not all arguments having one of these forms are so obviously fallacious as these examples, however, and since some propositions do necessarily imply their converses, we can easily go astray. For example, universal negative and particular affirmative propositions do necessarily imply their converses, and the following arguments are both perfectly valid:

No men are quadrupeds.
_____
No quadrupeds are men.

Some men are heroes.
_____
Some heroes are men.

Informal Fallacies

Informal fallacies are conveniently, but not comprehensively or systematically, grouped into two categories. One group consists of *fallacies of relevance*—arguments that tend to be improperly evaluated either because relevant premises are omitted or because irrelevant premises are introduced. The other group consists of *linguistic fallacies*—arguments that tend to be improperly evaluated because of an ambiguity or other obscurity in their formulation.

Fallacies of Relevance

Consider once again the argument:

1. If capitalism is a better economic system than socialism, then capitalist countries will have a greater gross national product than socialist countries.
2. Capitalist countries do have a greater gross national product than socialist countries.

Capitalism is a better economic system than socialism.

Let us assume that the arguer realizes that this argument is not valid. But let us assume that he nonetheless assigns greater weight to it than is warranted. This might happen for one or both of two reasons. First, the arguer might underestimate the importance of factors other than the prevailing economic system in producing a large gross national product. He might, for example, have overlooked such factors as the richness of natural resources, the availability of manpower and skilled technicians, the availability of funds for capital investment, the industrial base at the time the prevailing economic system was instituted, the cooperativeness of other countries, and so forth. If so, he would undoubtedly think that his premises give greater evidence for the conclusion than is in fact the case.

Second, the arguer might have overlooked some of the conventional criteria for determining the desirability or excellence of an economic system. Most of us, for example, would hesitate to call an economic system 'desirable' unless it permits a high degree of social freedom, minimizes class conflict, avoids highly inflationary fiscal policies, promotes relatively full employment, etc. But if the arguer were unaware of these additional criteria for a good economic system, he would again feel that his premises gave stronger support to the conclusion than they actually do.

When an argument is believed to carry more weight than it actually does because we have overlooked factors relevant to the conclusion, the argument is said to be a *fallacy of neglected aspect*. This fallacy is very common and one of the most difficult to avoid.

Another popular fallacy of relevance is *the fallacy of wishful thinking*. This fallacy occurs when we fail to give an argument due credit because we want its conclusion to be false or when we give an argument more credit than it deserves because we want its conclusion to be true. The person who says "God must exist; otherwise, life would be unbearable" commits the fallacy of wishful thinking. Unfortunately, truth has no respect for human desires or fears; and except in those special cases where an argument is about our feelings, our feelings are irrelevant to an evaluation of its logical worth.

One particularly noteworthy form of the fallacy of wishful thinking is called the *circumstantial ad hominem*. (The Latin component in this term means 'to the man.') This fallacy consists of playing upon the interests of the persons to whom an argument is addressed in order to win favor for the conclusion. Take, for example, the politician who argues that a given group ought to support a specific measure because that measure is in their own best interests and because what is good for them is good for the country. If the interests of the group addressed do in fact coincide with those of the country and if the interpreters accept the conclusion because the arguer has convincingly demonstrated this, no fallacy of any kind is committed. If, however, the arguer succeeds in winning support for the argument because the interpreters want to believe that what is good for them is good for the country, the fallacy of circumstantial ad hominem has been committed.

Another fallacy of relevance is the *fallacy of arguing beside the point*. This fallacy is committed when two different issues become confused and an argument in support of one position is mistakenly assumed to be an argument in support of a second. In the deliberations of a trial jury, jurors will often debate not only the issue of the defendant's guilt or innocence but also other issues such as the seriousness of the crime, the circumstances in which it was allegedly committed, or the consequences of allowing the accused to go free. These related issues can easily become confused with the central question of the defendant's guilt or innocence. For example, premises bearing on the seriousness of the alleged crime may also be interpreted as bearing on the guilt of the accused, though they are in fact irrelevant to his guilt. The fallacy of arguing beside the point is particularly common in loose, informal discussions.

Still another fallacy of relevance is called the *abusive ad hominem*, in which we underrate the merits of an argument because of logically irrelevant beliefs concerning the arguer. Sometimes, of course, beliefs concerning the arguer are logically relevant or even indispensable to the evaluation of an argument. If someone argues that he is an idealist and cites his past behavior as evidence, beliefs about his past behavior are obviously relevant. If a witness argues in court that Jones murdered Smith because he saw Jones do it, obviously we will have to determine the reliability of the witness. If, finally, somebody asks us to accept a certain proposition as true because he is an authority on the subject, we must determine his competence. This is why we say that the abusive ad hominem is committed only when *logically irrelevant* beliefs about the arguer are allowed to influence our judgment.

For example, many critics of the Warren Report argued at length, among other things, that Oswald could not have been the sole assassin of former President Kennedy because he did not have the time or ability to fire the required number of shots. Supporters of the Warren Report often answered by accusing these critics of being publicity hounds, of exploiting the assassination of Kennedy for personal gain, of giving the country a bad image, etc. In the heat of the fray, it was all too often forgotten that even if all these accusations were true, the logical merit of the critics' arguments would be totally unaffected. None of the major critics was personally involved in the events under debate, none claimed to have been an eyewitness, and none asked to be believed on his own authority. They argued, and the logical merit of their arguments must be assessed by determining the relationship between their premises and their conclusion, not by an inquiry into their character, motives, or intentions. These latter considerations, if relevant at all, are relevant only in alerting us to the need of examining their arguments closely. If we have reason to believe that an arguer is guilty of malice, wishful thinking, an intent to deceive, etc., it pays to be on our guard. No argument, however, is unsound simply because we dislike the arguer.

Unfortunately, the tendency to abuse one another rather than to examine one another's arguments is very strong. In debates between a theist and an atheist, for instance, the theist will often find himself accused of being a "weakling" or using God as a "crutch," whereas the atheist will often find himself accused of being "arrogant" or "inflating his own self-importance." A moment's calm reflection suffices to expose the irrelevance of considerations like these. God's existence obviously does not depend on anyone's special virtues or vices. But when feelings run high, abuse will often pass as argument.

Our final example of fallacies of relevance is the *fallacy of illegitimate appeal to authority*. Not all appeals to authority are illegitimate. If the subject matter falls within an area for which expert opinion is available and if the competence of the authority can be demonstrated, an arguer's appeal to authority is not illegitimate. If, however, the area is one in which there are no recognized authorities or if the alleged authority has no special competence in that area, the appeal is illegitimate. An instance of this fallacy would be the attempt to prove or disprove the existence of God by citing famous scientists who believed or disbelieved in his existence, since there is no good reason to believe that expertise in the sciences gives anyone special competence on the question of God's existence. Another example would be an attempt to prove a point by appealing to popular belief or the authority of numbers. History amply demonstrates that popular beliefs are as often wrong as right. In the words of Socrates, the seeker after truth will completely disregard "the opinion of the many."

Linguistic Fallacies

Linguistic fallacies are informal fallacies that make an argument appear to be stronger or weaker than it is because of some imperfection in its formulation. One of the most common linguistic fallacies is the *fallacy of equivocation*. This fallacy is committed whenever (1) some crucial term in an argument has two or more cognitive meanings, (2) the soundness of the argument depends upon the term's being used with the same cognitive meaning throughout, and (3) the component propositions in the argument are implausible unless the term is interpreted as having different cognitive meanings in different occurrences. The following argument is a classic example:

1. Death is the end of life.
2. The end of a thing is its perfection.

Death is the perfection of life.

For premise 1 to be plausible 'the end' must be interpreted to mean the final event in a series of events. For premise 2 to be plausible 'the end' must be interpreted to mean the accomplishment of a thing's purpose or goal. And when the premises are properly interpreted the argument has no force at all; its plausibility derives wholly from the fact that the crucial term 'the end' has two different cognitive meanings.

Another linguistic fallacy is called the *fallacy of division,* which rests on the mistaken inference that a property belonging to a class or group as a whole necessarily belongs to every member individually. Consider the following argument:

1. All nations ought to disarm.
2. The United States is a nation.

The United States ought to disarm.

If the term 'all nations' in premise 1 is being used distributively to mean that every single nation ought to disarm—unilaterally if necessary—the argument is valid. But if, as is more likely, 'all nations' is being used collectively to mean that the community of nations should disarm as a group, then the premises imply only that the United States must disarm if all other nations do the same. In this second case, the conclusion as stated does not follow from the premises, and anybody who thinks it does has committed the fallacy of division.

The opposite of the fallacy of division is the *fallacy of composition.* This fallacy is committed when we infer that a property belonging to each member of a group or class must belong to the group or class as a whole. Consider, for example,

1. Atomic bombs do more damage than conventional bombs.
2. Only conventional bombs are being used in this war.

The damage done by the bombs in this war is less extensive than it would be if atomic bombs were used.

If this argument appears to be sound, it is because its wording does not make clear whether 'atomic bombs' is being used distributively or collectively; for although one atomic bomb will do more damage than one conventional bomb, whether a group of atomic bombs will do more damage than a group of conventional bombs depends on the numbers of each used.

Still another common linguistic fallacy is called the *fallacy of arguing in a circle,* or the *fallacy of begging the question.* This fallacy is committed when the conclusion of the argument is itself a premise, either explicitly or implicitly. A classic example is the following:

> To allow every man unbounded freedom of speech must always be, on the whole, advantageous to the state; for it is highly conducive to the interests of the community that each individual should enjoy a liberty, perfectly unlimited, of expressing his sentiments.

Although the premise of this argument has a linguistic formulation wholly different from the conclusion, close examination reveals that both express the same proposition. And since an argument must by definition consist of at least two different propositions, the passage, strictly speaking, does not constitute an argument. The author has merely stated a proposition in two different ways and improperly linked these statements with the word 'for.'

Although most fallacies of begging the question are due to linguistic confusion, some, especially those in extended discourse, must be attributed to faulty memory. By the time we get to the conclusion, we have forgotten our starting point. In a book-length argument, for instance, the author may begin by assuming the existence of God, make a number of inferences for which the existence of God is a crucial premise, and then conclude by proving the existence of God on the basis of these inferences.

Another linguistic fallacy is the *fallacy of false precision*. This fallacy is committed when we judge a proposition to be more accurate than it really is simply because it is expressed in precise mathematical language. Due to the extensive use of mathematics in the advancèd sciences and the growing prestige of these sciences, this fallacy has become increasingly common in the twentieth century. Suppose, for example, that someone announces that 73.5% of all pornography circulating in the United States is sadistic. The precision of this figure might easily lead us to believe that it is a thoroughly accurate report of the findings of some highly scientific inquiry. Yet, given the extreme vagueness of the terms 'pornography' and 'sadistic,' a figure of this precision could be obtained only through an inquiry in which these terms had been experimentally defined so as to permit mathematical tabulation; and in all likelihood these experimental definitions would be highly controversial. Suppose, for example, that this figure had been obtained by an experimenter who submitted to five persons one hundred items that he deemed pornographic and asked these five persons to indicate which they judged to be sadistic. In this case the experimental definition of 'pornography' is, in effect, any item the experimenter judges to be pornographic; and the experimental definition of 'sadistic' is any item the five judges felt was sadistic. Obviously, the results of such a study would be subject to a wide margin of error despite the precision of the figure reported.

Our last example of a linguistic fallacy is called the *black and white fallacy*. This fallacy is committed when we mistakenly infer that a disjunctive proposition must be true because we assume that its disjuncts are contradictories when in fact they are merely contraries. Two propositions are *contradictories* when it is impossible for both to be true and also impossible for both to be false. On the other hand, two propositions are *contraries* when it is impossible for both to be true but possible for both to be false. Consider, for example, the following disjunction:

John is my friend or John is not my friend.

The disjuncts of this proposition—namely, 'John is my friend' and 'John is not my friend'—are contradictories, since they can not both be true nor can they both be false. Consider by contrast the disjunction:

John is my friend or John is my enemy.

The disjuncts of this proposition—namely, 'John is my friend' and 'John is my enemy'—may at first appear to be contradictories. When we look more closely, however, we see that they are merely contraries. Although both propositions can not be true, both may be false: John may be neither friendly nor unfriendly but simply indifferent.

Here is another example of a proposition that may give rise to the black and white fallacy:

John is a hero or John is a coward.

Once again it is clear that these propositions are contraries. They can not both be true. If John is a hero he can not be a coward, and conversely. But both disjuncts may be false. By definition a hero is someone who is braver than the average man; and a coward someone who is less brave than the average man. Therefore, if John were an average man, he would be neither a hero nor a coward.

The black and white fallacy is often committed in connection with arguments called *Dilemmas*. Dilemmas take the following form:

1. $(p \rightarrow q) \cdot (r \rightarrow s)$
2. $\underline{p \vee r}$

   $q \vee s$

For example,

1. If John is a good student, he does not need an instructor's guidance; and if he is a bad student, he can not benefit from it.
2. Either John is a good student or he is a bad student.

   Either John does not need an instructor's guidance or he can not benefit from it.

Since Dilemma is a valid argument form, this particular argument is valid; conceivably it is also sound. The second premise, however, should be carefully examined. In all likelihood the person who accepted this argument as sound would be guilty of the false inference that all students necessarily fall into one of the two categories: good or bad. Actually most students are average and do not fall into either category. 'John is a good student' and 'John is a bad student,' therefore, are not contradictories, but merely contraries.

EXERCISES FOR CHAPTER NINE

A. Which of the following passages can reasonably be regarded as containing arguments? Express these arguments as clearly and as succinctly as possible, taking care to make implicit premises explicit. Which arguments are deductive and which are non-deductive? (Some passages may contain more than one argument.)

1. A man can not be both honest and a politician. Jones is a politician.
2. If ignorance is bliss, then 'tis folly to be wise.
3. Since ignorance is bliss, 'tis folly to be wise.
4. Nuclear testing should be stopped. The consequences of atomic war are too horrible to contemplate.
5. Since most undergraduates have never learned to think clearly, they ought to take a course in logic.
6. Only an innocent fool could have remained unaware of the crookedness of the Long gang. Smith is neither innocent nor a fool.
7. You argue that the Soviet Union is more belligerent than the United States. The reverse is true. The United States defense outlays represent more than half of the federal budget. In Russia the figure is from ten to fifteen percent.

8. The sales tax is manifestly unjust. Everybody, whether rich or poor, pays the same tax on whatever he purchases.

9. Every man does what gives him pleasure. Therefore, all men are selfish.

10. Currently the government is investigating the American Telephone and Telegraph Company. Could it be that AT&T should be investigating the government? The United States Post Office, a government-operated monopoly, has tripled the price of postage during a period when AT&T has only doubled the cost of local telephone calls and actually decreased the cost of long-distance calls.

11. Everyone now alive has two parents, each of whom in turn had two parents. It follows that in our grandparents' day there were four times as many people as there are today.

12. "And immortality makes this other difference, which, by the by, has a connection with the difference between totalitarianism and democracy. If individuals live only seventy years, then a state, or a nation, or a civilisation, which may last for a thousand years, is more important than an individual. But if Christianity is true, then the individual is not only more important but incomparably more important, for he is everlasting and the life of a state or a civilisation, compared with his, is only a moment." (C. S. Lewis, *Mere Christianity*)

13. "When in 1930 I emerged from a respectable American university as a respectably well-educated young man, no hint had reached me that private property was other than a human institution evolved by the human brain. If I and my young contemporaries throughout the following years wasted much of our fire on social propositions involving the abolition of private ownership, then we did so in perfect faith that such a course would free mankind of many a frustration. No part of the curriculum of our psychology, sociology, or anthropology departments had presented us with the information that territoriality—the drive to gain, maintain, and defend the exclusive right to a piece of property—is an animal instinct approximately as ancient and powerful as sex.

"The role of territory in general animal behaviour lies today beyond scientific controversy; then it was unknown. We of the Class of 1930 had to emerge into a world of tumultuous evaluation without benefit of this most salient observation. Similarly, we could not know, as we bemused ourselves with the attractions of the classless state, that hierarchy is an institution among all social animals and the drive to dominate one's fellows an instinct three or four hundred million years old." (Robert Ardrey, *African Genesis*)

14. "The object of reasoning is to find out, from the consideration of what we already know, something else which we do not know. Consequently, reasoning is good if it be such as to give a true conclusion from true premises, and not otherwise. Thus the question of its validity is purely one of fact and not of thinking. *A* being the premises and *B* the conclusion, the question is whether these facts are really so related that if *A* is, *B* is. If so, the inference is valid; if not, not. It is not in the least the question whether, when the premises are accepted by the mind, we feel an impulse to accept the conclusion also. It is true that we do generally reason correctly by nature. But that is an accident; the true conclusion would remain true if we had no impulse to accept it; and the false one would remain false, though we could not resist the tendency to believe in it." (Charles Peirce, "The Fixation of Belief")

15. "The problem is, in a broad sense, political: given that the bulk of mankind are certain to commit fallacies, is it better that they should deduce false conclusions from true premises or true conclusions from false premises? A question of this sort is insoluble. The only true solution seems to be that ordinary men and women should be taught logic, so as to be able to refrain from drawing conclusions which only *seem* to follow. When it is said, for example, that the French are 'logical,' what is meant is that, when they accept a premise, they also accept everything that a person totally destitute of logical subtlety would erroneously suppose to follow from the premise. This is a most undesirable quality, from which, on the whole, the English-speaking

nations have, in the past, been more free than any others. But there are signs that, if they are to remain free in this respect, they will require more philosophy and logic than they have had in the past. Logic was, formerly, the art of drawing inferences; it has now become the art of abstaining from inferences, since it has appeared that the inferences we naturally feel inclined to make are hardly ever valid. I conclude, therefore, that logic ought to be taught in schools with a view to teaching people not to reason. For, if they reason, they will almost certainly reason wrongly." (Bertrand Russell, *Sceptical Essays*)

16. "Just as a bell struck with a hammer emits a characteristic note, so every atom put in a flame or in an electric arc or discharge tube, emits a characteristic light, which the spectroscope will resolve into its separate constituents." (James Jeans, *The Universe Around Us*)

17. "Nobody can be healthful without exercise, neither natural body nor politic; and certainly, to a kingdom or estate, a just and honourable war is the true exercise. A civil war, indeed, is like the heat of a fever; but a foreign war is like the heat of exercise, and serveth to keep the body in health; for in a slothful peace, both courages will effeminate and manners corrupt." (Francis Bacon, *Essays*)

18. "Suppose that by a subscription of the rich the eighteen-pence or two shillings, which men earn now, were made up to five shillings: it might be imagined, perhaps, that they would then be able to live comfortably, and have a piece of meat every day for their dinner. But this would be a very false conclusion. The transfer of three additional shillings a day to each labourer would not increase the quantity of meat in the country. There is not at present enough for all to have a moderate share. What would then be the consequence? The competition among the buyers in the market of meat would rapidly raise the price from eight-pence or ninepence to two or three shillings in the pound, and the commodity would not be divided among many more than it is at present." (Thomas Malthus, *Essay on Population*)

19. "The manner of questioning witnesses remains to be con-

sidered. In this part of our duty, the principal point is to know the witness well: for if he is timid he may be frightened; if foolish, misled; if irascible, provoked; if vain, flattered; if prolix, drawn from the point." (Quintilian, *Institutes of Oratory*)

B. Which of the following passages give grounds for believing that a fallacy has been committed? Identify the fallacies by name.

1. Punishment is degrading. Therefore, it can work no moral improvement.
2. You say that you do not believe that those who object to birth control have the right to impose their views by force of law on others. Are you implying that force of law is not proper? What force do you recommend other than law?
3. "The extent of the decline in higher education is reflected in the fact that Jews today represent 3.1 percent of all students in higher education, as contrasted with 13.5 percent in 1935. During this twenty-seven-year period, the Jewish proportion of the population decreased merely from 1.6 to 1.1 percent. There is no way of accounting for this drastic decline in a country with an expanding economy and growing opportunities—except by discrimination." (Moshe Decter, "The Status of the Jews in the Soviet Union," *Foreign Affairs*, January, 1963)
4. Most heroin addicts began by smoking marijuana. I submit, therefore, that most marijuana smokers are on the way to heroin addiction.
5. Every natural event has an external cause; therefore, the universe must have an external, or supernatural, cause.
6. The personnel manager of a large corporation rated his staff according to a set of established criteria of excellence with a view to adjusting salaries to national norms. When he discovered that the results called for substantial salary increases across the board, he decided that he must have made mistakes all the way down the line and reevaluated the entire staff.
7. There can be no question that Professor Smith is outstand-

ing in his field. He comes from one of the best universities in the country.

8. His poems are obviously in bad taste, since every sensitive critic condemns them on this score.

9. There is "an interesting relationship between difference in age between husband and wife and marital satisfaction. . . . Where the wife was older than the husband the difference was considered negative. A free hand curve of the type $(x - h)^2 = -2p(y - k)$ gives a correlation index of $+.60$ with an error of $.06$, indicating that such a parabola fits the data rather well. For men, the axes of the parabola must be rotated toward the left through an angle of about $10°$. In terms of the data themselves, these facts indicate that the women were satisfied with their husbands when their husbands were from zero to five years older than they, and that their satisfaction tended to diminish at about an equal rate when this difference was increased, regardless of whether it was they or their husbands who were the older. The men tended to be most satisfied with their wives when they were from zero to ten years older than their wives, but their dissatisfaction with their wives tended to increase more rapidly when their wives were older than they, than when they were older than their wives." (Jessie Bernard, "Factors in the Distribution of Success in Marriage," *American Journal of Sociology*)

10. "But, once originated, the conception of the constancy of the order of Nature has become the dominant idea of modern thought. To any person who is familiar with the facts upon which that conception is based, and is competent to estimate their significance, it has ceased to be conceivable that chance should have any place in the universe, or that events should depend upon any but the natural sequence of cause and effect. We have come to look upon the present as the child of the past and as the parent of the future; and, as we have excluded chance from a place in the universe, so we ignore, even as a possibility, the notion of any interference with the order of Nature. Whatever may be men's speculative doctrines, it is quite certain that every intelligent person guides his life and risks his fortune upon

the belief that the order of Nature is constant, and that the chain of natural causation is never broken." (T. H. Huxley, *Lectures on Evolution*)

11. In any war we undertake, we must either win or lose; but since we are the strongest military power on the face of the earth, we can not lose. Why, then, should we fear to confront the enemy out of fear of war?

12. Social harmony requires that we cultivate an attitude of cooperativeness, whereas progress requires that we cultivate competitiveness. We must choose, therefore, between harmony or stagnation.

13. "My answer to Miss Gustafson's letter replying to my attack on the 'cow fetishists' who are trying to outlaw kosher slaughtering is the same I gave to the 'Humane Legislation' lobbyists who ganged up on me in Albany last Tuesday.

"Except for some token campaigning against rodeos, you concentrate all your attacks on Jewish slaughterhouses and Jewish religious practices. You never talk about inhumane practices in non-Jewish slaughterhouses, nor do you introduce any bills about hunting or any other manifestation of cruelty to animals.

"Do you wonder why I question the real motives of some of the self-proclaimed 'Friends of Animals'?" (Seymour Posner, letter to the editor, in the New York *Post*, March 2, 1967)

14. Dr. X argues that adherents of the view according to which smoking causes lung cancer are "Puritans." They are the same people who tell you that drinking causes cancer of the throat and sexual intercourse cancer of the cervix. Their premise is that anything a man does for pleasure must be sinful and prevented by law if necessary.

15. "Seeing that eye and hand and foot and every one of our members has some obvious function, must we not believe that in like manner a human being has a function over and above these particular functions?" (Aristotle, *Nicomachean Ethics*)

16. We must avoid entangling commitments abroad. Washington and Monroe were not wrong.

17. Men native to countries of inclement weather, where the conditions of life are severe, are usually robust in health. One may conclude that the hardships such people are forced to undergo in youth are important causal factors in the production and sustaining of good health.
18. Far too much fuss has been made about the U-2 spy plane incident. The Russians are just as deeply engaged in espionage against the United States.
19. During the Democratic Administration both gross national income and employment have risen to the highest levels we have ever known. What better reason is there for voting Democratic?
20. "The only proof capable of being given that an object is visible is that people actually see it. The only proof that a sound is audible is that people hear it. . . . In like manner, I apprehend, the sole evidence it is possible to produce that anything is desirable is that people do actually desire it." (John Stuart Mill, *Utilitarianism*)
21. "No reason can be given why the general happiness is desirable except that each person, so far as he believes it to be attainable, desires his own happiness. . . . Each person's happiness is a good to that person, and the general happiness, therefore, a good to the aggregate of all persons." (John Stuart Mill, *Utilitarianism*)
22. Mr. X is a long-standing member of one of the most corrupt political machines in the country. I leave it to you to draw the appropriate conclusion.
23. Whatever is subject to law is subject to a governing will. Since Nature obeys laws, Nature herself is subject to a governing will.
24. It may interest the Senator's constituency to know that except for the Communist *Daily Worker* he is alone in attacking my proposal.
25. If you are a true music lover, you will love Bach. Jones loves Bach. I conclude that he is a true music lover.
26. "And first, where that I affirm the empire of a woman to be a thing repugnant to nature, I mean not only that God by the order of his creation hath spoiled woman of authority and dominion, but also that man hath seen, proved

and pronounced just causes why that it should be. Man, I say, in many other cases blind, doth in this behalf see very clearly. For the causes be so manifest, that they cannot be hid. For who can deny but it repugneth of nature that the blind shall be appointed to lead and conduct such as do see? That the weak, the sick, and impotent persons shall nourish and keep the whole and strong, and finally, that the foolish, mad and phrenetic shall govern the discreet and give counsel to such as be sober of mind? And such be all women, compared unto man in bearing of authority. For their sight in civil regiment is but blindness, their strength weakness, their counsel foolishness, and judgment frenzy, if it be rightly considered." (John Knox, *Regiment of Women*)

27. A good soldier is ready to sacrifice his life for his country; so one who is ready to sacrifice his life for his country is a good soldier.

28. The proof of the Creator is the created world.

29. If one marries, one's wife will be either beautiful or ugly. If beautiful, she excites jealousy. If ugly, she disgusts. Therefore, it is best not to marry.

30. If a number is divisible by two, it is an even number. Therefore, since forty-six is an even number, it is divisible by two.

31. American Indians are disappearing. Therefore, Chief Sitting Bull is disappearing.

Deductive Arguments: Truth-Functions

In this and the next chapter we shall be concerned solely with deductive arguments—that is to say, with arguments alleged to be valid. Our aim is to introduce techniques for determining whether an allegedly valid argument is in fact valid. In this chapter our concern will be further limited to arguments whose validity is alleged to follow entirely from truth-functional relationships among their non-compound components. Other deductive arguments will be discussed in Chapter Eleven.

In testing the validity of arguments we will use the following symbols, introduced in Part One:

the propositional variables: p, q, r . . . w

the propositional abbreviations: A, B, C . . . W

the logical operators:

- — called the 'symbol of negation' and read 'It is not the case that . . .' or '. . . not . . .'
- · called the 'symbol of conjunction' and read '. . . and . . .'
- v called the 'symbol of disjunction' and read '. . . or . . .'
- → called the 'conditional symbol' and read 'If . . . then . . .'
- ↔ called the 'biconditional symbol' and read '. . . if and only if . . .'

In addition we shall use truth tables. If you do not fully recall the truth-table definitions of the logical operators and the use of truth tables to classify sentences, review Sections II and III of Chapter Five before proceeding further.

I • TRUTH-TABLE TESTS OF VALIDITY

When an argument is valid by virtue of truth-functional relationships among its non-compound components, the argument is said to be 'truth-functionally valid.' When an argument is not valid by virtue of truth-functional relationships among its non-compound components, it is said to be 'truth-functionally invalid.' More specifically, an argument is *truth-functionally valid* if, given its logical form, there is no combination of truth values for the non-compound components that will render the conjunction of the premises true and the conclusion false. On the other hand, an argument is *truth-functionally invalid* if there is even one combination of truth values for the non-compound components that will render the conjunction of the premises true and the conclusion false. If an argument is truth-functionally valid, it is valid without qualification. An argument that is truth-functionally invalid, however, may be valid by virtue of certain logical features of its non-compound components to be discussed in the following chapter.

One effective technique for determining whether an argument is truth-functionally valid or invalid involves the use of truth tables. In constructing truth tables for this purpose, we proceed as follows: First, we count the number of non-compound components in the argument and make an exhaustive list of their possible combinations of truth values in a set of guide columns. Next, we write a heading for each premise and for the conclusion to the right of the guide-column headings. Finally, we determine the truth value for each premise and the conclusion, given the truth value of the non-compound components indicated in each row of the guide columns. Thus, the truth table for the valid argument form *Modus Ponens*

1. p → q
2. p
___
q

is as follows:

	p	q	p → q	p	q
(1)	T	T	T	T	T
(2)	T	F	F	T	F
(3)	F	T	T	F	T
(4)	F	F	T	F	F

Once a truth table has been constructed for a given argument, it is easy to determine whether the argument is valid. We merely examine each row and ask: Given the combination of truth values for the non-compound components indicated by the guide columns, are the premises true and the conclusion false? If for every row the answer is negative, the argument is valid. Thus, since in no row of the truth table for Modus Ponens do we find a case in which the premises are all true and the conclusion false, Modus Ponens is a valid argument form, and, of course, every argument having that form is valid.

If, on the other hand, there is even one row where the premises are all true and the conclusion false, the argument form—and consequently all arguments having that form—are truth-functionally invalid. Consider, for example, the invalid argument form Affirming the Consequent:

1. p → q
2. q
___
p

Its truth table is

	p	q	p → q	q	p
(1)	T	T	T	T	T
(2)	T	F	F	F	T
(3)	F	T	T	T	F
(4)	F	F	T	F	F

As row 3 of this table indicates, one combination of truth values for the non-compound components of arguments having this form does render the premises true and the conclusion false. Thus arguments Affirming the Consequent are truth-functionally invalid.

Truth tables can be used in another equally effective way to test the validity of an argument. First, we put the argument into its corresponding conditional—that is, a conditional whose antecedent is the conjunction of the argument's premises and whose consequent is the conclusion. Second, as outlined in Part One, we determine whether the corresponding conditional is a tautology. If the corresponding conditional is a tautology, the argument is valid; if the corresponding conditional is not a tautology, the argument is truth-functionally invalid. Consider, for example, the truth table for the corresponding conditional of the argument form Modus Ponens:

	p	q	$((p \to q) \cdot p) \to q$		
(1)	T	T	T	T	T
(2)	T	F	F	F	T
(3)	F	T	T	F	T
(4)	F	F	T	F	T

Since this conditional is a tautology, the argument form to which it corresponds is valid. Consider now the truth table for the corresponding conditional of the argument form Affirming the Consequent:

	p	q	$((p \to q) \cdot q) \to p$		
(1)	T	T	T	T	T
(2)	T	F	F	F	T
(3)	F	T	T	T	F
(4)	F	F	T	F	T

Since this conditional is not a tautology, arguments of this form are truth-functionally invalid.

These two truth-table techniques are closely related. Both highlight the all-important point that the validity of an argument does not depend in any way on the truth or falsity of its components.

The validity of an argument depends wholly upon its logical form—or, what for all practical purposes comes to the same thing, the meaning of its logical operators as contextually defined in truth tables.

II • SHORTER TRUTH-TABLE TESTS OF VALIDITY

Although the truth-table techniques discussed in the last section are highly instructive and thoroughly effective, the person who has understood their rationale will find that it is often possible to prove an argument truth-functionally valid or invalid without constructing a complete truth table.

Shorter Proofs of Invalidity

Consider the invalid argument form Denying the Antecedent:

1. $p \rightarrow q$
2. $-p$
   _____
   $-q$

If we inspect the complete truth table for this argument form we will discover that there is a row in which a given combination of truth values for its non-compound components renders the premises true and the conclusion false. Having discovered this row we know that the argument is invalid; there is no need to examine the other rows. If, therefore, we can discover such a row without constructing a complete truth table, our proof of invalidity is equally complete. Let us, therefore, write down the headings of a truth table for an argument of this form, placing a 'T' under the heading for each premise and an 'F' under the heading for the conclusion as follows:

p	q		$p \rightarrow q$	$-p$	$-q$
			T	T	F

Now, let us ask whether there is some combination of truth values for the non-compound propositions that justifies this assignment of truth values to the premises and conclusion. In this case, it is clear that such an assignment exists and it is not necessary to construct a truth table to find it. Since the conclusion is the proposition '−q,' 'q' must obviously be assigned the truth value 'T' to justify the entry under the conclusion. And since the second premise '−p' can be true only if 'p' is false, 'p' must obviously be assigned the truth value 'F.' And since this assignment of truth values to the two non-compound components 'p' and 'q' not only renders the conclusion false and the second premise true but also renders the first premise true, we know that there does exist a combination of truth values for the non-compound propositions that renders all of the premises true and the conclusion false.

In the case of some extended arguments the successful use of this method may require considerable trial and error. The fact that we do not succeed in proving an argument invalid by this method is not, therefore, conclusive evidence that the argument is valid. Nonetheless, the shorter method often saves us considerable time and effort.

Shorter Proofs of Validity

The shorter truth-table method of proving validity, unlike the shorter method of proving invalidity, requires that we examine every row. We may, however, prove the validity of an argument without making an entry under every component of the argument in every row. Let us explain. To prove an argument valid by truth tables we must show that there is no possible combination of truth values for the non-compound propositions that renders all of the premises true and the conclusion false. And since each row represents one possible combination of truth values for the non-compound propositions, each row must be examined. But since any row in which either one of the premises is false or the conclusion is true represents a combination of truth values for the non-compound propositions which cannot possibly render the conjunction of the premises true and the conclusion false, to prove an argument valid it suffices to show that in every row there is either an 'F' under the heading for one premise or a 'T' under the heading for the conclusion. In other words, if no row can prove an argument truth-functionally invalid, the argument is valid. And no row can prove an argument truth-functionally invalid if in that row either the conclusion is true or one of the premises is false. If, therefore, we have discovered that the conclusion is true or that a premise is false in a given row, there is no need to make any other entry in that row.

Suppose, then, that we are given an argument having the form

1. p v q v r
2. −p
3. −q
   _____
   r

and that we have constructed a partial truth table for it as follows:

	p	q	r	p v q v r	−p	−q	r
(1)	T	T	T				
(2)	T	T	F				
(3)	T	F	T				
(4)	T	F	F				
(5)	F	T	T				
(6)	F	T	F				
(7)	F	F	T				
(8)	F	F	F				

Since we know that no row in this table can be used to prove this argument invalid if the conclusion 'r' is true, we can save considerable time by filling in the column under 'r' first. Since 'r' is true in rows 1, 3, 5 and 7, there is no need to determine the truth value of the premises in these rows. We already know that these rows cannot be used to prove the argument invalid. If we then fill in the column under the premise '−p' in the remaining rows, we find that this premise is false in rows 2 and 4; so both of these rows can be eliminated from further consideration. If we then fill in the column under '−q' in the two remaining rows, we find that we can eliminate row 6 from consideration, since here, too, a premise is false. To show that the argument is not invalid—and therefore valid—the only row that must still be considered is row 8. And since 'p,' 'q,' and 'r' are all false in this row, the first premise as a whole (which is a disjunction of 'p,' 'q,' and 'r') is false. And since there is not a single row that may be used to prove the argument truth-functionally invalid, the argument is clearly valid.

Let us, therefore, adopt the convention of placing a check mark to the right of any one entry that by itself shows the impossibility of the premises' all being true and the conclusion false in a given row. If we use this convention, we can effectively prove the above argument valid by this much abbreviated truth table:

	p	q	r	p v q v r	−p	−q	r
(1)	T	T	T				T✔
(2)	T	T	F		F✔	F	
(3)	T	F	T				T✔
(4)	T	F	F		F✔	F	
(5)	F	T	T				T✔
(6)	F	T	F		T	F✔	F
(7)	F	F	T				T✔
(8)	F	F	F	F✔	T	T	F

If the conclusion or one of the premises in an argument is a non-compound proposition, it is usually best, when employing this shorter method, to begin by filling in the column for this non-compound proposition. If the argument has no non-compound component, it is often best to begin with whichever component is least complex. There are, however, no hard and fast rules; and in this regard the shorter method of proving validity is like the shorter method of proving invalidity.

III • ELEMENTARY VALID ARGUMENT FORMS

Since every valid argument is one whose premises necessarily imply its conclusion, every valid argument form provides us with a *valid rule of inference*. That is, if we are given certain propositions and if we know that these propositions correspond to the premises in an argument form known to be valid, we can properly infer a conclusion corresponding to the conclusion of the valid argument form. Thus, if we are given the two propositions

1. If John is in the library then he is working.
2. John is in the library.

We are entitled to infer

John is working.

by virtue of the valid argument form Modus Ponens.

The greater our knowledge of valid argument forms, therefore, the greater our ability to make valid inferences. The number and complexity of valid argument forms, however, is without limit and no one could be expected to learn or remember them all. Fortunately, no such prodigious feats of learning and memory are required, since most legitimate inferences from a given set of propositions can be discovered, if not directly then indirectly, through the use of a relatively small number of simple or elementary valid argument forms. Thus we have yet another method for proving the validity of arguments. This method has the advantage of being quicker than the other methods, especially when we are dealing with arguments having many non-compound components. Even when an argument has as few as five non-compound components, its truth table has thirty-two rows; and when an argument has six non-compound components, its truth table has sixty-four rows!

Suppose, then, that we are given an argument abbreviated to:

1. $A \cdot B$
2. $(A \vee C) \rightarrow D$
   $\overline{A \cdot D}$

and we wish to determine whether the conclusion is necessarily implied by the premises. Even though we have never encountered an argument of this form before and can not immediately see that it is valid, we may nonetheless derive the conclusion from the premises through a sequence of inferences, each of which is justified by an elementary valid argument form. In using this method, the conclusion is ordinarily written to the right of the last premise, from which it is separated by a diagonal:

 1. A · B
 2. (A v C) → D / A · D

In the proof itself each inference is placed on a separate line, numbered, and justified by citing the preceding line or lines from which it is derived and the elementary valid argument form that authorizes the inference. The proof for our sample argument might go as follows:

 1. A · B
 2. (A v C) → D / A · D
 3. A   1, Simplification
 4. A v C   3, Addition
 5. D   2, 4, Modus Ponens
 6. A · D   3, 5, Conjunction

The notation to the right on line 3 indicates that the inference is made from premise 1 and is authorized by the elementary valid argument form known as *Simplification*. According to this rule, which follows from the meaning of the conjunction sign, if a conjunction is true, then so is every component conjunct. Thus, if 'A · B' is true, we are justified in inferring the truth of 'A' or 'B' singly. The notation to the right on line 4 shows that the inference to 'A v C' is made from line 3 and is authorized by the elementary valid argument form known as *Addition*. According to this rule, which follows from the meaning of the sign of disjunction, if a given proposition is true, then so is any disjunction of which it is a component. The notation to the right on line 5 shows that the inference to 'D' is made from lines 2 and 4 and is justified by the elementary valid argument form Modus Ponens. Finally, the notation to the right on line 6 shows that the inference to 'A · D' follows from lines 3 and 5 by virtue of the elementary valid argument form known as *Conjunction*, according to which if two or more propositions are each true singly then the conjunction of these propositions is also true.

It should be noted that the argument

1. $(A v C) \rightarrow D$
2. $A v C$

$\overline{D}$

is a genuine instance of Modus Ponens:

1. $p \rightarrow q$
2. p

$\overline{q}$

even though 'A v C' is itself a compound proposition. Propositional variables, we have noted, stand for any proposition whatsoever, simple or compound. Consequently, any argument is an instance of a given argument form provided only that (1) each different variable in the argument form corresponds to a different proposition in the argument and (2) each occurrence of the same variable corresponds to an occurrence of the same proposition.

It follows that a given argument may be a genuine instance of more than one argument form. For example, the argument

1. $(A v C) \rightarrow D$
2. $A v C$

$\overline{D}$

is an instance not only of Modus Ponens but also of the argument form

1. $(p v q) \rightarrow r$
2. $p v q$

$\overline{r}$

and in addition of the invalid argument form

1. p
2. q

$\overline{r}$

The problem in proving the validity of an argument is not to find any argument form of which it is an instance but to find some argument form that is useful in proving its validity.

Since the principle of this method of proving validity consists in breaking down complex arguments whose validity we do not immediately see into a sequence of relatively simple arguments whose validity is obvious, any argument form that we immediately see is valid could function as an elementary valid argument form. For classroom purposes, however, we stipulate that only the following will count as elementary valid argument forms:

Modus Ponens:
$$\begin{array}{l} p \rightarrow q \\ \underline{p} \\ q \end{array}$$

Modus Tollens:
$$\begin{array}{l} p \rightarrow q \\ \underline{-q} \\ -p \end{array}$$

Dilemma:
$$\begin{array}{l} (p \rightarrow q) \cdot (r \rightarrow s) \\ \underline{p \vee r} \\ q \vee s \end{array}$$

Simplification:
$$\frac{p \cdot q}{p} \qquad \frac{p \cdot q}{q} \qquad \frac{p \cdot q \cdot r}{p} \qquad \frac{p \cdot q \cdot r}{q} \qquad \text{etc.}$$

The common principle underlying the use of these argument forms as rules of inference is as follows: given a conjunction, we are authorized to infer any of its conjuncts.

Addition:
$$\frac{p}{p \vee q} \qquad \frac{p}{p \vee q \vee r} \qquad \frac{p}{q \vee p \vee r} \qquad \text{etc.}$$

The common principle underlying the use of these argument forms as rules of inference is as follows: given a proposition, we are authorized to infer any disjunction of which it is a disjunct.

Conjunction:

p	p	p	
q	q	q	
p·q	r	r	etc.
	p·q·r	s	
		p·r·q·s	

The common principle underlying the use of these argument forms as rules of inference is as follows: given two or more propositions separately, we are authorized to infer their conjunction.

Disjunction:

p v q	p v q	p v q v r	
−p	−q	−p	etc.
q	p	−r	
		q	

The common principle underlying the use of these argument forms as rules of inference is as follows: given a disjunction and the negation of all but one of its disjuncts, we are authorized to infer the remaining disjunct.

Hypothetical
Implication:

p → q	p → q	p → q	
q → p	q → r	q → r	
p → q	r → s	r → s	etc.
	p → s	s → t	
		p → t	

The common principle underlying the use of these argument forms as rules of inference is as follows: given any series of conditionals in which the antecedent of the second is the consequent of the first, the antecedent of the third (if there is a third) is the consequent of the second, etc., we are authorized to infer a conditional whose antecedent is the antecedent of the first and whose consequent is the consequent of the last.

Observe that compound components of propositions derived by the use of one of these rules of inference must often be enclosed in parentheses. One reason for the parentheses is to avoid ambiguity. If, for example, we are given 'A · B' and wish to make a derivation by the rule of Addition

$$\frac{p}{p \lor q}$$

we can not write an ambiguous formula such as 'A · B v C.' The correct derivation would be '(A · B) v C.' A second—and in this context more important—reason for the use of parentheses is to exhibit clearly the correspondence between the argument form invoked and the argument that expresses the inference. Suppose, for example, that one invokes the rule of Addition

$$\frac{p}{p \lor q}$$

to justify the derivation expressed by the argument

$$\frac{A \lor B}{A \lor B \lor C}$$

The conclusion of this argument is not ambiguous. Nonetheless, the inference is not justified by the rule invoked. The conclusion of the argument form has only two first-order components, whereas the conclusion of the argument has three, and there is no way of knowing whether 'p' corresponds to 'A' alone or to 'A v B.' Thus the correct derivation is

$$\frac{A \lor B}{(A \lor B) \lor C}$$

where the parentheses reduce the number of first-order components to two and clearly indicate that 'p' corresponds to 'A v B.'

Of course, the inference from 'A v B' to 'A v B v C' is valid, but like many other valid inferences it is not justified by the elementary argument forms stipulated. To prove its validity we need an additional rule of derivation of a kind to be discussed next.

IV • LOGICAL EQUIVALENCE

Two sentences are cognitively equivalent if both have the same cognitive meaning, or express the same proposition. Sometimes cognitive equivalence is due to principles of grammar. For example,

> John loves Mary.
> Mary is loved by John.

Other times, cognitive equivalence is due to the meanings assigned to certain categorematic terms. For example,

> Socrates is human.
> Socrates is a man.

Some sentences, however, are equivalent simply because of their logical forms, or the meanings assigned to their logical operators. For example, the standard use of the operators 'It is not the case that' and 'not' guarantees the equivalence of

> Socrates is human.
> It is not the case that Socrates is not human.

In cases like these the equivalence is called 'logical equivalence.'

If two sentences are equivalent by virtue of principles of grammar or the meaning of their categorematic terms, a sentence used to assert their biconditionality will, of course, express a true proposition. No one would question the truth of

> John loves Mary if and only if Mary is loved by John.
> Socrates is human if and only if Socrates is a man.

When, however, two sentences are equivalent by virtue of their logical form, a sentence used to assert their biconditionality will be not only true but tautologically true. For example, the truth table for 'Socrates is human if and only if it is not the case that Socrates is not human' is as follows:

S	$S \leftrightarrow --S$
T	T TF
F	T FT

Since the column indicating the truth value of the proposition as a whole consists of nothing but 'T's,' this biconditional is a tautology. Thus, *logical equivalence* may be defined as follows: Two sentences are logically equivalent if and only if the assertion of their biconditionality is a tautology.

If two propositions are logically equivalent, either can replace the other without change of truth value. And just as every elementary valid argument form provides a rule of inference, so every tautological assertion of biconditionality gives a rule of replacement. Certain rules of replacement are classified as elementary and used along with elementary valid argument forms to prove the validity of complex or extended arguments. Consider an argument abbreviated as follows:

1. $A \rightarrow B$
2. $--A$
   —————
   B

This argument, though perfectly valid, cannot be proved valid by the use of the elementary valid argument forms cited in the last section. It can, however, be proved valid by supplementing the rules of inference with the rule of replacement called *Double Negation* as follows:

1. $A \rightarrow B$
2. $--A \: / \: B$
   —————
3. A   2, Double Negation
4. B   1, 3, Modus Ponens

Below is a complete list of allowable elementary rules of replacement.

Double Negation:	$p \leftrightarrow --p$
Tautology:	$p \leftrightarrow (p \vee p)$
	$p \leftrightarrow (p \cdot p)$
Transposition:	$(p \rightarrow q) \leftrightarrow (-q \rightarrow -p)$
Conditionality:	$(p \rightarrow q) \leftrightarrow -(p \cdot -q)$
	$(p \rightarrow q) \leftrightarrow (-p \vee q)$
Biconditionality:	$(p \leftrightarrow q) \leftrightarrow ((p \cdot q) \vee (-p \cdot -q))$
	$(p \leftrightarrow q) \leftrightarrow ((p \rightarrow q) \cdot (q \rightarrow p))$
Exportation:	$((p \cdot q) \rightarrow r) \leftrightarrow (p \rightarrow (q \rightarrow r))$
Distribution:	$(p \cdot (q \vee r)) \leftrightarrow ((p \cdot q) \vee (p \cdot r))$
	$(p \vee (q \cdot r)) \leftrightarrow ((p \vee q) \cdot (p \vee r))$

De Morgan's Laws:

(1) $-(p \cdot q) \leftrightarrow (-p \vee -q)$
$-(p \cdot q \cdot r) \leftrightarrow (-p \vee -q \vee -r)$
  etc.

(2) $-(p \vee q) \leftrightarrow (-p \cdot -q)$
$-(p \vee q \vee r) \leftrightarrow (-p \cdot -q \cdot -r)$
  etc.

The principles underlying these rules of replacement are respectively: (1) the negation of a conjunction has the same truth value as a disjunction of the negations of its conjuncts, and conversely; (2) the negation of a disjunction has the same truth value as a conjunction of the negations of its disjuncts, and conversely.

Commutation:

(1) $(p \vee q) \leftrightarrow (q \vee p)$
$(p \vee q \vee r) \leftrightarrow (q \vee r \vee p)$
  etc.

(2) $(p \cdot q) \leftrightarrow (q \cdot p)$
$(p \cdot q \cdot r) \leftrightarrow (q \cdot r \cdot p)$
  etc.

The principles underlying these rules of replacement are respectively: (1) the order in which the disjuncts of a disjunction appear is irrelevant to the truth value of the disjunction; (2) the order in which the conjuncts of a conjunction appear is irrelevant to the truth value of the conjunction.

Association:
    (1) $(p \vee (q \vee r)) \leftrightarrow (p \vee q \vee r)$
        $((p \vee q) \vee r) \leftrightarrow (p \vee (q \vee r))$
        etc.
    (2) $(p \cdot (q \cdot r)) \leftrightarrow (p \cdot q \cdot r)$
        $((p \cdot q) \cdot r) \leftrightarrow (p \cdot (q \cdot r))$
        etc.

The principles underlying these rules of replacement are respectively: (1) the grouping, or punctuation, of the disjuncts of a disjunction is irrelevant to the truth value of the disjunction; (2) the grouping, or punctuation, of the conjuncts of a conjunction is irrelevant to the truth value of the conjunction.

All these rules are justified by the meanings of the relevant logical operators alone. A failure to see that the right-hand and left-hand components in the biconditionals above are logically equivalent is a sign that one has imperfectly mastered the meaning of these operators. For example, one has not fully understood the conditional sign if one does not see, as the first version of the rule of Conditionality says, that a conditional is true if and only if it is not the case that the antecedent is true and the consequent false, or if one fails to see, as the second version of the rule says, that a conditional is true if and only if either the antecedent is false or the consequent is true. Similarly, one has not fully understood conjunctions and disjunctions if one does not see, as the rule of Commutation says, that the order in which their components occur is irrelevant to their truth values, or if one does not see, as the rule of Association says, that their components may be grouped in any way at all without affecting their truth values.

Note that while rules of inference apply exclusively to whole lines in a proof of validity, rules of replacement can apply either to whole lines or to parts of a line. If, for example, someone used the inference rule Simplification to derive 'A' from '(A · B) → C,' this would be a misuse of the rule. '(A · B) → C' asserts that *if* 'A' and 'B' are both true, then 'C' is true; it does not assert that 'A' or 'B' is true. If, on the other hand, one used the rule of replacement Transposition to substitute '(A → B) → C' for '(−B → −A) → C,' the step would be perfectly legitimate. Since 'A → B' and '−B → −A' are logically equivalent, either can replace the other in any occurrence. If the proposition expressed by one is true (or false), the proposition expressed by the other is also true (or false), and the substitution cannot affect the truth value of any more complex proposition of which either is a component.

Note also that while rules of inference are one-way rules, rules of replacement are two-way rules. For example, from 'A · B' one can derive either 'A' or 'B' by the rule of Simplification, but one cannot derive 'A · B' from 'A' or 'B' singly. Transposition, on the other hand, permits us not only to replace 'A → B' by '−B → −A,' but also to replace '−B → −A' by 'A → B.'

V • PROBLEMS OF SYMBOLIZATION

The symbolic apparatus employed in this chapter constitutes a kind of artificial language governed by rules far more strict than those governing the use of natural languages. This artificial language has many incontestable advantages over natural languages. One of these advantages is precision. For example, while the English operator 'or' is ambiguous, serving sometimes as a symbol of exclusive disjunction and sometimes as a symbol of inclusive disjunction, the logical operator 'v' is perfectly precise. A second advantage of our logical vocabulary is the clarity with which it permits us to represent the logical structure of propositions. To anyone familiar with this artificial language the structure of a formula such as '((A v B) → (C v D)) → E' is far clearer than the structure of an ordinary English sentence used to express a proposition so symbolized. A third advantage is the relative simplicity of the symbolic language, which is free not only of distracting non-cognitive meanings but even of categorematic terms. A fourth advantage—which is largely the consequence of these first three—is the ease with which this language permits us to trace the logical relationships among propositions. It is far easier, for example, to establish the validity or invalidity of an argument formulated in symbols than of one formulated in ordinary English.

We must remember, however, that this artificial language is not a substitute for natural languages. Its primary purpose is not to replace natural languages but rather to help us understand certain logical features of natural languages themselves. Moreover, the artificial language and the techniques devised for its use can not serve their primary purpose unless sentences in ordinary language are correctly translated. In most cases correct translation is a relatively simple matter, but there are some sentences whose correct symbolic translation is not immediately obvious.

In troublesome cases, four general techniques may prove helpful. The first is to reword the sentence so that it contains only standard English operators. Consider, for example, the sentence 'He will come unless he is ill.' A little reflection reveals that this sentence, which contains the non-standard operator 'unless,' can be translated without loss of meaning into a sentence containing none but the standard English operators 'if . . . then . . .' and 'not,' thus: 'If he is not ill, then he will come.' This rewording makes the correct symbolic formulation of this sentence clear: '$-I \rightarrow C$.'

The second technique is to translate the troublesome sentence directly into whatever likely symbolic formulation comes to mind, to read the symbolic formulation back into English using only standard English operators, and then to compare the meaning of the reformulation with that of the original sentence. For example, it might seem at first that the correct translation of 'Neither John nor Henry will come' would be '$-J \vee -H$.' If this symbolic formulation is read back into English, however, we get 'It is not the case that John will come or it is not the case that Henry will come,' which clearly does not have the same meaning as the original sentence. We may then try '$-J \cdot -H$,' which reads 'It is not the case that John will come and it is not the case that Henry will come.' If we can see that this sentence is indeed equivalent to the original in cognitive meaning, we know that the corresponding symbolic translation is correct.

The third technique, which is essentially a refinement of the second, is to translate the troublesome English sentence into some likely symbolic formulation, to construct a truth table for this symbolic formulation, and then to ask whether the proposition expressed by the original English sentence has the same truth value as the symbolic formulation for each possible combination of truth values of the non-compound components. Consider again 'Neither John nor Henry will come.' If we formulated this sentence as '$-J \lor -H$,' the incorrectness of our translation would be revealed by its truth table:

	J	H		$-J$	$\lor$	$-H$
(1)	T	T		F	F	F
(2)	T	F		F	T	T
(3)	F	T		T	T	F
(4)	F	F		T	T	T

According to the second row of the truth table the proposition expressed by the symbolic formulation would be true if John came but Henry did not, and according to the third row the proposition would be true if Henry came but John did not. Clearly, however, the proposition expressed by the original English sentence would not be true under these circumstances, and consequently this formulation is incorrect.

A fourth method for testing the adequacy of a proposed symbolization is to translate the proposed symbolization into a logical equivalence. For example, if it is not clear that '$-J \cdot -H$' is a proper symbolization of 'Neither John nor Henry will come,' it may help to convert '$-J \cdot -H$' to '$-(J \lor H)$' by means of De Morgan's Laws. If a given formulation is correct, so is every logically equivalent formulation. But not all logically equivalent formulations are as readily recognized as correct or incorrect. For some of us the correctness of symbolizing 'Neither John nor Henry will come' as '$-(J \lor H)$' is more readily apparent than the correctness of symbolizing it as '$-J \cdot -H$.' Similarly, for most of us the correctness of symbolizing 'He will come unless he is ill' as '$-I \to C$' is easier to see than the correctness of symbolizing it with the logically equivalent formula '$I \lor C$,' obtained by applying successively the rules of Conditionality and Double Negation.

In translating conditionals, however, care must be exercised in the use of these methods, since the meaning of '. . .→ . . .' is not identical with the ordinary English meaning of 'If . . . then. . . .' For example, 'If Socrates is human, then Socrates is mortal' and 'H → M' are both false if the antecedent is true and the consequent false; but the English proposition would ordinarily be regarded as having an indeterminate truth value for the other possible combinations of its components' truth values, whereas 'H → M' would be true for all the other combinations. Thus, if we use the truth-table method to determine the adequacy of a translation for an English conditional, the only relevant row in the appropriate truth table is the one indicating the part of the meaning of 'If . . . then . . .' and '. . .→ . . .' that is common to both formulations.

Suppose, for example, that one is tempted to formulate 'John will pass the course only if he attends classes' as 'A → P.' The complete truth table for this formulation is

	A	P		A → P
(1)	T	T		T
(2)	T	F		F
(3)	F	T		T
(4)	F	F		T

If we used the truth-table method uncritically we might declare this formulation incorrect because the original English sentence could not be considered true just because 'John attends classes' is false as indicated in rows three and four.

In fact this formulation *is* incorrect, but for another reason: According to the second row of the truth table—which alone exhibits the meaning common to 'If . . . then . . .' and '. . .→ . . .'—if 'John attends classes' is true and 'John passes the course' is false, then the formulation as a whole is false. But in fact the original statement itself could be true even if its components had these truth values. The original sentence is intended to assert not that attending classes is a *sufficient condition* of passing but rather that it is a *necessary condition*—not that if John attends classes he will pass his course but rather that if John does not attend classes he will not pass. The instructor who tells John

that he will pass only if he attends classes has not uttered a falsehood if he fails John for having neglected to turn in a term paper.
Thus the correct formulation is '— A → — P,' or a logical equivalence of this such as 'P → A.'

VI • SOME ODDITIES OF OUR ARTIFICIAL LANGUAGE

A consequence of the disparity in meaning between the logical operator '→' and the English operator 'If . . . then . . .' is
that some conditionals which strike most of us as nonsensical
when stated in English turn out to be tautologies when formulated with the aid of '→.' For example, by the use of truth tables
it is easy to show that the following sentences and all sentences
of the same form are tautologies:

If Lincoln was assassinated, then if some cats are black
Lincoln was assassinated.
If Lincoln was not assassinated, then if Lincoln was assas-
sinated some cats are black.

Propositions of these forms are sometimes called the *paradoxes of
material implication,* 'material implication' being a technical term
once used to refer to the kind of conditionality expressed by '→.'
Another oddity of our symbolic language is that it allows us
to derive any conclusion whatsoever from any set of *logically
inconsistent premises*—that is, premises whose conjunction is a
logical self-contradiction. If, for example, we are given 'The moon
is made of green cheese' and 'The moon is not made of green
cheese,' whose conjunction 'M · — M' is obviously a self-contradiction, we can legitimately derive 'God is dead.' An argument with
the premises 'M' and '— M' and the conclusion 'G' is perfectly
valid. This can be shown as follows:

1. M
2. — M / G
3. M v G   1, Addition
4. G   3, 2, Disjunction

(That arguments with inconsistent premises are valid may also be seen by noting that if an argument has inconsistent premises it is impossible for all of the premises to be true.) In ordinary discourse, however, we would say that nothing can be legitimately inferred from a set of inconsistent premises.

Despite these peculiarities of our logical language, its substantial practical worth is unimpaired. In most cases the validity or invalidity of arguments containing the standard English operator 'If . . . then . . .' will be preserved when translated into the symbolic language and tested for validity or invalidity according to the rules of that language. And when this is not the case, the arguments are as a rule patently unsound.

Similarly, although the rules of the artificial language compel us to regard arguments with inconsistent premises as valid, we are not permitted to regard an argument as sound merely because it is valid. For an argument to be sound, its premises must give evidence for the conclusion; but logically inconsistent premises do not support any conclusion. Moreover, the artificial language itself provides us with a simple means of determining whether or not an argument's premises are logically consistent: we simply conjoin the premises, construct a truth table for their conjunction, and examine the truth table to see whether this conjunction is a logical self-contradiction.

EXERCISES FOR CHAPTER TEN

A. Construct complete truth tables for the following argument forms and determine whether they are valid or invalid.

1. p
   ___
   p v q

2. p · q
   _____
   q

3. 1. p → q
   2. q → r
   _____
   p → r

4. 1. p → q
   2. q → r
   _____
   r → p

5. 1. −p v q
   2. −q v r
   _____
   r → p

6. 1. (p ↔ q) → r
   2. −r
   _____
   −(p ↔ q)

7. 1. (p → q) · (r → s)
   2. −p v −r
   _____
   −q v −s

8. 1. (p → q) ↔ (−q → −p)
   2. −q
   _____
   −p

B. Prove the following argument forms invalid by the shorter method discussed in the text:

1. p → q
   _____
   q → p

2. p → q
   _____
   p ↔ q

3. 1. (p v q) v r
   2. −p
   _____
   r

4. 1. p → q
   2. q → r
   3. r → s
   _____
   q v r

5. 1. p v −q
   2. −(−r · s)
   _____
   −q → r

C. Prove the following arguments valid by the shorter truth-table method discussed in the text:

1. 1. J
   2. K
   3. (K v L) → M
   ——————
   J · M

2. 1. R → (S v T v V)
   2. R
   3. −S
   4. −V
   ——————
   T

3. 1. (D → E) · (F → G)
   2. H
   3. D v F
   ——————
   E v G v A

4. 1. (L v A) → B
   2. B → G
   3. A · −G
   ——————
   −L

D. What elementary valid argument form justifies each step in the following proofs of validity:

1. 1. J · K
   2. (K v L) → M / J · M
   3. K
   4. K v L
   5. M
   6. J
   7. J · M

2. 1. A → B
   2. B → C
   3. C → D
   4. −D / −A
   5. A → D
   6. −A

3. 1. R → (S v T v V)
   2. R
   3. −S
   4. −V / T
   5. S v T v V
   6. T

4. 1. (L v A) → B
   2. B → G
   3. A · −G / −(L v A)
   4. −G
   5. −B
   6. −(L v A)

5. 1. (D → E) · (F → G)
   2. H
   3. D v F / (E v G) v A
   4. E v G
   5. (E v G) v A

6. 1. R → W
   2. W → S
   3. S → T / (R → T) v V v W
   4. R → T
   5. (R → T) v V v W

E. Identify the rule of replacement that justifies each of the replacements below:

1. $\dfrac{(A \vee B \vee C) \to D}{(C \vee A \vee B) \to D}$

2. $\dfrac{(A \vee B \vee C) \to -\!-D}{(A \vee B \vee C) \to D}$

3. $\dfrac{A \leftrightarrow B}{(A \to B) \cdot (B \to A)}$

4. $\dfrac{A \to (B \to C)}{(A \cdot B) \to C}$

5. $\dfrac{(A \vee B) \to C}{-(A \vee B) \vee C}$

6. $\dfrac{-(A \vee B) \to C}{(-A \cdot -B) \to C}$

7. $\dfrac{A \cdot A}{A}$

8. $\dfrac{A \vee A}{A}$

9. $\dfrac{(K \cdot L) \to (M \cdot P)}{-(M \cdot P) \to -(K \cdot L)}$

10. $\dfrac{S \vee (A \cdot C)}{(S \vee A) \cdot (S \vee C)}$

11. $\dfrac{T \cdot (W \vee R)}{(T \cdot W) \vee (T \cdot R)}$

12. $\dfrac{P \to (Q \to R)}{-P \vee (Q \to R)}$

13. $\dfrac{-P \vee (Q \to R)}{-P \vee (-Q \vee R)}$

14. $\dfrac{-P \vee (-Q \vee R)}{-P \vee -Q \vee R}$

15. $\dfrac{(A \cdot B) \vee (-A \cdot -B)}{A \leftrightarrow B}$

F. Prove the validity of the following arguments using the allowable elementary valid argument forms and rules of replacement:

1. 1. $-(G \vee B) / -B$

2. 1. $-(G \vee -B) / B$

3. 1. $-R \vee S$
   2. R / S

4. 1. $C \to D / C \to (D \vee R)$

5. 1. $J \to B$
   2. $-J \to R$
   3. $-B / R$

6. 1. $A \to K$
   2. $L \cdot M$
   3. $A \vee -M / L \cdot K$

7. 1. S → T
   2. U → −T / S → −U

8. 1. (D v E) → (F · G · H)
   2. E / G · H

9. 1. (G v E) → (F · H)
   2. −F / −G

10. 1. M → N
    2. N → O
    3. O → P
    4. P → −O / −(M · O)

11. 1. A → B
    2. B → (C → (M v O))
    3. M ↔ O
    4. −(M · O) / −(B · C)

12. 1. R → S / (R · F) → S

13. 1. L → M
    2. M → R
    3. −−L → −R / −L

14. 1. (D → E) → K
    2. −(L v K) / D

15. 1. J ↔ M
    2. M → (L · K)
    3. −L / −J

G. Abbreviate the sentences below, using the suggested notations:

1. If it is neither possible nor desirable to undertake this adventure, there is no point in even talking about it. (P, D, T)
2. I am not willing to talk about this adventure unless it is both possible and desirable. (P, D, T)
3. I am willing to talk about this adventure provided that it is both desirable and possible. (P, D, T)
4. I am willing to talk about this adventure only if it is both desirable and possible. (P, D, T)

5. An act that is not performed freely is neither right nor wrong. (F, R, W)
6. If an act is neither right nor wrong, then punishment and reward are both unjust. (R, W, P, R)
7. Only if an act is performed freely, is punishment or reward just. (F, P, R)
8. Murder and treachery cannot be good without regret being bad. (M, T, R)
9. A prudent ruler ought not to keep faith when by so doing he would defeat his own interests. (P, K, D)

Deductive Arguments: Quantification

In this chapter we shall introduce techniques for testing deductive arguments whose validity is alleged to follow wholly or in part from the internal structure of their non-compound components. A classic example of arguments like these is

1. All humans are mortal.
2. Socrates is human.

   Socrates is mortal.

This argument is valid, but if we symbolized it using the techniques introduced in the last chapter, it would appear:

1. H
2. S

   M

And so symbolized, its validity cannot be proven.

To test the validity of the arguments dealt with in this chapter we use the following familiar symbols:

the property variables: ϕ and ψ
the property constants: A . . . W
the individual variables: x, y, and z
the individual constants: a . . . w
the existential quantifiers: (∃x), (∃y), and (∃z)
the universal quantifiers: (x), (y), and (z)
the logical operators: ·, v, →, ↔, and −

I • TESTING SYLLOGISMS FOR VALIDITY

The simplest class of arguments whose validity or invalidity may be tested by the techniques we are about to introduce are called 'syllogisms.' *Syllogisms* are arguments that consist of exactly two premises and contain exactly three categorematic terms. The component propositions may be either affirmative or negative and either universal, particular, or singular. The predicate of the conclusion is called the *major term*. The subject of the conclusion is called the *minor term*. The third term, which does not appear in the conclusion but which appears twice in the premises, is called the *middle term*. In the syllogism

1. All humans are mortal.
2. Socrates is human.

Socrates is mortal.

'Mortal' is the major term; 'Socrates,' the minor term; and 'human' the middle term. The first premise, since it contains the major term, is called the *major premise*. The second premise, since it contains the minor term, is called the *minor premise*. Conventionally, the major premise of a syllogism is stated first. This convention is a useful one, but the techniques for proving the validity of a syllogism work equally well, regardless of the order in which the premises are stated.

The component propositions of a syllogism can all be symbolized as indicated in Chapter Four. The singular propositions 'Socrates is human' and 'Socrates is mortal,' like other simple singular propositions, can be symbolized with the aid of property constants and individual constants, thus: 'Hs' and 'Ms.' The universal affirmative proposition 'All humans are mortal,' like all others of its kind, can be symbolized with the aid of property constants, an individual variable, and the universal quantifier, thus: $(x)(Hx \to Mx)$.

Proving Validity

In proving the validity of syllogisms we can use the rules of inference and rules of replacement discussed in the last chapter. However, since these rules do not permit inferences from or to quantified propositions, we must introduce additional rules permitting us to convert quantified propositions into non-quantified propositions and vice versa.

Consider again the syllogism

1. All humans are mortal.
2. Socrates is human.

   Socrates is mortal.

which we shall abbreviate to

1. $(x)(Hx \rightarrow Mx)$
2. $Hs \, / \, Ms$

Premise 1 asserts that if any individual whatsoever has the property of being human it also has the property of being mortal; and obviously what is true of *all individuals* is true of *any one named individual* such as Socrates. But since premise 1 is quantified, we can not infer the conclusion directly. We therefore use a rule called *Universal Specification,* which permits us to drop the quantifier in a universal proposition and substitute any name of any individual for the individual variable. This rule allows us to prove our paradigm argument as follows:

1. $(x)(Hx \rightarrow Mx)$
2. $Hs \, / \, Ms$
3. $Hs \rightarrow Ms$ 1, Universal Specification
4. Ms 3, 2, Modus Ponens

The rule of Universal Specification may be used in two other ways as well. The second application of this rule permits us to infer that what is true of *all individuals* is true of *any arbitrarily selected individual*. This application of Universal Specification is ordinarily used in conjunction with a second rule of inference known as *Universal Generalization,* which permits us to infer that what is true of *any arbitrarily selected individual* is true of *all individuals*. If we let a circled individual variable stand for any arbitrarily selected individual, the second application of the rule of Universal Specification and the rule of Universal Generalization can be symbolized respectively as follows:

$$\frac{(x)(\phi x \rightarrow \psi x)}{\phi \text{ⓧ} \rightarrow \psi \text{ⓧ}}$$

$$\frac{\phi \text{ⓧ} \rightarrow \psi \text{ⓧ}}{(x)(\phi x \rightarrow \psi x)}$$

Thus, the validity of the syllogism

    1. All humans are mortal.
    2. All Greeks are human.
    <u>All Greeks are mortal.</u>

can be demonstrated as follows:

    1. $(x)(Hx \rightarrow Mx)$
    2. $(x)(Gx \rightarrow Hx) / (x)(Gx \rightarrow Mx)$
    3. $H\text{ⓧ} \rightarrow M\text{ⓧ}$ 1, Universal Specification
    4. $G\text{ⓧ} \rightarrow H\text{ⓧ}$ 2, Universal Specification
    5. $G\text{ⓧ} \rightarrow M\text{ⓧ}$ 4, 3, Hypothetical Implication
    6. $(x)(Gx \rightarrow Mx)$ 5, Universal Generalization

The distinction between 'all individuals' symbolized by '(x)' and 'any arbitrarily selected individual' symbolized by 'ⓧ' is subtle, and the theoretical justification of the argument forms that depend on this distinction is a highly technical matter on which logicians differ. With these technical matters we shall not be concerned here. There are two observations, however, that may prove helpful. First, at the very least there is a formal difference between propositions of the form '$(x)(\phi x \rightarrow \psi x)$' and propositions of the form '$\phi \circledR \rightarrow \psi \circledR$,' since the former are quantified and the latter are not. In the second place, all of us have at one time or another made inferences of the kind authorized by the argument forms expressed with the aid of these formulas. When, for example, a mathematician who is familiar with the properties of all triangles teaches a student those properties by drawing a triangle on the blackboard, he is relying on the principle that what is true of all triangles is true of the triangle he has drawn on the blackboard for purposes of illustration. Conversely, the student who learns in this way has inferred that the properties belonging to the arbitrarily chosen triangle used for illustration belong to all triangles.

The third use of Universal Specification permits us to infer that what is true of *all individuals* is true of *some one unnamed individual*. If we use circled constants to refer to some one unnamed individual, this application of the rule can be illustrated symbolically as follows:

$$\frac{(x)(Hx \rightarrow Mx)}{H\circleda \rightarrow M\circleda} \qquad \frac{(x)(Hx \rightarrow Mx)}{H\circledb \rightarrow M\circledb} \qquad \frac{(x)(Hx \rightarrow Mx)}{H\circledc \rightarrow M\circledc} \quad \text{etc.}$$

This third application of Universal Specification is used in conjunction with two other rules. The first rule, called *Existential Specification*, permits us to infer that what is true of *at least one individual* is true of *some one unnamed individual*. Symbolically:

$$\frac{(\exists x)(Hx \rightarrow Mx)}{H\circleda \rightarrow M\circleda} \qquad \frac{(\exists x)(Hx \rightarrow Mx)}{H\circledb \rightarrow M\circledb} \qquad \frac{(\exists x)(Hx \rightarrow Mx)}{H\circledc \rightarrow M\circledc} \quad \text{etc.}$$

The second rule, called *Existential Generalization,* permits us to infer that what is true of *some one unnamed individual* is true of *at least one individual*. Symbolically:

$$\frac{H\circleda \rightarrow M\circleda}{(\exists x)(Hx \rightarrow Mx)} \qquad \frac{H\circledb \rightarrow M\circledb}{(\exists x)(Hx \rightarrow Mx)} \qquad \frac{H\circledc \rightarrow M\circledc}{(x)(Hx \rightarrow Mx)} \quad \text{etc.}$$

Thus, the valid syllogism

1. All humans are mortal.
2. Some humans are fools.
   _____
   Some mortals are fools.

can be proved valid as follows:

1. $(x)(Hx \to Mx)$
2. $(\exists x)(Hx \cdot Fx) / (\exists x)(Mx \cdot Fx)$
3. $H\,\textcircled{a} \cdot F\,\textcircled{a}$ 2, Existential Specification
4. $H\,\textcircled{a} \to M\,\textcircled{a}$ 1, Universal Specification
5. $H\,\textcircled{a}$ 3, Simplification
6. $M\,\textcircled{a}$ 4, 5, Modus Ponens
7. $F\,\textcircled{a}$ 3, Simplification
8. $M\,\textcircled{a} \cdot F\,\textcircled{a}$ 6, 7, Conjunction
9. $(\exists x)(Mx \cdot Fx)$ 8, Existential Generalization

The justification for the third application of the rule of Universal Specification is clear: what is true of all individuals is certainly true of some one unnamed individual. And the need for this third application of the rule can be seen by noting that neither of its other applications would permit us to derive the conclusion from the premises of our sample argument. Since the premises say nothing about any one named individual, the first application of Universal Specification can not be used at all. As for the second application of the rule, we could properly use it to infer 'H $\textcircled{x}$ → M $\textcircled{x}$' from premise 1; but if line 4 read 'H $\textcircled{x}$ → M $\textcircled{x}$' rather than 'H $\textcircled{a}$ → M $\textcircled{a}$,' then line 6 could not be derived; and if line 6 can not be derived, neither can the conclusion.

Existential Specification and Universal Generalization are alike in that each has only a single application. The rule of Existential Generalization, however, is like the rule of Universal Specification in that it has three applications. Not only does it permit us to infer that what is true of some one unnamed individual is true of at least one individual, but it permits us to infer that what is true of *some one named individual* is true of *at least one individual* and that what is true of *any arbitrarily selected individual* is true of *at least one individual*. The following arguments illustrate respectively the second and third applications of Existential Generalization:

1. $(x)(Hx \rightarrow Mx)$
2. $Hs / (\exists x)(Hx \cdot Mx)$

3. $Hs \rightarrow Ms$ 1, Universal Specification
4. Ms 3, 2, Modus Ponens
5. $Hs \cdot Ms$ 2, 4, Conjunction
6. $(\exists x)(Hx \cdot Mx)$ 5, Existential Generalization

1. $(x)(Ax \rightarrow Bx)$
2. $(x)(Bx \rightarrow Cx) / (\exists x)(Ax \rightarrow Cx)$
3. $A\circledx \rightarrow B\circledx$ 1, Universal Specification
4. $B\circledx \rightarrow C\circledx$ 2, Universal Specification
5. $A\circledx \rightarrow C\circledx$ 3, 4, Hypothetical Implication
6. $(\exists x)(Ax \rightarrow Cx)$ 5, Existential Generalization

Care must be taken in the use of Existential Specification. Existential Specification need not ordinarily be used more than once. But if it is used more than once, the second inference must be to a circled constant not hitherto used in the proof. If this restriction is not observed, many invalid arguments will test valid. Suppose, for example, one is given the clearly invalid syllogism:

1. Some birds have wings.
2. Some spiders have wings.

   Some birds are spiders.

In symbols:

1. $(\exists x)(Bx \cdot Wx)$
2. $(\exists x)(Sx \cdot Wx) / (\exists x)(Bx \cdot Sx)$

If we failed to observe the restriction on the use of Existential Specification, this syllogism could be proved valid as follows:

3. $B\circleda \cdot W\circleda$ 1, Existential Specification
4. $S\circleda \cdot W\circleda$ 2, **Existential Specification (erroneous)**
5. $B\circleda$ 3, Simplification
6. $S\circleda$ 4, Simplification
7. $B\circleda \cdot S\circleda$ 5, 6, Conjunction
8. $\exists x (Bx \cdot Sx)$ 7, Existential Generalization

The reason step 4 is erroneous is that the symbol '(a)' has already been used in step 3 to indicate that there exists some one unnamed individual that is both a bird and winged and there is no information in the premises to indicate, as line 4 asserts, that this individual (a) which is both a bird and winged is in addition a spider. Note that step 4 would not be invalid if the symbol '(a)' had not been previously used; but given the fact that it has already been used, the only warranted inference would be to some formula containing a different circled constant such as 'S (b) · W (b),' where the use of a different circled constant indicates that the individual denoted is not necessarily the individual denoted by the previously used symbol '(a).' And when a symbol other than '(a)' is used in step 4 the conclusion can not be derived.

Proving Invalidity

Since the validity or invalidity of an argument depends wholly on its logical form and in no way on any truth of fact, an argument can be proved invalid by showing that it is possible for the premises to be true and the conclusion false not only in the universe as we know it but in any conceivable universe. If, therefore, we can show that in a universe containing only one individual—a universe which, however difficult to picture, is nonetheless logically conceivable—it is possible for the premises of an argument to be true and the conclusion false, the argument is invalid. This fact about the conditions under which an argument is invalid provides a relatively simple technique for proving invalidity.

Consider, for example, an argument abbreviated to

1. $(x)(Ax \rightarrow Bx)$
2. $(x)(Cx \rightarrow -Ax)$
$(x)(Cx \rightarrow -Bx)$

In a universe assumed to contain only one individual, whom we shall baptize 'a,' this argument would be equivalent to

1. Aa $\rightarrow$ Ba
2. Ca $\rightarrow$ $-$Aa

Ca $\rightarrow$ $-$Ba

And since the following assignment of truth values:

Aa $-$ False
Ca $-$ True
Ba $-$ True

renders the premises true and the conclusion false, the original argument is invalid.

Sometimes, however, we can not prove an invalid argument invalid when we assume a universe of only one individual. In such cases, to prove its invalidity we must assume a universe of more than one individual. Consider, for example, the invalid argument:

1. $(x)(Ax \rightarrow Bx)$
2. $(\exists x)(Ax \cdot Cx)$

$(x)(Cx \rightarrow Bx)$

If we assume a universe with only one individual, this argument is equivalent to

1. Aa $\rightarrow$ Ba
2. Aa $\cdot$ Ca / Ca $\rightarrow$ Ba

which can be proved valid as follows:

3. Aa	2, Simplification
4. Ba	1, 3, Modus Ponens
5. Ba v $-$Ca	4, Addition
6. $-$Ca v Ba	5, Commutation
7. Ca $\rightarrow$ Ba	6, Conditionality

If, however, we assume a universe of exactly two individuals, the original argument is equivalent to

1. $(Aa \rightarrow Ba) \cdot (Ab \rightarrow Bb)$
2. $(Aa \cdot Ca) \: v \: (Ab \cdot Cb)$
$$\overline{(Ca \rightarrow Ba) \cdot (Cb \rightarrow Bb)}$$

which can be proved invalid by the following assignment of truth values:

$$Aa - False$$
$$Ba - False$$
$$Ca - True$$
$$Ab - True$$
$$Bb - True$$
$$Cb - True$$

Thus, the premises of the original argument do not guarantee the truth of the conclusion under all conceivable circumstances and the argument is invalid.

Note that when we assume a universe of two or more individuals, universal premises are equivalent to conjunctions, whereas particular premises are equivalent to disjunctions. For example, on the assumption of a universe of two individuals, the proposition 'All humans are mortal' is equivalent to '$(Ha \rightarrow Ma) \cdot (Hb \rightarrow Mb)$,' whereas 'Some humans are fools' is equivalent to '$(Ha \cdot Fa) \: v \: (Hb \cdot Fb)$.'

Note also that although most invalid arguments we are likely to encounter in ordinary discourse can be proved invalid by assuming a universe of only one or only two individuals, some invalid arguments can not be proved invalid without assuming a universe with a relatively large number of individuals. Moreover, in some cases considerable trial and error is involved in finding an assignment of truth values needed to prove invalidity. Failure to prove invalidity by this method can not, therefore, be taken as conclusive evidence that a given argument is in fact valid.

II • TESTING NON-SYLLOGISTIC ARGUMENTS FOR VALIDITY

The techniques used to test the validity of syllogisms can also be used to test the validity of a large variety of other arguments.

For example, the following argument is not a syllogism, since it contains four rather than three categorematic terms:

1. All professionals are intelligent or well-educated.
2. Jones is a professional.

   Jones is intelligent or well-educated.

This argument can, however, be symbolized and proved valid as follows:

1. $(x)(Px \to (Ix \vee Ex))$
2. $Pj \: / \: Ij \vee Ej$
3. $Pj \to (Ij \vee Ej)$ 1, Universal Specification
4. $Ij \vee Ej$ 3, 2, Modus Ponens

Another example of a non-syllogistic argument is

1. All babies are illogical.
2. All illogical persons are despised.
3. No despised persons can manage crocodiles.

   No babies can manage crocodiles.

This argument can be symbolized and proved valid as follows:

1. $(x)(Bx \to Ix)$
2. $(x)(Ix \to Dx)$
3. $(x)(Dx \to -Mx) \: / \: (x)(Bx \to -Mx)$
4. $B\textcircled{x} \to I\textcircled{x}$ 1, Universal Specification
5. $I\textcircled{x} \to D\textcircled{x}$ 2, Universal Specification
6. $D\textcircled{x} \to -M\textcircled{x}$ 3, Universal Specification
7. $B\textcircled{x} \to -M\textcircled{x}$ 4, 5, 6, Hypothetical Implication
8. $(x)(Bx \to -Mx)$ 7, Universal Generalization

This last argument is traditionally called a 'sorites.' Though not themselves syllogisms, sorites can be broken down into a chain of syllogisms, in which the conclusion of one is a premise in a second; the conclusion of the second, a premise in a third, and so on. Thus, the sample argument could also be written

All babies are illogical.
All illogical persons are despised.

All babies are despised.
No despised persons can manage crocodiles.

No babies can manage crocodiles.

Since arguments containing more than three categorematic terms are more complex than syllogisms, tests of their validity or invalidity are often more complicated. Moreover, there are many non-syllogistic arguments, especially arguments containing relational terms and requiring multiple quantification, that can only be tested with much more elaborate techniques than it is possible to discuss in this text.

III • PROBLEMS OF SYMBOLIZATION

In symbolizing the class of arguments discussed in this chapter we must observe several points. First, non-explicative synonyms count as a single term and are given the same symbol. Consider, for example, the argument:

1. All wealthy men are hard workers.
2. Jones is a rich man.

Jones is a hard worker.

This argument can not be proved valid if the terms 'wealthy man' and 'rich man' are represented by different symbols. But the argument is intuitively valid, and its validity can be easily demonstrated once the synonymy of 'wealthy man' and 'rich man' is formally recognized by symbolizing the two terms in the same way.

When a term and an explicative synonym of that term both occur in a single argument, however, each term must be differently symbolized. Otherwise, we do violence to the intended meaning of the arguer. Consider, for example, the argument:

1. All bachelors are unmarried men.
2. John is a bachelor.

   John is an unmarried man.

If 'bachelors' and 'unmarried men' were both assigned the symbol 'B,' the formulation would be

1. $(x)(Bx \rightarrow Bx)$
2. Bj

   Bj

which is read: for any x if x is a bachelor then x is a bachelor; John is a bachelor; therefore, John is a bachelor. Clearly this formulation does not express the meaning intended by the arguer.

Second, a word should be said about a few troublesome non-standard English operators. One of these is 'only' and its synonym 'none but.' Consider the sentences:

Only members may attend.
None but members may attend.

Because these sentences are obviously universal affirmative and because the terms directly following their non-standard operators are the grammatical subjects of the sentences in which they occur, we may be tempted to translate them as follows:

$(x)(Mx \rightarrow Ax)$

This translation, however, is erroneous. Reading back into English, we get: for any x, if x is a member, then x may attend. In other words, being a member is a sufficient condition of attendance. But this is not the meaning of the original sentence. According to the original sentence, being a member is a necessary condition of attendance; nothing is said about its being a sufficient condition. If the committee in charge of a club function says that only members may attend, the committee's intent is to forbid members from bringing non-members, not to assure members that they will be admitted under any circumstances. A member who has been told 'Only members may attend' can not reasonably infer that he will be admitted even if he is drunk, or insulting to other members, or improperly dressed. The correct translation, therefore, is

$$(x)(-Mx \rightarrow -Ax)$$

or its equivalent by the rule of Transposition:

$$(x)(Ax \rightarrow Mx)$$

As this last formulation makes evident, the term following 'only' or 'none but' is a logical predicate, not a logical subject.

Another pair of non-standard English operators frequently mistranslated and for similar reasons, is 'Not all . . .' and its synonym 'All . . . not.' Consider, for example, the sentences

Not all members may attend.
All members may not attend.

Since 'not' is a standard sign of a negative proposition and 'all' the standard sign of a universal proposition, we might easily be led to translate these sentences as if they were synonymous with the universal negative 'No members may attend.' In fact, however, 'Not all members may attend' and 'All members may not attend' both express the particular negative proposition 'Some members may not attend.' The proposition expressed by 'No members may attend' is false if even a single member may attend; but the proposition expressed by 'Not all members may attend' and 'All members may not attend' is false only if every member may attend. The correct translation, therefore, is

$$(\exists x)(Mx \cdot -Ax)$$

The non-equivalence of 'Not all members may attend' (or 'All members may not attend') and 'No member may attend' is perhaps even more clearly seen by observing that the function of the former is to deny, or contradict, the universal proposition 'All members may attend.' Since, however, 'No member may attend' is not the contradictory but simply the contrary of 'All members may attend,' it can not be used in this way. Club functions to which some members are admitted and others excluded are not uncommon. Thus, 'All members may attend' and 'No member may attend' could both be false.

Still another pair of operators to note is 'all except' and its synonym 'all but.' A sentence introduced by either term expresses a double proposition. For example, 'All except employees are invited to compete' says both that if anyone is an employee he is not invited to compete and that if anyone is not an employee he is invited to compete. It may therefore be symbolized

$$(x)(Ex \rightarrow -Ix) \cdot (x)(-Ex \rightarrow Ix)$$

Logically equivalent translations are

$$(x)(Ix \leftrightarrow -Ex)$$
$$(x)(-Ix \leftrightarrow Ex)$$

Third, a few words are in order concerning sentences with more than one subject or predicate. Most of these sentences can by symbolized as conjunctions or disjunctions of two or more quantified propositions. For example, 'All citizens and resident aliens are subject to the draft' can be properly symbolized

$$(x)(Cx \rightarrow Sx) \cdot (x)(Rx \rightarrow Sx)$$

Not infrequently, however, it is easier to test the validity of arguments expressed by sentences like these if they are symbolized as single quantified expressions. Thus, the sample sentence may be symbolized alternatively:

$$(x)((Cx \lor Rx) \rightarrow Sx)$$

Note, however, that in translating such sentences, we may be misled by the English operators 'and' and 'or.' 'All citizens *and* resident aliens are subject to the draft' can not, for instance, be properly symbolized

$$(x)((Cx \cdot Rx) \to Sx)$$

The inaccuracy of this formula may be seen from its English reading: for any x, if x is a citizen and a resident alien, then x is subject to the draft.

Note, too, that not all sentences with more than one subject or predicate can be accurately translated as a conjunction or a disjunction of two quantified expressions. For example, 'All officers are either appointed or elected' can not be translated

$$(x)(Ox \to Ax) \text{ v } (x)(Ox \to Ex)$$

which says that either all officers are appointed or all officers are elected. The proposition is correctly symbolized as

$$(x)(Ox \to (Ax \text{ v } Ex))$$

which is read: for any x, if x is an officer then x is appointed or elected.

Finally, a word should be said about the use of *parameters*— that is, expressions like 'all times . . .' 'all places . . .' 'all instances. . . .' These expressions are often useful in putting sentences into standard sentence form. For example, 'Every time I take an examination I get a headache,' may be rewritten in standard form as

All times I take an examination are times I get a headache.

Similarly, 'Whenever there is heavy unemployment, there is political unrest' may be rewritten

All cases of heavy unemployment are cases of political unrest.

EXERCISES FOR CHAPTER ELEVEN

A. Prove the following syllogisms valid:

1. 1. $(x)(Cx \rightarrow -Dx)$
   2. $Dc \, / -Cc$
2. 1. $(x)(Rx \rightarrow Sx)$
   2. $(x)(Sx \rightarrow Tx) \, / \, (x)(Rx \rightarrow Tx)$
3. 1. $(x)(Ax \rightarrow Bx)$
   2. $(\exists x)(Cx \cdot Ax) \, / \, (\exists x)(Cx \cdot Bx)$
4. 1. $(x)(Lx \rightarrow Ux)$
   2. $(x)(Vx \rightarrow -Ux) \, / \, (x)(Lx \rightarrow -Vx)$
5. 1. $(x)(Tx \rightarrow -Rx)$
   2. $(x)(-Rx \rightarrow Sx) \, / \, (x)(Tx \rightarrow Sx)$

B. Prove the following syllogisms invalid:

1. 1. $(x)(Sx \rightarrow Bx)$
   2. $(x)(Cx \rightarrow Sx) \, / \, (x)(Sx \rightarrow Cx)$
2. 1. $(x)(Rx \rightarrow Lx)$
   2. $(\exists x)(Mx \cdot Lx) \, / \, (\exists x)(Rx \cdot Mx)$
3. 1. $(x)(Ax \rightarrow Bx)$
   2. $(x)(Cx \rightarrow Ax) \, / \, (x)(Bx \rightarrow Cx)$
4. 1. $(\exists x)(Tx \cdot -Kx)$
   2. $(\exists x)(Kx \cdot -Mx) \, / \, (\exists x)(Tx \cdot -Mx)$
5. 1. $(\exists x)(Ax \cdot Bx)$
   2. $(\exists x)(Cx \cdot -Bx) \, / \, (x)(Cx \rightarrow -Ax)$

C. Prove the validity of the following non-syllogistic arguments:

1. 1. $(x)((Px \vee Rx) \rightarrow Sx)$
   2. $(x)(Tx \rightarrow Px) \, / \, (x)(Tx \rightarrow Sx)$
2. 1. $(x)(Ox \rightarrow (Tx \vee Ux))$
   2. $(\exists x)(Ox \cdot -Ux) \, / \, (\exists x)(Tx \cdot Ox)$
3. 1. $(\exists x)(Bx \cdot Sx)$
   2. $(x)(Sx \rightarrow Rx)$
   3. $(x)(Rx \rightarrow -Gx) \, / \, (\exists x)(Bx \cdot -Gx)$

D. Prove the invalidity of the following non-syllogistic arguments:

1. 1. $(x)((Rx \lor Tx) \to (Ax \lor Bx))$
   2. $(\exists x)(Tx \cdot -Ax) / (\exists x)(Rx \cdot Bx)$
2. 1. $(x)((Cx \to (Px \lor Qx))$
   2. $(\exists x)(Cx \cdot -Gx) / (\exists x)(Px \cdot -Gx)$
3. 1. $(\exists x)(Ax \cdot Bx \cdot -Cx)$
   2. $(x)(Ax \to Tx)$
   3. $(\exists x)(Ax \cdot -Bx)$
   4. $(x)(Rx \to Bx) / (\exists x)(Rx \cdot -Tx)$

E. Put the following sentences into standard English sentence form.

1. The unexamined life is not worth living. (Socrates, *Apology*)
2. Only the brave deserve the fair.
3. All marriages do not end in divorce.
4. He who lives by the sword shall perish by the sword.
5. John and Mary do everything together.
6. Every sin is not venial.
7. All true music lovers appreciate Bach.
8. Not everybody who appreciates Bach is a true music lover.
9. Governments would be harmless only in case they consisted of saints.
10. Whenever it rains it pours.
11. Death is always a shock.
12. All but cowards will fight for their country.
13. None but chauvinists will fight for their country in an unjust war.

F. Abbreviate the following sentences, using the suggested symbols.

1. Doctors, lawyers, and teachers are all professionals. (Dx, Lx, Tx, Px)
2. No one who knew the man would vote for him. (Px: x is person; Kx: x knows him; Vx: x votes for him)
3. No one would vote for him unless he knew him. (Px: x is a person; Vx: x votes for him; Kx: x knows him)

4. Only a fool or a knave would vote for him. (Fx, Kx, Vx)
5. Harry will vote for him if and only if Harry is a fool. (h: Harry; V: will vote for him; F: is a fool)
6. No candidate who shows contempt for hippies or who refuses to solicit the Negro vote will get the nomination. (Cx, Hx, Sx, Nx)
7. A candidate may show contempt for hippies or refuse to solicit the Negro vote and still get the nomination; but if he hopes to get the nomination he can not do both. (Cx, Hx, Sx, Nx)
8. Politicians are not all dishonest. (Px, Dx)

Laws of Nature

In the preceding two chapters we were concerned with validity. In the remaining chapters of this book our concern will be not with validity but with soundness. Of these two concepts soundness is much broader than validity. Whereas deductive arguments alone may be evaluated as valid or invalid, all arguments may be evaluated as sound or unsound. From a practical point of view soundness is also a much more important concept. If we know that an argument is valid, we know that its conclusion may be logically derived from its premises; but the fact that an argument is valid gives us no good reason to believe that its conclusion is true. If, however, we know that an argument is sound, we do have good reason to believe that its conclusion is true—and for most purposes this knowledge is obviously much more useful.

It is important to note, however, that whereas 'validity' in its technical meaning is perfectly precise, 'soundness' is not. As we know, an argument is sound only if it is clearly expressed, the premises give evidence for the conclusion, and we have reason to believe that the premises are true. But no one can say with precision how clearly an argument must be expressed, how much evidence the premises must give for the conclusion, or how much reason we must have for believing its premises are true to justify calling it 'sound.' Although, therefore, we often say flatly that an argument is either "sound" or "unsound," strictly speaking soundness is not a matter of "either . . . or . . ." but of "more or less."

In Chapters Thirteen through Sixteen we shall spell out spe-

251

cific criteria for evaluating the soundness of different classes of arguments. However, since most arguments contain laws of nature and since the specific criteria for evaluating the soundness of these arguments often depend upon how these laws are interpreted, it will be necessary to devote a preliminary chapter to laws of nature.

For our purposes in this text, *laws of nature* are defined as material propositions affirming a universal relationship between at least two phenomena with an unlimited number of instances. Examples are: 'Water freezes at 32° F.,' 'All men have lungs,' 'Copper conducts electricity,' 'Whenever there is a high level of unemployment, there is political unrest.'

I • CAUSAL LAWS

Many laws of nature are non-causal. It will be convenient, however, to begin our discussion with an analysis of causal laws. Like all laws of nature, causal laws are universal propositions. Each affirms a universal or invariant relationship between a cause and an effect. Moreover, causal laws are like other laws of nature in that all authorize some inference from the presence or the absence of one phenomenon to the presence or absence of a second phenomenon. More specifically, every causal law says at the very least either (1) that the presence of the cause is an unfailing sign of the presence of the effect or (2) that the absence of the cause is an unfailing sign of the absence of the effect. For example, the causal law 'Severing a man's head from his body produces death' is a universal proposition authorizing us to infer that every time a man's head is severed from his body he dies. And 'Oxygen is a cause of fire' is a universal proposition authorizing us to infer that where there is no oxygen there is no fire.

The distinction between a cause whose presence is an unfailing sign of the presence of an effect and a cause whose absence is an unfailing sign of the absence of an effect is closely related to the distinction between a sufficient condition and a necessary condition. The causal law 'Severing a man's head from his body is a cause of death,' for example, says that severing a man's head from his body is a sufficient condition of death. In symbols:

$$(x)(Sx \rightarrow Dx)$$

The causal law 'Oxygen is a cause of fire,' on the other hand, says that oxygen is a necessary condition of fire. In symbols:

$$(x)(-Ox \rightarrow -Fx)$$

Note carefully that the causal law 'Severing a man's head from his body is a cause of death' can not reasonably be interpreted as saying that severing a man's head from his body is a necessary condition of death. It is obvious that death occurs in many other ways. Neither can the causal law 'Oxygen is a cause of fire' reasonably be interpreted to say that the presence of oxygen is a sufficient condition of fire. If it were, all of us would have burned to death before we were even born. Some causal laws, however, state that a given cause is both a necessary and sufficient condition of its effect. When this is the case, the causal law is symbolized as a biconditional, thus:

$$(x)(Cx \leftrightarrow Ex)$$

As we shall see in later chapters, the distinction between the three kinds of causal laws is of the utmost importance, since the evidence required to support causal laws is of a different kind in each case. Unfortunately, speakers are rarely explicit about their intended meaning, and most sentences expressing causal laws must be interpreted by asking which kind of causal relationship is best supported by the available evidence.

The conventional symbolizations for the three types of causal laws have many logical equivalents. For example, the standard formulation of a causal law expressing a sufficient condition

$$(x)(Cx \rightarrow Ex)$$

is equivalent by the rule of Transposition to

$$(x)(-Ex \rightarrow -Cx)$$

which is read: if the effect is absent then the cause is absent. Similarly, the standard symbolization of a causal law expressing a necessary condition

$$(x)(-Cx \rightarrow -Ex)$$

is equivalent by the rule of Transposition to

$$(x)(Ex \rightarrow Cx)$$

which is read: if the effect is present then the cause is present. These two equivalences are highly instructive. They reveal respectively that if one kind of event is a sufficient condition of a second then the second is a necessary condition of the first, and that if one kind of event is a necessary condition of a second then the second is a sufficient condition of the first.

Although every cause is clearly a condition of some second phenomenon—namely, its effect—as the term 'cause' is ordinarily used, not all conditions of a given phenomenon are causes. There are three principal reasons for this.

First, it is ordinarily assumed that causes must exist either prior to or at the same time as their effects. Conditions, on the other hand, may follow the phenomena of which they are conditions. For example, from the fact that an acorn is a cause—in the sense of a necessary condition of a tree's being an oak—it follows by the rule of Transposition that being an oak is a sufficient condition of having once been an acorn. In other words, being an oak is an unfailing sign of having once been an acorn, and a proposition of the form 'x is now an oak' permits us to infer a proposition of the form 'x was once an acorn.' Being an oak is not, however, regarded as a cause of having been an acorn.

Second, many phenomena that are conditions of one another are regarded as symptoms or effects of a common cause rather than as cause and effect. For example, the tidal movements of large bodies of water and the positions of these bodies of water relative to the moon are ordinarily regarded as common effects of the rotation of the earth and the orbiting of the moon around the earth, and it would strike us as odd if these two phenomena were called causes of one another. Yet, a given tidal movement of a body of water is an unfailing sign of, or a sufficient condition for inferring, a particular position of that body of water relative to the moon, and conversely. That is, each phenomenon is a necessary and sufficient condition of the other. Similarly, the symptoms of a particular disease may be so related that the presence of one is a certain sign of, or a sufficient condition for inferring, the presence of another. However, in calling them 'symptoms' we are clearly denying that they are causally related. By definition 'symptoms' are effects, not causes. Two phenomena are ordinarily said to be common effects rather than cause and effect whenever we are aware of a third phenomenon whose presence is sufficient to account for both.

Finally, consider the relationship between having one's head attached to one's shoulders and suffering from a head cold. The first phenomenon is obviously a necessary condition of the second. It is also contemporary to the second phenomenon and not related to it as a common effect of some third phenomenon. Are these two phenomena, however, causally related? Most of us would hesitate to say one way or the other. On the one hand, the relationship does not seem to correspond fully to our preanalytic notion of a causal relationship. On the other hand, there appears to be no good reason for denying that they are causally related; no obvious and well established defining property of a causal relationship appears to be absent. Clearly there must be some property with respect to which 'causality' and its cognate terms are labile. This property is the relational property of being deemed especially important in the light of some practical goal or human interest. Our practical interest in regard to head colds, for instance, is to eliminate them without causing undue stress; and if we hesitate to say that having one's head attached to one's shoulders is a cause, this is because chopping people's heads off, though an effective remedy, is not a desirable one. By contrast, we would not hesitate to attribute head colds to viruses insofar as a remedy for head colds that consisted in eliminating viruses would strike us as both feasible and desirable.

The absence or presence of this labile property is sometimes suggested in ordinary discourse by the terms 'a cause' and 'the cause.' Having one's head attached to one's shoulders qualifies as 'a cause' of the suffering associated with head colds because it is a necessary condition of the suffering, because it is not later in time than the suffering, and because it is not related to the suffering as a common effect of a third condition. But it is not 'the cause' of head-cold suffering, because given our practical needs and interests it can safely be forgotten.

The close relationship of 'the cause' to human interests, needs, or desires emerges even more clearly from the following example. Suppose that a number of students, having eaten in a college dining hall, suffer from food poisoning. The college dietician would identify 'the cause' in terms of a particular dish served: let us say it was the canned peas. Her chief practical interest is merely to prevent a recurrence of food poisoning among the students, and to effect this end she can simply throw out her remaining stock of canned peas. The manufacturer of the canned peas, however, will not identify 'the cause' as canned peas. His practical interest is to see that no future peas bearing his label will produce food poisoning, and for this purpose he must isolate and eliminate the specific factor in processing that caused the food poisoning. 'The cause' for him might turn out to be a chemical fertilizer used by one of his suppliers. For the doctor who is called in to treat the student victims, 'the cause' will be neither the canned peas nor the chemical fertilizer but rather a specific bacterium in the peas for which there is or might be an effective antidote.

As these examples illustrate, whenever the effect is something undesirable or something we wish to eliminate or prevent, 'the cause' will ordinarily be a necessary condition. When, however, the effect is something desirable or something we wish to bring into being, 'the cause' will ordinarily be a sufficient condition. For instance, if a successful writer said, "My success is due to talent and hard work," this statement must be interpreted to mean that talent and hard work suffice to explain his success—that anybody as talented and industrious as he was would also be successful. It can not be interpreted as saying that talent and hard work are necessary conditions for success. We can not tell from what the author has said whether he believes that talent and hard work are also necessary for everyone's success, or whether, on the other hand, he believes that even a lazy and untalented writer could be successful if he had a good publicity agent or if he could produce books shrewdly calculated to appeal to the current public taste.

In order to avoid confusion, we hereby stipulate that in this text statements of the form 'C is the cause of E' will mean

1. C is a necessary condition, a sufficient condition, or a necessary and sufficient condition of E.
2. C is either temporally prior to or contemporary with E.
3. C and E are not common effects or symptoms of a third phenomenon that explains both.

When we wish to stress that a cause so defined is of particular importance in the light of some human need, goal, or interest, we will use the term *pragmatic cause*. Causal laws that identify a pragmatic cause will be called *pragmatic causal laws*.

II • GENERAL, THEORETICAL, AND QUANTITATIVE LAWS

As already noted, many laws of nature are not causal laws. For example, 'Every oak was once an acorn' and 'Every movement of the tides is related to the position of the moon vis-a-vis the earth' are both laws of nature, since both are material propositions affirming a universal relationship between at least two phenomena with an unlimited number of instances. Yet, neither is a causal law. The first does not qualify because the oak is temporally posterior to the acorn; the second, because the movements of the tides and the position of the moon vis-a-vis the earth are effects of a common cause.

The distinction between causal and non-causal laws, however, provides only one of several useful principles of classification. A second distinction—that between *general laws* and *specific laws*—corresponds to the distinction between general and specific terms, and like the latter it is entirely relative. For example, 'All animals are mortal' is specific relative to 'All living beings are mortal' but general relative to 'All men are mortal.'

A third distinction is that between *theoretical laws* and *ob-*

servational laws. This distinction corresponds to the distinction between theoretical terms and observational terms; and like the latter it is not only relative but vague. In practice, however, correct classification does not usually pose serious problems. The laws of atomic behavior and genetic development, for example, are agreed to be theoretical laws, since atoms and genes have never been directly observed. 'Every oak was once an acorn' and 'Decapitation is a cause of death,' by contrast, are generally agreed to be observational laws.

Our fourth and final distinction is between qualitative laws and quantitative laws. *Qualitative laws* say simply that every instance of one property is an instance of a second property. Thus, 'All swans are white' and 'Decapitation is a cause of death' are both qualitative laws. The first proposition says simply that every individual who has the property of being a swan also has the property of being white; the second, that every individual who is decapitated dies.

Quantitative laws fall into two categories. The first, called *statistical laws,* assert that every complex phenomenon of a given kind has a certain percentage of components with a certain property that distinguishes them from the other components. For example: 'In every sufficiently long series of trials in which a fair die is repeatedly tossed, any given face of the die will turn up approximately one out of six times' and 'Whenever round and wrinkled peas are inbred, approximately three fourths of the progeny will be round.' The second type of quantitative laws, called *laws of functional dependence,* relate every variation in the degree to which one property is present in a given phenomenon to a variation in the degree to which a second property is present. For example, 'Every increase in the temperature of a physical body involves an increase in the movement of its molecules' and 'Every variation in the distance of the moon from a large body of water corresponds to a variation in the ebb or flow of the tides in that body of water.' Properties related by laws of functional dependence are called *variables,* and the laws relating these variables to one another are often expressed in precise mathematical formulas.

In daily life most of the laws of nature we invoke are qualitative rather than quantitative, and as a rule they are relatively specific and observational. This is not true, however, in the sciences. In scientific discourse the proportion of highly general, theoretical, and quantitative laws is far greater than in ordinary discourse, and the proportion tends to mount from the less developed to the more advanced sciences. Since one goal of every science is a comprehensive understanding of its subject matter, the presence of highly general laws is not surprising. Obviously, Newton's law of gravity, which applies to all physical bodies and is therefore more general than Kepler's laws of planetary motion and Galileo's laws of falling bodies near the surface of the earth, represented an important advance in the science of physics. Since another aim of the sciences is mathematical precision, the presence of many quantitative laws is also readily understood. Why, however, scientific explanations are so often framed in terms of theoretical laws is largely an unsolved problem. That the sciences do use many theoretical laws successfully is beyond dispute. But why and how laws formulated in terms of unobserved entities can be used to explain directly observed phenomena is still far from clear.

III • APPROXIMATE LAWS OF NATURE

We said earlier that universality is a defining property of 'law of nature.' There is, however, a problem here. Consider, for example, 'Smoking causes lung cancer.' Most of us are convinced that the statistics on smoking and lung cancer point to some kind of causal relationship. Yet, we all know that the relationship between smoking and lung cancer does not hold in all instances. Smoking can not be a necessary condition of lung cancer, since many nonsmokers die of this disease. Nor can smoking be a sufficient condition of lung cancer, since many smokers do not become its victims. And since smoking is neither a necessary nor a sufficient condition, it clearly can not be both. Consider also: 'Poverty causes crime,' 'Carelessness causes accidents,' 'Broken homes cause juvenile delinquency.' In each case the stated cause and the stated effect occur together far more often than we would expect if no causal relationship were involved. But in none of these cases is the relationship between stated cause and stated effect universal.

Must we, then, qualify our definition to allow for non-universal laws of nature? The answer to this question is negative. Sentences of the kind in question are susceptible to one or both of two interpretations, each of which is wholly compatible with the universality of laws of nature. First, some may be interpreted as quantitative laws. For example, many persons believe that in any large human population every increase in smoking is accompanied by an increase in lung cancer. When this is the case, 'Smoking causes lung cancer' may be regarded as a loose expression of a quantitative law. Second, some of these sentences express what we shall call *approximate laws of nature.* For example, many persons who are perfectly aware that the relationship between smoking and lung cancer as such is not universal nonetheless believe that some element associated with smoking is universally related to lung cancer. In such cases 'Smoking causes lung cancer' may be interpreted as a loose or vague expression of a universal qualitative law of nature.

In general, sentences of the kind under discussion are most plausibly interpreted in the second way, and it is important that we be perfectly clear about the difference between approximate and non-approximate laws of nature. The difference is *not* that the latter are universal and the former non-universal. When properly interpreted, all laws of nature are universal. The difference resides rather in the fact that some laws of nature can be *stated* with more precision than others. Whereas non-approximate laws of nature represent relatively complete and precise knowledge of causal relationships, approximate laws of nature express relatively incomplete and vague knowledge of causal relationships. Contrast, for example, the non-approximate law of nature 'The tubercule bacillus causes tuberculosis' with the approximate law 'Smoking causes lung cancer.' The first sentence means quite simply what it says, since the tubercule bacillus is a relatively simple and precisely defined phenomenon whose presence in a given instance can be determined by standard tests. But the second sentence is another matter; for 'smoking' is not as clear or precise an expression as 'tubercule bacillus.' There are, after all, pipe-smokers, cigarette-smokers, and cigar-smokers. Some smokers inhale; some do not. Different smokers are exposed to different kinds of tobacco, tar, and other chemical substances. And insofar as anyone who says "Smoking causes lung cancer" is certainly aware of at least some of these complexities, it is not reasonable to assume that he wishes to assert that smoking *as such* causes lung cancer. His intent is rather to assert that some as yet unidentified element often associated with smoking is the cause of lung cancer. For a complex and vaguely defined phenomenon that figures in an approximate law of nature we shall use the term *gross condition*—or, if we wish to be more specific, *gross cause* or *gross effect*.

Approximate laws of nature are usually based on statistical correlations. These must be carefully distinguished from quantitative laws. The latter, as we know, are universal propositions affirming either that *every* complex phenomenon of a certain kind has a certain percentage of components with a given property, or else that *every* variation of magnitude in a given property of some phenomenon is accompanied by a variation of magnitude in another property. *Statistical correlations,* on the other hand, are always particular and affirm merely that a certain percentage of individuals in some one closed class have a given property. If, for example, we are told that in a given study of three thousand heavy smokers twenty percent died of lung cancer, we are being given a statistical correlation, not a quantitative law.

Statistical correlations must also be carefully distinguished from the approximate laws of nature they support. For example, the approximate law of nature 'Smoking causes lung cancer' no doubt rests upon statistical correlations such as 'Twenty percent of heavy smokers who have been investigated died of lung cancer.' But whereas statistical correlations are merely particular statements about a closed class, approximate laws of nature interpret those facts and impute to them a universal significance. (The conditions under which statistical correlations justify approximate laws of nature will be discussed in the following chapter.)

EXERCISES FOR CHAPTER TWELVE

A. Which of the passages below express or imply laws of nature? Formulate any laws of nature expressed or implied as succinctly as possible. Classify as causal or non-causal, qualitative or quantitative, approximate or non-approximate. If quantitative, indicate whether they are laws of statistical frequency or laws of functional dependence. If causal, indicate whether they are pragmatic or non-pragmatic. Are the alleged causes best regarded as necessary, sufficient, or necessary and sufficient conditions of their effects? Which of the laws of nature are theoretical?

1. Last year the train to Chicago left at 12:03 P.M. This year it leaves at 12:05 P.M.
2. Night invariably follows day.
3. According to Freud guilt feelings are the product of innate aggressive energies that have been frustrated in the course of experience and redirected toward the self.
4. Between one and two percent of all men are color-blind.
5. In a study of one thousand men it was discovered that seventeen were color-blind.
6. No psychologist or social scientist can predict that any given individual will commit suicide. But it can be predicted with certainty that the percentage of persons committing suicide in May will be higher than the percentage of persons committing suicide in November.
7. The law for the velocity of the bob of a simple pendulum along the path of its motion says that, "if v_0 is the velocity of the bob at the lowest point of its motion, h the height of the bob above the horizontal line through this point, and k a constant, then at any point along the arc of its motion the bob has a velocity v such that $v^2 = v_0{}^2 - kh^2$." (Ernest Nagel, *The Structure of Science*)
8. Race riots are caused by poverty.
9. Race riots are caused by inadequate policing.

10. Race riots are caused by the generalized moral decay among American citizens.

11. Race riots are caused by the disintegration of family life among American Negroes.

12. Race riots are caused by hatred for the American way of life stirred up by Communist agitators.

13. Race riots are caused by social injustice.

14. Race riots occur in the summer when the climate is intolerable. It would cost society less to equip every Negro household with an air conditioner than to pay the damages for the riots.

15. Race riots are due to the high unemployment rate among Negro youth.

16. Race riots are merely an excuse for looting.

17. Many American Negroes can not reasonably look forward to any satisfaction greater than that of taking revenge on their oppressors, and this satisfaction is often so intense that they are prepared to risk their lives for its sake. Give them a chance for a normal life with the amenities, pleasures, and satisfactions that accompany it, and race riots will be a thing of the past.

18. If you want to know why there are race riots, read a little American history. If the North had not been so eager to reintegrate the South into the mainstream of American life after the Civil War, the North would have made it a condition of reentrance into the Union that the South solve the racial problem justly, and the bitterness which today manifests itself in race riots would not have developed.

19. If the American people had generally recognized the wisdom of segregation, there would be no race riots today. Instead, the American people has been seduced by pseudo-democratic slogans and utopian ideals whose only fruit is violence.

Generalization

The term 'generalization' is ambiguous; sometimes it is used to denote approximate or non-approximate 'laws of nature.' For example, 'All swans are white' is a generalization. At other times it denotes an argument based on the inference that something true of one or more members of a certain class is also true of one or more other members of that class. The argument

All the swans I have ever seen are white.

All swans are white.

is a generalization in this second sense, since it expresses a claim that what is true of a limited sample of observed swans is true of all swans. The two meanings of the term 'generalization' are related, since the conclusion of most generalizing arguments is a law of nature. But the two meanings ought not to be confused, for generalizing arguments do not always have general conclusions. If, for example, someone argued that because Dr. Smith, Dr. Jones, and Dr. White all have good incomes, Dr. Brown must also have a good income, he would be generalizing even though the conclusion is a singular proposition. In this chapter we shall examine the more common forms of generalizing arguments, and unless the context indicates otherwise the term 'generalization' will be used to denote such arguments.

265

I • ARGUMENTS FROM A FAIR SAMPLE

Arguments from a fair sample are based upon a principle known as *the principle of induction*. This principle may be stated as follows: If in a certain number of observed instances the presence or absence of one phenomenon has been uniformly associated with the presence or absence of a second, we may then infer that the presence or absence of the first is regularly associated with the presence or absence of the second in all instances whether observed or unobserved. The status of this principle is a matter of dispute. In particular, philosophers debate whether this principle can itself be defended by rational argument. Nonetheless, it not only underlies much of our scientific knowledge but is essential to our daily conduct. In past experience when persons have jumped from the observation platform of the Empire State Building, they have crashed to their death on the pavement below. The person who ignored this lesson of past experience and jumped from the Empire State Building in the expectation of floating to heaven would be cruelly disappointed.

Arguments from a fair sample are used exclusively to establish non-approximate observational laws of nature. If a law of nature asserts that phenomenon A is a sufficient condition of phenomenon B, then an argument from a fair sample in support of this law will assume the following logical form:

1. S is a fair sample of A consisting of x number of instances.
2. In every instance of S, B has been present.

$$(x)(Ax \rightarrow Bx) \quad [\text{Alternatively: } (x)(-Bx \rightarrow -Ax)]$$

If a law of nature asserts that A is a necessary condition of B, the pattern will be:

1. S is a fair sample of B consisting of x number of instances.
2. In every instance of S, A has been present.

$$(x)(-Ax \rightarrow -Bx) \quad [\text{Alternatively: } (x)(Bx \rightarrow Ax)]$$

If a law of nature asserts that a phenomenon A is a necessary and sufficient condition of B, then the pattern is:

1. S_1 is a fair sample of A consisting of x number of instances.
2. S_2 is a fair sample of B consisting of x number of instances.
3. In every instance of S_1, B has been present.
4. In every instance of S_2, A has been present.

$(x)(Ax \leftrightarrow Bx)$
[Alternatively: $(x)(Ax \rightarrow Bx) \cdot (x)(Bx \rightarrow Ax)$]

Often arguments from a fair sample are incompletely stated. If somebody argues that all swans are white because all the swans he has ever seen are white, there is every reason to suppose that he believes the swans he has seen constitute a fair sample of swans. Similarly, if someone argues

A hundred persons suffering from mental illness in a New York clinic were examined and each found to have had traumatic childhood experiences.

Traumatic childhood experiences are a cause of mental illness.

he clearly believes that these hundred cases are a fair sample of the mentally ill.

If we can not assume an implicit premise to the effect that the samples cited in the two arguments are fair samples, the arguments are no better than the following:

All the men I have ever seen are white.

All men are white.

A hundred persons suffering from mental illness in a New York clinic were examined and each found to have undergone shock treatment.

All persons suffering from mental illness undergo shock treatment.

It is therefore extremely important that implicit premises asserting that a certain number of observed instances constitutes a fair sample be made explicit and that the evidence for them be carefully examined.

Since the conclusion of our sample argument about swans must be interpreted to assert that being a swan is a sufficient condition of being white, the argument may be reformulated and abbreviated as follows:

1. All the swans I have ever seen constitute a fair sample of S.
2. All the swans I have ever seen are W.

$$(x)(Sx \rightarrow Wx)$$

Since many persons have had traumatic childhood experiences without suffering mental illness, the conclusion of the second argument would be most plausibly construed as asserting that traumatic childhood experiences are a necessary rather than a sufficient condition of mental illness. The argument might be reformulated and abbreviated as follows:

1. A hundred cases of mentally ill persons examined in a New York clinic constitute a fair sample of M.
2. All the cases of M examined were observed to have suffered from T.

$$(x)(-Tx \rightarrow -Mx)$$

The term 'fair sample' is characterized by both vagueness of family resemblance and linear vagueness. Its vagueness of family resemblance follows from the fact that its strict intension consists of a disjunctive property whose components are three meaning criteria. Its linear vagueness follows from the fact that each of these meaning criteria is itself characterized by linear vagueness. In a paradigm all three meaning criteria will be present to a high degree, but there are many borderline cases in which one or more of these criteria are either not present or present in only a limited degree.

The first and most important of these criteria is as follows: Of two samples of a given class, that sample is fairer which contains instances from a larger number of its significant subclasses.

Thus a sample of swans consisting of European swans, Australian swans, American swans, and so forth would ordinarily be considered fairer than a sample consisting exclusively of European swans.

It is important to note, however, that the significance of a subclass in the context of any given argument from a fair sample is relative to the conclusion of that argument. If, for example, we wish to establish that all swans are white, subclasses of swans defined in terms of geographical location are more significant than subclasses defined in terms of brain size. If, however, we wished to establish that no swan can be taught tricks, subclasses defined in terms of brain size would be more significant than subclasses defined in terms of geographical location.

If we use 'C' for the class named by the subject of the conclusion and 'E' for the phenomenon the conclusion says is universally related to C, a *significant subclass* may be defined as follows: Of two subclasses of C, one subclass is more significant than the other if accumulated knowledge gives us reason to believe that the properties of the first are more relevant to E than the properties of the second. Since, for example, we know that the color of animal species often varies with geographical location, we have good reason to suppose that geographical location is relevant to the color of swans. We have no good reason, however, for believing that brain size is related to the color of swans.

Samples chosen selectively so as to satisfy this first criterion are called *representative samples.*

The second criterion may be stated as follows: Of two samples of a given class, that sample is fairer which contains the larger number of instances chosen unselectively, or at random. Samples chosen to satisfy this second criterion are called *random samples.* In general, representative samples are superior to random samples, but when our knowledge of significant subclasses is incomplete random sampling is often indispensable. For example, our knowledge of significant subclasses of swans relative to the conclusion 'All swans are white' is limited. We do know that geographical location is relevant, and zoologists can specify a few other relevant properties. But many of the properties responsible for the color of any given animal species are still unknown, and we cannot be sure that a sample of swans designed to establish that all swans are white is fair unless we have reason to believe that the sample includes instances of swans that exhibit these unknown properties. This is why we invoke the second criterion. Its rationale is that the larger and the more random the sample the greater the likelihood that it will include any subclasses genuinely related to E of which we may be ignorant. Thus, a random sample of a thousand swans is superior to a random sample of a hundred swans.

The third criterion may be stated as follows: Of two samples of a given class, that sample is fairer which contains the larger number of instances from within each known significant subclass. To illustrate, a sample of swans consisting of a hundred European swans, a hundred Australian swans, a hundred American swans, and so forth is a fairer sample than one consisting of ten swans from each of these subclasses. The need for this third criterion follows from the fact that almost every significant subclass is itself divisible into subclasses and that often the significance of a subclass is due not to the defining properties of that subclass itself but rather to the defining properties of one of its subclasses. For example, since some Australian swans have been discovered to be black, the purported law of nature 'All swans are white' is false. But since not all Australian swans are black, the color of Australian swans can not be due simply to their being Australian, and a small sample of Australian swans would be less likely to include significant subclasses of Australian swans than a large sample. In fact, since black Australian swans are much rarer than white Australian swans, the falsity of 'All swans are white' would probably not be discovered unless the sample of Australian swans was fairly large.

The knowledge which permits us to determine what subclasses are significant relative to a given conclusion is ordinarily knowledge about some class of which the class cited in the conclusion is itself a subclass. As already indicated, it is because swans are a subclass of animals and because the color of animal species is known to vary with geographical location that subclasses defined by geographical location are significant relative to 'All swans are white.' And it should be noted that knowledge of this kind bears not only on decisions with regard to significant subclasses but also on decisions with regard to the size of the samples required. For example, since collies are a subclass of animal species and since it is known that anatomical properties such as having a tail are less variable among animal species than a property such as color, a relatively small sample of collies that gives little support to 'All collies are brown' might give considerable support to 'All collies have tails.'

II • ARGUMENTS FROM STATISTICAL CORRELATIONS

Whereas arguments from a fair sample proceed from the assertion of a uniform relationship between the pertinent phenomena in the observed instances to the assertion of a non-approximate law of nature, arguments from statistical correlations proceed from the assertion of a statistical relationship between the pertinent phenomena in the observed instances to the assertion of a merely approximate law of nature. Arguments from statistical correlations, however, are like arguments from a fair sample in that they are based on observation of a limited sample and in that their conclusions are invariably observational laws of nature.

Arguments from statistical correlations are also like arguments from a fair sample in that they are often incompletely stated. Consider the following argument:

In a study of mentally ill persons who had undergone psychoanalysis for two years it was observed that two-thirds showed complete recovery or marked improvement.

Psychoanalysis cures mental illness.

By itself this argument is no sounder than

In a study of persons suffering from head colds who had taken Dr. Quack's pink pills for two weeks it was observed that two-thirds showed complete recovery or marked improvement.

Dr. Quack's pink pills cure head colds.

In other words, no statistical correlation by itself supports even an approximate law of nature. Statistical correlations are significant and support laws of nature only if certain conditions are met, and an argument from a statistical correlation is complete only if its premises assert that these conditions hold.

These conditions can best be stated with the help of the terms 'experimental group' and 'control group.' An *experimental group* is any set of observed instances cited in support of a law of nature in which the asserted condition is present. If we wish to establish the law of nature 'Smoking causes lung cancer,' the experimental group will consist of persons known to be smokers. If we wish to establish the law of nature 'Psychoanalytic treatment causes recovery from mental illness,' the experimental group will consist of mentally ill persons who have undergone psychoanalytic treatment. A *control group* is any set of observed instances in which the alleged condition is absent. Thus, a set of nonsmokers would be a control group relative to 'Smoking causes lung cancer,' and a set of mentally ill patients who had not undergone psychoanalytic treatment would be a control group relative to 'Psychoanalysis is a cause of recovery from mental illness.'

These, then, are the conditions which a statistical correlation must satisfy to be significant: (1) The experimental group must be a fair sample. (2) It must be possible to specify an appropriate control group. (3) The percentage of cases in which the effect is present must be significantly higher in the experimental group than in the control group. (4) The control group must be a fair sample.

Thus, to refute an argument for the conclusion 'Psychoanalysis is a cause of recovery from mental illness' based on a correlation between psychoanalytic treatment and recovery in a given experimental group, we can do any of four things. First, we can attempt to show that the experimental group is biased. A somewhat skeptical psychoanalyst once remarked that psychoanalysts tend to choose as patients those who are about to recover anyway. If he were right, an experimental group of mentally ill persons undergoing psychoanalysis would be a biased sample of the mentally ill and the correlation would have little or no significance. Second, we can challenge the arguer to specify a control group. If we have no information about the percentage of mentally ill persons who do not undergo psychoanalysis but who nonetheless recover, the fact that two thirds of the mentally ill who undergo psychoanalysis recover is without significance. Third, we can attempt to establish that the percentage of mentally ill persons who recover after psychoanalytic treatment is not significantly higher than the percentage of mentally ill persons who recover from mental illness without undergoing psychoanalysis. Finally, we can question the fairness of the control group. If the control group consisted exclusively of severe psychotics, the correlation would once again be of little or no significance.

Experimental and control groups may be selected either randomly or representatively. Sometimes both are selected the same way; sometimes one is randomly selected and the other representatively selected. In carefully controlled experiments, however, it often happens not only that both groups are representatively selected but that each contains the same number of instances from each significant subclass. In these cases, the experimental and control groups are said to be *matched*. For example, a matched pair of experimental and control groups for testing the causal law 'Psychoanalytic treatment is a cure for mental illness' would include an equal number of instances from subclasses of mentally ill persons defined by such properties as severity of illness, duration of illness, nature of illness, intelligence, socio-economic level, age, prognosis, and so on—all of which could conceivably be gross causes of recovery.

The advantages of matching experimental and control groups can be seen in the following hypothetical cases. Suppose that a study based on random samples of smokers and nonsmokers revealed that twenty percent of the smokers contracted lung cancer as against only two percent of the nonsmokers. These results would be significant and would strongly indicate that smoking is a gross cause of lung cancer. But a phenomenon like lung cancer may have several gross causes, and this study would give us no information about other gross causes or about their relative importance. Suppose, then, that a second study based on matched groups reveals the same percentage disparity between the occurrence of lung cancer in the total experimental group and the occurrence of lung cancer in the total control group but at the same time reveals an even greater percentage

disparity between the occurrence of lung cancer in the total experimental group and the occurrence of lung cancer in a sub-
control group defined in terms of exposure to air pollution. This
would clearly indicate both that exposure to air pollution is also
a gross cause of lung cancer and that it is relatively more important.

III • ANALOGICAL ARGUMENTS

In analogical arguments, unlike arguments from a fair sample
and arguments from statistical correlations, the conclusions may
be either singular or general and may be either observational or
theoretical. Regardless of the type of conclusion, however, all
analogical arguments are based on the inference that if one individual or class shares one or more properties with a second
individual or class, certain other properties of the first are also
shared by the second.

Thus, if we believed that individuals a, b, c, and d share
properties X and Y and we further believed that individuals a,
b, and c possess property Z, we might infer that d also possesses
Z. In symbols:

1. a, b, and c are X, Y, and Z
2. d is X and Y

   d is Z

An argument with this pattern is

1. John, Bill, and David are young, rich, and irresponsible.
2. Robert is young and rich.

   Robert is irresponsible.

Properties asserted in the premises to be common to all the
individuals or classes involved are called *premised analogies*.
Properties imputed to the subject of the conclusion are called

inferred analogies. Individuals or classes identified in the conclusion are called the *analogical subject;* those not named in the
conclusion, the *analogical base.* In the sample argument, the
analogical subject is Robert; the analogical base, John, Bill, and
David. The premised analogies are the properties of being young
and rich; the inferred analogy, the property of being irresponsible. Analogical arguments may of course include any
number of individuals or classes in their analogical bases or
subjects and may include any number of premised or inferred
analogies.

Analogical arguments are susceptible to two interpretations,
depending on whether the arguer is prepared to accept the analogical base as a fair sample of the class defined by the premised
analogies. If, for example, the author of the sample argument
above believed that John, Bill, and David were a fair sample of
the young and rich, his argument would have the following
implicit pattern:

John, Bill, and David are a fair sample of the young and rich.
John, Bill, and David are irresponsible.
___
All young and rich persons are irresponsible.
Robert is young and rich.
___
Robert is irresponsible.

If, however, the author did not believe that the analogical base
was a fair sample of the class defined by the premised analogies,
the implicit logical pattern of his argument would be

1. Some young and rich persons are irresponsible.
2. Robert is young and rich.
___
Robert is irresponsible.

When interpreted in this second way, the premises of an
analogical argument give meager support for the conclusion, and
thus the first interpretation is generally to be preferred. Even if
the first interpretation does violence to the arguer's intent, re-
casting the argument along these lines often has the advantage

of making explicit certain issues that are relevant to the soundness of the argument and that should therefore be taken into account. For example, the soundness of the sample argument above depends almost entirely upon the degree to which John, Bill, and David are typical of the young and rich. If we can show that they do not constitute a fair sample, the argument gives little support for the conclusion.

Sometimes, however, the second and weaker interpretation is the only appropriate one. This is especially true when an analogical argument is introduced in the early stage of some inquiry with the intent less of establishing the conclusion beyond reasonable doubt than with the intent of suggesting an hypothesis worthy of further exploration but not susceptible to confirmation by reference to a fair sample. Consider, for example, the following argument first introduced by the classical atomists:

1. Trellises and like physical objects observed to contain empty space permit sound to pass through them.
2. Apparently solid objects permit sound to pass through them.

Apparently solid objects contain empty space.

In this case the analogical base consists of trellises and similar objects observed to contain empty space; the premised analogy is the property of permitting sound to pass. If this argument were interpreted in the first way, it would assume the following form:

Trellises and like physical objects are a fair sample of physical objects permitting sound to pass through them.
Trellises and like physical objects contain empty space.

All objects permitting sound to pass through them contain empty space.
Apparently solid objects permit sound to pass through them.

Apparently solid objects contain empty space.

Since, however, apparently solid objects are obviously a significant subclass of objects permitting sound to pass, it is most unlikely that anybody would subscribe to the first premise of the above argument. The argument must, therefore, be given the second interpretation:

1. Some objects permitting sound to pass through them contain empty space.
2. Apparently solid objects permit sound to pass through them.

Apparently solid objects contain empty space.

Not only is this interpretation more likely to represent the arguer's intent but, more important, it is the only plausible one, since the conclusion, like those of all arguments referring to theoretical or unobservable entities, can not be reasonably supported by an argument from a fair sample.

When this second interpretation of analogical arguments is appropriate, the analogical base is called an *analogical model,* and the argument itself is called an *argument from an analogical model.* The chief use of arguments from an analogical model, as suggested earlier, is in proposing hypotheses for further con-firmation. We must not assume, however, that the premises of an argument from an analogical model give no evidence for the conclusion. In the absence of any evidence to the contrary, the fact that some objects permitting sound to pass through them contain empty space is partial grounds for believing that all such objects contain empty space. If it were not, the conclusion of the argument would not even be an hypothesis worth considering. Similarly, we must not assume that the conclusion of arguments from analogical models can not be supported by additional evidence. But we must remember that the evidence cited in the premises is only partial and that additional evidence for the conclusion will not be based on a fair sample.

Correct interpretation of analogical arguments is often a very delicate matter. For example, it has been argued

1. Clocks and other human artifacts are orderly systems and products of an intelligent being.
2. The universe is an orderly system.

The universe is the product of an intelligent being.

Since systems of order do exist that are not observably products of intelligent beings (for example, the solar system and bee hives), human artifacts are not in fact a fair sample of orderly systems, and many of the persons who propose this argument quite properly regard it as merely suggestive. They argue, in effect, that since some systems of order are caused by the agency of intelligent beings, an intelligent designer of the universe is an hypothesis worth considering. Many persons who propose this argument, however, find it so compelling that we must assume an implicit premise to the effect that human artifacts do constitute a fair sample of orderly systems.

When an analogical argument is properly interpreted in the first way, the crucial premise is likely to be the implicit premise asserting that the analogical base is a fair sample of the class defined by the premised analogy, and this premise must be evaluated in the way that any such proposition is evaluated. When, however, an argument proceeds from an analogical model, four principal criteria are relevant to its evaluation.

(1) The number of significant analogies between the analogical model and the analogical subject. The greater the number of significant analogies between human creations and the universe, for example, the stronger is the argument for an intelligent creator of the universe. If the universe and human artifacts are alike not only in being orderly systems but also in conducing to human well-being, an argument premising both of these analogies would be stronger than an argument premising only one. (2) The frequency with which the premised analogy and the inferred analogy are known to occur together. For example, the greater the percentage of instances of order known to be due to human intelligence, the stronger is the sample argument. (3) The possibility of eliminating rival explanations of the property imputed to the analogical subject in the premises. For example, the order in the universe has been explained by many scientists as a product of evolutionary process rather than as a product of superhuman intelligence. But if grave defects can be shown in this rival explanation, the original argument becomes relatively stronger. (4) The number of significant disanalogies between analogical model and analogical subject. Since, for example, many products of human intelligence are the result of a joint effort

among human beings, an argument from these products to the existence of a single superhuman creator of the universe is weaker than it would be if every human artifact were the product of a single intelligence.

In conclusion it should be pointed out that analogies play a far greater role in our thinking than we are ordinarily aware, since the plausibility of many beliefs we hold is due almost entirely to a tacit or half-conscious appeal to some analogical model. For example, many people believe that creative persons draw on a store of sexual energy in their work and consequently have a less active sex life than non-creative persons. This belief is largely based on the assumption that the sum of energy in the human psyche is fixed, which in turn rests on the analogical model of a closed physical system in which energy may be redirected but neither augmented nor reduced. Whether this belief is justified or not is irrelevant here. The point is that many beliefs to which we subscribe rest upon implicit arguments from analogical models. And although arguments of this kind are often weaker than other generalizing arguments, they deserve careful attention.

EXERCISES FOR CHAPTER THIRTEEN

A. What generalizations are stated or implied in the following passages? What evidence, if any, is given for them? Is the evidence adequate? What additional data might help to confirm or disconfirm the generalizations?

1. "In 1888, a doctor claimed that summer diarrheas of infancy are due to poisonous milk. An opponent claimed, on the other hand, that the high infant mortality was due to the growing use of the baby perambulator, since the death rate among children had increased since the baby cab had come into fashion. The first doctor replied that he withdrew his claim, but thought he could claim, with a right equal to that of his opponent, that the high infant mortality

was due to the growing use of umbrellas." (Morris R. Cohen and Ernest Nagel, *Introduction to Logic and Scientific Method*)

2. Monday I drank rum and soda. Tuesday I drank whiskey and soda. Wednesday I drank gin and soda. Thursday I drank brandy and soda. In each case I had a hangover the following day. The cause must be the soda.

3. If you want a long life get married. The death rate for bachelors in a three-year period was almost two-thirds greater than that among husbands.

4. "It is three times as dangerous to be a pedestrian while intoxicated as to be a driver. This is shown by the fact that last year 13,943 intoxicated pedestrians were injured and only 4,399 intoxicated drivers." (Quoted in W. Allen Wallis and Harry V. Roberts, *Statistics: A New Approach*)

5. A medical doctor reported that out of a group of carefully screened subjects, a significant percentage who were given harmless placebos, or bogus pills, complained of trembling, vomiting, stomach pain, etc. Also, a significant percentage of those given placebos in place of their usual drugs experienced the same benefit from the placebos as they normally did from their drugs. This included diabetic patients who had been on sulfa drugs. The doctor concluded that the 'suggestive effect' of drug taking is as important as the pharmacological properties of the drugs in controlling disease.

6. "His procedure was straightforward. He used a local advertisement for good and poor sleepers and offered to pay for two nights of laboratory sleep. All the volunteers were selected by a carefully worded questionnaire. They answered such questions as, 'How long does it take you to fall asleep at night?' The response was considerable, and the men were selected so that he had two well-matched groups, all of whom met some health standards, and none of whom represented real extremes of insomnia or exaggerated somnolence.

"They were men between twenty and forty. The two groups were matched so that each contained people of comparable ages, education, and athletic proclivities. The spectrum included laborers, students, doctors, and professionals—men who had never gone to school beyond eighth grade and those with advanced degrees. Some were physically inactive, others very active. There were sixteen men in each group. Each person came to sleep in the lab for one night of acclimation before his night of recording, and was asked to fill out two questionnaires. . . .

". . . The group of good sleepers averaged a total of 6½ hours of sleep, while the poor sleepers obtained an average of 5¾. The poor sleepers took longer to fall asleep and awakened twice as often during the night.

"Although the two groups differed in the amount of sleep they got, the experimenters had actually expected a far greater divergence. . . . On questioning, the good sleepers had accurately estimated how long they took to fall asleep at night. In the laboratory the average for the group was about seven minutes. On the other hand, the poor sleepers had apparently exaggerated on the questionnaire—suggesting that the group would average about an hour before sleep onset. As it turned out, the group fell asleep in fifteen minutes on the average. . . .

"Pronounced physiological differences are associated with . . . the poor sleeper's difficulty in falling asleep. High body temperature and somewhat faster pulse suggested that the poor sleeper was more aroused before sleep, and closer to a waking state during sleep than was the good sleeper. . . .

". . . [Personality tests showed that] the poor sleepers were more anxious, introverted, hypochondriacal, and emotionally disturbed than were the good sleepers." (Gay Gaer Luce and Julius Segal, *Sleep*)

7. "In spite of all our effort at education, the American people are becoming more ignorant. . . . Women college graduates, people of forty-five to forty-nine, have had barely enough children to replace their parents; high school graduates, same age, four-fifths enough children for replacement . . . BUT women, same age, with *fourth grade educa-*

tion or less, have had nearly twice the number necessary to replace the parents. Fourth-graders are practically doubling their numbers every generation; college women are dying out fifty percent every generation." (Quoted in W. Allen Wallis and Harry V. Roberts, *Statistics: A New Approach*)

8. "Dr. Robert Seashore of Northwestern University stated in 1938 that the average college student has a recognition vocabulary of 176,000 words, instead of the 15,000 words which are often credited to the 'average intelligent adult.' He arrived at the figure by taking the third word from the top of the first column of each even-numbered page in a standard dictionary, and then dividing the words into two groups: commonly used and rarely used. Giving the two groups to his undergraduate and graduate classes to define, he determined that the average student recognition vocabulary was 62,000 basic words and 114,000 derived words." (Harold A. Larrabee, *Reliable Knowledge*)

9. The death rate for tuberculosis is higher in Arizona than in any other state. The climate is obviously not so good as the Arizona Chamber of Commerce would like us to believe.

10. For a twenty-day period following a change of police commissioners in New York City the crimes reported by the police increased by better than a third over a comparable period in the preceding year. A critic of the commissioner concluded that the increase was due to his inefficiency.

B. Opponents of the view that smoking causes lung cancer have argued, among other things, that: (1) the rate of lung cancer among bald men is three or four times higher than among men with hair; (2) there is no positive correlation between smoking and lung cancer in female populations; (3) there are a number of male populations (for example, the Japanese) where there is no positive correlation between smoking and lung cancer; (4) lung cancer is much more common in urban areas than in rural areas, though the average number of cigarettes smoked in rural areas is only slightly lower than the number smoked in urban areas. To what extent, if any, do these data undermine the claim that smoking causes lung cancer? Explain your answer.

C. The following passages indicate two ways in which statistical correlations that relate advertising to sales may be deceptive. Can you think of still other ways in which data of this kind may be subject to misinterpretation?

1. "I always showed prospective clients the dramatic improvement that followed when Ogilvy, Benson & Mather took accounts away from old agencies—'in every case we have blazed new trails, and in every case *sales have gone up.*' But I was never able to keep a straight face when I said this; if a company's sales had not grown more than sixfold in the previous twenty-one years, its growth had been less than average." (David Ogilvy, *Confessions of an Advertising Man*)

2. "One of the biggest advertisers in the world recently engaged an illustrious firm of management engineers to study the relationship between his advertising and his profit. The statistician who made the study fell into a trap which is curiously common: he assumed that the only significant variable was the *amount of money* spent on advertising from year to year. He was not aware that a million dollars' worth of effective advertising can sell more than ten million dollars' worth of ineffective advertising." (David Ogilvy, *Confessions of an Advertising Man*)

D. The following passages all raise questions concerning the fairness of the sample Kinsey used in his *Sexual Behavior in the Human Female*. Do you think the criticisms are justified? What additional information would you like to have to determine the fairness of his sample?

1. "In 1953 Dr. Alfred C. Kinsey and his associates at Indiana University published *Sexual Behavior in the Human Female,* based upon extensive interviews with 5,940 female volunteers, of whom 1,840 were college students from 16–20, 2,480 women who had been married, and 649 women of twenty-six years and over who had never married. Of the sample, fifty-eight percent were single, when only about twenty percent of the female population over fourteen were

single; ninety percent were urban, when only sixty-four percent of the population in 1950 were urban; and over half had had some college education. Dr. Kinsey himself pointed out that his conclusions were 'least likely to be applicable' to age groups over fifty; persons with no more than grammar school education; the previously married; all Catholics; devoutly Jewish groups; laboring groups; rural people; persons born before 1900; and to the Southeastern quarter of the United States, the Pacific Northwest, and the high plains and Rocky Mountain areas. He defended the use of volunteers rather than random sampling on the ground that the latter sort of interviewing would have led to too large a percentage of refusals to discuss intimate personal matters." (Harold A. Larrabee, *Reliable Knowledge*)

2. "The aim of any comprehensive study of a phenomenon is to throw light on its determinants, so that it can be completely and accurately understood. Now there are obvious social characteristics of American women which are presumably central to their behavior, and which are not comprehended at all under the traditional groupings by age, education, religion, etc., which were used for the male. It will probably occur to any reader that one manifest determinant of a large area of feminine behavior is the presence or absence of motherhood, and the extent to which a woman must care for children. Another clearly apparent social characteristic which affects many aspects of woman's behavior is her status as an independent wage-earner, or as a dependent non-working wife or daughter. Conceivably these factors have no relation to sexual behavior, but the presumption is so strong that they do, and they have been so saliently mentioned in most discussions of the problem, that we find it disappointing that their effects are not reported on in the present volume. It is even conceivable that the interpretation of some of the differences within the female sample, and of some of the differences between males and females which are now attributed to other factors would be substantially revised, if we could determine the effects of such characteristics as we have named and examine the representativeness of Kinsey's sample in that light. Is it not likely, for

example, that the large group of women with post-graduate training are for the most part professionally employed? If this be so, the nature and frequency of their sexual activities may implicitly reflect their occupational status rather than some of the other factors which have been examined. And were this found to be true, their heavy over-representation in Kinsey's sample would tend to distort the overall findings." (Herbert Hyman and Paul B. Sheatsley, "The Scientific Method," in *An Analysis of the Kinsey Reports*)

3. "Statistics show that more than twice as many women (forty-four percent) who had no previous experience with orgasm as those who had (nineteen percent), failed to reach orgasm in the first year of marriage. On the basis of these statistical data, Kinsey ventures the judgment that 'it is doubtful if any therapy (sic) has ever been as effective as early experience in orgasm, in reducing the incidences of unresponsiveness in marital coitus, and in increasing the frequencies of response to orgasm in that coitus.' This is an unequivocal statement. But the question promptly arises—did the women who had pre-marital experience with orgasm have the experience because they had an innate drive and capacity for orgasm, or did they acquire a competence in orgasm because of their pre-marital experience?" (Iago Galdston, "So Noble an Effort Corrupted," in *An Analysis of the Kinsey Reports*)

E. Identify the analogical base or model, the analogical subject, the premised analogy or analogies, and the inferred analogy or analogies of the arguments stated or implied in the following passages. Appraise these arguments according to whichever of the criteria outlined in the text appear relevant.

1. The philosopher Epicurus argued that since no man had ever observed intelligence except in a human body, the gods must have bodies.

2. "By what conceivable standard can the policy of price-fixing be a crime, when practiced by businessmen, but a public benefit, when practiced by the government? There are many industries in peacetime—trucking, for instance—

whose prices are fixed by the government. If price-fixing is harmful to competition, to industry, to production, to consumers, to the whole economy, and to the 'public interest' —as the advocates of the antitrust laws have claimed—then how can that same harmful policy become beneficial in the hands of the government? Since there is no rational answer to this question, I suggest that you question the economic knowledge, the purpose, and the motives of the champions of antitrust." (Ayn Rand, *Capitalism: The Unknown Ideal*)

3. "The naive acceptance of the game theory as a pattern for dealing with international conflicts may be not only due to the credulity of politicians and generals in the omnipotence of the new science; it may also stem from the American pattern of social and economic life, which fits into and reinforces the concepts of game theory. This pattern is well known: competition within the framework of law, i.e., accepted rules. If the small business goes under because the corporation is stronger and has escalated competition by de-escalating prices beyond the resistance power of the small firm, this surely should apply to the conflict between U.S.A., Inc., and Uncle Ho's grocery store. The trouble is that Uncle Ho does not abide by the rules. Possibly, he may be thinking in altogether different concepts, though having been to the West, he may express them in 'models' as well. His model, one would guess, is the rice paddy, or swamp: the heavier your boots, the deeper you sink." (Mordecai Roshwald, "The Cybernetics of Blunder," in *The Nation*, March 13, 1967)

4. "Because the prevailing intellectual model for coming to terms with our world is no longer tenable, we are the victims of forces we cannot control. The point can perhaps be illustrated by an analogy. Boyle's Law of Gases is based on their molecular nature, and affirms (in part) that any gas will fill uniformly whatever space may be available to it, exerting uniform pressure in every direction. An increase in temperature will cause this pressure to rise in a uniform manner in every direction. The situation is stable and vectorless. The assumption, of course, is that the size and

mass of the individual molecules is so small that for all practical purposes the gas may be considered a continuum. Now, the political model of the eighteenth-century liberalism may be seen to apply to humanity in the same way Boyle's Law applies to a gas. Humanity is seen as an aggregation of individual molecules whose aggressive pressures, expressed as discrete individual forces, are so small and diffuse as to effectively cancel one another out. The whole is in a stable state. But the moment large-scale organization and mass media emerge, something undreamed of in the eighteenth century happens: the body politic loses its molecular structure. As vectors are introduced and as connections are made, the old model ceases to be applicable. The bombardment of the larger units against one another and the container's walls produces shocks and patterns with which the old model fails to cope." (Henry S. Kariel, "Private Acts and Public Goals: The Ideological Vacuum," in *The Nation,* April 18, 1966)

5. "We may observe a very great similitude between this earth which we inhabit and the other planets, Saturn, Jupiter, Mars, Venus, and Mercury. They all revolve around the sun, as the earth does. . . . They borrow all their light from the sun, as the earth does. Several of them are known to revolve round their axis like the earth, and, by that means, must have a like succession of day and night. Some of them have moons that serve to give them light in the absence of the sun, as our moon does to us. They are all, in their motions, subject to the same law of gravitation as the earth is. From all this similitude, it is not unreasonable to think that those planets may, like our earth, be the habitation of various orders of living creatures. There is some probability in this conclusion from analogy." (Thomas Reid, *Essays on the Intellectual Powers of Man*)

6. "Much of the argument against comprehensive schools proceeds by analogy. The critics point to the low standards characteristic of many American high schools. These low standards are not in dispute. But there are many possible explanations besides the comprehensive character of these schools: for example, the anti-highbrow and anti-academic

('anti-egghead') tradition of American life, the acute shortage of teachers (especially male teachers), the low quality of many of the teachers (amounting sometimes almost to illiteracy), the insistence on automatic 'social promotion' by age-groups and the lack of grading by ability, an excessive attachment to Deweyism and 'life-adjustment' education at the expense of more basic academic disciplines, the overwhelming preference for vocational courses, and so on. All or any of these influences, none of which are or need be reproduced in English comprehensive schools, may be responsible for the lower standards." (C. A. R. Crosland, *The Future of Socialism*)

7. "I am the father of two daughters. When I hear this argument that we can't protect freedom in Europe, in Asia, or in our own hemisphere and still meet our domestic problems, I think it is a phony argument. It is just like saying that I can't take care of Luci because I have Lynda Bird. We have to take care of both of them and we have to meet them head on." (Lyndon Johnson, *The New York Times*, February 3, 1968)

8. If the thirteen American colonies were able to unite, there is no reason that the countries of Europe can not unite today.

9. "One tradition, going back to the classical liberalism of the eighteenth century and embodied in the economic theory of Adam Smith, holds that man is a self-sufficient and egoistic being whose actions are based on a calculus of personal interest. For reasons of efficiency, he comes together with others of his kind to form a social compact and live as a community. He remains faithful to the compact because he foresightedly recognizes that he benefits through the arrangement, gaining the profits of division of labor and related economies of cooperation. He is engaged, to use game theoretic terminology, in a lifelong bargaining game of partial cooperation.

"But however well this portrait may have corresponded to the shopkeeper of Adam Smith's day, as a universal picture of man it is woefully inadequate. In reality, as any sociologist or anthropologist or psychologist knows, man is first and last a social being. His mores, language, habits, expectations, even the innermost structure of his personality, are shaped by his culture. He sets goals, and fulfills himself most successfully, only in a social context. Men do not form political communities merely because, by some accident of nature, they lack the abilities to fulfill their private goals individually. They do so because, as Aristotle long ago asserted, their highest potentialities are *political* in nature. Men only realize themselves fully through participation in the political life of the community. Such participation, in a state formed on democratic principles, aims at the achievement of *social* values. Hence, Game Theory, by sharpening and reinforcing the image of man as a maximizer of egoistic value, badly distorts the nature of our society." (Robert Paul Wolff, *The Rhetoric of Deterrence*, an unpublished manuscript)

10. The last seven United States Presidents to have been elected in even-numbered years in multiples of twenty have died in office: Harrison, 1840; Lincoln, 1860; Garfield 1880; McKinley, 1900; Harding, 1920; Roosevelt, 1940; Kennedy, 1960. Therefore, the U.S. president elected in 1980 will die in office.

11. "The Christian says, 'Creatures are not born with desires unless satisfaction for those desires exists. A baby feels hunger: well, there is such a thing as food. A duckling wants to swim: well, there is such a thing as water. Men feel sexual desire: well, there is such a thing as sex. If I find in myself a desire which no experience in this world can satisfy, the most probable explanation is that I was made for another world. If none of my earthly pleasures satisfy it, that does not prove that the universe is a fraud.'"
(C. S. Lewis, *Mere Christianity*)

12. A reporter who pressed Robert Welch, leader of the John Birch Society, to name the Communist conspirators in Washington, reported the following answer:
"Suppose I'm walking on a golf course with the president of the club and we see divots all along the way. I say to him 'You've got some members who don't care about the course.' He asks me to name them. I tell him 'I can't name

them, but they must be here.' "   (James Wechsler, the New York *Post*, October 11, 1965)

13. "Theology teaches that the sun has been created in order to illuminate the earth. But one moves the torch in order to illuminate the house, and not the house in order to be illuminated by the torch. Hence it is the sun which revolves around the earth, and not the earth which revolves around the sun." (Besian Array, doctor of the Sorbonne, writing in 1671)

Confirmation

Propositions are often classified as facts or hypotheses. If the evidence for a proposition is deemed sufficiently strong that there is no practical need for further evidence, it is called a *fact*. If the evidence is strong enough to warrant further investigation but not sufficiently strong to warrant more than tentative acceptance, it is called an *hypothesis*.[1] This distinction between fact and hypothesis is not always clear-cut, however. What one inquirer considers a fact another may consider an hypothesis, and what passes as a fact in one context of inquiry may rank as an hypothesis in another. Even a single researcher in a single context of inquiry may be unsure about the proper classification of a given proposition. Moreover, every non-tautologous proposition is hypothetical to some degree, since it is always logically conceivable that circumstances arise in which its truth will be questioned and further evidence sought. A 'fact,' therefore, may be alternatively defined as a well-confirmed hypothesis.

Despite this relativity and vagueness, the distinction between

[1] The term 'fact' is ambiguous. As used in this chapter, it refers to a proposition. Often, however, it is also used to refer to an actual, rather than imaginary, event or state of affairs. Even when used of propositions it is ambiguous. In addition to the meaning given above, 'fact' sometimes refers, as in earlier chapters in this text, to a true material or definitional proposition (as opposed to a tautologous proposition). At other times, it refers to propositions affirming that something does or does not exist (as opposed to value judgments, or assertions relating to what ought or ought not to exist).

facts and hypotheses is a useful one. Some propositions are obviously better confirmed than others, and it is highly desirable to have some brief and simple way of indicating this kind of relationship between propositions. The distinction is particularly useful in discussing confirmation, since only propositions for which the available evidence is considered inadequate (that is, hypotheses) need to be confirmed and only better confirmed propositions (that is, facts) may be used to confirm them.

Depending upon their nature, hypotheses may be confirmed in one or more of the following ways. (1) Sometimes hypotheses are confirmed by direct observation. For example, 'There is a desk in the room,' 'The cupboard is bare,' and 'All the apples in this barrel are green' can be so confirmed. Although the concept of direct observation is not easy to analyze, confirmation by this method is for most practical purposes unproblematic, and the method is listed here simply for the sake of completeness. (2) If an hypothesis is a law of nature it is often confirmed either by an argument from a fair sample or by an argument from a statistical correlation in the manner discussed in the last chapter. (3) Sometimes hypotheses are confirmed by what we shall call *arguments by subsumption*. The premises in an argument of this kind cite one or more well-confirmed non-approximate laws of nature and one or more other facts intended to show that the hypothesis is a special case of the law or laws cited. If you were uncertain whether a particular piece of wire could conduct electricity, your doubts might be banished by the argument below:

1. All copper conducts electricity.
2. This piece of wire is copper.

   This piece of wire conducts electricity.

(4) The fourth method of confirmation seeks to show that an hypothesis is worthy of belief because it has explanatory power. Arguments based on this method are called *hypothetical confirmatory arguments*. Suppose that on the basis of an unreliable report you entertain hypothetically the proposition 'John is ill' (John being a fellow student). To confirm this proposition you might seek to determine whether John is attending classes. If he is not, the hypothesis has been confirmed to some extent. In effect, you have argued

1. If John were ill, he would be absent from classes.
2. John is absent from classes.

   John is ill.

Hypothetical confirmatory arguments are based on the principle that any fact explained by an hypothesis constitutes partial evidence for that hypothesis. (5) Finally, one may try to show that of two or more rival hypotheses all but one is unacceptable. Arguments based on this method are called *arguments by elimination*. For example,

1. Either John is absent from classes because he is ill or he is absent because his classes bore him.
2. John is not absent because his classes bore him.

   John is absent because he is ill.

In this chapter each of the last three methods of confirmation will be discussed in turn.

I • ARGUMENTS BY SUBSUMPTION

The conclusion, or hypothesis confirmed, in an argument by subsumption may be either a singular proposition or a law of nature. Thus,

1. All copper conducts electricity.
2. This piece of wire is copper.

   This piece of wire conducts electricity.

is a confirmation of the singular proposition 'This piece of wire conducts electricity.' The argument

1. All animals are mortal.
2. All men are animals.

   All men are mortal.

is a confirmation of the law of nature 'All men are mortal.'

294 PART TWO: ARGUMENT

The conclusion of an argument by subsumption may also be either an observational hypothesis, as in the above examples, or a theoretical hypothesis. If, for example, one accepted as fact the proposition 'Every instance of order is the creation of an intelligent being' one might then argue to a theoretical conclusion, as follows:

1. Every instance of order is the creation of an intelligent being.
2. The universe is an instance of order.

The universe is the creation of an intelligent being.

Finally, the laws of nature under which the conclusion is subsumed may be either observational or theoretical. For example, the law of nature 'All copper conducts electricity,' used in the argument above to support the hypothesis 'This piece of wire conducts electricity,' is an observational law. But if a student in a science course were asked to confirm 'All copper conducts electricity' in an argument by subsumption, the relevant laws of nature would have to be highly theoretical laws of the kind commonly encountered in physics and chemistry (among others, laws relating to the crystal structure of metals).

Some arguments by subsumption are much more complicated than the above examples. Many, in fact, can not be precisely stated except in highly technical language and require a fairly large number of premises. For example, it is possible to construct an argument by subsumption whose major premise is Newton's law of gravity and whose conclusion is Kepler's laws of planetary motion. It is also possible to construct an argument by subsumption whose major premise is again Newton's law of gravity and whose conclusion is Galileo's law of falling bodies. In these cases it is necessary to introduce complex mathematical formulas and a large number of auxiliary premises (including the laws of motion) linking the hypothesis to the premised law. The essential logical features, however, are the same as in the simpler examples cited. In each case we assert that the individual or class cited by the subject of the conclusion is a member or subclass of a larger class and that what is universally true of the premised class is true of its individual members or subclasses. Since all physical bodies are subject to the law of gravity, so are the planets and so are falling bodies near the surface of the earth. Kepler's laws of planetary motion and Galileo's law of falling bodies are essentially instances of the law of gravity which take account of special circumstances relating to the subclasses with which each law deals.

Some philosophers have maintained that arguments by subsumption are strictly circular. In order to establish the truth of the assertions regarding the premised classes it is necessary to establish the truth of the assertion about the members or subclasses cited in the conclusion. If we did not know that the conclusion were true, we could not know that the premised laws were true. Consequently, arguments by subsumption, unlike arguments from a fair sample, yield no new knowledge. If, for example, we did not know that all men are mortal, we could not know that all animals are mortal; similarly, if we did not know that Kepler's and Galileo's laws were true, we could not know that Newton's law of gravity is true. On this view, the proposition 'All animals are mortal' is merely a shorter way of saying 'Ants are mortal,' 'Storks are mortal,' 'Bears are mortal,' 'Men are mortal,' and so on. Similarly, Newton's law of gravity is merely a telescoped expression for all the more specific laws—such as Kepler's and Galileo's discoveries—regarding the movements of physical bodies.

Supporters of this view point out that man's knowledge of his own mortality preceded his knowledge of animal mortality and that historically Kepler's and Galileo's discoveries preceded Newton's discovery. They also point out that we could not know beyond all doubt that all animals are mortal unless we knew beyond all doubt that all men are mortal and that we could not know beyond all doubt that Newton's law of gravity is true unless we knew beyond all doubt that Kepler's and Galileo's laws are true. Both of these observations are correct, but neither supports the conclusion. The historical order of their discovery has nothing to do with the logical relationships between propositions. And since it is generally agreed that no law of nature can be known to be true beyond any possible doubt, the second observation is beside the point.

In deciding whether an argument by subsumption is circular,

the key question is whether evidence for the truth of the premised
laws can be presented even though we have no evidence or less
evidence for the truth of the conclusion. Consider again the proposition 'All animals are mortal.' Obviously we may argue for
this law of nature directly by an argument from a fair sample.
And if we can argue from a fair sample of animals to the conclusion that all animals are mortal without including in our
sample the subclass of men, the argument by subsumption from
'All animals are mortal' to 'All men are mortal' need not be circular, since we do not need probable evidence of the truth of the
second law in order to have probable evidence of the truth
of the first. Need we then include the subclass of men in a
fair sample of animals relative to the conclusion 'All animals
are mortal'? The answer is that we need not. The omission of
men from the sample of animals used to support a conclusion of
mortality would not substantially affect the fairness of the sample,
since man is not a significant subclass of animals relative to the
asserted conclusion. This is not only because we have no reason
to believe that the properties defining the subclass of men are
relevant but also because we have good reason to believe that
they are irrelevant. Everything we know suggests that the properties of animals related to their mortality are not those properties
defining man as a subclass of animals (i.e., man's specific differences) but rather properties all animals share with one another. If, therefore, we insisted that the subclass of men be included in a representative sample of animals, we would be in
much the same position as someone who insisted that we included subclasses of swans defined by brain size in a sample
used to test 'All swans are white.' Of course, this judgment of
relevance could be mistaken and a random sample that included
instances from the subclass of men would somewhat strengthen
an argument for the mortality of animals. But the subclass of man
represents such a small proportion of the class of animals that
even a very large random sample of animals would be statistically
unlikely to include instances from the subclass of man.

Moreover, even if man were a significant subclass of animals
and even if the class of men were a much larger segment of the
class of animals than it is, a fair sample used to establish the
mortality of animals would not necessarily have to include men.
Many arguments from a fair sample have passed muster despite

such defects. Soundness, it must be remembered, is a matter of degree.

Finally, it should be pointed out that if an argument from a fair sample supporting the major premise of an argument by subsumption has even the slightest evidential weight when the sample excludes the subclass referred to in the conclusion of that argument, the argument by subsumption is not circular. The most that can be conceded to the position under criticism is that an argument by subsumption would be circular in the highly unlikely case that the evidence for the major premise were exactly the same as the evidence for its conclusion. If, for instance, the only evidence we had for the mortality of animals was the mortality of men—if we argued exclusively from the mortality of men to the mortality of animals and then back to the mortality of men—we would indeed be arguing in a circle. In such a case our fair sample of animals would be identical with our sample of men. But merely to state this possibility is to indicate its improbability. This is simply not the way we ordinarily argue for the major premise of a typical argument by subsumption.

The upshot of this discussion is that arguments by subsumption may as genuinely advance our understanding of nature as arguments from a fair sample. Past experience with human beings strongly and directly supports the law of nature 'All men are mortal.' But the likelihood of that law of nature being true is even greater because all men are animals and all animals are mortal.

II • HYPOTHETICAL CONFIRMATORY ARGUMENTS

The pattern of hypothetical confirmatory arguments is

1. If H then E
2. E
   _____
   H

where 'H' stands for the hypothesis and 'E' for what is technically called the *explicandum*—that is, the fact or facts the hypothesis is alleged to explain. The example cited at the beginning of the chapter was

1. If John were ill, he would be absent from classes.
2. John is absent from classes.

John is ill.

Another example is

1. If apparently solid objects contained different degrees of empty space, sound would pass more readily through some than through others.
2. Sound does pass more readily through some apparently solid objects than through others.

Apparently solid objects contain different degrees of empty space.

Hypothetical confirmatory arguments are closely related to arguments from analogical models and have a similar implicit structure. The plausibility of arguments of both kinds rests upon the assumption that what is true of some members of a class may also be true of other members of that class. For example, the first sample argument assumes that since some absences from class are due to illness, John's absence may be due to illness; the second assumes that since physical objects observed to contain empty space permit sound to pass through them more or less readily because of the amount of empty space they are observed to contain, then physical objects not observed to contain empty space may permit sound to pass through them more or less readily for the same reason.

One difference between the two kinds of arguments is that hypothetical confirmatory arguments do not explicitly identify their analogical models. A second difference relates to function: arguments from analogical models are ordinarily used to suggest hypotheses, whereas hypothetical confirmatory arguments are designed to confirm them. Neither of these differences, however, is of great significance when it comes to evaluating arguments of these two kinds. The first is not important because hypothetical confirmatory arguments can not be properly assessed until the implicit analogical model is made explicit. The second is not important because any fact explained by an hypothesis, including any fact that may have led us to formulate the hypothesis in the first place, gives some evidence for the hypothesis and therefore partially confirms it.

Consequently, the criteria for evaluating hypothetical confirmatory arguments are essentially the same as those for evaluating arguments from analogical models.

(1) How many facts can the hypothesis be shown to explain? The hypothesis that apparently solid objects contain different proportions of empty space explains not only the fact that sound passes more readily through some than through others but also that apparently solid objects of equal volume often have different weights. Clearly a hypothetical confirmatory argument whose explicandum cited both of these facts would be stronger than a hypothetical confirmatory argument that cited only one. Consider also the argument

1. If John were ill, then he would be absent, would have told his instructors he was ill, would have consulted a doctor, and would look unwell.
2. John is absent, has told his instructors he is ill, has consulted a doctor, and does look unwell.

John is ill.

This argument, whose explicandum cites four facts, is obviously much stronger than our earlier hypothetical confirmatory argument with the same conclusion whose explicandum cited only the fact of absence from classes.

It should be noted that every time the explicandum of a hypothetical confirmatory argument is augmented by an additional fact, the implicit logical structure of the argument is augmented by an additional analogical model. For example, the analogical model tacitly invoked to explain that sound passes more readily through some apparently solid objects than others is that of trellises and like objects which are observed to permit sound to pass in proportion to the amount of empty space they contain, whereas the analogical model tacitly invoked to explain that apparently solid objects of equal volume have different weights is that of sponges and like objects whose weight is correlated with their porousness, or the amount of empty space they contain. Similarly, the analogical model invoked to explain John's absence from class is the fact that many absences from class are due to illness, whereas the analogical model invoked to explain John's having told his instructors he was ill is the fact that many students who are ill do advise their instructors of this fact.

(2) In what percentage of cases are the premised and the inferred analogy associated in the analogical model? Contrast, for example, the following arguments:

1. If John were ill, then he would be absent from classes.
2. John is absent from classes.

John is ill.

1. If John were attending a funeral, then he would be absent from classes.
2. John is absent from classes.

John is attending a funeral.

In both cases the premised analogy is absence from classes; but the first argument is stronger than the second because the percentage of cases in which absence from classes and the inferred analogy, illness, are associated is far greater than the percentage of cases in which absence from classes and the inferred analogy, attendance at funerals, are associated.

(3) Can rival hypotheses for the explicandum be eliminated? Absence from class, for example, can be explained by a large number of hypotheses other than illness: attendance at a funeral, lack of interest, celebration of a religious holiday, etc. But if we can show that these other hypotheses are inadequate in a particular case, we strengthen the evidence for the favored hypothesis.

(4) How compatible is the hypothesis with relevant facts? If, for example, we hypothesize illness as an explanation of John's

absence from class and then discover that John looks perfectly fit, our hypothesis will be weakened. More will be said about the last two criteria in the next section.

III • ARGUMENTS BY ELIMINATION

Arguments designed to confirm an hypothesis by eliminating rival hypotheses are called *arguments by elimination.* Here are a few examples:

1. Either Oswald acted alone in assassinating President Kennedy or Oswald conspired with others.
2. Oswald did not act alone.

   Oswald conspired with others.

1. Either yellow fever is communicated by direct contact between yellow fever victims or it is communicated by mosquito bites.
2. Yellow fever is not communicated by direct contact.

   Yellow fever is communicated by mosquito bites.

1. Either John is absent because he is ill or he is absent because he is bored.
2. John is not absent because he is bored.

   John is absent because he is ill.

For the sake of simplicity the sample arguments above list only two rival hypotheses, although there are, of course, many other possibilities in each case. Note that for each increase in the number of rival hypotheses listed in the disjunctive premise there will be a corresponding increase in the number of negative premises, since each rival explanation will have to be eliminated separately.

The soundness of an argument by elimination depends upon two factors: (1) the evidence adduced to support the negative premises and (2) the completeness with which the rival hypotheses, or possible explanations of the explicandum, have been catalogued in the disjunctive premise.

The question raised by 1 is essentially: How can hypotheses be disconfirmed? There are four principal methods. First, an hypothesis can be disconfirmed by direct observation. If, for example, someone hypothesizes that a certain island is uninhabited, we can disconfirm this hypothesis by visiting the island and observing that it does in fact have inhabitants. This method of disconfirmation, like the corresponding method of direct confirmation, is of relatively little logical interest and is listed only for the sake of completeness.

Second, hypotheses may be disconfirmed by citing evidence based on an appropriate fair sample or statistical correlation. For example, it was demonstrated that yellow fever is not communicated through direct human contact by showing that when a sample of healthy persons were exposed to yellow fever victims but not to mosquitoes none of the healthy persons contracted yellow fever.

Third, hypotheses may be disconfirmed by *negative arguments by subsumption*. For example,

1. No one who listens attentively in class and argues with his instructors is bored by his classes.
2. John does listen attentively and does argue with his instructors.

John is not bored.

Finally, an hypothesis may be disconfirmed by a *hypothetical disconfirmatory argument*. The pattern of such arguments is

1. If H then S
2. −S

−H

where 'H' stands for the hypothesis and 'S' for a proposition describing some state of affairs whose nonoccurrence casts doubt on the truth of the hypothesis. An example would be

1. If Oswald assassinated Kennedy, then Oswald would have shown signs of hostility to Kennedy.
2. Oswald did not show signs of hostility to Kennedy.

Oswald did not assassinate Kennedy.

The plausibility of hypothetical disconfirmatory arguments, like that of hypothetical confirmatory arguments, rests on a tacit appeal to analogical models. In the sample argument the analogical model consists of assassins known to have shown hostility to their victims. The crucial criteria for evaluating hypothetical disconfirmatory arguments are: (1) the number of states of affairs cited whose nonoccurrence would cast doubt on the hypothesis and (2) the percentage of cases in which the premised analogy and the inferred analogy have occurred together. Thus, according to 1, the following argument is stronger than the sample argument above:

1. If Oswald assassinated Kennedy, then Oswald would have shown signs of hostility to Kennedy and would have arranged to flee Dallas immediately after the assassination.
2. Oswald did not show signs of hostility to Kennedy and did not arrange to flee Dallas immediately after the assassination.

Oswald did not assassinate Kennedy.

According to 2, if it could be shown that ninety-five percent of known political assassins have shown signs of hostility to their victims, the sample argument would be stronger than if we could establish that only fifty percent of known political assassins had behaved this way.

The second basic problem posed by arguments by elimination—how to determine the adequacy of the catalogue of possible explanations in the disjunctive premise—is one of the most vexing in the logic of inquiry. In the first place, no one has yet succeeded in framing a precise definition of 'possible explanation.' In the second place, no one has yet succeeded in specifying general procedures for testing the completeness of any list of possible explanations.

Speaking loosely, however, we may say that a 'possible explanation' is one that does not seem unreasonable to an intelligent person who is well informed about the phenomenon to be explained. Alternatively, we may say that a 'possible explanation' is any hypothesis that might reasonably appear in an inconclusive argument whose conclusion asserts the reality of the phenomenon to be explained. The relevant argument will often be a weak hypothetical confirmatory argument or an argument from an analogical model. For example, since some absences from classes are due to illness, possibly John's absence is due to illness. Since some infectious diseases are known to be caused by insect bites, perhaps yellow fever is also caused by insect bites. Often, too, especially when the possible explanation is a law of nature, the relevant argument will be based on a statistical correlation. Since yellow fever is known to be unusually common in tropical countries infested with mosquitoes, yellow fever may well be caused by mosquitoes.

As to the completeness of any catalogue of possible explanations, we can say only that in general it will depend on three factors: (1) how much we know about the phenomenon to be explained, (2) how much we know about related phenomena, and (3) our insight into the connections between the phenomenon to be explained and related phenomena. Thus, if we know that yellow fever is an infectious disease and that most yellow fever victims inhabit areas heavily infested with mosquitoes, if we know that some infectious diseases are caused by mosquitoes, and if we are able to make a mental connection between these items of information, our catalogue of possible explanations of yellow fever will be more complete than would otherwise be the case. There is no logical guarantee, however, that any catalogue is ever complete.

In conclusion it should be noted that the classification of arguments in this and the preceding chapter is based on their explicit patterns. Often, however, the explicit pattern of a given argument is very different from its implicit pattern. As we have already seen, for example, arguments from analogical models and hypothetical confirmatory arguments have essentially the same implicit pattern.

Often, too, the explicit pattern of an argument is misleading. For example, many arguments in ordinary discourse whose explicit pattern is hypothetical confirmatory are best analyzed as arguments by subsumption. The person who believes that every instance of order is an instance of intelligent creation might well argue

> 1. If the universe has an intelligent creator, the universe would exhibit order.
> 2. The universe does exhibit order.
>
> ---
>
> The universe has an intelligent creator.

But since he would also subscribe to the stronger argument by subsumption

> 1. Every instance of order is an instance of intelligent creation.
> 2. The universe is an instance of order.
>
> ---
>
> The universe has an intelligent creator.

the latter argument much better represents his true intent.

Finally, an argument of a given explicit pattern often implicitly combines several different kinds of argument. For example, every argument from a representative sample is implicitly based on an argument by elimination. When we insist that a representative sample of swans selected to establish 'All swans are white' include subclasses defined by geographical location, we do so because we wish to eliminate the possibility that the color of swans is due to a specific geographical location. In effect, we are proceeding from the following assumption:

> Either the whiteness of swans is a consequence of their specific geographical location or it is a consequence of some property present in all swans.

And our hope is to eliminate the possibility that whiteness is due to a specific geographical location by showing that the color of swans does not vary with geographical location.

EXERCISES FOR CHAPTER FOURTEEN

Classify the following arguments. Evaluate them according to the criteria outlined in the text.

1. If human beings had an innate proclivity for war, it would be unnecessary to spend so much time training them in war-like virtues. The mere fact that societies do find this necessary proves that no such innate proclivity exists.

2. "A person can have all the energy in the world, and sleep very little—yet once in twenty-four hours he must sleep. The most elemental explanation for this inevitable rest is given by mothers to tired children: 'You must sleep to restore energy.' Doctors pronounce the same message for patients in slightly more sophisticated language. For as long as scientists have worried about the purpose of sleep, the same theory has recurred. Sleep must be restorative, and vast expenditures of mental and muscular energy finally, so to speak, poison us into slumber so that the body may rebuild its supplies. There is one flaw in this plausible idea that bothers everyone. Why does an Olympic runner sleep no more than a lazy sales clerk, and why doesn't he fall asleep after his four-mile sprint, instead of waiting for nightfall?" (Gay Gaer Luce and Julius Segal, *Sleep*)

3. "The uncanny time sense of the honeybee may in a general way indicate how people may set mental clocks to wake themselves, to check on dinner in the oven, or make a phone call. The great Austrian naturalist Karl von Frisch found he could train bees to come for food at a particular hour each day. Did they tell the time by the light of the sun, geography, the earth's turning? Von Frisch designed a simple test. Paris-trained bees were flown to New York. If they relied on outside cues for time, they would have been fooled, but they came to the assigned feeding place on Paris time, exactly 24 hours later. Several hives of

trained bees have since been flown between New York, California, and Paris with the same results—showing that they contain a day clock within them. Left in a new place, however, they will slowly adjust to the local time, as will man." (Gay Gaer Luce and Julius Segal, *Sleep*)

4. "A. Lacassagne, in his important book, *Peine de Mort*, shows that homicides are rarest in those countries where capital punishment is most rigorously enforced. I do not want to press this, however, as the relation of cause and effect is proverbially difficult to trace in social affairs. . . . I prefer to rely on syllogistic reasoning. . . . The fact that capital punishment is only invoked to meet the highest flights of public resentment is unequivocal proof that popular sentiment regards it as the most terrible of all punishments. Whether popular sentiment on this matter is well grounded or not is another question. I shall shortly endeavor to show that it is not; but in the meantime I am only concerned to note the attitude of popular sentiment, and to draw the obvious corollary that the punishment which popular sentiment regards as the most terrible is necessarily that which the public are most desirous to avoid, and therefore that which has the greatest deterrent effect." (Hugh S. R. Elliot, quoted in Raziel Abelson, *Ethics and Metaethics*)

5. "How powerful and mysterious is the pull of the home-place on animal behaviour has been the subject of many a human meditation. . . .

"Eugène Marais, an untrained South African naturalist, once performed a homely experiment that by careful laboratory extension might give us a quantitative measurement for the power of animal nostalgia. Marais observed two columns of red ants moving along an African roadside. They proceeded in opposite directions, as ants do, one towards the nest and one away from it. The column leaving the nest was unburdened; each ant of the returning column carried from a neighbouring field a seed very nearly as large as itself.

"To begin his experiment, Marais scratched a narrow ditch across the path of the two columns and filled the little ditch with water. On either side of the ditch there immediately gathered a milling mass of frustrated ants, confused as only ants can be when they encounter an unexpected obstacle. Marais then offered them a way. He placed a straw across the ditch for a bridge. And then he sat back to observe the startling climax.

"The unencumbered ants proceeding *away from the nest* tried the bridge, hesitated, explored its uncertainties again, backed away, and in the end rejected its hazards. But the column of ants each handicapped by the burden of a gigantic seed hesitated not at all and proceeded nimbly and with confidence across the swaying straw. They were going home." (Robert Ardrey, *African Genesis*)

6. A paint salesman wished to convince a farmer that his product was superior to the products of his competitors. To prove this he painted one side of the farmer's barn with his own product, two other sides with competing products, and left one side unpainted. To insure that the test was fair, he used flat red paint on all three sides. A year later he and the farmer took a look at the three sides of the barn. On one side, painted with a competitor's product, the paint had blistered and cracked. On another side, also painted with a competitor's product, the paint had faded and in some places worn off. But the side painted with his product showed no defects. The salesman expected to contract, but the farmer was unconvinced and refused to order.

7. "First, we may consider what sort of evidence may reasonably be looked for as an indication that the religious sentiment is rooted in a particular instinct. There are several different kinds of evidence which are relevant. In the first place, if an instinct is not uniformly in action during the whole of the lifetime of the individual but has a period of development and decay, we should expect to find that, so far as it is based on that instinct, the religious sentiment shows similar variations. Secondly, so far as it is based on an instinct, we should expect to find the religious sentiment expressing itself in language characteristic of the sentiment normally developed from that instinct. Thirdly, we should

expect to find religious practice particularly concerned with
the suppression of the normal behaviour characteristic of
that instinct. Fourthly, we might expect to find a tendency
for religion of a highly emotional but ill-controlled type to
develop into an uncontrolled normal exercise of the instinct.

"We find, in fact, that all of these tests yield positive results when applied to religion and the sex-instinct. Certain
types of religious excitement and certain phases of religious
development show a correspondence with the times of the
crises of the sex-life. The expressions of religious emotion
(particularly those of the mystics) are very generally in the
language of human love. Religion has, on the whole, tended
to attach a great value to chastity. Finally, there is a
tendency for religious excitement of a certain kind to pass
into sexual license. At the same time, a closer examination
of these facts does not lead us to suspect that religion is
merely a development from the sex-instinct. On the contrary, the indications are clearly in the opposite direction."
(Robert H. Thouless, *An Introduction to the Psychology of
Religion*)

8. "Now the Nile, when it overflows, floods not only the Delta,
but also the tracts of country on both sides of the stream
which are thought to belong to Libya and Arabia, in some
places reaching to the extent of two days journey from its
banks, in some even exceeding that distance, but in others
falling short of it.

"Concerning the nature of the river, I was not able to
gain any information either from the priests or from
others. I was particularly anxious to learn from them why
the Nile, at the commencement of the summer solstice, begins to rise, and continues to increase for a hundred days—
and why, as soon as that number is past, it forthwith retires
and contracts its stream, continuing low during the whole
of the winter until the summer solstice comes round again.
On none of these points could I obtain any explanation
from the inhabitants, though I made every inquiry, wishing
to know what was commonly reported—they could neither
tell me what special virtue the Nile has which makes it

so opposite in its nature to all other streams, nor why, unlike every other river, it gives forth no breezes from its surface.

"Some of the Greeks, however, wishing to get a reputation for cleverness, have offered explanations of the phenomena of the river, for which they have accounted in three different ways. Two of these I do not think it worth while to speak of, further than simply to mention what they are. One pretends that the Etesian winds cause the rise of the river by preventing the Nile-water from running off into the sea. But in the first place it has often happened, when the Etesian winds did not blow, that the Nile has risen according to its usual wont; and further, if the Etesian winds produced the effect, the other rivers which flow in a direction opposite to those winds ought to present the same phenomena as the Nile, and the more so as they are all smaller streams, and have a weaker current. But these rivers, of which there are many both in Syria and Libya, are entirely unlike the Nile in this respect.

"The second opinion is even more unscientific than the one just mentioned, and also, if I may so say, more marvellous. It is that the Nile acts so strangely, because it flows from the ocean, and that the ocean flows all round the earth.

"The third explanation, which is very much more plausible than either of the others, is positively the furthest from the truth; for there is really nothing in what it says, any more than in the other theories. It is, that the inundation of the Nile is caused by the melting of snows. Now, as the Nile flows out of Libya, through Ethiopia, into Egypt, how is it possible that it can be formed of melted snow, running, as it does, from the hottest regions of the world into cooler countries? Many are the proofs whereby any one capable of reasoning on the subject may be convinced that it is most unlikely this should be the case. The first and strongest argument is furnished by the winds, which always blow hot from these regions. The second is, that rain and frost are unknown there. Now, whenever snow falls, it must of necessity rain within five days; so that, if there were snow, there must be rain also in those parts. Thirdly, it is certain that the natives of the country are black with the heat, that the kites and the swallows remain there the whole year, and that the cranes, when they fly from the rigours of a Scythian winter, flock thither to pass the cold season. If then, in the country whence the Nile has its source, or in that through which it flows, there fell ever so little snow, it is absolutely impossible that any of these circumstances could take place.

"As for the writer who attributes the phenomenon to the ocean, his account is involved in such obscurity, that it is impossible to disprove it by argument. For my part I know of no river called Ocean, and I think that Homer, or one of the earlier poets, invented the name, and introduced it into his poetry.

"Perhaps, after censuring all the opinions that have been put forward on this obscure subject, one ought to propose some theory of one's own. I will therefore proceed to explain what I think to be the reason of the Nile's swelling in the summer time. During the winter, the sun is driven out of his usual course by the storms, and removes to the upper parts of Libya. This is the whole secret in the fewest possible words; for it stands to reason that the country to which the Sun-god approaches the nearest, and which he passes most directly over, will be scantest of water, and that there the streams which feed the rivers will shrink the most.

"To explain, however, more at length, the case is this. The sun, in his passage across the upper parts of Libya, affects them in the following way. As the air in those regions is constantly clear, and the country warm through the absence of cold winds, the sun in his passage across them acts upon them exactly as he is wont to act elsewhere in summer, when his path is in the middle of heaven —that is, he attracts the water. After attracting it, he again repels it into the upper regions, where the winds lay hold of it, scatter it, and reduce it to a vapour, whence it naturally enough comes to pass that the winds which blow from this quarter—the south and south-west—are all winds the most rainy. And my own opinion is that the sun does not get rid of all the water which he draws year by year from the Nile, but retains some about him. When the winter begins to soften, the sun goes back again to his old place in the middle of the heaven, and proceeds to attract water equally from all countries. Till then the other rivers run big, from the quantity of rain-water which they bring down from countries where so much moisture falls that all the land is cut into gullies; but in summer, when the showers fail, and the sun attracts their water, they become low. The Nile, on the contrary, not deriving any of its bulk from rains, and being in winter subject to the attraction of the sun, naturally runs at that season, unlike all other streams, with a less burthen of water than in the summer time. For in summer it is exposed to attraction equally with all other rivers, but in winter it suffers alone. The sun, therefore, I regard as the sole cause of the phenomenon." (Herodotus, *The Persian Wars*)

9. When the Copernican hypothesis was first proposed, it was rejected for a number of reasons, of which we shall mention two. First, if the earth revolved around the sun once a year, the position of the fixed stars relative to the earth would be different at different times of the year; but no such difference could be observed. Second, if the earth moved from East to West, as the hypothesis also maintained, an object projected vertically into the air from the earth's surface would fall to the west of the point from which it was projected; but this does not happen.

10. A psychiatrist had a patient who claimed he was dead. To persuade his patient of his mistake the psychiatrist got him to admit that dead men do not bleed and then pricked his finger. At this point the patient said, "Dead men do bleed, after all."

11. "Contrary to expectation, the peak seasons for suicide are not autumn and winter when nature is at its most depressing, but spring and early summer, when nature is at its best and life seems most worthwhile. . . . Various explanations for these seasonal fluctuations have been advanced, for example, that the increasing temperature in late spring

and early summer leads to greater excitability. . . . If this was so, the incidence of suicide ought to be higher in hot than in cool springs and summers. . . . No such correlation has been established. Durkheim believed that with the increasing length of the day social life became more intense and suicide more frequent in consequence. This explanation is not convincing because in some respects social contacts are closer in winter. . . . It has been suggested that it may be the manifestation of one of the rhythmical biological changes which play an important part in animal life although they are much less conspicuous in man. It has often been reported that depressive illness is more common in spring than in the rest of the year. This would partly account for the seasonal increase . . . but there must be other factors also." (Erwin Stengel, *Suicide and Attempted Suicide*)

12. A common explanation of suicide-attempts is that the person who attempts suicide is making an appeal for help to others. "One would at least expect suicidal attempts to be rare in a society indifferent or hostile to its individual members, if the appeal-effect plays as important a part as has been assumed here. No such society now exists. Even in prison, a suicidal attempt calls forth reactions similar to those observed in the community at large. However, not long ago there existed a society which was openly hostile to its members, *i.e.*, the German concentration camps. Several reports about the behaviour of the inmates have been published by medical observers who were themselves members of those communities. All of them noted the rarity of suicidal attempts. There was less agreement about the occurrence of suicide." (Erwin Stengel, *Suicide and Attempted Suicide*)

13. "Let me restate this argument in more formal terms. On the basis of detailed observation of the dreams of many patients, we arrive at the hypothesis that 'dreams are wish-fulfilments.' From this hypothesis we deduce that starving men should dream of food. If this can be shown to be so, our hypothesis is supported; if this can be shown not to be

so, our hypothesis is decisively disproved. Now Freud does not provide us with experimental evidence of any kind; he relies on anecdotal evidence of the most unreliable variety, second-hand, selective, and incomplete. Little value can be attributed to it. Fortunately we have more recent reports of adequately controlled, well-carried-out experiments into human starvation, experiments in which the participants lost almost a quarter of their body weight. Detailed records were made of their dreams, and comparisons with properly-fed individuals failed to show any tendency, however small, for the starving subjects to report more food-dreams than the control group." (H. J. Eysenck, *Uses and Abuses of Psychology*)

14. "Such data as are available, particularly from the study of identical and fraternal twins, seem to favour rather strongly the view that heredity plays a very conspicuous part indeed in the causation of neurotic disorders.

"This view of neuroticism as hereditarily determined may seem to run counter to our discussion of the recovery rate among neurotics, which appeared reasonably high both with and without psychotherapy. How, it may be asked, can there be any kind of recovery if neuroticism is caused by inherited factors? The answer is that one must carefully distinguish between neuroticism, *i.e.*, the inherited emotional instability which predisposes a person to form neurotic symptoms under stress, and ultimately to have a nervous breakdown; and *neurosis*, the result of the imposition of emotional stress on a nervous system predisposed to react through the neurotic mechanisms. Neurosis may appear in a person showing little emotional instability, through overwhelmingly strong environmental stress; it may fail to appear in a person strongly predisposed, because of lack of environmental stress." (H. J. Eysenck, *Uses and Abuses of Psychology*)

15. "While walking one night with Dr. Frink, we accidentally met a colleague, Dr. P., whom I had not seen for years, and of whose private life I knew nothing. We were naturally very pleased to meet again, and on my invitation, he ac-

companied us to a cafe, where we spent about two hours in pleasant conversation. To my question as to whether he was married, he gave a negative answer, and added, 'Why should a man like me marry?'

"On leaving the cafe, he suddenly turned to me and said, 'I should like to know what you would do in a case like this: I know a nurse who was named as co-respondent in a divorce case. The wife sued the husband for divorce and named her as co-respondent, and *he* got the divorce.' I interrupted him saying, 'You mean *she* got the divorce.' He immediately corrected himself, saying, 'Yes, she got the divorce,' and continued to tell how the excitement of the trial had affected this nurse to such an extent that she became nervous and took to drink. He wanted me to advise him how to treat her.

"As soon as I had corrected his mistake, I asked him to explain it, but, as is usually the case, he was surprised at my question. He wanted to know whether a person had no right to make mistakes in talking. I explained to him that there is a reason for every mistake, and that if he had not told me that he was unmarried, I should say that he was the hero of the divorce case in question, and that the mistake showed that he wished he had obtained the divorce instead of his wife, so as not to be obliged to pay alimony and to be permitted to marry again in New York State.

"He stoutly denied my interpretation, but his emotional agitation, followed by loud laughter, only strengthened my suspicions. To my appeal that he should tell the truth 'for science' sake,' he said, 'Unless you wish me to lie, you must believe that I was never married, and hence, your psychoanalytic interpretation is all wrong.' He, however, added that it was dangerous to be with a person who paid attention to such little things. Then he suddenly remembered that he had another appointment and left us.

"Both Dr. Frink and I were convinced that my interpretation of his *lapsus linguae* was correct, and I decided to corroborate or disprove it by further investigation. The next day, I found a neighbor and old friend of Dr. P., who confirmed my interpretation in every particular. The divorce was granted to Dr. P.'s wife a few weeks before, and a nurse was named as co-respondent. A few weeks later, I met Dr. P., and he told me that he was thoroughly convinced of the Freudian mechanisms." (A. A. Brill, *Psychoanalysis: Its Theories and Practical Applications*, pp. 225-26)

Explanation

The premises of confirmatory arguments, as we saw in the last chapter, are offered as evidence for the truth of the conclusion; and in every case the conclusion is taken to be an hypothesis. In explanatory arguments, on the other hand, the conclusion is taken to be a fact, and the premises are offered as an answer to the question: Why is the conclusion true?

Explanatory arguments are like confirmatory arguments by subsumption in that when completely expressed the premises of both consist of at least one law of nature and at least one proposition that subsumes the phenomenon to be explained under the law or laws cited. The chief difference is that the major premises of confirmatory arguments are by definition non-approximate, whereas the major premises of explanatory arguments may be approximate or non-approximate.

If the laws cited in an explanatory argument are non-approximate and the conclusion follows deductively, the explanation is said to be *complete*. If, for example, we observed that a piece of paper turned red when dipped in a certain solution, we might explain this phenomenon by the complete explanatory argument:

1. All instances in which litmus paper is dipped in an acid solution are instances in which the paper turns red.
2. This is an instance of a piece of litmus paper dipped in an acid solution.

This piece of paper turns red.

If, however, the laws cited in an explanatory argument are approximate laws based on statistical correlations or if the conclusion does not follow deductively, the explanation is said to be *incomplete*. For example,

1. Heavy smokers contract lung cancer.
2. John is a heavy smoker.

John contracted lung cancer.

is an incomplete explanation because premise 1 is only an approximate law. It is not smoking as such but some as yet unidentified element associated with smoking that explains why John contracted lung cancer. Similarly,

1. Every time John gets angry, he becomes violent.
2. John was angry.

John gave Joe a black eye.

is an incomplete explanation. In this case, however, the incompleteness is due to the fact that the premises are too general to permit us to deduce the conclusion. The premises permit us to deduce the occurrence of an act of violence but not the specific form of violence stated in the conclusion.

Often an explanation will be incomplete both because the law cited is approximate and because the conclusion as stated does not follow deductively. If, for example, one assumed as true the proposition 'Oswald assassinated Kennedy' and asked why, almost any modestly plausible answer would be incomplete for both reasons. The most common explanation is that Oswald was unbalanced, resented persons in positions of authority, and wished to demonstrate his own importance. This explanation obviously relies on an implicit law of nature: that persons with these traits are more prone to acts of violence than well-balanced persons who are at peace with the world and who are firmly convinced of their own worth. But this law is clearly only approximate. And even if the law were universal, it would still not explain why Oswald's violence took the form of political assassination or why his target should have been Kennedy rather than another political figure.

Because of the relativity of the distinction between facts and hypotheses, upon which the distinction between explanatory arguments and hypothetical confirmatory arguments rests, a given argument will often be confirmatory in some of its token occurrences and explanatory in others. Thus, if in a given context 'This piece of wire conducts electricity' is assumed to be true, the following argument by subsumption, cited in the last chapter as an example of a confirmatory argument, would be an instance of an explanatory argument:

1. All copper conducts electricity.
2. This piece of wire is copper.

This piece of wire conducts electricity.

Moreover, the logical relationship between premises and conclusion in an argument of either type is totally unaffected by its classification as explanatory or hypothetical confirmatory. This classification is based on the intent of the arguer rather than on the logical form of the argument.

The difference between explanation and confirmation is thus far from fundamental in the logic of inquiry, and some of the material in this chapter will duplicate the material of the last. In the last chapter, however, we emphasized the formal patterns of confirmatory arguments, whereas here we shall focus on stages in the process of inquiry.

I • CLARIFYING THE PURPOSE OF INQUIRY

Every explanatory inquiry begins with a question of the form 'Why is X the case?' and is successfully terminated only when this question has been given an appropriate answer. Sometimes questions of this form are perfectly straightforward and there is no problem about the kind of answer desired. Often, however, questions of this kind are susceptible to more than one interpretation. In such cases it is important that we be clear about the proper interpretation of the question. If an inquirer is not clear about this in his own mind, he may easily become distracted by

320 PART TWO: ARGUMENT

side issues; and if a group of inquirers have not agreed upon the meaning of the question, they may well find themselves disputing at cross purposes.

For example, the question 'Why did Oswald kill Kennedy?' may be a request for Oswald's motives. If so, an explanation of the kind cited in the last section would be appropriate. But the questioner may take it for granted that Oswald had the motives commonly attributed to him, in which case the question is probably a request for an explanation of these motives. If so, an appropriate answer might cite such circumstances as Oswald's having been reared in a broken home, having come from a lower-class background, having been taught to regard violence as a sign of masculinity, etc. On occasion, the question 'Why did Oswald kill Kennedy?' could even be a request for an explanation of the objective circumstances that made it possible for Oswald to kill Kennedy, whatever his motives may have been. In this case an appropriate explanation might center on such questions as a President's need to make himself available to the public, the adequacy or inadequacy of Secret Service protection, and the ready public availability of rifles and other deadly weapons. Of course, these three kinds of explanation are related. If Oswald had had a different background, he would probably have been a different kind of person; if he had been a different kind of person, he would probably not have wanted to kill Kennedy; and if the circumstances had been different, he would probably not have been able to kill Kennedy. Thus, the question 'Why did Oswald kill Kennedy?' could be a request for an answer to all three of the more specific questions: 'Why did Oswald want to kill Kennedy?' 'Why was Oswald the kind of person who wanted to kill Kennedy?' and 'What were the circumstances that made it possible for him to kill Kennedy?'

Consider, too, the question 'Why do human beings have lungs?' This question has two principal interpretations. On the one hand, it may be a request for an account of the evolutionary process by which men acquired lungs. On the other hand, it may be a request for an account of the function or purpose that the lungs serve. In the former case, the appropriate answer will be framed in terms of what are called *genetic laws* or *developmental laws*.

In the latter case, the appropriate answer will be in terms of what are called *functional laws* or *teleological laws*.

Consider, finally, the question 'Why did St. Thomas Aquinas believe in the existence of God?' If put to a sociologist, the answer might stress the fact that St. Thomas was born in a Christian culture and was indoctrinated to believe in God at an early age. If put to a psychologist, the answer might stress some alleged human need for a divine surrogate father. If put to a philosopher, the question would probably be answered by citing the five proofs of the existence of God to be found in St. Thomas' published work.

As the above examples illustrate, a question initiating an explanatory inquiry may be ambiguous in that it is susceptible to several different kinds of interpretations, or complex in that it must be broken down into several sub-questions. The problem of interpreting a particular question, however, may be of a different order. Often, what must be decided is the level of generality the inquiry demands. Although this distinction is not hard and fast, we may say that inquiry has two primary goals: (1) *practical understanding*—knowledge enabling us to avert or remedy undesirable states of affairs and to preserve or bring about desirable states of affairs—and (2) *comprehensive understanding*—knowledge of relatively general laws with extensive explanatory power under which a wide variety of phenomena and a great number of more specific laws can be subsumed. If the aim of inquiry is comprehensive understanding, an appropriate explanation will ordinarily be at a high level of generality. If the aim is practical, an appropriate explanation will ordinarily be at a much lower level of generality. If, for example, an electrician's apprentice asks why a particular piece of wire conducts electricity, his goal is probably the practical one of identifying electrical conductors. Consequently, an explanation of the kind cited on page 319 would be appropriate. But if the same question were asked in a physics or a chemistry class, we may assume that the goal is comprehensive understanding. Consequently, the appropriate explanation would cite properties of the wire shared by all electrical conductors, whether copper or not, and the relevant laws of nature would be of a corresponding level of generality.

Practical understanding and comprehensive understanding are not, of course, antithetical goals. On the contrary, they are often complementary. Although, therefore, the purpose of inquiry may and often does require a single explanation at some one determinate level of generality, it may and often does require both a general explanation and a more or less systematic and specific elaboration of this general explanation. For example, to the question 'Why has the rate of suicide greatly increased in the Western world during the last hundred and fifty years?' an appropriate general answer might be: because the social conditions of modern life have led to an increase in the percentage of persons experiencing acute distress, and because whenever there is an increase in the percentage of persons suffering acute distress there is an increase in suicide. This answer, however, might well have to be supplemented by citing specific forms of distress and the specific social institutions engendering them: increasing financial insecurity due to the competitiveness and cyclical fluctuations of modern economic institutions; increasing anxiety and confusion due to the corrosion of traditional morality; increasing frustration due to advertising and the spread of democratic ideals (expectations rising faster than the possibility of satisfying them); increasing loneliness or alienation due to (1) the breakdown of the family, (2) extensive urbanization and the anonymity of city life, and (3) widespread industrialization and the impersonality of corporate industrial organizations; and so on.

II • CATALOGUING POSSIBLE EXPLANATIONS

The second step in explanatory inquiry is to catalogue possible explanations. This step is of the utmost importance, for there is no greater source of error in explanatory reasoning than failure to consider all possible explanations. Sometimes this failure may be attributed to the poorly advanced stage of knowledge in the general area of inquiry and to the poverty of the human imagination. For example, in the seventeenth century Galileo set himself the task of explaining why water in an ordinary suction or lift pump could not be made to rise more than approximately thirty-four feet. Since hydraulics was a poorly developed science at this time, there were no available well-confirmed generalizations that explained this phenomenon. Galileo was therefore obliged to argue from analogical models, extending generalizations for other better understood phenomena to the behavior of columns of water. He reasoned as follows: a column of water is analogous to a suspended coil of wire, and since a suspended coil of wire will break of its own weight if it is extended a sufficient distance, a column of water extended thirty-four feet also breaks of its own weight. As we know today, this explanation is incorrect. Water in a suction pump fails to rise more than thirty-four feet not because it breaks of its own weight but rather because of air pressure. The correct explanation, however, did not even occur to Galileo.

Some historians of science have characterized Galileo's failure even to consider the correct explanation as an unaccountable shortcoming of an otherwise brilliant mind. After all, they point out, Galileo knew that air had weight and correctly surmised that the rise and fall of feathers and balloons was related to air pressure. Why, then, they ask, did Galileo take a suspended coil of wire as his model rather than a feather or a balloon? Why did he argue

> Because some solid bodies break of their own weight, a column of water breaks of its own weight

rather than

> Because the rise and fall of some solid bodies is related to air pressure, the rise and fall of a column of water is related to air pressure.

Since Galileo was one of the most imaginative men in the history of science, why did his imagination fail him here?

These questions are misplaced. Galileo's explanation happened to be the wrong one, but it is remarkable that it should have occurred to him at all. If we do not see this, it is only because we have the advantage of hindsight. It is enormously difficult to see significant analogies between such different phenomena as suspended coils of wire, feathers, and balloons, on the one hand, and a column of water in a suction pump, on the other. The psychological processes by which such connections are made are extremely obscure, and most insights of this kind, even mistaken ones, are the prerogative of genius.

The unavailability of appropriate well-confirmed laws of nature and failure of imagination are not, however, the only reasons for overlooking possible explanations. A third and equally common reason is a natural human tendency to overwork familiar analogical models and to take a proprietary interest in the first hypothesis that comes to mind as if it were a pet to whom we had special obligations. It is well known that if researchers in different disciplines jointly inquire into some phenomenon of common interest, each tends to interpret that phenomenon in terms of the conceptual schemes most familiar to him in his own domain.

Research into typhus is an example of an inquiry that was hindered because of a misleading but familiar analogical model. Researchers in this field were thoroughly acquainted with earlier studies of yellow fever and knew that mosquitoes communicated yellow fever by injecting their saliva into the victim while sucking his blood. When they discovered that typhus was communicated by lice, they assumed that lice communicated the virus of typhus in the same way. It was some time before it even occurred to them to consider other possible explanations, and even longer before they discovered that lice communicate the virus through their excreta rather than through their saliva.

Often the tendency to overwork familiar models is abetted by ignorance of established facts and by wishful thinking. This is particularly true when the phenomenon to be explained is one that deeply engages our feelings. For example, most Americans, if asked why large numbers of Cubans came to the United States after the Castro revolution, would answer unhesitatingly that the refugees had come to escape political repression. In fact, most Americans would not even have considered other possible explanations. That this explanation should be the first to occur to them is easily understood, since the migrations most familiar to

Americans are those of earlier immigrants whom history books commonly represent as having come to the United States in pursuit of freedom. That most Americans would not seek an alternative explanation is also easily understood, since the favored explanation accords with their anti-Castro feelings and since American news media rarely cover events of this kind in depth.

We can see, however, that an impartial investigator would at least consider other possible explanations. It is well known that Cuba is a poorer country than the United States; it would therefore be reasonable to suppose that a desire for improved material well-being was a substantial factor in the Cuban exodus. If the United States were to waive the immigration quota for the citizens of some equally poor but politically free country, give immigrants from these countries work permits, help them find jobs, provide them with a monthly stipend until jobs were found, and establish schools where their children could be taught in their native language—all steps the United States has taken to help Cuban immigrants—it would be surprising indeed if the number of emigrants from that country failed to increase.

Similarly, some political conservatives have explained the high suicide rate in Denmark by arguing that Denmark is a socialistic or welfare state, that such states weaken the moral fiber of the populace, and that the morally weak are more prone to suicide than the morally strong. President Eisenhower in a famous press interview almost precipitated an international incident by suggesting this explanation of the high Danish suicide rate. The analogical model here is the familiar conservative explanation of other social ills, such as unemployment and race riots, in terms of individual moral weakness begot by government "coddling." However, the impartial investigator who has made a serious attempt to familiarize himself with the literature on suicide will not accept this explanation without first considering other possibilities as well. It is known, for example, that suicide rates generally increase with age and that Denmark has an unusually high percentage of aged citizens. It is also known that the suicide rate tends to vary inversely with the homicide rate and that Denmark has an unusually low homicide rate. Since we have no reason to believe that the aged and the non-homicidal are morally weaker than the young and the homicidal, here are at least two possible explanations unrelated to moral fiber worth considering.

The above remarks are not intended to suggest that Americans or conservatives are particularly guilty of overlooking possible explanations that do not fit their preconceptions or habitual models of thinking. This is a universal human tendency. Neither are these remarks intended to suggest that the popular American explanation of the post-Castro immigration or the popular conservative explanation of the high suicide rate in Denmark are wholly incorrect (though they are undoubtedly oversimplified). The point is rather that all of us have a strong tendency to attach greater weight to certain explanations than is logically warranted and that one of the best ways of correcting this tendency is to seek out other possible explanations and to force our favorite explanation into active competition with them. Galileo might have discovered that his explanation of why a column of water in a suction pump rises only thirty-four feet was wrong without ever conceiving of the true explanation. There can be no doubt, however, that he would have been far more cautious about accepting his erroneous explanation had an explanation in terms of air pressure occurred to him. Similarly, the explanation of the post-Castro emigration from Cuba as a flight from political repression could be put to many tests even by those who are unable to think of other explanations; but it is unlikely that the person who is unaware of alternative explanations will feel a compelling urge to question his own.

III • ANALYZING POSSIBLE EXPLANATIONS AND COLLECTING FURTHER DATA

If the explicandum is relatively simple and the purpose of inquiry has been clearly defined, chances are that the possible explanations will be of more or less the same kind, at more or less the same order of generality, and reasonably precise. In such cases it is possible to pass directly to the final stage of inquiry, confirming or disconfirming each possible explanation by appropriate tests. When, for example, inquiry had reached the stage that one asked:

> Does a column of water in a suction pump break of its own weight or does it fail to rise because of air pressure?

or

> Is yellow fever communicated by direct contact between human victims or by mosquito bite?

or

> Is typhus communicated by the excreta or by the saliva of the louse?

researchers had little left to do except to test each of these possible explanations.

But if the phenomenon to be explained is complex and multifaceted and if the purpose of inquiry is to achieve the fullest possible understanding at all levels, the possible explanations are likely to be extremely heterogeneous and often very vague. In such cases confirmation or disconfirmation must be preceded or accompanied by painstaking analysis of these possible explanations and a careful search for relevant data.

Suppose, for example, that we set ourselves the task of explaining why men commit suicide. Common sense tells us that suicide is due to financial reverses, physical suffering, unrequited love, involvement in scandal, etc. Statisticians tell us that suicide is more common among the aged than among the young, more common in groups with a low homicide rate than in groups with a high homicide rate, more common among men than among women, more common in countries at peace than in countries at war, more common among the *nouveaux riches* than among persons of established wealth, more common in rich countries than in poor countries, more common among Protestants than among Catholics, more common among whites than among Negroes, more common in the cities than in the country, more common among the divorced and the widowed than among the married, etc. Psychologists tell us, among other things, that suicide is due to the fact that innate aggressive drives have been thwarted and the energy of these drives has been turned inward. Sociologists tell us, among other things, that suicide is due to lack of social cohesion. Political liberals often ascribe suicide to forms of acute distress preventable by wise government action, while political conservatives often ascribe suicide to moral weakness engendered by unwise government intervention in men's lives.

And so it is with practically all the pressing questions of human interest: Why do men go to war? Why are some countries rich and others poor? Why are there depressions? Why is there a high rate of unemployment? Why is there a high rate of crime? Why are there race riots? In every case if we take the trouble to examine the views held by reasonably intelligent men with a reasonably good knowledge of the phenomenon to be explained, we discover a bewildering variety of possible explanations of different kinds and different levels of generality, many of which are extremely vague. Our problem, therefore, is not only to determine which of the possible explanations is correct but to clarify the possible explanations and determine how they are related to one another. What is called for is not simply confirmation or disconfirmation but interpretation and analysis. And to this end it will often be necessary to accumulate a vast supply of relevant data.

What, for example, do we mean by 'aggressive energy turned inward,' 'lack of social cohesion,' 'acute distress,' 'moral weakness'? What ascertainable facts will be taken as evidence that an individual has aggressive drives and that these have been turned inward, that a society lacks social cohesion, or that an individual is in acute distress or morally weak? Are these highly general and vague explanations compatible with one another? Must we choose between them or do they each explain some aspect of the complex phenomenon of suicide? If these explanations are not compatible in their conventional interpretations, can they be made compatible by introducing suitable qualifications?

What interpretation should be put on the various statistical correlations? Are the aged, the widowed, and the divorced more prone to suicide than the young and the married because they tend to be lonely? Is loneliness a part of what is meant by lack of social cohesion? Is the fact that the suicide rate decreases in time of war to be interpreted as a consequence of the fact that war tends to produce a high degree of social cohesion or as a consequence of the fact that in wartime people have a suitable outlet for aggressive drives? Is the fact that proportionately more Protestants commit suicide than Catholics to be attributed to greater social cohesion among Catholics? Or should it be attributed to a Protestant propensity to turn aggressive drives inward? (Freud held that Protestants tend to experience a greater sense of guilt and individual worthlessness than Catholics, and that this experience is evidence of aggressive drives turned inward.) Is the high rate of suicide in prosperous countries due to a lack of social cohesion following from urbanization and industrialization or is it due simply to the fact that the populations of these countries are longer-lived and consequently have a higher percentage of older citizens?

What shall we make of specific common-sense explanations? We say that one man committed suicide because he was wiped out in a stock market crash; another, because he was suffering from a terminal cancer; still another, because he was disappointed in love; and a fourth, because he had fallen into the hands of the enemy and feared being tortured into giving information that would have led to the death of his comrades. One common denominator in each of these cases is some form of distress or suffering. But distress is at most a necessary condition of suicide; many men in similar situations do not take their own lives. Shall we say, then, that the crucial difference between those who commit suicide and those who do not is moral weakness and that suicide must finally be explained as a combination of distress and moral weakness? If so, shall we say that the man who kills himself to avoid giving information to an enemy is morally weak or shall we say that self-inflicted death under these circumstances is not an instance of suicide?

And how are we to relate these specific common-sense explanations to the highly general and theoretical explanations in terms of aggression turned inward or lack of social cohesion? Is the man who commits suicide to spare himself the agony of a terminal cancer or to avoid giving the enemy information really

committing suicide because he is a member of a socially inco-
hesive society or because his aggressive drives have been
directed inward? Or are these explanations less comprehensive
than their proponents believe?

Although analysis or interpretation is obviously not the same
thing as testing, the two procedures are closely related and
usually proceed apace. The gathering of statistics on suicide, for
example, gives us greater insight into the nature of suicide and
at the same time provides evidence for or against possible explanations. Since the explanation in terms of aggressive energy
turned inward explains both why suicide and homicide rates tend
to vary inversely and why the suicide rate decreases in times of
war, this possible explanation has considerable explanatory
power and is to that extent confirmed. On the other hand, since
there are good reasons to question the view that women,
Catholics, Negroes, and other groups with low suicide rates are
morally stronger than men, Protestants, whites, and other groups
with high suicide rates, the explanation in terms of moral weakness appears to be inconsistent with the facts and is to that extent
disconfirmed. In the present state of knowledge, however, no
hypothesis has been highly confirmed and few can be entirely
ruled out.

IV • EXPLAINING PHENOMENA IN THE SOCIAL SCIENCES

In great part the explanatory power of the more advanced
sciences such as physics and chemistry has been achieved by the
discovery of highly general and theoretical laws from which
specific, observational laws can be deduced. And more often than
not, these highly general, theoretical laws are quantitative laws
of functional dependence—that is to say, laws that relate an increase or decrease in one measurable property to an increase or
decrease in one or more other measurable properties, every unit
of increase or decrease in one variable being matched to a unit
of increase or decrease in the other variables. Almost all the
great historical discoveries in these sciences were of this char-

acter. For example, Boyle's law states that at constant tempera-
tures the pressure of a gas varies inversely with its volume: if
the pressure is increased by half, the volume decreases by half,
and conversely. Similarly, Galileo analyzed the velocity of falling
bodies in terms of units of time and units of distance, relating
these variables to one another in precise mathematical formulas.

Although the extent to which the newer social sciences will
in time be able to match the achievements of the more advanced
physical sciences is still an open question, it is evident that the
social sciences have adopted similar goals and even much of the
vocabulary of the physical sciences. For example, social scientists
have borrowed the term 'variable,' using it in much the same
sense that we have been using the terms 'gross condition' and
'possible explanation.' Thus in sociology and psychology, age,
religion, homicide rate, race, social cohesion, aggressive energy
turned inward, etc., are all referred to as 'variables' in relation to
suicide.

It would appear that progress in the social sciences is impeded
by two principal factors: (1) the large number of variables involved in the phenomena studied, and (2) the difficulty of
measuring these variables. Boyle's law is framed in terms of
only three variables—temperature, pressure, and volume—all of
which are relatively easy to measure. But there are literally
dozens of variables related to suicide, and many of them—for
example, social cohesion and aggressive energy turned inward—
are very hard to measure. The result is that the social sciences
can presently boast of very few precise laws of functional dependence. For the most part they have been able to formulate
only what we shall call *approximate laws of functional dependence,* of which the inverse relationship between suicide and
homicide is an example. These approximate laws of functional
dependence differ from laws of functional dependence proper in
either or both of two ways: First, they may not be truly universal
as stated. Though most groups with a high homicide rate have a
low suicide rate, there are exceptions. The English have a low rate
of homicide and also a low rate of suicide. Second, even if the law
is universal, it may not be possible to relate each determinate
measurable change in one variable to a determinate measurable
change in the others. If homicide considerably increases, suicide

332 PART TWO: ARGUMENT

usually decreases. But we do not know how much the rate of homicide must increase for the suicide rate to decrease, nor can we accurately predict from the magnitude of the increase in suicide what the magnitude of decrease in homicide will be.

It has sometimes been argued that the attempt to apply the methods of the established sciences in studies of human behavior is misguided. Critics say that this attempt can only result in misleading simplifications. Sometimes these critics focus on the extensive use of experimental definitions that seem to narrow the subject of inquiry unduly. For example, as pointed out in Part I, when a statistically-minded researcher such as Kinsey defines sexuality, he does so in terms of mathematically measurable units of sexual behavior. In Kinsey's case, it was the number of contacts. Human feelings were neglected. On other occasions, the criticism focuses on the extensive use of *deductive models*—that is to say, a relatively small set of assumptions from which a large number of deductions can be made. Such models, critics say, force us to ignore relevant variables and are often based on assumptions known to be false. For example, many laws in classical economics were derived from a deductive model which assumed that all men are motivated in their economic behavior exclusively by the desire for profit and that all men act rationally in the pursuit of this end. Given these assumptions, many laws could be deduced. But since these assumptions are known to be contrary to fact, critics argue that the entire deductive system based on this model is tainted.

To these criticisms social scientists usually answer by pointing out that whereas physics and chemistry are hundreds of years old, most of the social sciences have emerged only in the twentieth century. Thus, the present shortcomings of the social sciences may be more reasonably attributed to their youth than to any peculiarity in their subject matter. More specifically, social scientists argue that the use of simplifying experimental definitions and simplifying deductive models is as common in the advanced sciences as in the social sciences and need not be misleading. For example, in framing his laws of falling bodies, Galileo deliberately neglected the variable of air resistance. Yet this omission did not lead to any misunderstanding. On the contrary, given Galileo's laws and given a measure of the deviation of falling bodies from the behavior demanded by these laws, it is possible to calculate the precise value of the neglected variable. Similarly, laws deduced from the classical economic model can be checked against the facts; and any disparity between the deduced laws and the facts serves both as a forcible reminder that the model was simplified and as a spur to further research. Moreover, if this model had been so misleading as the critics maintain, how can we account for the fact that economists are better able to predict economic changes today than they were when the model was first introduced?

EXERCISES FOR CHAPTER FIFTEEN

A. Give at least two interpretations of each of the following questions:

1. How can we account for World War II?
2. Why do fish have gills?
3. Why did Lincoln sign the Emancipation Proclamation?
4. Why are men cruel to one another?
5. Why did Adam eat the forbidden fruit?

B. Give as many possible explanations for the following phenomena as occur to you:

1. statistical reports according to which there is a rising incidence of teen-age crime
2. school drop-outs
3. wars
4. inflation
5. a high level of productivity by the assembly workers in an automobile company

C. Can you think of an explanation for each of the following:

1. In a famous experiment conducted in 1927 at the Hawthorne Works of the Western Electric Company to determine what factors improved productivity, experimental groups were given first better lighting, then longer rest periods, then a shorter work day, then food during morning rest periods, then more pay, etc. In every case there was a carefully matched control group denied these advantages. Curiously, however, the productivity of both experimental and control groups increased, and in the same measure.

2. In the early days of political polling a very large number of conservative victories that failed to materialize were predicted.

D. Comment on the following passages in the light of the discussion in this chapter. If the passage contains an argument evaluate the argument.

1. Soldiers do not fight because they have aggressive impulses; they fight because they have been drafted.

2. "'Poverty' is not an isolated variable which operates in precisely the same fashion wherever found; it is only one in a complex of identifiably interdependent social and cultural variables. Poverty as such and consequently limitation of opportunity are not enough to produce a conspicuously high rate of criminal behavior. Even the notorious 'poverty in the midst of plenty' will not necessarily lead to this result. But when poverty and associated disadvantages in competing for the cultural values approved for *all* members of the society are linked with a cultural emphasis on pecuniary success as a dominant goal, high rates of criminal behavior are the normal outcome. Thus, crude (and not necessarily reliable) crime statistics suggest that poverty is less highly correlated with crime in southeastern Europe than in the United States. The economic life-chances of the poor in these European areas would seem to be even less promising than in this country, so that neither poverty nor its association with limited opportunity is sufficient to

account for the varying correlations. However, when we consider the full configuration—poverty, limited economic opportunity, and the assignment of cultural goals—there appears some basis for explaining the higher correlation between poverty and crime in our society than in others where rigidified class structure is coupled with *differential class symbols of success.*" (Robert K. Merton, *Social Theory and Social Structure*)

3. A senator received in a primary election a higher percentage of votes in cities where he had not campaigned than in cities where he had. A newspaper commented editorially that the senator would have done better if he had stayed at home altogether.

4. "Intersexuals are individuals who cannot be said to belong completely to either sex, though they have some of the physical features of both. . . .

   "Despite their bisexual appearance, intersexuals are not necessarily bisexual in their desires. One might expect that their sexual impulses would follow the pattern of their internal sex glands. . . . But it does not work out like that. An intersexual's desires are more likely to fall in line with the sex in which he is reared than to conform to the sex to which his endocrine glands belong. Many of them are brought up as boy or girl on the basis of an arbitrary decision made immediately after birth after an inspection of the genitals. Sometimes the decision runs contrary to the true sex as reflected in the internal organs. . . .

   "[A study] shows that of thirty-nine intersexuals reared as males thirty-four showed definite sexual desires. In all thirty-four cases their desires followed the normal male pattern, although twenty-three of them had either mixed or female sex glands. . . . This is strong evidence . . . that heterosexuality and homosexuality are attitudes acquired by psychological conditioning." (D. J. West, *Homosexuality*)

5. "Kallman, an American authority on human heredity, has achieved a remarkable investigation on male homosexual twins. The study of twins enables the investigator to sort out the effects of hereditary and environmental influences.

There are two types of twins. Dizygotic or ordinary twins
. . . are no more alike than ordinary brothers and sisters.
Monozygotic or identical twins . . . have precisely the
same hereditary endowment. . . . Ordinary twins and
identical twins are both brought up in similar environments,
but only the identical twins have the additional factor of
precisely the same inheritance.

"In the end [Kallman] secured eighty-five homosexually-
inclined twins. . . . Of these eighty-five, forty were identical twins, and of these forty, Kallman succeeded in tracing
the brothers of thirty-seven. He found that all thirty-seven
twin brothers were homosexually inclined. . . .

"In striking contrast the brothers of the ordinary, non-
identical twins showed no particular homosexual trend.
Twenty-six were traced, and only three [were homosexually
inclined.] This represents an incidence no higher than that
of the population at large." (D. J. West, *Homosexuality*)

6. "It is quite common these days for social workers to look
for deep psychological causes when faced with ordinary
day-to-day problems, whereas there may be no such causes
at all. Just because a man commits some minor kind of
crime it does not necessarily mean that he does it because
he was forced to study Latin at school; he may steal food
for no reason other than that he is hungry." (W. J. Reich-
man, *Use and Abuse of Statistics*)

7. "The soundness of your charge depends on certain basic
assumptions. You have assumed, first, that man by nature
is a passive, inert animal who will arouse himself to effort
only when prodded by the threat of deprivation; second,
that assistance will only corrode what will power man does
possess; and, third, that any effort to tamper with this
simple input-output mechanism will only serve to warp
the fabric of our society. I do not believe that either our
common experience or contemporary social science will
support these assumptions.

"If your assumptions were true, we would have to conclude that the lowest economic groups—those people who
are existing right at the level of subsistence—are the most
active and productive individuals in our society. But sur-

veys show that the poor belong to the fewest number of social groups, are the least active in public affairs, finish the fewest years of school, and make the smallest economic contribution to the nation. In other words, those people who are closest to the struggle for survival and who, according to your assumptions, ought to have the most incentive to be active, are the most inactive and least productive members of the community.

"Look at it the other way around. Those two gentlemen whom conservatives defer to so often, Barry Goldwater and William Buckley, were not born with hunger staring them in the face, yet they are energetic and productive persons. The same holds for the Kennedys, the Rockefellers, the Fords, and several million other wealthy Americans. Although they were all born into families with so-called 'womb to tomb' security surpassing anything a government could provide, most of them are useful citizens. According to your theory, these fortunate individuals should be contentedly languishing in their penthouses doing absolutely nothing. But this isn't the case.

"Men labor for many things: security, power, prestige, the joy of workmanship. Few of us work just for food and shelter. Once people are sure of the material essentials of life, they normally find other, usually more creative outlets for their physical and intellectual energies.

"But let's not be satisfied with our own observations. The social sciences, notably psychology and anthropology, are in general agreement that man is an innately active creature. For example, recent anthropological studies have discovered that the natives of certain islands of the South Pacific, long described by armchair authorities as living in blissful indolence, work and work hard despite the fact that they, almost uniquely in the world, are furnished by nature with all the material necessities. In a set of experiments involving the more 'civilized' peoples of the West, subjects were paid twenty dollars an hour to lie motionless in a dark room. Most couldn't take it for more than a few hours; their body chemistry was such that they had to be doing things.

"Now let's examine the effects of the welfare programs you have called into question. For example, let's look at social insurance, far and away the largest welfare program. By means of the various programs within our social-security system—old-age insurance, disability insurance, medical insurance for the aged—the risk of those expenses which often beset people through no fault of their own is spread over the entire population. This coverage against accidents, such as injuries on the job, and inevitabilities, such as old age and retirement, is not government charity. The benefits are paid out of a trust fund to which all participants contribute during their working years. You don't hear people accuse commercial insurance policies of destroying individual initiative and character. Since public insurance operates on the same principles, there is no basis for such accusations here either." (Neil Staebler and Douglas Ross, *How to Argue with a Conservative*)

8. "One of the procedures which showed a high correlation with ulcers involved training the monkeys to avoid an electric shock by pressing a lever. The animal received a brief shock on the feet at regular intervals, say, every twenty seconds. It could avoid the shock if it learned to press the lever at least once in every twenty-second interval. It does not take a monkey very long to master this problem; within a short time it is pressing the lever far oftener than once in twenty seconds. Only occasionally does it slow down enough to receive a shock as a reminder.

"One possibility, of course, was that the monkeys which had developed ulcers under this procedure had done so not because of the psychological stress involved but rather as a cumulative result of the shocks. To test this possibility we set up a controlled experiment, using two monkeys in 'yoked chairs' in which both monkeys received shocks but only one monkey could prevent them. The experimental or 'executive' monkey could prevent shocks to himself and his partner by pressing the lever; the control monkey's lever was a dummy. Thus both animals were subjected to the same physical stress (*i.e.*, both received the same number of shocks at the same time), but only the 'executive' monkey was under the psychological stress of having to press the lever.

"We placed the monkeys on a continuous schedule of alternate periods of shock-avoidance and rest, arbitrarily choosing an interval of six hours for each period. As a cue for the executive monkey we provided a red light which was turned on during the avoidance periods and turned off during the 'off' hours. The animal soon learned to press its lever at a rate averaging between fifteen and twenty times a minute during the avoidance periods, and to stop pressing the lever when the red light was turned off. These responses showed no change throughout the experiment. The control monkey at first pressed the lever sporadically during both the avoidance and rest sessions, but lost interest in the lever within a few days.

"After twenty-three days of a continuous six-hours-on, six-hours-off schedule the executive monkey died during one of the avoidance sessions. Our only advance warning had been the animal's failure to eat on the preceding day. It had lost no weight during the experiment, and it pressed the lever at an unflagging rate through the first two hours of its last avoidance session. Then it suddenly collapsed and had to be sacrificed. An autopsy revealed a large perforation in the wall of the duodenum—the upper part of the small intestine near its junction with the stomach, and a common site of ulcers in man. Microscopic analysis revealed both acute and chronic inflammation around this lesion. The control monkey, sacrificed in good health a few hours later, showed no gastrointestinal abnormalities. A second experiment using precisely the same procedure produced much the same results. This time the executive monkey developed ulcers in both the stomach and the duodenum; the control animal was again unaffected." (Joseph V. Brady, "Ulcers in 'Executive' Monkeys," in *Scientific American*, October, 1958)

9. ". . . Elliot Smith . . . asserted that man's original nature could be studied if one observed those primitive peoples who by physical isolation or manner of life were most thoroughly cut off from all influence of civilization. The

Eskimo, living on the frigid periphery of human existence, became a favourite object of such studies. The Yahgans of Tierra del Fuego became another such favourite, for the remoteness and hostility of the Yahgan environment could scarcely be rivalled anywhere on earth. . . . These and other peoples in tropical hideaways . . . all revealed natures much the same—gentle, shy, extremely timid and entirely non-aggressive. . . .

"The conclusion appears inarguable. His method was irreproachable, his evidence overwhelming. His error however was total, for like most scientific error it lay in the premise. The assumption that people living under remote conditions untouched by civilization will reveal like walking museum pieces the original nature of man, is quite false. The conclusion that the shy, timid, amiable, non-aggressive nature of pristine man has been revealed by the character of these people is a logical sequitur simply to a false premise. What has been revealed is nothing more than that people living where nobody else wants to live may quite possibly suffer from non-aggressive dispositions.

". . . All that has been actually demonstrated by this loosely disciplined but immensely popular raid into the outposts of man's nature has been that timid people tend to live at unfashionable addresses." (Robert Ardrey, *African Genesis*)

10. "Hippies may be produced by the combination of a dominant mother and a weak or absent father, according to some social scientists.

" 'Hippies are looking for involvement on a group level— to escape the dominant mother,' says Richard A. Koenigsberg, a lecturer in psychology at Manhattan Community College, who is giving a summer course on hippies at the New School for Social Research.

" 'If you love one person, there's a chance that this person will bug you like your mother did,' he says. 'But on the group level—be-ins, love-ins and so forth—there's no such risk.'

"Harry Silverstein, sociologist and co-director of the Creative Arts-Alienated Youth Project in the East Village, finds a functional absence of the father in the hippie background:

"'He's there, but he didn't take the large, effective role he could have. There's a notable absence of conflict with parents, but also a lack of affectionate deep relationships in the home. Hippies have grown up in the middle ground between the two—and that may be what middle-class life is all about.'" (John Leo, "Dominant Mothers Are Called the Key to Hippies," in the New York *Post*, August 6, 1967)

11. "Why does the human animal come in different colors?

"The answer to racial differentiation, according to a Brandeis University biochemist, probably involves the ultraviolet rays of the sun and the body's production of vitamin D, the 'sunshine vitamin.'

"Humans make vitamin D in their skin in the presence of the ultraviolet rays of sunlight. . . . Too little vitamin D leads to the bone deformities of rickets, spinal curvature, decalcification of adult bone, etc. Too much leads to calcification of soft tissue including blood vessels and can cause a fatal kidney disease. . . .

"Variations in skin hue, according to the thesis of Prof. W. Farnsworth Loomis, are the result of the evolutionary adaptive process to protect the species from making too much or too little vitamin D.

"'Having evolved in the tropics,' Loomis writes, 'early hominids . . . were probably deeply pigmented and covered with fur, as are most other tropical primates. . . .

"'As they moved farther and farther north, their more deeply pigmented infants must have been especially likely to develop the grossly bent legs and twisted spines characteristic of rickets, deformities which would cripple their ability to hunt game,' thus encouraging the survival of and procreation by the lighter-skinned.

"Distribution of pigment shows a fairly consistent shading off to lighter skin, the greater the distance from the Equator. 'The only exception to the correlation between latitude and skin color in the Old World is the Eskimo,' Loomis notes. But since his natural diet of fish and meat supplies plenty of vitamin D, he did not have to evolve a

white skin to survive." (Barbara Yuncker, "The Colors of
Man—A Scientist's View," in the New York *Post*, August 5,
1967)

12. Nine months after the 1965 blackout in New York the New
York birth rate took a big jump. The same thing happened
in southern Italy nine months after a similar blackout. An
unidentified Italian sociologist was reported by the Italian
news agency Ansa to have commented as follows: "One
thing seems certain, and that is that the phenomenon assumes the character of defiance of natural adversity, a
prompt reassertion of human vitality over it." (Comment
reported in *The New York Times*, August 30, 1967)

13. "Anyone who starts experimenting in parapsychology is
very likely to begin with an experimental set-up which
later reflection or criticism by other people will convince
him was not adequate to cut out the possibility of explanations alternative to ESP. He may, for example, begin with
some such arrangement as this. The experimenter sits at
a table with the percipient on the opposite side facing him.
The experimenter looks at each card in turn, keeping its
face carefully turned away from the percipient, and writes
down some symbol indicating what is on its face, *e.g.*,
+ for a cross. The percipient calls out what he thinks is
the picture on the face and the experimenter writes that
down too in another column. He may encourage the
percipient by telling him he is right, or even by telling him
what the card was after his guess, irrespective of whether
that guess was right or wrong. There may be a small audience, including perhaps friends or relatives of the percipient sitting behind the experimenter so that they too
know what card he has looked at. At the end of each experiment, the experimenter counts up how often the symbol
in the column of guesses is the same as that in the column
of targets. If this is sufficiently greater than the number
of right guesses to be expected by chance this is taken as
evidence of telepathic communication between experimenter and percipient.

   "It is in reality evidence that some cause is operating to
produce correspondence between the guesses of the per-

cipient and the cards looked at by the experimenter. Whether or not that cause is of some form of extra-sensory perception depends on the adequacy of the precautions taken to exclude other causes." (Robert H. Thouless, *Experimental Psychical Research*)

14. "Negative evidence from a long-term study in Hawaii suggests that the 'so-called races [of man] are not really very much different from each other' genetically, a conference on the biology of human variation was told here yesterday.

    "The study of a larger sampling of the state's population was unable to detect any evidence of hybrid vigor or the genetic effects related to it, said the geneticist who made the report.

    "The phenomenon of hybrid vigor has been observed in plants and animals. A cross between two distinctly different genetic strains sometimes produces offspring hardier or bigger than either parent.

    "If there are comparably important genetic differences among the races of man, Dr. Chin S. Chung said, it might be possible to find evidence of hybrid vigor and related effects in a reasonably large multiracial human population.

    "The groups involved in the sample were Caucasian, Hawaiian, Chinese, Japanese, Philippine, Puerto Rican and Korean. . . . The population of Hawaii offered an excellent sample for a study of this kind because, at an estimate, about a third of the marriages in the state were interracial." (Harold M. Schmeck, Jr., *The New York Times*, February 12, 1965)

15. "What causes migrating birds to migrate? 'All theories of the causes of bird migration,' says Dean Amadon of the American Museum of Natural History, 'have serious shortcomings.' Lack of food and extreme cold provide obvious stimuli; but some birds in warm climates fly north in response to wet or dry conditions. One theory holds that migrations began when the continents were closer together. But the continental drift, if it occurred, must have been so long ago that only primitive types of birds were present. Mallard ducks of non-migrating varieties were hatched from eggs in Finland, and promptly migrated

southward; and anaesthetized birds transported long distances have returned home, indicating that memory is not the cause." (Harold A. Larrabee, *Reliable Knowledge*)

16. "To the question 'Why have so few in Germany embraced the principle of liberal democracy?' Dahrendorf provides and then dismisses two popular answers. It is neither the fault of 'Hitler' (short for the influence of individual men or events), nor the fault of 'Tacitus' (by which he means all explanations founded on 'national and immutable character'). The development of German society is to blame: the industrial revolution which blotted out early liberalism with state capitalism rather than produce a politically conscious bourgeoisie; the survival of an elite with a largely agrarian and feudal outlook; the 'cultural pessimism' of the nineteenth century and afterward, which saw Germany as 'the late nation' whose young culture was being poisoned in the cradle by jealous neighbors." (Neal Ascherson, *The New York Review of Books*, February 1, 1968)

17. "The authors of *The Negro Family* take at face value Census Bureau statistics that record illegitimacy rates for whites at about three percent, for Negroes at about twenty-two percent. More careful consideration, *in the context of other well-known facts*, would reveal not so much a careless acceptance by Negroes of promiscuity and illegitimacy, as a systematic inequality of access to a variety of services and information.

"If we do not attribute the seven-to-one difference in illegitimacy rates to Negro family instability as a subcultural trait, what does account for these differences? Here, very briefly, are a few pieces of additional data:

"*Reporting.* Illegitimate births are significantly underreported, and more underreported for whites than for nonwhites. This is true, first, because reporting is dependent upon discriminatory white sources. Second, white illegitimate births occur more often in private hospitals, are attended by sympathetic—and white—doctors, and involve the cooperation of social agencies, all of which work consciously to help the white unmarried mother conceal the fact of illegitimacy.

"*Shotgun marriages.* A large portion of first-born children are conceived 'illegitimately,' with the parents marrying before the child's birth. Such marriages are less frequent among Negroes because of the man's financial insecurity.

"*Abortion.* It is estimated that more than one million illegal and unreported induced abortions are performed each year. Authorities agree that one-fourth to one-half of these are performed for unmarried women, and that the overwhelming majority of abortion patients are white. Abortions alone account for most of the differences in the census illegitimacy figures.

"*Contraception.* Access to contraceptive information and services is also unequally distributed in favor of whites. The extent of inequality is not known, but if the differential were as low as two to one in favor of whites, we would be able to conclude that 'illegitimate intercourse'—if we may push the terminology this far—is about the same among Negroes and whites." (William Ryan, "Savage Discovery: The Moynihan Report," in *The Nation*, November 22, 1965)

18. "When Nelya Mikhailova, a former Russian army master sergeant stared and frowned at her recruits during World War II, they jumped. Now, when the middle-aged woman stares and frowns at apples, they jump. When she looks at a drinking glass, it trembles, and when she stares at a clock it stops. According to the Moskovskaya Pravda Newspaper, Miss Mikhailova has the power of telekinesis—mind over matter. . . .

"A reporter for the newspaper who went to visit Miss Mikhailova . . . came away convinced her powers are genuine. Scientists who have studied Miss Mikhailova's unusual ability have confirmed its authenticity.

"At the first seance she started off simply—by staring at the cap of a fountain pen. Nothing happened. Then she stared harder, her face furrowed in concentration. The cap began to crawl across the table cloth, the reporter said. Suspicious of a trick, he inverted a wine glass over the pen cap to be certain she was not moving it with her breath or using strings. Miss Mikhailova stared again and the cap jumped from side to side inside the glass. 'Perhaps a magnet?' the reporter asked himself. No. Miss Mikhailova then began to move the non-metallic wine glass. 'I have been hypnotized,' the reporter thought. No. Miss Mikhailova has been filmed in action, and a movie camera can not be hypnotized.

"For the camera and for scientists who watched her, Miss Mikhailova outdid herself. She stared at the pendulum of a clock and first stopped it and then speeded it up. She moved a piece of bread, an apple and some matches across a table until they fell on the floor. She stared at a group of glasses and moved just one of them—the one that had been pointed to.

"The scientists offered a variety of theories to explain her powers. One suggested she could generate static electricity, another that her powers were based on electromagnetic forces and a third that she put forth her own gravitational field.

"Miss Mikhailova herself does not know the answer." (Reported from Moscow, in the New York *Post*, March 26, 1968)

19. "In fact, there are two problems to be resolved if we want to know the reasons for Hitler's success. We need to know what were the means Hitler used, and we need to know why nobody stopped him, either in his rise to power or in the pursuit of his policies once he had become Chancellor." (James Joll, *The New York Review of Books*, February 15, 1968)

20. "Darwin had already raised the question of the survival value of fighting, and he has given us an enlightening answer: It is always favorable to the future of a species if the stronger of two rivals takes possession either of the territory or of the desired female. As so often, this truth of yesterday is not the untruth of today but only a special case. . . . Unless the special interests of a social organization demand close aggregation of its members, it is obviously most expedient to spread the individuals of an animal species as evenly as possible over the available habitat. To use a human analogy: if, in a certain area, a larger number of doctors, builders, and mechanics want to

exist, the representatives of these professions will do well to settle as far away from each other as possible.

"The danger of too dense a population of an animal species settling in one part of the available biotope and exhausting all of its source of nutrition and so starving can be obviated by a mutual repulsion acting on the animals of the same species, effecting their regular spacing out, in much the same manner as electrical charges are regularly distributed all over the surface of a spherical conductor. This, in plain terms, is the most important survival value of intra-specific aggression." (Konrad Lorenz, *On Aggression*)

21. "Of the natural narcotics, stimulants and hallucinators there is, I believe, not a single one whose properties have not been known from time immemorial. . . . The fact is strangely significant; for it seems to prove that, always and everywhere, human beings have felt the radical inadequacy of their personal existence, the misery of being their insulated selves and not something else, something wider, something in Wordsworthian phrase, 'far more deeply interfused.' " (Aldous Huxley, *The Devils of Loudun*)

Moral Arguments

Philosophers generally agree that any arguments whose conclusions contain a moral term are moral arguments. But they do not agree on the proper definition of 'moral terms.' It is reasonably clear that in a definition by genus and specific difference the proper genus would be 'value term.' But value terms fall into a bewildering variety of groups. Some—such as 'delicious' and 'unappetizing'—express personal tastes or private preferences. Some—such as 'beautiful' and 'ugly'—are aesthetic. Others—such as 'true' and 'false'—are logical. Still others—such as 'criminal neglect' and 'justifiable homicide'—are legal. Again, some —such as 'good government' and 'free society'—are political. And it is not at all clear how or to what extent moral terms may be distinguished from other value terms. Many philosophers have argued that moral terms are essentially different from these other species; but few have specified at all precisely the respects in which they differ, and those who have do not agree among themselves. Aristotle suggested that moral terms are a subclass of political terms. And some contemporary philosophers maintain that moral terms are not essentially different from terms like 'delicious' and 'unappetizing.'

If an attempt were made to give a definition by classification, similar problems would be encountered. Most moral terms fall into one of three categories: (1) terms, like 'right' and 'wrong' or 'ought' and 'ought not,' used to evaluate specific acts or courses of behavior, (2) terms, like 'brave' and 'cowardly' or 'honest' and 'deceitful,' used to evaluate character, and (3) terms, like 'good' and 'bad' or 'desirable' and 'undesirable,' used to evaluate things or states of affairs having to do with the welfare of some individual or group. Most of these terms, however, have nonmoral as well as moral uses. We say, for instance, "I dialed the wrong number" and "I have a bad headache." And how these nonmoral uses differ from the moral uses is also a matter of sharp debate.

In view of these difficulties a precise definition of 'moral term' and consequently 'moral argument' would be too controversial to serve a useful purpose in an elementary logic test, and none will here be offered. Although this is regrettable, it is not fatal. Despite these controversies over the strict intension of 'moral term,' there is substantial agreement on the denotations of 'moral term' and 'moral argument.' Just as most of us can recognize swans even though we can not define 'swan,' so most of us can recognize moral terms and moral arguments even though we can not define the terms used to denote them. Our pre-analytic notions are too dense and tangled to permit precise and noncontroversial definitions, but they are not so dense or tangled that we can not agree on a large number of paradigm cases. In this chapter, therefore, we shall simply ignore problems relating to the identification of moral arguments.

I • THE PATTERNS OF MORAL ARGUMENTS

Since moral terms fall into three categories, moral arguments may also be divided into three categories: those dealing with human behavior; those dealing with human character; and those dealing with some state of affairs deemed desirable or undesirable. The conclusion of a moral argument might be: 'Smith ought to return the book he borrowed'; 'Jones is a coward'; 'That society is best which affords to citizens the greatest freedom.' Arguments with these three kinds of conclusions generally pose similar problems; but since arguments relating to human behavior are widely considered to be of central importance in moral discourse, our discussion will center on them.

In analyzing arguments of this kind it is necessary to distinguish among three kinds of judgments. The first are *singular moral judgments*—for example, 'Smith ought to return the book he borrowed'—concerned with an individual act or course of behavior. The second are *moral rules*—for example, 'One ought to keep promises'—which express general rules of behavior and which are normally supported by an appeal to a higher-order general rule. The third are *ultimate moral principles*—for example, 'One ought to do that which promotes the greatest happiness of the greatest number'—which are normally used to support moral rules but which are not themselves supported by a higher-order moral generalization.

As we shall see in greater detail in the following section, ultimate moral principles usually function as general definitions of 'a morally right act' (or its non-explicative synonyms, such as 'an act that ought morally to be performed'). The most commonly invoked ultimate moral principle is the one cited above—'One ought to do that which promotes the greatest happiness of the greatest number'—known as the *utilitarian principle*. But many others have been advanced. Among them are

> One ought to conform one's behavior to the conventional moral rules.
> One ought to promote one's own best interests.
> One ought to act in accordance with the will of God.
> One ought to act according to rules that may be willed as universal laws.

Often a given set of moral rules is regarded as a specific definition of 'a morally right act' relative to some ultimate moral principle. However, since moral rules follow from ultimate moral principles only on condition that we can adduce evidence showing that behavior in accordance with these rules does have the property cited in the relevant ultimate moral principle, for our purposes moral rules will be regarded as implicit material propositions asserting that the recommended behavior conforms to an ultimate moral principle.

The simplest and perhaps the most common argument patterns in moral discourse are arguments by subsumption. For example,

1. One ought to do that which promotes the greatest happiness of the greatest number.
2. Promise-keeping promotes the greatest happiness of the greatest number.

One ought to keep promises.

1. One ought to keep promises.
2. Jones promised to return the book.

Jones ought to return the book.

In the first sample argument the first premise is an ultimate moral principle and the conclusion is a moral rule. In the second argument the first premise is a moral rule and the conclusion a singular moral judgment. In both arguments the second premise is a factual proposition linking the conclusion to the major premise. By a *factual proposition* in this context, however, we do not mean a proposition considered to be beyond reasonable doubt but rather a non-tautologous proposition asserting that something is or is not the case as opposed to an evaluative proposition asserting that something ought or ought not to be the case.

The soundness of any moral argument by subsumption obviously depends on the truth or falsity of the factual premise and on the adequacy of the moral rule or ultimate moral principle. In addition, the soundness of any moral argument by subsumption whose major premise is a moral rule will depend upon the soundness of some further argument by subsumption whose major premise is an ultimate moral principle. If, for example, we wish to determine the soundness of the argument whose conclusion is 'Jones ought to return the book,' it is necessary to show not only that the factual premise 'Jones promised to return the book' is true but also that the moral rule 'One ought to keep promises' is acceptable. And to show that the moral rule is acceptable one must be able to subsume it under an ultimate moral principle which gives a general definition of the key term 'ought.'

It must be noted that there are many cases in which a simple argument by subsumption such as those illustrated above will not adequately support a moral judgment. This can happen for either or both of two reasons. First, moral rules frequently conflict, and an act in accordance with one may violate a second. Suppose, for example, that Smith has promised to lend a deadly weapon to Jones and that Jones comes to Smith in a sudden fit of madness demanding that the promise be kept. Suppose, further, that Smith has reason to believe that Jones intends to use this weapon to kill a stranger whom Jones falsely believes to have wronged him. If Smith does not keep his promise, he violates the moral rule enjoining us to keep promises. On the other hand, if Smith does keep his promise under these circumstances, he violates another moral rule which forbids us to aid or abet a second party in a senseless killing. To allow for such cases a moral rule such as 'One ought to keep promises' is ordinarily interpreted to mean not 'One ought to keep *every* promise' but rather 'One ought to keep promises except on those occasions when keeping a promise would violate a moral rule that takes precedence.' And when so interpreted moral arguments have a more complex pattern than indicated above. The pattern of our second sample argument will not be

1. One ought to keep promises.
2. Jones promised to return the book.

Jones ought to return the book.

but rather

1. One ought to keep promises except on those occasions when keeping a promise would violate a moral rule that takes precedence.
2. Jones promised to return the book.
3. There are no circumstances such that by returning the book Jones will violate some moral rule that takes precedence.

Jones ought to return the book.

or else

1. One ought always to do that which given the particular circumstances will promote the greatest happiness of the greatest number.
2. Given the particular circumstances Jones will promote the greatest happiness of the greatest number by returning the book.

Jones ought to return the book.

Second, the ultimate moral principles invoked in moral arguments are often more complex than the ones cited above. Ultimate moral principles, as we said before, usually function as definitions; and the ones cited above are similar to the definitions of 'a bachelor' or 'a quadrilateral' in that they cite none but defining properties. Many moral philosophers have argued, however, that the correct definition of 'a right act' is more like the definition of 'poem' in that its intension must include a disjunctive property citing meaning criteria. For example, it has been held that in determining whether an act is right we must invoke not only the utilitarian principle of maximizing human well-being but two other principles as well. The first, called the *principle of justice,* may be loosely formulated as follows: if any two groups or individuals are treated differently, we must be able to specify a difference between them that justifies discriminatory treatment. The second, the *principle of desert,* may be loosely formulated as follows: in the distribution of goods the more deserving should be favored over the less deserving. According to the utilitarians these alleged meaning criteria are merely specifications of the meaning of 'a right act.' Properly speaking, they are moral rules, not meaning criteria, since we accept them only because behavior in accordance with them does in fact promote the greatest happiness of the greatest number. Opponents of the utilitarians, however, argue not only that these principles are coordinate with, or equal in status to, the utilitarian criterion but that sometimes they conflict in the same way that moral rules conflict, an act conforming to one being contrary to another. On occasion one can maximize human well-being only by arbitrarily discriminating against some group or individual or by favoring the less deserving. If these philosophers are right, moral arguments will often require the introduction of premises that assign relative weights to the various meaning criteria that define 'a right act.'

II • THE DEFINITION OF MORAL TERMS

For reasons indicated in the last section the soundness of every moral argument depends in the last analysis on the adequacy of the relevant moral principle. What this means, in effect, is that showing an act to be right or wrong is essentially a matter of showing that it has the defining properties of 'a right act' or 'a wrong act.' It has sometimes been said that moral arguments differ in this respect from nonmoral arguments, but this view is mistaken. The soundness of an argument in support of the conclusion 'This piece of metal is gold' depends no less upon the adequacy of the implied definition of 'gold' than the soundness of a moral argument depends upon the adequacy of the definition supplied by the relevant moral principle. Nonetheless, moral terms are far more controversial than many nonmoral terms, and it is not surprising that in discussions of moral arguments particular emphasis is placed upon questions of definition. What, then, are the major positions with regard to the nature of ultimate moral principles? Although many more answers to this question have been proposed than we can discuss in an elementary text, the most common answers can be grouped under three headings.

According to one view—sometimes called *definism*—the problem of defining moral terms is simply a matter of making explicit or formulating precisely the rules that guide actual usage. The definist argues that all but an insignificant percentage of human beings do in fact have the same pre-analytic notion of 'a right act.' Disagreement arises only because our analysis of that notion is faulty. Many utilitarians are definists, holding that their definition of 'a morally right act' is the only accurate unfolding of the ordinary use of the term. Utilitarian definists are aware, of course, that other philosophers have proposed different ultimate moral principles; but, they argue, each of these alternative proposals is based on linguistic confusion.

For example, the utilitarian might argue that to see the inadequacy of defining 'a right act' as one that accords with the conventional moral rules, we need only observe that conventional moral rules often conflict and that when they do our natural reaction is to ask which moral rule must be upheld in order to achieve the greatest good. The utilitarian might also argue that those who define 'a right act' as an act in accord with the will of God have simply confused the proposition

For any x if x may properly be called 'God,' then x approves of right acts.

with the proposition

For any x if x may properly be called 'a right act,' then x is in accord with the will of God.

These people say that an act is right because it accords with the will of God, but what they really mean is that an act accords with the will of God because it is right. The proof of their real intent, says the utilitarian, is that they would refuse to call any being 'God' unless he approved of acts that promoted the greatest happiness of the greatest number. For it is generally agreed that if there were a being otherwise like God except that he delighted in human suffering, he would by definition not be God. Similarly, it is generally agreed that if the Bible urged men to rape and murder, it could not by definition be a revelation from God. And since we can not determine whether anything may properly be called 'God' or 'a revelation from God' without invoking the utilitarian principle, this principle must be correct. If the theological definition were assumed as correct, the result would be a vicious circle.

According to a second view, called *emotivism,* general moral definitions are purely persuasive and can not be rationally justified in any way. Those who hold this view argue that since moral terms are invariably emotive, the primary purpose of moral discourse is expressive or directive. The man who says "x is right" is saying something like, "I approve of x; do so as well." Emotivists concede that, given ultimate moral principles, we can justify moral rules and other lower-level moral judgments by argument; but, they argue, ultimate moral principles themselves can not be justified at all. If asked to explain why we defined 'a morally right act' as an act that maximizes human well-being, the only honest answer we could give is "because I personally approve of such acts and wish to exploit the favorable emotive meaning of the definiendum to persuade others to adopt my personal attitudes."

As a rule, emotivists reject the view that human beings share closely similar pre-analytic notions of moral terms. What is relevant to a proper understanding of the use of crucial moral terms, they say, is not some alleged half-unconscious but nonetheless universally shared awareness of their meanings but rather the substantial variability of human attitudes together with the nearly universal tendency of human beings to exploit emotive terms for their own purposes.

Most emotivists also make a sharp distinction between evaluative terms and purely factual terms. A disagreement about the proper definition of a purely factual term can always in principle be resolved by rational methods—either by appealing to accepted usage or by showing that a given use of the term advances the purpose of some factual inquiry. If somebody defines 'bachelor' as a married male, we can show him his error by citing the relevant rules of linguistic usage. And if somebody challenges us to justify a judicative definition of 'gold' or some other purely factual term, we can argue that these definitions advance our understanding of the subject matter to which they are relevant. But neither method is open to us in resolving disagreements about the definition of a moral term. The definists are wrong in thinking that there are relevant rules of linguistic usage by which one of the many proposed general definitions of 'a right act' may be justified. And since the ultimate purpose of moral discourse is expressive and directive, moral definitions can not be justified judicatively. If I define 'a right act' as one that promotes the greatest happiness of the greatest number and you define 'a right act' as one that is in the best interests of the agent, each of us has expressed his own attitude and thereby fulfilled the purpose our respective definitions were intended to fulfill. There is no further shared purpose such as the desire to advance our common understanding of some subject in terms of which these different definitions could be rationally judged. Given that our attitudes are what they are, each of us has an equal right to his own definition. In fact, if we assume that these definitions do accurately reflect our respective attitudes, neither of us would be logically justified in accepting the other's definition. The man who said "One ought to promote the greatest happiness of the greatest number" even though he did not favor acts promoting this end would seriously mislead us about his true attitudes. It would be as if he said: "One ought to promote the greatest happiness of the greatest number; but I do not approve of doing so" —which, of course, is pure nonsense.

According to the third position—which for want of a more accurate label we shall call *moral pragmatism*—the emotivists are right in saying that moral terms are emotive and that consequently moral definitions express basic moral attitudes. It would indeed be misleading to assent to a definition of a moral term with favorable emotive meaning if we did not approve of what the definiens denotes, or to assent to a definition of a moral term with unfavorable emotive meaning if we did not disapprove of what the definiens denotes. The pragmatist also agrees that in almost any society there are individuals whose basic moral attitudes differ from those of the majority and are unlikely to be modified by rational argument. The pragmatist insists, however, that there is far greater agreement in basic moral attitudes than the emotivist typically allows; that given this substantial agreement, moral disputes can be reconciled by rational arguments; and that those who bemoan the fact that some individuals will fail to be persuaded by such arguments are simply unrealistic. The purpose of moral discourse is not to secure universal agreement on moral issues. That, he says, is a highly utopian ideal. Even the scientist is satisfied with general consensus within the scientific community. Moreover, given substantial agreement on basic moral attitudes, the serious practical obstacles to moral consensus are not difficulties in defining moral terms but rather difficulties attendant upon the resolution of relevant factual or logical issues.

Consider any of the pressing moral issues of our day: birth control, capital punishment, racism, anti-Semitism, and so forth. If we peruse the literature on these subjects, we only rarely encounter rationally insuperable disagreement on moral principles. In practically every case the essential points of difference are factual or logical. Take the use of contraceptive devices. Those who oppose the dissemination of contraceptive devices usually argue that this is contrary to the will of God, that 'a wrong act' can be defined without logical circularity as one contrary to the will of God, that there is no serious problem of overpopulation because modern technology is capable of producing enough wealth to provide for all, that if there were a serious problem of overpopulation it could be adequately met by discouraging early marriages and encouraging the use of methods of birth control sanctioned by the Catholic Church, that children in large families are psychologically healthier than those in small families, and so on. Each of these arguments turns on a point of logic or a point of fact; and although it is logically conceivable that the parties to this dispute could all agree on the relevant factual and logical issues without agreeing on the moral issue as well, it is highly improbable. And so it is with all other major moral problems. Can one picture a proponent of capital punishment agreeing that capital punishment does not deter crime, that many innocent men have been executed by the state, that the institution of capital punishment seriously discriminates against the poor who can not afford expensive lawyers, and that when a state legalizes the taking of human life it sets an example that many private citizens are quick to follow? Can one imagine a racist whose beliefs about Negroes and the consequences of discrimination do not differ from the beliefs of those who oppose racism? These questions are, of course, rhetorical. The major obstacles to the resolution of moral disputes are not difficulties peculiar to the nature of moral definitions. The major obstacles are exactly the same as those that impede agreement on factual issues: ignorance, superstition, illogicality, and the all-too-human propensity toward wishful thinking or rationalization.

Moreover, although the pragmatist agrees with the emotivist in regarding moral definitions as persuasive, he does not agree that moral definitions are *essentially* persuasive. And although the pragmatist also agrees with the definist that most people do have very similar pre-analytic notions of 'right' and 'wrong,' he does not agree that moral definitions are *essentially* reportive. According to the pragmatist the ultimate function of moral discourse is to facilitate the resolution of painful conflicts of interest. Consequently, moral definitions are *essentially* judicative. To show that a moral definition is adequate we must be able to show that if in any given society everybody consistently behaved in the manner the definition sanctions, the result would be a substantial reduction in painful conflicts of interest.

III • SOME COMMON PITFALLS IN MORAL REASONING

In this section we should like to call attention to three especially common pitfalls in moral discourse.

The first is the improper or uncritical use of emotive terms. In purely informative discourse we can ordinarily dispense with emotive terms, substituting non-emotive terms with roughly equivalent cognitive meanings. In moral discourse, however, this is less easily done. If we wish to say that a man is brave, that it is wrong to tell lies, or that freedom is a good, we are virtually compelled to use emotive language, since ordinary language rarely provides us with non-emotive terms of equivalent cognitive content. Moreover, if we were to coin a new term or stretch the meaning of an existing non-emotive term to serve this purpose, the substituted term would soon acquire the emotive force of the original. Some time ago, for example, in an effort to avoid value judgments, psychologists began to apply terms such as 'mature' and 'immature' to certain kinds of behavior that had formerly been characterized with moral epithets, and this practice has spread rather widely throughout the American public. The result is that for most Americans today 'mature' and 'immature' are as strongly emotive as 'good' and 'bad.'

Unfortunate though the unavoidability of emotive terms may be, it is a fact with which we must come to grips—and one that imposes upon us a special responsibility to specify as precisely as possible our intended cognitive meaning. All too often because of their rich emotive and pictorial meaning, terms that figure in moral discourse give us a comfortable feeling of familiarity, and we do not even ask what cognitive meaning they have. When, for example, someone says that he is against anti-Semitism, we ordinarily feel that we know exactly what he is talking about. Yet, the cognitive meaning of 'anti-Semitism' is far from clear. Almost everybody would agree that the person who believes Jews ought to be killed or denied civil rights enjoyed by other citizens in the same country is an anti-Semite. But what about the anti-Zionist? What about the person who believes that the

Jewish religion is rationally unfounded and says so publicly? What about the person who believes that because of historical circumstances Jews have developed a high incidence of certain undesirable character traits such as aggressiveness and deviousness? What about the person who refuses to associate with Jews socially but is adamantly opposed to any discrimination except at the social level? If one attempts to answer these questions by paying close attention to how the word is actually used, one will quickly discover that there are no simple answers. The term is not only ambiguous but vague and labile as well.

For example, some persons view anti-Zionism as a sufficient condition of 'anti-Semitism'; others take it to be a meaning criterion; and still others insist that it is not even a part of the term's contingent intension. Unless, therefore, the intended cognitive meaning of 'anti-Semitism' is clearly specified, an argument in which a token of this term occurs can not be clearly understood or properly evaluated.

Of course, the person who strongly disapproves of anti-Zionism will be strongly tempted to define 'anti-Semitism' persuasively so as to make all anti-Zionists anti-Semites by virtue of the term's meaning. And it is conceivable that a definition along these lines could be justified judicatively. Great care must be exercised, however, to avoid confusing a persuasive or judicative definition of a term with an analysis of its conventional meaning. And if one chooses to express one's views on a controversial issue with the aid of terms one has judicatively defined, one must be prepared not only to make one's chosen meaning for that term explicit but also to state the justification for that choice.

The above example illustrates how the emotive force of a term can mask obscurities in its cognitive meaning. Often, however, an argument can go astray because the disputants prematurely conclude that an emotive term is hopelessly obscure. Suppose, for instance, that a Russian and an American are discussing the relative merits of Soviet and American life. Each of them claims that life in his own society is better because his society is more free. At some point in the discussion the two men might come to the conclusion that they attached wholly different meanings to the term 'free.' The American, for example, might say that by 'freedom' he meant the right to criticize his government publicly, the right of an employer to hire an employee at any salary the employee is willing to accept, the right of a manufacturer to sell his product at a free-market price, etc. The Russian might say that by 'freedom' he meant, among other things, the right of any able-bodied man to employment, the right of all citizens to free medical care, and the right of all qualified students to free higher education.

Now, if at this point the disputants decided that the discussion could proceed profitably only if they abandoned the term 'free,' this might be premature. To be sure, they do disagree about the specific meaning of the term, but it could well be that they share a common pre-analytic notion of its meaning which permits agreement at a higher level of generality. For instance, they might after reflection come to agree that an ideally free man would be someone who could do anything he wanted to do without in-curring penalties or suffering ill consequences, and that one measure of a free society is the extent to which the situation of its citizens approximates that of the ideally free man. After all, if a man says that he is not free to do something he seems always to mean either (1) that he can not do it at all or (2) that he will suffer in some way for doing it. The man who desires good medical care but can not get it because he has no money and good free medical care is not available illustrates 1. So does a man who is not free to take a job because no one will hire him. Illustrations of 2 would include the man who is not free to express his political views because he would be sent to prison or lose his job and the man who is not free to hire another at a salary the other is willing to take because he would get into trouble with the law or the labor union.

After further reflection the two men might agree that it is not always desirable that people be able to do what they want to do. In any non-utopian society human wants will undoubtedly con-flict. It is therefore good that society tries to prevent people from doing certain things and penalizes them when they do. Who would want to abandon penalties for murder? In view of this the American and the Russian might decide that what they really mean by a 'free' society is not simply one in which the greatest possible number of men may do what they want without penalty, but rather one in which they can do what they want without penalty, provided they do not infringe on the vital interests of other citizens.

After still further reflection the two men might agree that yet another qualification in their definition would be desirable. If a society is to offer any great measure of freedom in the sense so far specified, its social and economic institutions must dispose citizens to want only those things they can have without damage to the vital interests of others. Consequently, a free society would be (1) one in which citizens may do what they want without penalty, provided that they do not damage the vital interests of others, and (2) one whose social institutions dispose people to want only those things which do not damage the interests of others.

Of course, this last definition of a free society could be still further refined, and agreement on it would not of itself permit a resolution to the original controversy between the two men. But if analysis of the term 'freedom' led to mutual agreement on a general definition such as this, the disputants would be in a far more favorable position to resolve the controversy than would have been possible if they had simply abandoned the term at an earlier stage. For agreement at this level of generality places the controversy in a framework that makes it easier to identify the relevant factual or logical issues.

The second common error in moral reasoning is a tendency to oversimplify moral rules by stating them without the appropriate qualifications. We saw in the last section that moral rules such as 'One ought to keep promises' must usually be qualified. To take another example, let us suppose that somebody argues for desegregation of public schools on the grounds that all men deserve equal opportunities. The rule of equal opportunities is so often appealed to, especially in America, that many persons hold it "sacred" in some unspecifiable meaning of that term and will no doubt regard anyone who appears to "tamper" with it as "undemocratic." Yet, the simple fact is that nobody really believes all men deserve equal opportunities. At the very least this moral rule must be qualified, and quite possibly the interests of clarity would best be served if we never appealed to it at all. Who, for instance, believes that the mentally retarded are entitled to the opportunity of enrolling in a first-rate university along with those of great intellectual capacity? Who believes that a third-rate singer is entitled to the opportunity of singing at the Metropolitan along with a first-rate singer? In order to take account of these cases, perhaps the rule of equality could be restated: All men are entitled to equal opportunities provided they are all equally capable of benefiting from them and equally deserving. But even these qualifications are insufficient. Most persons believe that parents have the right to give their children superior advantages if they possibly can; and very few persons, at least in America, would wish to deprive parents of this right, even though in practice this means that some children will have greater opportunities than others with the same innate capabilities or merits. To allow for such exceptions, the rule of equality would have to be modified once again. Perhaps it could be stated: All men are entitled to equal opportunities provided (1) they are equally capable of benefiting from them and equally deserving and (2) the granting of equal opportunities does not have undesirable social consequences.

Even so stated it is unlikely that the rule could withstand further criticism, but it is not necessary to carry the analysis further in order to see that moral rules are frequently couched in oversimplified language. Those who hope to be clear about moral issues will have to subject moral rules to careful analysis and when necessary abandon them, even at the risk of being branded a "dangerous intellectual."

The third common pitfall in moral reasoning is a tendency to overwork and misuse analogies. Take, for example, the problem of determining the proper nature and degree of student participation in policy making at an American college. A military man is likely to construe a college as a kind of miniature military organization with a chain of command running from the board of trustees at the top of the pyramid to the students at the bottom, and it may seem self-evident to him that students have no right to participate in the formation of college policy. An industrialist or a businessman, on the other hand, will tend to consider the board of trustees and the administration as management, the faculty as clerks or assembly workers, and the students as customers or clients. In this case it will seem clear that the trustees and the administration must retain ultimate control but that the students must be catered to and given what they want. A convinced liberal democrat, however, is likely to regard a college as a community of faculty and students and to take it for granted that decisions ought to be made by a majority vote in faculty-student committees (to which representatives of the administration might be invited as nonvoting members since it is their duty to execute the policies determined by the legislative body). All these analogies have grave defects, yet it is surprisingly easy to be misled by them.

An even cruder instance of analogical reasoning was implicit in a display at a college football game during the height of the cold war. Spread across the front of a fraternity were two banners, one directly below the other, reading "Beat Yale" and "Beat Russia." Similarly, it has been argued that we ought to take decisive measures against a Communist move in the cold war because if somebody hits you, you hit back. Of course, if one is already committed to a policy of strong action as the proper method for resolving differences between the "free world" and Communist countries, these analogies will probably be welcomed as effective propaganda. If, however, one is interested in determining what policy ought to be adopted, these analogies are next to useless. The ways in which the cold war is similar to a football game or a fist fight are few and insignificant; the ways in which they differ are numerous and of the utmost importance. In a football game or a fist fight nobody is likely to get hurt except the parties directly involved, and even the participants are unlikely to get hurt seriously. By contrast, if the cold war becomes a hot war millions of men will probably die. In a football game there are accepted rules and an umpire to see that both parties observe them. There are few generally accepted rules of international relations, however, and there is no umpire to enforce observance of those rules that do exist. Finally, if one is struck physically, one usually does not have time to think and responds more or less instinctively. Moves in the cold war ordinarily leave time for reflection. Hopefully, we shall respond to them with due regard for the rules of logic and in full knowledge of all available and relevant facts.

EXERCISES FOR CHAPTER SIXTEEN

Examine the following arguments. What is the pattern of the argument? What moral principles or moral rules seem to be involved? Has the author overlooked any relevant moral rules? Do the rules involved require qualification? What factual issues are relevant?

1. "A man drowned his incurably ill child, suffering from tuberculosis and gangrene of the face. He had nursed her with devoted care, but one morning after sitting up with her all night, could no longer bear to see her suffering. The jury returned a verdict of 'not guilty' of murder. In the course of his summing-up Mr. Justice Branson said: 'It is a matter which gives food for thought when one comes to consider that, had this poor child been an animal instead of a human being, so far from there being anything blameworthy in the man's action in putting an end to its suffering, he would actually have been liable to punishment if he had not done so.'" (Glanville Williams, *The Sanctity of Life and the Criminal Law*)

2. "An American explorer in the Amazon was appalled by the practice of slavery among the Indians. A missionary in the region to whom he spoke of the matter said:

   "'You see, my friend, slavery cannot be abolished. Our economy is built on it. As long as each tree will produce thirty kilos of rubber, there is no hope of relief. Slavery must always be deplored, but must never be abolished. At best we compromise, and make the life of the slaves a little less brutal.'

   "'If this were known in the United States—surely something could be done.'

   "'My poor friend!—the United States buys all our rubber!'" (Leonard Clark, *The Rivers Ran East*)

3. "The only proper purpose of a government is to protect

man's rights, which means: to protect him from physical violence. A proper government is only a policeman, acting as an agent of man's self-defense, and, as such, may resort to force *only* against those who *start* the use of force. The only proper functions of a government are the police, to protect you from criminals; the army, to protect you from foreign invaders; and the courts, to protect your property and contracts from breach or fraud by others, to settle disputes by rational rules, according to objective law. But a government that *initiates* the employment of force against men who had forced no one, the employment of armed compulsion against disarmed victims, is a nightmare infernal machine designed to annihilate morality: such a government reverses its only moral purpose and switches from the role of protector to the role of man's deadliest enemy, from the role of policeman to the role of a criminal vested with the right to the wielding of violence against victims deprived of the right of self-defense. Such a government substitutes for morality the following rule of social conduct: you may do whatever you please to your neighbor, provided your gang is bigger than his." (Ayn Rand, *Atlas Shrugged*)

4. "What should we think of an individual who proclaimed: 'I am morally and intellectually superior to all other individuals, and, because of this superiority, I have a right to ignore all interests except my own'? There are, of course, plenty of people who *feel* this way, but if they proclaim their feeling too openly, and act upon it too blatantly, they are thought ill of. When, however, a number of such individuals, constituting the population of some area, collectively make such a declaration about themselves, they are thought noble and splendid and spirited. They put up statues to each other and teach school-children to admire the most blatant advocates of national conceit." (Bertrand Russell, *Common Sense and Nuclear Warfare*)

5. "Pacifism is very noble and war is very horrible indeed. But in our present state of society, people who announce that they will not bear arms to resist aggression are only

inviting aggression; if everyone acted thus, the good people in the world would be exterminated by the bad ones. Those who are pacifists today have lived to be so and are able to preach their doctrine, because in the period 1939–45 there were enough people who were *not* pacifists: the Allied armies made their pacifism possible by defending them against a tyranny which, had it been victorious, would have taken away most of their liberties, including their right to preach pacifism." (Quoted in John Hospers, *Human Conduct*)

6. "Suppose that, during 1942 and 1943, the firm of J. A. Topf & Sons, manufacturers of refractory furnaces, had sent recruiters to the technical institutes of Germany, seeking engineers to take part in the design and production of very large furnaces for Government installations at Auschwitz, Sobibor, Chelmno, etc. . . .

"We who . . . are appalled by the indiscriminate agony created in Vietnam by what Dow Chemical produces [napalm] can see no shred of justification for any university's abetting Dow Chemical's misdeeds; nor can we see any sense in which freedom of speech or freedom of anything else (save to corrupt) can meaningly be invoked here." (Rudolph von Abele, letter to the editor, in *The New Republic,* November 18, 1967)

7. "There is a vast empire governed by a monarch whose strange conduct is very proper to confound the minds of his subjects. He wishes to be known, loved, respected, obeyed; but never shows himself to his subjects, and everything conspires to render uncertain the ideas formed of his character.

"The people subjected to his power have of the character and laws of their invisible sovereign such ideas only, as his ministers give them. They, however, confess that they have no idea of their master, that his ways are impenetrable, his views and nature totally incomprehensible. These ministers, likewise, disagree upon the commands they pretend have been issued by the sovereign, whose instruments they call themselves. They announce them differently to each province of the empire. They defame one another, and mutually treat each other as imposters and false teachers. The decrees and ordinances they take upon themselves to promulgate are obscure; they are enigmas, little calculated to be understood, or even divined by the subjects for whose instruction they were intended. The laws of the concealed monarch require interpreters; but the interpreters are always disputing upon the true manner of understanding them. Besides they are not consistent with themselves; all they relate of their concealed prince is only a thread of contradiction. They utter concerning him not a single word that does not immediately confute itself. They call him supremely good; yet there is no one who does not complain of his decrees. They suppose him infinitely wise; and under his administration everything appears to contradict reason and good sense. They extol his justice; and the best of his subjects are generally the least favored. They assert he sees everything; yet his presence avails nothing. He is, they say, the friend of order; yet throughout his dominions all is in confusion and disorder. He makes all for himself, and the events seldom answer his designs. He foresees everything, but cannot prevent anything. He impatiently suffers offence, yet gives every one the power of offending him. Men admire the wisdom and perfection of his works; yet his works, full of imperfection, are short of duration. He is continually doing and undoing: repairing what he has made, but is never pleased with his work. In all his undertakings he proposes only his own glory; yet is never glorified. His only end is the happiness of his subjects; and his subjects, for the most part, want necessaries. Those, whom he seems to favor, are generally least satisfied with their fate; almost all appear in perpetual revolt against a master, whose greatness they never cease to admire, whose wisdom to extol, whose goodness to adore, whose justice to fear, and whose laws to reverence, though never obeyed!

"This empire is the world; this monarch God; his ministers are the priests; his subjects mankind." (Paul Henri d'Holbach, *Good Sense*)

8. "Why should government-guaranteed incomes make the

poor any more shiftless than unearned or inherited incomes make the rich?

"It is questionable whether the percentage of bums among the dependent poor would match the proportion of playboys among the idle rich." (Malvine Cole, letter to the editor, in *The New York Times*, January 2, 1967)

9. A New York high school introduced a course in Swahili, one of the major languages of Negro Africa. A champion of the program was reported to have said that the course constituted "a positive step in the betterment of race relations. Any move in opposition can only be interpreted as racist." (*The New York Times*, November 18, 1967)

10. "I was taught in school that a logical conclusion can be no better than the premise it is based upon. And I was also taught, what many people forget, that a premise cannot be any better than the conclusion which it validly implies.

"Like Spinoza, we can set down innocent-seeming axioms:

Axiom: A basic goal is 'freedom of the individual to pursue his own interests so long as he does not interfere with the freedom of others to do likewise.'

"From premises like these we are supposed to deduce that the draft is a bad thing, that graduated tax structures based on income are a perversion of democracy, that the farm program is a mess, that government expenditure is now much too high, and that its trend should be slowed down in order to minimize arbitrary power.

"Well, who would confess to being against an increase in freedom all around, when such a movement can be identified and shown to be possible? We are all against simple sin. However, every one of the hard issues upon which Congress and the citizenry have to vote involves delicate quantitative questions of whose freedom and well-being is to be increased and at what cost to the freedom, well-being and opportunities of others.

"We live in an interdependent world. . . . Consider the homely example of traffic regulations. Stoplights involve coercion over my free will. The tyranny of government has reared its ugly head. All power corrupts, as some sage almost said in a letter to his friend. Of course, this is all balderdash." (Paul Samuelson, "The Case Against Goldwater's Economics," in *The New York Times Magazine*, October 25, 1964)

11. "Inevitably, every drug represents an experiment that continues until some time after it is put on the market. Almost no one is satisfied with the preliminary toxicity tests, in which two or more species of animals get a new drug in doses much stiffer than those intended for human therapy. If the animals fare badly—e.g., develop cancers or kidney failures—the drug is promptly abandoned. This is a prudent way of experimenting, to be sure, but in some cases it is undoubtedly much too cautious for the good of medicine. No one knows how many valuable drugs have been passed up because of discouraging tests on animals.

"Quinine, for example, would probably never reach the market if it were discovered today. Repeated doses cause blindness in dogs, though not in human beings. Aspirin, too, would be quickly eliminated because it harms rat embryos. Besides, it is only mildly effective in its original role as a pain-killer, yet most specialists now agree that it is the best weapon available against rheumatoid arthritis." (George A. W. Boehm, "He Is Shaking 'Food and Drug' Well Before Using," in *The New York Times Magazine*, May 15, 1966)

12. "We may sum up this discussion in a few words. Science has not given men more self-control, more kindliness, or more power of discounting their passions in deciding upon a course of action. It has given communities more power to indulge their collective passions. . . . Men's collective passions are mainly evil; far the strongest of them are hatred and rivalry directed toward other groups. Therefore at present all that gives men power to indulge their collective passions is bad. That is why science threatens to cause the destruction of our civilization." (Bertrand Russell, *Icarus, or the Future of Science*)

13. "Undoubtedly for those who use marijuana so frequently and so excessively as to become social derelicts, society pays a large cost. In the first place, these unfortunates use

either private or public resources for their medical and social care. In the second place, and of greater consequence, our relatively limited medical, hospital and welfare personnel and facilities used for those victims of marijuana are unavailable for others whose illness or poverty is more deserving of our compassion. The social balance sheet bears charges which ought not to be in the reckoning.

"From the foregoing facts, it does appear that the marijuana problem is of social and not merely of private consequence. J. S. Mill to the contrary notwithstanding, there is no such thing as a vice which is purely private in its total aspect. He who overindulges in any way with respect to drugs, with respect to food, with respect to liquor, with respect to sensuality, alters the lives of others than himself and his private associates. He is unavailable for civic obligation which rests upon him. He bears a responsibility for the unavailability of social and medical services gravely needed by others.

"Yet against the impressive considerations just stated, one must weigh—and in my opinion weigh more heavily—the social costs of trying to limit by law private indulgence in vice. Every attempt of the law to detect, prosecute and punish wrong represents an expenditure not merely of time, effort, manpower and money, but also a concession to the forces of coercion as distinguished from persuasion. Moreover, law enforcement in the area of what some regard as private morality and private consumption almost inevitably entails the use of despicable, or, at any rate, unworthy enforcement measures. Informers, undercover operators, blackmailers, and often corrupt enforcement authorities have opportunities far more dangerous than in the suppression of conventional types of crime.

"In the end, liberty tends to be sacrificed for the supposedly greater advantage of health, safety and morals. To some, including myself, the sacrifice is inconsistent with our ultimate political beliefs." (Charles E. Wyzanski, Jr., "Marijuana: It's Up to the Young to Solve the Problem," in *The New Republic*, October 21, 1967)

14. There is a story about the abolitionist Wendell Phillips, who was approached by a group of Southern clergymen.

"Are you Wendell Phillips?" one of them asked.

"Yes," he replied.

"Are you the great abolitionist?"

"I am not great, but I am an abolitionist."

"Are you the one who makes speeches in Boston and New York decrying slavery?"

"Yes, sir. I am."

"Why don't you go to Kentucky and make speeches there?"

After a pause, Phillips asked: "Are you a clergyman?"

"Yes, I am," was the reply.

"Are you trying to save souls from hell?"

"Indeed."

"Well, why don't you go there?"

15. An attorney may consult law books at will. A physician may look up cases in medical books. So why aren't students permitted the use of textbooks during examinations?

16. Students have no right to participate in decisions regarding curricula. Would you care to be treated in a hospital where methods of therapy were determined by a committee of patients and doctors?

17. "It is often asked: 'But what if a country cannot find a sufficient number of volunteers?' Even so, this would not give the rest of the population a right to the lives of the country's young men. But, in fact, the lack of volunteers occurs for one of two reasons: (1) If a country is demoralized by a corrupt, authoritarian government, its citizens will not volunteer to defend it. But neither will they fight for long, if drafted. For example, observe the literal disintegration of the Czarist Russian army in World War I. (2) If a country's government undertakes to fight a war for some reason other than self-defense, for a purpose which the citizens neither share nor understand, it will not find many volunteers. Thus a volunteer army is one of the best protectors of peace, not only against foreign aggression, but also against any warlike ideologies or projects on the part of a country's own government.

"Not many men would volunteer for such wars as Korea or Vietnam. Without the power to draft, the makers of our foreign policy would not be able to embark on adventures of that kind. This is one of the best practical reasons for the abolition of the draft." (Ayn Rand, *Capitalism: The Unknown Ideal*)

18. "This leads us to the third—and the worst—argument, used by some 'conservatives': the attempt to defend capitalism on the ground of *man's depravity.*

"This argument runs as follows: since men are weak, fallible, non-omniscient and innately depraved, no man may be entrusted with the responsibility of being a dictator and of ruling everybody else; therefore, a free society is the proper way of life for imperfect creatures. Please grasp fully the implications of this argument: since men are depraved, they are *not good enough for a dictatorship;* freedom is all that they deserve; if they were perfect, they would be worthy of a totalitarian state.

". . . dictatorships—this theory declares—and all the other disasters of the modern world are man's punishment for the sin of relying on his intellect and of attempting to improve his life on earth by seeking to devise a perfect political system and to establish a *rational* society. This means that humility, passivity, lethargic resignation and a belief in Original Sin are the bulwarks of capitalism. . . .

"The cynical, man-hating advocates of this theory sneer at all ideals, scoff at all human aspirations and deride all attempts to improve men's existence. 'You can't change human nature,' is their stock answer to the socialists. Thus they concede that socialism *is* the ideal, but human nature is unworthy of it; after which, they invite men to crusade for capitalism. . . . Who will fight and die to defend his status as a miserable sinner? If, as a result of such theories, people become contemptuous of 'conservatism,' do not wonder and do not ascribe it to the cleverness of the socialists." (Ayn Rand, *Capitalism: The Unknown Ideal*)

19. "For this [the Johnson Administration] to support and boast of the Peace Corps is as though Murder, Inc., were to sponsor an orphanage and point to this as extenuation of

its other activities." (Gerald D. Berreman, *The Nation*, February 26, 1968)

20. "In a letter published on February 27, Robert M. Byrn of the Fordham law faculty asked, 'If destruction of the fetus is justified because of a substantial risk that the child will be born defective, then should not post-natal destruction of a defective child also be justified?'

"Mr. Byrn's question assumes that a fetus during the early months of pregnancy is a human being, as the already born child is. His own church taught the contrary for seven centuries, and the system of secular law he professes taught the contrary for six.

". . . in 1869, Pius IX amended the canon law so as to treat abortion during the early months of pregnancy on a par with abortion during the later months.

"The pre-1869 canonical dividing point was forty days after conception if the fetus was male, eighty if female, but as it was usually impossible to ascertain the sex to which the fetus had belonged, the eighty-day rule was the one normally applied. The Anglo-American rule of quickening was more liberal because, though the time of this phenomenon varies from one woman to another, it rarely occurs so soon as eighty days after conception.

"Eugenic abortion is not, as Mr. Byrn fears, a program for breeding *Supermenschen* but of preventing the birth of monsters. Now that science has, in some cases, armed us with the power to detect and prevent monstrous births, many Jews and Christians will interpret the command 'Be fruitful and multiply' (Genesis i, 28) as restricted, in the object of the reproduction commanded, to the 'image' and 'likeness' of God mentioned in the preceding verses (Genesis i, 26–27). . . .

"One prosecuted under a state abortion statute who had acted upon this religious belief should be sustained, I think, in a defense based on the free exercise of religion clause of the First Amendment, made applicable to the states by the Fourteenth." (Cyril C. Means, Jr., letter to the editor, in *The New York Times*, April 16, 1965)

21. "We have now recognized the necessity to the mental well-

being of mankind (on which all their other well-being depends) of freedom of opinion and freedom of the expression of opinion, on four distinct grounds; which we will now briefly recapitulate.

"First, if any opinion is compelled to silence, that opinion may, for aught we can certainly know, be true. To deny this is to assume our own infallibility.

"Secondly, though the silenced opinion be an error, it may and very commonly does, contain a portion of truth; and since the general or prevailing opinion on any subject is rarely or never the whole truth, it is only by the collision of adverse opinions that the remainder of the truth has any chance of being supplied.

"Thirdly, even if the received opinion be not only true, but the whole truth; unless it is suffered to be, and actually is, vigorously and earnestly contested, it will, by most of those who receive it, be held in the manner of a prejudice, with little comprehension or feeling of its rational grounds. And not only this, but, fourthly, the meaning of the doctrine itself will be in danger of being lost, or enfeebled, and deprived of its vital effect on the character and conduct: the dogma becoming a mere formal profession, inefficacious for good, but cumbering the ground, and preventing the growth of any real and heartfelt conviction, from reason or personal experience." (John Stuart Mill, *On Liberty*)

22. "Should the wealth of churches be taxed? The question, which has been raised with increasing frequency in the United States in recent years, came to the fore again last week. . . .

"The practice of exempting Christian churches from paying taxes was begun in the fourth century by the Emperor Constantine, as part of his plan to make Christianity the official religion of the Empire. He reasoned that if the state taxed churches, it would in effect be taxing itself.

"A similar situation arose in the American Colonies and in the period immediately after the American Revolution, when the various states had their own established religions.

"The custom of exempting churches from taxation survived disestablishment in the late eighteenth and early nineteenth centuries, but the development of a fair legal means for preserving the exemption has not always been smooth.

"In recent years a growing number of persons—especially Protestant churchmen—have begun to argue that present formulas are inadequate. . . .

"One of the principal arguments against relief for religious organizations is that it is a patently unconstitutional subsidy of religion that forces nonbelievers to pay higher taxes.

"It is also argued that financially hard-pressed state and local governments can no longer afford to exempt church-owned real estate and other resources from taxes.

"Two main arguments are used by those who favor tax exemptions. Roman Catholics have argued most fervently that the power to tax is the power to control or destroy, and that tax exemption for religious groups is essential to the separation of church and state.

"The other argument is that religious groups, like charities, schools and other tax-exempt organizations, provide useful social services that the Government would otherwise have to assume itself, and that religion enriches society through those who choose to participate in it." (Edward B. Fiske, "Religion: To Tax, or Not to Tax?" in *The New York Times*, May 28, 1967)

23. Below is the text of a statement broadcast on the Vatican radio the day after Mrs. Robert Finkbine, an American, had an abortion performed legally under Swedish law in Stockholm. Mrs. Finkbine, who had taken the child-deforming drug thalidomide, feared that the child would be abnormal, and her doctors confirmed that view:

"A crime has been committed. What happened yesterday morning at the Caroline Hospital in Stockholm, Sweden, cannot be defined otherwise. Morally, objectively it is a crime; and all the more serious because it was committed legally. The motives adduced are false and captious pretexts, and they do not justify it.

"There was no uncertainty, no doubt whatsoever that

378 PART TWO: ARGUMENT

the victim was a human being. It was simply ascertained, it is reported, that the child Mrs. Finkbine carried in her womb would have seriously threatened the mental and physical life of the mother, had it been born deformed.

"The child was killed as if it had been an aggressor, against whom self-defense is more than justified; but a mother's womb is the natural abode of the child yet unborn. And whoever limits himself simply to live there where nature has destined him cannot be considered an aggressor, a threat to someone else's life.

"It is not the child's fault if his existence or his physical and mental makeup endangers others, even his mother; he has not desired life, and even less asked for life. It is therefore arbitrary to consider him as an intruder and sentence him to capital punishment.

"It is sad to think there are laws that authorize such things. Everyone has his own ideas regarding civilization, but all agree that man is the foundation, subject and end of all true civilization. No one doubts that what happened yesterday in Stockholm was prompted by humanitarian feelings, but only an aberration can prompt to kill for humanitarian purposes." ("Is Abortion Ever Justified?" in *U.S. News and World Report,* September 3, 1962)

24. "Chastity is the most unpopular of the Christian virtues. There is no getting away from it: the old Christian rule is, 'Either marriage, with complete faithfulness to your partner, or else total abstinence.' Now this is so difficult and so contrary to our instincts, that obviously either Christianity is wrong or our sexual instinct, as it now is, has gone wrong. One or the other. Of course, being a Christian, I think it is the instinct which has gone wrong.

"But I have other reasons for thinking so. The biological purpose of sex is children, just as the biological purpose of eating is to repair the body. Now if we eat whenever we feel inclined and just as much as we want, it is quite true that most of us will eat too much: but not terrifically too much. One man may eat enough for two, but he does not eat enough for ten. The appetite goes a little beyond its biological purpose, but not enormously. But if a healthy young man indulged his sexual appetite whenever he felt inclined, and if each act produced a baby, then in ten years he might easily populate a small village. This appetite is in ludicrous and preposterous excess of its function.

"Or take it another way. You can get a large audience together for a strip-tease act—that is, to watch a girl undress on the stage. Now suppose you came to a country where you could fill a theatre by simply bringing a covered plate on to the stage and then slowly lifting the cover so as to let every one see, just before the lights went out, that it contained a mutton chop or a bit of bacon, would you not think that in that country something had gone wrong with the appetite for food?" (C. S. Lewis, *Mere Christianity*)

25. "Strictly speaking, every man is free at any time to say whatever he wishes, whether he is in a totalitarian or a democratic society. What he is not always free to do is to say it *to* someone else. In short, he is not free to *communicate*. Freedom of speech really is freedom of communication. It is not a private right unrelated to the rights of others, but a relation between men in which the listener is fully as significant as the speaker. Indeed, we may go one step further. Freedom of speech, to be genuine, must be reciprocal—the listener must be free in turn to become the speaker. In other words, when we speak about the right of free speech, we are really talking about the right of free men to enter into the *cooperative* relationship of communication. It follows from this that men can only bring about freedom of speech cooperatively. It is contrary to the very concept of free speech to speak of forcing or tricking a man into it. . . .

"It [also] follows from the above that the old phrase, 'free marketplace of ideas,' is a quite inadequate description of the political forum in a democracy. The image of a marketplace of ideas derived, of course, from the classical economic concept of a free economic marketplace, in which goods compete for the money of the consumers. By analogy, the political forum is viewed as a market in which ideas are put up for sale, and compete for the assent of the citizens. In the forum, the ideas put forward may in some sense be viewed as 'competitors' for our assent. But the proponents of the ideas ought not to consider themselves as competing producers, on the analogy of economics. If they are genuinely devoted to the pursuit of truth, they will adopt an attitude quite different from that of a manufacturer seeking profits. The manufacturer is not expected by classical economics to exercise a personal censorship of his product, withdrawing it from the market as soon as he sees that a superior brand has appeared. The consumers can perform that function by ceasing to buy from him. In the political forum, on the other hand, the speaker genuinely devoted to the truth will withdraw his ideas as soon as *he* has been convinced of their falsehood. It is just this willingness to abide by the objective and universal criterion of truth that distinguishes genuine democratic debate from mere propaganda battles. However debased one may think the political debates have become in this country, still it would take a thorough cynic to see in them nothing more than advertising battles among competing brands. Contrary to what many men have thought, a thoroughgoing market mentality would be the death of democratic discourse." (Robert Paul Wolff, *The Rhetoric of Deterrence,* an unpublished manuscript)

26. "We may define 'faith' as a firm belief in something for which there is no evidence. We do not speak of faith that two and two are four or that the earth is round. . . . Christians have faith in the Resurrection; Communists have faith in Marx's theory of Value. Neither faith can be defended rationally, and each, therefore, is defended by propaganda and, if necessary, by war. The two are equal in this respect. If you think it immensely important that people should believe something which can not be rationally defended, it makes no difference what that something is. Where you control the government, you teach the something to the immature minds of children and you burn or prohibit books which teach the contrary. Where you do not control the government, you will, if you are strong

enough, build up armed forces with a view to conquest. . . .

". . . I admit at once that new systems of dogma, such as those of the Nazis and the Communists, are even worse than the old systems, but they could never have acquired a hold over men's minds if orthodox habits had not been instilled in youth. Stalin's language is full of reminiscences of the theological seminary in which he received his training." (Bertrand Russell, *Human Society in Ethics and Politics*)

382 ACKNOWLEDGMENTS (cont. from p. iv)

THE NEW YORK TIMES—For excerpt from George A. W. Boehm, "He Is Shaking 'Food and Drug' Well Before Using," *The New York Times Magazine*, © 1966 by The New York Times Company; for excerpt from Malvine Cole, "Incomes for the Poor," *The New York Times*, © 1967 by The New York Times Company; for excerpts from "Deserters: Problem for the Military," editorial, *The New York Times*, © 1967 by The New York Times Company; for excerpt from Edward B. Fiske, "Religion: To Tax or Not To Tax?" *The New York Times*, © 1967 by The New York Times Company; for excerpt from Joseph Lelyveld, "The Afrikaner Feels Lonely in the World," *The New York Times Magazine*, © 1966 by The New York Times Company; for excerpt from John Leo, "Dominant Mothers Are Called the Key to Hippies," *The New York Times*, © 1967 by The New York Times Company; for excerpt from Cyril C. Means, Jr., "Eugenic Abortion," *The New York Times*, © 1965 by The New York Times Company; for excerpt from Charles C. Moskos, Jr., "A Sociologist Appraises the G.I.," *The New York Times Magazine*, © 1967 by The New York Times Company; for excerpt from Oded I. Remba, "Socialism No Issue," *The New York Times*, © 1964 by The New York Times Company; for excerpt from Paul Samuelson, "The Case Against Goldwater's Economics," *The New York Times Magazine*, © 1964 by The New York Times Company; for excerpt from Harold M. Schmeck, Jr., "Hawaii Genetics Study Suggests Difference in the Races Is Slight," *The New York Times*, © 1965 by The New York Times Company; for excerpt from Alfred Soman, "Elections Not Sport," *The New York Times*, © 1968 by The New York Times Company; for excerpt from Theodore Winner, "Reality of Ghetto," *The New York Times*, © 1968 by The New York Times Company. All reprinted by permission.

PENGUIN BOOKS LTD.—For excerpts from H. J. Eysenck, *Uses and Abuses of Psychology;* for excerpt from Michael Harrington, *The Accidental Century;* for excerpts from Erwin Stengel, *Suicide and Attempted Suicide;* for excerpts from Robert H. Thouless, *Experimental Psychical Research;* for excerpt from D. J. West, *Homosexuality.* All reprinted by permission.

PUBLISHERS-HALL SYNDICATE—For excerpts from Sylvia Porter, "What is Inflation?" *New York Post,* and "Who Are the Unemployed?" *New York Post.* SYLVIA PORTER courtesy Publishers-Hall Syndicate.

ROUTLEDGE & KEGAN PAUL LTD.—For excerpts from Harry M. Johnson, *Sociology: A Systematic Introduction.* Reprinted by permission.

SCHOCKEN BOOKS INC.—For excerpts from C. A. R. Crosland, *The Future of Socialism.* Reprinted by permission of Schocken Books Inc. Copyright © 1956, 1963 by C. A. R. Crosland.

SCIENCE—For excerpt from W. Farnsworth Loomis, "Skin-Pigment Regulation of Vitamin-D Biosynthesis in Man," *Science*, Vol. 157, pp. 501–06, August 4, 1967. Copyright © 1967 by the American Association for the Advancement of Science. Reprinted by permission.

SCIENTIFIC AMERICAN—For excerpt from Joseph V. Brady, "Ulcers in 'Executive Monkeys,'" *Scientific American.* Copyright © 1958 by Scientific American, Inc. All rights reserved.

SCOTT, FORESMAN AND COMPANY—For excerpts from R. S. Peters, *Ethics and Education.* © George Allen & Unwin Ltd., 1966. Published by Scott, Foresman and Company.

U.S. NEWS & WORLD REPORT—For excerpts from "Is Abortion Ever Justified?" *U.S. News & World Report,* September 3, 1962. Copyright © 1962 by *U.S. News & World Report.*

W.C.C. PUBLISHING COMPANY, INC.—For excerpt from Martin G. Berck, "A Bircher Defines His Society's Aims," *New York Herald Tribune.* Reprinted by permission of W.C.C. Publishing Company, Inc.

THE WORLD PUBLISHING COMPANY—For excerpts from Ayn Rand, *Capitalism: The Unknown Ideal.* Reprinted by permission of The World Publishing Company. Copyright © 1946, 1962, 1964, 1966 by Ayn Rand (an NAL book).

Glossary

Most of the terms defined below are terms used in the text of *Meaning and Argument*. Some, however, are not used in this book but are included because students may encounter them in their general reading. Similarly, most of the definitions given are those adopted by the author in the main body of the text. But on occasion widely used alternative definitions are also given. Entries for terms not used in the text as well as alternative definitions of terms that are used in the text have been italicized.

ABSTRACTNESS: A term is abstract if and only if it is used to designate a trait or an activity of a thing or event or of a class of things or events. (Abstractness is contrasted with concreteness.)

ABUSIVE AD HOMINEM: (1) a fallacious argument designed to discredit some position by introducing logically irrelevant considerations relating to its advocate or advocates; (2) a fallacious inference to the effect that some position is weaker than it actually is because of logically irrelevant beliefs concerning its advocate or advocates.

AD HOC HYPOTHESIS: *an hypothesis whose explanatory power is limited to the fact or facts it was introduced to explain.*

AD HOMINEM: an informal fallacy of relevance having two forms known respectively as 'circumstantial ad hominem' and 'abusive ad hominem.' (The Latin means literally 'to the man.')

ADDITION: (1) an elementary valid rule of inference based on the following principle: if a proposition is given, we are authorized to infer any disjunction of which it is a disjunct; (2) an elementary

383

valid argument form exemplifying this rule of inference. For example,

$$\frac{p}{p \lor q} \qquad \frac{p}{p \lor q \lor r} \qquad \frac{p}{r \lor q \lor p}$$

AFFIRMING THE CONSEQUENT: the invalid argument form

$$\frac{p \to q}{q}$$
$$\frac{}{p}$$

(See also FALLACY OF AFFIRMING THE CONSEQUENT.)

AMBIGUITY: (1) A class term or a singular name is ambiguous if and only if it has two different strict intensions. (2) A property term is ambiguous if and only if its corresponding class term is ambiguous. (3) A sentence is ambiguous if and only if it contains an ambiguous term or has a grammatical construction that permits two different interpretations. (See also TYPE-AMBIGUITY, TOKEN AMBIGUITY, CONTEXTUAL AMBIGUITY, USER AMBIGUITY, AMPHIBOLY.)

AMPHIBOLY: an ambiguous sentence whose grammatical construction permits two different interpretations.

ANALOGICAL ARGUMENT: an argument based on the inference that if one individual or class shares one or more properties with a second individual or class, one or more other properties of the first are also shared by the second.

ANALOGICAL BASE: individuals or classes identified in the premises of an analogical argument but not named in the conclusion.

ANALOGICAL MODEL: the analogical base in an argument from an analogical model.

ANALOGICAL SUBJECT: an individual or class named in the conclusion of an analogical argument.

ANTECEDENT: (1) a first-order component of a conditional proposition which when expressed in standard sentence form immediately follows the word 'if' in the logical operator 'If . . . then . . .'; (2) a sentence or group of sentences used to express an antecedent in sense 1.

APPROXIMATE LAW OF FUNCTIONAL DEPENDENCE: a law of functional dependence that is either not truly universal as stated or fails to relate each determinate measurable change in one variable to a determinate measurable change in the others.

APPROXIMATE LAW OF NATURE: an imprecisely stated law of nature in which the cause and the effect as stated are not universally related to one another.

ARGUMENT: a group of propositions consisting of a conclusion, the proposition the argument is alleged to establish, and one or more premises, propositions the arguer offers as evidence for the conclusion. (This term is also used loosely to refer to a set of sentences expressing an argument.)

ARGUMENT FORM: (1) the pattern of a class of arguments that is symbolized solely with the aid of logical constants and logical variables; (2) a symbolic formula expressing an argument form in sense 1.

ARGUMENT BY ELIMINATION: an argument one of whose premises is a disjunction, whose other premises deny all but one of the disjuncts, and which is used to confirm an hypothesis.

ARGUMENT BY SUBSUMPTION: (1) a deductive argument whose premises cite one or more laws of nature and which is intended to show that the state of affairs identified by the conclusion is a special case of the law or laws cited; (2) a moral argument whose premises cite one or more moral rules or ultimate moral principles and from which the conclusion follows deductively.

ARGUMENT FROM AN ANALOGICAL MODEL: an analogical argument whose analogical base can not be plausibly construed as a fair sample relative to the conclusion.

ARGUMENT FROM A STATISTICAL CORRELATION: an argument proceeding from an assertion of a statistical correlation to the assertion of an approximate law of nature.

ARGUMENTATIVE DISCOURSE: discourse used to express inferences.

ARGUMENTUM AD BACULUM (APPEAL TO THREATS): *an argument designed to encourage the fallacious inference that its conclusion is true because an interpreter's failure to accept it as true would have undesirable consequences for him. (The Latin means literally 'argument to the club.')*

ARGUMENTUM AD IGNORANTIAM (APPEAL TO IGNORANCE): *an argument or inference resting on the fallacious belief that a given proposition must be true or false because there is no evidence for or against it. (For example, 'God must exist, since there is no evidence to the contrary.' The Latin means literally 'argument to ignorance.')*

ARGUMENTUM AD MISERICORDIAM (APPEAL TO PITY): *an argument designed to win acceptance for its conclusion by playing upon the interpreter's sympathy for an individual or group cited in the conclusion. (The Latin means literally 'argument to pity.')*

ARGUMENTUM AD POPULUM (APPEAL TO THE PEOPLE): *an argument designed to win acceptance for the conclusion by playing upon prejudices or base emotions attributed to the lower classes or the uneducated. (The Latin means literally 'argument to the people.')*

ARGUMENTUM AD VERECUNDIAM: see FALLACY OF ILLEGITIMATE APPEAL TO AUTHORITY.

ARISTOTELIAN LOGIC: the logical system devised by the Greek philosopher Aristotle in the fourth century B.C. It differs from modern symbolic logic in that it is primarily concerned with syllogisms and makes relatively little use of special symbols.

ARTIFICIAL SIGN: A sign is artificial if and only if (1) it is a product or creation of human beings, (2) it is used for the purpose of communication, and (3) it has acquired its meaning through some kind of convention, agreement, or understanding among its users.

ASSOCIATION: the elementary rules of replacement

$$(1) \quad (p \lor (q \lor r)) \leftrightarrow (p \lor q \lor r)$$
$$((p \lor q) \lor r) \leftrightarrow (p \lor (q \lor r))$$
etc.

$$(2) \quad (p \cdot (q \cdot r)) \leftrightarrow (p \cdot q \cdot r)$$
$$((p \cdot q) \cdot r) \leftrightarrow (p \cdot (q \cdot r))$$
etc.

The principles underlying these rules of replacement are respectively: (1) the grouping, or punctuation, of the disjuncts of a disjunction is irrelevant to the truth value of the disjunction; (2) the grouping, or punctuation, of the conjuncts of a conjunction is irrelevant to the truth value of the conjunction.

ASYMMETRICAL TERM: A relational term is asymmetrical if and only if the knowledge that it may be correctly attributed to one of the relata permits us to infer that it can not be attributed to the others.

ATTRIBUTIVE CLASS TERM: a class term used to say something about an already identified subject of discourse. (Attributive class terms are contrasted with class names.)

ATTRIBUTIVE PROPERTY TERM: a property term used to say something about an already identified subject of discourse. (Attributive property terms are contrasted with property names.)

BEHAVIORAL DEFINITION: an experimental definition of mental phenomena in terms of publicly observable behavioral responses to publicly observable environmental stimuli that may be experimentally manipulated.

BICONDITIONAL: (1) a truth-functional compound proposition whose first-order components when expressed in standard sentence form are connected by the logical operator 'if and only if'; (2) a sentence expressing a biconditional in sense 1.

BICONDITIONALITY: the elementary rules of replacement

$$(1) \quad (p \leftrightarrow q) . \leftrightarrow ((p \cdot q) \vee (-p \cdot -q))$$
$$(2) \quad (p \leftrightarrow q) \leftrightarrow ((p \rightarrow q) \cdot (q \rightarrow p))$$

BLACK AND WHITE FALLACY: an inference that a disjunctive proposition must be true because of the mistaken assumption that its disjuncts are contradictories when in fact they are merely contraries.

BORDERLINE CASE: (1) A borderline case relative to a class term is an individual whose inclusion in the denotation of the term is not clearly apparent or about whose inclusion different users of the term disagree. (2) A borderline case relative to a property term is a borderline case in sense 1 of the property term's corresponding class term.

CATEGOREMATIC TERM: a property term, a class term, or a singular name. (Categorematic terms are contrasted with syncategorematic terms.)

CAUSAL LAW: A sentence having the form 'C is the cause of E' (where 'C' stands for a cause and 'E' for an effect) expresses a causal law if and only if (1) C is a necessary condition, a sufficient condition, or a necessary and sufficient condition of E, (2) C is either temporally prior to or contemporary with E, and (3) C and E are not common effects or symptoms of a third phenomenon that explains both.

CEREMONIAL MEANING: A sentence has ceremonial meaning insofar as it can be reasonably interpreted as a sign of the speaker's regard for social etiquette or the amenities of human intercourse.

CIRCULAR DEFINITION: a definition whose definiens contains either the definiendum itself or a non-explicative synonym of the definiendum.

CIRCUMSTANTIAL AD HOMINEM: an informal fallacy of relevance that tends to elicit the support of the addressee because one of the premises indicates that the state of affairs identified by the conclusion would be in his interests.

CLASS NAME: a class term that is used to name a subject of discourse. (Class names are contrasted with attributive class terms.)

CLASS TERM: a verbal token that refers to a set of things or events with one or more common properties. (This term is also used loosely to refer to a verbal type whose tokens are usually class terms in the sense defined.)

CLOSED CLASS: a class for which all members may be explicitly identified or enumerated.

COGNITIVE MEANING: (1) A sentence has cognitive meaning if and only if it may properly be qualified as true or false. (2) A term has cognitive meaning if and only if it may be used to help express the cognitive meaning of a sentence.

COLLECTIVE NOUN: a common noun used to refer collectively to a group as a single unit rather than distributively to every member of the group.

COMMUTATION: the elementary rules of replacement

(1) $(p \lor q) \leftrightarrow (q \lor p)$, $(p \lor q \lor r) \leftrightarrow (p \lor r \lor q)$, etc.
(2) $(p \cdot q) \leftrightarrow (q \cdot p)$, $(p \cdot q \cdot r) \leftrightarrow (p \cdot r \cdot q)$, etc.

The principles underlying these rules of replacement are respectively: (1) the order in which the disjuncts of a disjunction appear is irrelevant to the truth value of the disjunction; (2) the order in which the conjuncts of a conjunction appear is irrelevant to the truth value of the conjunction.

COMPLETE EXPLANATORY ARGUMENT: an explanatory argument whose premises necessarily imply the conclusion.

COMPLETE STRICT INTENSION: any set of defining properties in a term's strict intension that gives a reasonably full account of the term's cognitive meaning.

COMPOUND: (1) A sentence is compound if and only if it contains one or more other sentences as components. (2) A proposition is compound if and only if it is expressed by a compound sentence.

COMPREHENSIVE CLASSIFICATION: a classification in which the subclasses cited include every member of the genus being classified.

CONCLUSION: The conclusion of an argument is the proposition the argument is alleged to establish.

CONCRETENESS: A term is concrete if and only if it is used to refer to a thing or event conceived as having an independent existence in a space-time continuum or to a class of things or events whose members are so conceived. (Concreteness is contrasted with abstractness.)

CONDITION: (1) One phenomenon is a condition of a second if the presence of the first is a reliable sign of the presence of the second or if the absence of the first is a reliable sign of the absence of the second. (2) One class of phenomena is a condition of a second if the presence of a member of the first is a reliable sign of the presence of a member of the second or if the absence of a member of the first is a reliable sign of the absence of a member of the second. (See also SUFFICIENT CONDITION and NECESSARY CONDITION.)

CONDITIONAL: (1) a compound proposition which consists of two first-order components and which is expressed in standard sentence form with the use of the logical operator 'If . . . then . . .'; (2) a compound sentence expressing a conditional in sense 1.

CONDITIONALITY: the elementary rules of replacement

$$(1)\ (p \to q) \leftrightarrow -(p \cdot -q)$$
$$(2)\ (p \to q) \leftrightarrow (-p \lor q)$$

CONJUNCT: a first-order component of a conjunction.

CONJUNCTION: (1) a truth-functional compound proposition whose first-order components when expressed in standard sentence form are connected by the logical operator 'and'; (2) a compound sentence expressing a conjunction in sense 1; (3) an elementary valid rule of inference based on the following principle: if two or more propositions are given separately, we are authorized to infer the conjunction of these propositions; (4) an elementary valid argument form exemplifying this rule of inference. For example,

$$\begin{array}{ccc} p & p & \\ q & q & \text{etc.} \\ \hline p \cdot q & r & \\ & \hline & p \cdot q \cdot r \end{array}$$

CONNOTATION: see TOTAL INTENSION.

CONNOTATIVE DEFINITION: (1) a proposition or set of propositions presumed to give a reasonably full account of the meaning of a class term or a singular name by acquainting us with certain properties in its strict intension; (2) a proposition or set of propositions presumed to give a reasonably full account of the meaning of a property term by acquainting us with certain properties in the strict intension of its corresponding class term.

CONSEQUENT: (1) a first-order component of a conditional proposition which when expressed in standard sentence form follows the word 'then' in the logical operator 'If . . . then . . .'; (2) a sentence or group of sentences used to express a consequent in sense 1.

CONTEXTUAL AMBIGUITY: (1) A class term or a singular name is contextually ambiguous if and only if it is employed by a single class of users with two or more different strict intensions in different contexts. (2) A property term is contextually ambiguous if and only if its corresponding class term is ambiguous.

CONTEXTUAL DEFINITION: a definition whose definiens cites conditions that must obtain in order for propositions expressed by a certain class of sentences containing the definiendum to be true.

CONTINGENT INTENSION: a class term's set of contingent properties considered collectively.

CONTINGENT PROPERTY: (1) a property of a class term that belongs to all or nearly all the objects in its denotation but that is neither a defining property nor a meaning criterion; (2) *a property of a class term that belongs to all the objects in its denotation but is not a defining property.*

CONTINGENT PROPOSITION: *a proposition whose truth or falsity does not depend upon its logical form alone. (Contingent propositions are contrasted with formal propositions and are also called 'factual propositions.')*

CONTRADICTORIES: two propositions that can not both be true and also can not both be false. (For example, 'All men are mortal' and 'Some men are not mortal.')

CONTRARIES: two propositions that cannot both be true but may both be false. (For example, 'All elephants are grey' and 'No elephants are grey.')

CONTROL GROUP: a set of observed instances cited in support of a law of nature in which the alleged condition is absent. (For example, if we were testing the validity of the law of nature 'Smoking causes lung cancer,' our control group would be a set of non-smokers.)

CONVENTIONAL MEANING: an intended meaning of many tokens of a given verbal type.

CONVERSE: (1) The converse of a subject-predicate sentence is formed by interchanging subject and predicate. (For example, the converse of 'All men are mammals' is 'All mammals are men.') The converse of a conditional sentence is formed by interchanging antecedent and consequent. (For example, the converse of 'If he is a Communist then he supports socialized medicine' is 'If he supports socialized medicine then he is a Communist.') (2) A proposition expressed by a converse in sense 1.

CORRELATIVE TERMS: two terms each of which is defined by reference to the other.

CORRESPONDING CONDITIONAL: The corresponding conditional of an argument is a standard-form conditional whose antecedent is a conjunction of the argument's premises and whose consequent is the conclusion.

CORRESPONDING TERM: (1) A class term corresponds to a property term if and only if the designatum of the property term consists of the defining properties of the class term. (2) A property term corresponds to a class term if and only if its designatum consists of the defining properties of the class term.

DEDUCTIVE ARGUMENT: An argument is deductive if and only if the arguer believes that the premises necessarily imply the conclusion.

DEDUCTIVE IMPLICATION: see NECESSARY IMPLICATION.

DEDUCTIVE LOGIC: that branch of logic concerned with deductive arguments.

DEDUCTIVE MODEL: a relatively small set of assumptions from which a large number of significant deductions may be made.

DEFINIENDUM: the term being defined in a definition.

DEFINIENS: any term or terms used to define another term.

DEFINING PROPERTY: (1) A defining property of a class term or a singular name is any property whose absence in an object is a sufficient condition for not using that term to denote that object. (2) A defining property of a property term is any defining property of that term's corresponding class term. (When used strictly, 'defining property' is predicated of terms; on occasion, however, it is also predicated of classes.)

DEFINISM: a position in moral philosophy according to which the problem of defining moral terms is simply a matter of making explicit or formulating clearly the rules that guide actual usage.

DEFINITE DESCRIPTION: a singular name consisting of a common noun preceded by the word 'the' or some other singularizing expression.

DEFINITION BY CLASSIFICATION: a definition intended to give a reasonably full account of a term by citing subclasses.

DEFINITION BY GENUS AND SPECIFIC DIFFERENCE: a common form of connotative definition whose definiendum is a class name and whose definiens is a class name plus a property term. The class denoted by the class name in the definiens is purported to be a genus with respect to the class denoted by the definiendum, and the property term in the definiens is purported to designate a property that belongs to all members of the class denoted by the definiendum and that distinguishes them from all other members of the genus. (For example, 'Man is a rational animal.')

DEFINITIONAL PROPOSITION: a proposition whose truth or falsity can be fully determined from a knowledge of its propositional form and the cognitive meaning of the categorematic terms used to express it. (Definitional propositions are contrasted with formal propositions and material propositions.)

DE MORGAN'S LAWS: the elementary rules of replacement

(1) $-(p \cdot q) \leftrightarrow (-p \vee -q)$, $-(p \cdot q \cdot r) \leftrightarrow (-p \vee -q \vee -r)$, etc.

(2) $-(p \vee q) \leftrightarrow (-p \cdot -q)$, $-(p \vee q \vee r) \leftrightarrow (-p \cdot -q \cdot -r)$, etc.

The principles underlying these rules of replacement are respectively: (1) the negation of a conjunction has the same truth value as a disjunction whose disjuncts are negations of the conjuncts of the conjunction, and conversely; (2) the negation of a disjunction has the same truth value as a conjunction whose conjuncts are negations of the disjuncts of the disjunction, and conversely.

DENOTATION: the set of individuals a class term stands for.

DENOTATIVE DEFINITION: A definition designed to give an account of the meaning of a class term or its corresponding property term by acquainting us with instances in the denotation of the class term.

DENYING THE ANTECEDENT: the invalid argument form

$$p \rightarrow q$$
$$\frac{-p}{-q}$$

(See also FALLACY OF DENYING THE ANTECEDENT.)

DESIGNATUM: the property referred to by a property term.

DEVELOPMENTAL LAW OF NATURE: a law of nature used to explain the origin or development of some phenomenon.

DILEMMA: (1) the elementary valid argument form

$$(p \rightarrow q) \cdot (r \rightarrow s)$$
$$\frac{p \vee r}{q \vee s}$$

(2) the elementary valid rule of inference corresponding to the above argument form.

DIRECTIVE MEANING: A sentence has directive meaning insofar as it is a sign of a desire on the speaker's part to influence the behavior of others.

DISJUNCT: a first-order component of a disjunction.

DISJUNCTION: (1) a truth-functional compound proposition whose first-order components when expressed in standard sentence form are connected by the logical operator 'or'; (2) a sentence expressing a disjunction in sense 1; (3) an elementary valid rule of inference based on the following principle: if a disjunctive proposition and the negation of all but one of its disjuncts is given, we are authorized to infer the remaining disjunct; (4) an elementary valid argument form exemplifying this rule of inference. For example,

$$
\begin{array}{ccc}
\text{p} \vee \text{q} & \text{p} \vee \text{q} & \text{p} \vee \text{q} \vee \text{r} \\
-\text{p} & -\text{q} & -\text{p} \\
\hline
\text{q} & \text{p} & -\text{q} \\
 & & \hline
 & & \text{r}
\end{array}
$$

(See also INCLUSIVE DISJUNCTION and EXCLUSIVE DISJUNCTION.)

DISJUNCTIVE PROPERTY TERM: a complex property term whose components are linked with the word 'or.' (For example, 'being in rhyme or being in meter.')

DISTRIBUTION: the elementary rules of replacement

$$(1) \quad (p \cdot (q \vee r)) \leftrightarrow ((p \cdot q) \vee (q \cdot r))$$
$$(2) \quad (p \vee (q \cdot r)) \leftrightarrow ((p \vee q) \cdot (p \vee r))$$

DOUBLE NEGATION: the elementary rule of replacement

$$p \leftrightarrow --p$$

ELEMENTARY RULE OF REPLACEMENT: a tautologous biconditional propositional form insofar as it is considered as authorizing the replacement of either first-order component by the other when testing arguments for validity.

ELEMENTARY VALID ARGUMENT FORM: a valid argument form whose validity may be recognized with relatively little logical insight.

ELEMENTARY VALID RULE OF INFERENCE: a valid rule of inference corresponding to an elementary valid argument form which is used in proving the validity of complex or extended arguments.

EMOTIVE MEANING: (1) A term has emotive meaning if and only if its use is a sign that the speaker approves or disapproves of that which it names or designates. (2) A sentence has emotive meaning if and only if it is used to express the speaker's feelings or attitudes. (Sentences with emotive meaning are also said to be 'expressive.')

EMOTIVISM: a position in moral philosophy according to which general definitions of moral terms are purely or essentially persuasive.

EMPTY CLASS: see NULL SET.

EVOCATIVE MEANING: A sentence has evocative meaning insofar as it tends to arouse feelings in those to whom it is addressed.

EXCLUSIVE DISJUNCTION: a disjunction that is true if and only if one disjunct is true and the others false. (Exclusive disjunctions are opposed to inclusive disjunctions.)

EXISTENTIAL GENERALIZATION: a valid rule of inference used in proving the validity of arguments whose validity does not depend entirely upon truth-functional relationships among its non-compound propositions. The rule has three applications. It permits us to infer (1) that what is true of some one unnamed individual is true of at least one individual, (2) that what is true of some one named individual is true of at least one individual, and (3) that what is true of any arbitrarily selected individual is true of at least one individual.

EXISTENTIAL IMPORT: A proposition has existential import insofar as it affirms the existence of its subject. (For example, 'Some men are heroes' has existential import since a part of its intended cognitive meaning is to posit the existence of men.)

EXISTENTIAL PROPOSITION: (1) a proposition with existential import (For example, 'Some men are heroes.'); (2) a proposition that functions exclusively as an assertion of existence (For example, 'Men exist' and 'There are men.')

EXISTENTIAL QUANTIFIER: one of the logical constants '$(\exists x)$,' '$(\exists y)$,' '$(\exists z)$.' (The chief use of the existential quantifier is to replace the logical operator 'some' in symbolizing particular propositions expressed in standard sentence form.)

EXISTENTIAL SPECIFICATION: a valid rule of inference used in proving the validity of arguments whose validity does not depend entirely upon truth-functional relationships among their non-compound propositions. It authorizes us to infer that what is true of at least one individual is true of at least one unnamed individual.

EXPERIMENTAL DEFINITION: a judicative definition designed to render whatever the definiendum named or designated more amenable to experimental manipulation or more readily available to competent observers.

EXPERIMENTAL GROUP: a set of observed instances cited in support of a law of nature in which the asserted condition is present. (For example, if we are trying to establish the law of nature 'Smoking is a cause of lung cancer,' our experimental group would be a set of smokers.)

EXPLANATORY ARGUMENT: an argument by subsumption designed to explain, rather than to confirm, the conclusion or a non-deductive argument otherwise like an argument by subsumption designed to serve the same purpose. (See also COMPLETE EXPLANATORY ARGUMENT and INCOMPLETE EXPLANATORY ARGUMENT.)

EXPLICANDUM: a fact which some hypothesis is believed to explain.

EXPLICATIVE DEFINITION: a definition whose definiens is purported to be an explicative synonym of the definiendum. (Explicative definitions are also called more simply 'explications.')

EXPLICATIVE SYNONYM: a term with the same cognitive meaning as a second that may be used to analyze or explain the meaning of the second. (For example, 'closed plane figure with exactly three sides' is an explicative synonym of 'triangle.' See also NONEXPLICATIVE SYNONYMS.)

EXPORTATION: the elementary rule of replacement

$$((p \cdot q) \rightarrow r) \leftrightarrow (p \rightarrow (q \rightarrow r))$$

EXPRESSIVE MEANING: A sentence has expressive meaning insofar as it is a sign of the speaker's feelings or attitudes.

EXTENSION: see DENOTATION.

FACT: (1) an actual event or state of affairs (as opposed to something imaginary, legendary, fictional, etc.); (2) a proposition deemed sufficiently well-confirmed that there is no practical need for further evidence to support it (as opposed to an hypothesis); (3) a proposition affirming that something is or is not the case (as opposed to value judgments, or assertions relating to what ought or ought not to be the case); (4) A material or definitional proposition (as opposed to a formal proposition).

FAIR SAMPLE: a sample of a given class which is believed to offer a sound basis for generalizations about the class as a whole. To determine the relative fairness of two samples of a given class one invokes the following meaning criteria: (a) size of sample, (b) number of significant subclasses represented, (c) number of instances representing each significant subclass.

FALLACY: (1) a widely held but false belief; (2) an inference involving the mistaken judgment that certain premises give either more or less support for a conclusion than is in fact the case; (3) an argument or an argument form having some feature that tends to encourage fallacious inferences. (In logic the term is most often used in sense 2 or 3.)

FALLACY OF AFFIRMING THE CONSEQUENT: (1) the invalid argument form

$$\begin{array}{c} p \rightarrow q \\ \underline{q} \\ p \end{array}$$

(2) the fallacious inference that an argument of the form above is a valid deductive argument. (Note that many arguments having this invalid form are nonetheless sound probable arguments.)

FALLACY OF ARGUING BESIDE THE POINT: an informal fallacy of relevance committed when two different issues become confused and an argument in support of one is mistakenly inferred to be an argument in support of the second.

FALLACY OF ARGUING IN A CIRCLE: see FALLACY OF BEGGING THE QUESTION.

FALLACY OF BEGGING THE QUESTION: an informal fallacy whose conclusion is itself a premise, either explicitly or implicitly.

FALLACY OF COMPOSITION: an informal linguistic fallacy involving the mistaken inference that a property belonging to each member of a group or class must belong to the group or class as a whole.

FALLACY OF DENYING THE ANTECEDENT: (1) the invalid argument form

$$\frac{\begin{array}{l} p \rightarrow q \\ -p \end{array}}{-q}$$

(2) the fallacious inference that an argument of the form above is a valid deductive argument.

FALLACY OF DIVISION: an informal linguistic fallacy involving the mistaken inference that a property belonging to a class or group as a whole necessarily belongs to every member individually.

FALLACY OF EQUIVOCATION: an informal linguistic fallacy committed when (a) some crucial term in an argument has two or more cognitive meanings, (b) the soundness of the argument depends upon the term's being used with the same cognitive meaning throughout, and (c) the component propositions in the argument are implausible unless the term is interpreted as having different cognitive meanings in different occurrences.

FALLACY OF FALSE PRECISION: the mistaken inference that a proposition is more accurate than it really is simply because it is expressed in precise mathematical language.

FALLACY OF ILLEGITIMATE APPEAL TO AUTHORITY: a fallacious argument or inference occasioned by the mistaken belief that some individual or group who supports a given position on some issue has greater competence to pass on that issue than is in fact the case.

FALLACY OF NEGLECTED ASPECT: an argument believed to be more sound than it actually is because some factor or factors relevant to the conclusion have been overlooked.

FALLACY OF RELEVANCE: an informal fallacy in which either relevant premises are omitted or irrelevant premises introduced.

FALLACY OF WISHFUL THINKING: the mistaken inference that an argument is either more sound (or weaker) than it actually is because we wish the conclusion to be true (or false).

FALSE CONVERSION: a formal fallacy with one of the following three argument forms:

$$\frac{(x)(\phi x \rightarrow \psi x)}{(x)(\psi x \rightarrow \phi x)}$$

$$\frac{(\exists x)(\phi x \cdot -\psi x)}{(\exists x)(\psi x \cdot -\phi x)}$$

$$\frac{p \rightarrow q}{q \rightarrow p}$$

FALSE QUESTION: *A question designed to encourage the fallacious inference that something is the case simply because the question presupposes that it is the case. (For example, 'When did you stop beating your wife?')*

FIRST-ORDER COMPONENT: (1) a component of a truth-functional compound proposition that is directly relevant to the determination of the truth value of the proposition as a whole; (2) a sentence expressing a first-order component in sense 1.

FORMAL FALLACY: (1) an invalid argument form that has some superficial resemblance to a valid argument form; (2) an invalid argument that tends to express or occasion fallacious inferences because its logical form resembles that of a valid argument form.

FORMAL LOGIC: see DEDUCTIVE LOGIC.

FORMAL PROPOSITION: a proposition whose truth value can be determined from a knowledge of its propositional form alone.

FUNCTIONAL DEPENDENCE, LAW OF: a law of nature relating every variation in the degree to which one property is present in a given phenomenon to a variation in the degree to which a second property is present in that phenomenon.

FUNCTIONAL LAW OF NATURE: a law of nature used to explain some phenomenon by showing some purpose or end to which it contributes.

GENERALITY: (1) A class term is general relative to a second if and only if the second term has all of the defining properties of the first and in addition one or more other defining properties. (2) A property term is general if and only if its corresponding class term is general. (3) A definition is general with respect to a second if and only if the second provides an analysis of the definiens of the first. (Generality is contrasted with specificity.)

GENERALIZATION: (1) an argument based on the inference that something true of one or more members of a certain class is also true of one or more other members of that class; (2) a law of nature, either approximate or non-approximate.

GENETIC LAW OF NATURE: a law of nature used to explain the origin or development of some phenomenon.

GENUS: One class is a genus relative to a second if and only if the second has all of the defining properties of the first and in addition one or more defining properties, called 'specific differences,' that distinguish members of the second from other members of the first. (A class with respect to which a genus is a genus is called a subclass, or species. The plural of 'genus' is 'genera.')

GROSS CONDITION: a vaguely defined phenomenon cited in an approximate law of nature.

HYPOTHESIS: (1) a proposition for which the evidence is deemed sufficiently strong to warrant further investigation but not sufficiently strong to warrant more than tentative acceptance; (2) *a proposition expressed with the aid of a theoretical term.*

HYPOTHETICAL CONFIRMATORY ARGUMENT: an argument of the form

$$\frac{\begin{array}{l} H \to E \\ E \end{array}}{H}$$

(where 'H' stands for an hypothesis and 'E' for an explicandum) used to confirm an hypothesis.

HYPOTHETICAL-DEDUCTIVE METHOD: *a method of inquiry which consists in asking what observable states of affairs would obtain if a given hypothesis were true and investigating to see whether these states of affairs do actually obtain. (This term, though widely used, is somewhat misleading, since an argument expressing the results of an application of this method will be either an argument by subsumption or else a hypothetical confirmatory or hypothetical disconfirmatory argument. Arguments by subsumption, however, are not hypothetical, and hypothetical confirmatory arguments are not deductive.)*

HYPOTHETICAL DISCONFIRMATORY ARGUMENT: an argument of the form

$$\frac{\begin{array}{l} H \to S \\ -S \end{array}}{-H}$$

(where 'H' stands for an hypothesis and 'S' for a proposition identifying some state of affairs whose nonoccurrence casts doubts on the hypothesis) used to disconfirm an hypothesis.

HYPOTHETICAL IMPLICATION: (1) an elementary valid rule of inference based on the following principle: if we are given any series of conditionals in which the antecedent of the second is the consequent of the first, the antecedent of the third (if there is a third) is a consequent of the second, etc., we are authorized to infer a conditional whose antecedent is the antecedent of the first and whose consequent is the consequent of the last; (2) an elementary valid argument form that exemplifies this rule of inference. For example,

$$
\begin{array}{ccc}
p \to q & p \to q & p \to q \\
q \to r & q \to r & q \to r \\
\hline
p \to r & r \to s & r \to s \\
& \hline
p \to s & s \to t \\
& & \hline
& & p \to t
\end{array}
$$

IMPLICATION: One proposition or set of propositions implies a second if and only if it gives evidence for the second. (See also NECESSARY IMPLICATION and PROBABLE IMPLICATION.)

IMPLICIT PREMISE: an unexpressed premise.

INCLUSIVE DISJUNCTION: a disjunction which is true if and only if at least one disjunct is true. (Inclusive disjunctions are contrasted with exclusive disjunctions.)

INCOMPLETE EXPLANATORY ARGUMENT: an explanatory argument whose premises do not necessarily imply the conclusion either because the laws of nature cited are approximate laws of nature or because the conclusion is too specific relative to the premises.

INCOMPLETE STRICT INTENSION: A term has an incomplete strict intension if and only if its set of defining properties does not give a reasonably full account of its meaning.

INDIVIDUAL CONSTANTS: the lower-case letters of the alphabet 'a' through 'w' used in propositional abbreviations to replace singular names.

INDIVIDUAL VARIABLES: the symbols 'x,' 'y,' and 'z' used to stand for any individual whatsoever in propositional forms and propositional abbreviations.

INDUCTION, PRINCIPLE OF: a rule by which we infer that if in a certain number of observed instances the presence or absence of one phenomenon has been uniformly associated with the presence or absence of a second, the presence or absence of the first is regularly associated with the presence or absence of the second in all instances whether observed or unobserved.

INDUCTIVE ARGUMENT: *(1) an argument based on the principle of induction; (2) a non-deductive, or probable, argument.*

INDUCTIVE LOGIC: *(1) that branch of logic which is concerned with arguments based on the principle of induction; (2) that branch of logic which is concerned with non-deductive, or probable, arguments; (3) that branch of logic which is concerned with evaluating the soundness (as opposed to merely the validity) of arguments.*

INFERENCE: a mental process culminating in the belief that one or more propositions assumed to be true give evidence for some other proposition.

INFERRED ANALOGY: a property imputed to the subject of the conclusion in an analogical argument.

INFORMAL FALLACY: a fallacy that is not a formal fallacy. (See FORMAL FALLACY.)

INTENSION: see TOTAL INTENSION.

INTRANSITIVE TERM: A relational term is intransitive if when we know that X is related to Y and Y to Z by virtue of the property designated by the term we can infer that X does not stand in the same relation to Z.

INVALIDITY: (1) An argument is invalid if and only if it is alleged to be deductive and its logical form is such that it is possible for the conjunction of the premises to be true and the conclusion false. (2) An argument form is invalid if and only if there is an argument having that form with true premises and a false conclusion. (3) *An argument is invalid if and only if it is an instance of an invalid argument form (whether it is alleged to be deductive or not).*

JUDICATIVE DEFINITION: a redefinition of a term already in use introduced either to facilitate inquiry or to incorporate the results of inquiry into language. (See also WORKING DEFINITIONS and TERMINAL DEFINITIONS.)

LABILITY: (1) A class term is labile if and only if there is some class of users who are confused or undecided as to whether some property is most properly classified as a defining property, a meaning criterion, or a contingent property of the term. (2) A sentence is labile if and only if there is some class of users who are confused or undecided about whether it should be classified as a definitional sentence or a material sentence.

LAW OF NATURE: a material proposition affirming a universal relationship between at least two phenomena with an unlimited number of instances.

LINEAR VAGUENESS: (1) A class term is characterized by linear vagueness if and only if (a) the objects it denotes may be serially ordered according to the degree in which some defining property of that term is present; (b) this serial order is continuous with a more inclusive serial order of some related class term; and (c) there is no rule of usage specifying at what point in the continuum the less inclusive series is to be demarcated from the more inclusive series. (2) A property term is characterized by linear vagueness if and only if its corresponding class term is so characterized.

LINGUISTIC FALLACY: (1) an argument that tends to be improperly evaluated because of an ambiguity or other obscurity in its formulation; (2) a faulty inference occasioned by some ambiguity or obscurity in the formulation of a proposition.

LOGICAL CONSTANT: a logical operator or a punctuation mark used in propositional abbreviations or logical forms.

LOGICAL EQUIVALENCE: Two sentences are logically equivalent if and only if the assertion of their biconditionality is a tautology.

LOGICAL INCONSISTENCY: (1) A proposition is logically inconsistent if and only if it is a self-contradiction. (2) The premises of an argument are logically inconsistent if and only if their conjunction is a self-contradiction. (3) An argument is logically inconsistent if and only if the conjunction of its premises and its conclusion is a self-contradiction.

LOGICAL OPERATOR: (1) a standard logical operator in ordinary language or a syncategorematic term other than a standard logical operator used to serve a similar function; (2) a symbol used to replace a logical operator in sense 1 in propositional abbreviations and propositional forms.

LOGICAL VARIABLE: a propositional variable, a property variable, or an individual variable.

LOOSE INTENSION: the set of a class term's meaning criteria considered collectively.

MAJOR PREMISE: the premise in a syllogism that contains the major term.

MAJOR TERM: the predicate of the conclusion in a syllogism.

MATCHED SAMPLE: an experimental group and a control group representatively selected so as to include the same number of instances from each significant subclass.

MATERIAL IMPLICATION: a technical name for the truth function represented by the symbol of conditionality '→.'

MATERIAL PROPOSITION: a proposition whose truth value can not be determined without knowledge relating to whatever is denoted or designated by its categorematic terms. (Material propositions are distinguished from formal propositions and definitional propositions.)

MEANING CRITERION: (1) A meaning criterion of a class term is any property whose absence or presence in an object is relevant to a determination of the propriety of using that term to denote that object but whose absence is not a conclusive reason for excluding that object from the term's denotation. (2) A meaning criterion of a property term is a meaning criterion of its corresponding class term.

MIDDLE TERM: the categorematic term in a syllogism that appears twice in the premises.

MINOR PREMISE: the premise of a syllogism that contains the minor term.

MINOR TERM: the subject of the conclusion of a syllogism.

MODUS PONENS: (1) the elementary valid argument form

$$\frac{\begin{array}{c} p \rightarrow q \\ p \end{array}}{q}$$

(2) the elementary valid rule of inference corresponding to the above argument form.

MODUS TOLLENS: (1) the elementary valid argument form

$$\frac{\begin{array}{c} p \rightarrow q \\ -q \end{array}}{-p}$$

(2) the elementary valid rule of inference corresponding to the above argument form.

MORAL PRAGMATISM: a philosophical position according to which general moral definitions are essentially judicative and can be rationally justified by showing that behavior in accordance with them would result in a substantial reduction in painful conflicts of interest.

MORAL RULE: a moral judgment prescribing or forbidding a certain kind of behavior which is normally justified by an appeal to an ultimate moral principle.

NATURAL SIGN: a sign that is not an artificial sign. (See ARTIFICIAL SIGN.)

NECESSARY ARGUMENT: see DEDUCTIVE ARGUMENT.

NECESSARY CONDITION: (1) One phenomenon is a necessary condition of a second if the absence of the first is a reliable sign of the absence of the second. (2) One class of phenomena is a necessary condition of a second if the absence of a member of the first is a reliable sign of the absence of a member of the second.

NECESSARY IMPLICATION: One proposition or set of propositions necessarily implies a second if and only if it gives conclusive evidence for the second. (An argument expressing a necessary implication is a valid argument.)

NEGATION: a truth-functional compound proposition with a single first-order component which when expressed in standard sentence form either begins with the logical operator 'It is not the case that' or denies the truth of the first-order component by the use of the logical operator 'not.'

NOMINAL DEFINITION: (1) *a stipulative definition (as opposed to a reportive definition);* (2) *a reportive definition (as opposed to a judicative definition);* (3) *a nominative definition (as opposed to a judicative definition);* (4) *a synonymous definition (as opposed to a connotative definition).*

NOMINATIVE DEFINITION: A definition is nominative if and only if the definer introduces it for the purpose of naming or designating something for which he finds no adequate label already in existence.

NON SEQUITUR: *an argument whose premises do not imply the conclusion.*

NON-COGNITIVE MEANING: A phenomenon has non-cognitive meaning if and only if its occurrence permits us to make a reasonable inference concerning the existence or nature of some second phenomenon.

NON-COMPOUND: (1) a sentence that does not contain another sentence as a component; (2) a proposition expressed by a non-compound sentence.

NON-DEDUCTIVE ARGUMENT: (1) An argument is non-deductive if and only if the arguer believes that his premises give less than conclusive evidence for the conclusion. (2) *An argument is non-deductive if and only if its premises give less than conclusive evidence for the conclusion regardless of the arguer's beliefs.*

NON-EXPLICATIVE SYNONYMS: a pair of terms with the same cognitive meaning neither of which can be used to explain or analyze the meaning of the other. (For example, 'bashful' and 'shy.' Non-explicative synonyms are contrasted with explicative synonyms.)

NON-SYMMETRICAL TERM: A relational term is non-symmetrical if and only if the knowledge that it may correctly be attributed to one of the relata does not permit us to make any inference regarding the propriety of attributing it to the other relata.

NON-TRANSITIVE TERM: a relational term that is neither a transitive term nor an intransitive term.

NULL SET: the denotation of a class term that possesses no real members. (For example, the denotation of the class term 'centaur' is a null set.)

OBSERVATIONAL TERM: a term standing for something which may be immediately or directly experienced. (Observational terms are contrasted with theoretical terms.)

OPEN CLASS: a class whose members can not all be explicitly identified or enumerated.

OPERATIONAL DEFINITIONS: A subclass of contextual definitions in which a term is defined by specifying certain operations or tests that may be performed and certain observable results that must follow if the propositions expressed by a class of sentences containing this term are true.

OSTENSIVE DEFINITION: a form of denotative definition that involves pointing to one or more instances in the term's denotation.

PARADIGM CASE: (1) A paradigm case of a class term is an instance in its denotation which the users of that term easily recognize to be an instance and over whose inclusion in the term's denotation there is general agreement. (2) A paradigm case of a property term is a paradigm case in sense 1 of its corresponding class term.

PARADOXES OF MATERIAL IMPLICATION: the propositional forms

$$p \rightarrow (q \rightarrow p)$$
$$-p \rightarrow (p \rightarrow q)$$

PARAMETER: a term such as 'all places,' 'all times,' and 'all cases' used to express propositions in standard sentence form.

PARTICULAR PROPOSITION: a proposition expressed by a particular sentence.

PARTICULAR SENTENCE: a sentence whose subject is a class term and which is used to say that at least one individual in the denotation of its subject term possesses or lacks a given property. (When in standard sentence form a particular sentence begins with the logical operator 'some.')

PFRFORMATIVE MEANING: A sentence has performative meaning when it is more conspicuously an instance of doing than of saying. (For example, 'I now pronounce you man and wife.')

PERSUASIVE DEFINITION: a definition in which the definer exploits the emotive meaning of the definiendum or the definiens in order to arouse favorable or unfavorable attitudes toward something of which he personally approves or disapproves. (For example: 'Socialism' is economic democracy.)

PETITIO PRINCIPII: see FALLACY OF BEGGING THE QUESTION.

PICTORIAL MEANING: the ideas, images, or mental pictures that a term tends to evoke in the minds of its users or interpreters.

POST HOC; ERGO, PROPTER HOC: *the fallacious inference that simply because one event follows a second, the first event is a cause of* the second. (*The Latin means literally 'after the fact; therefore, because of the fact.'*)

PRAGMATIC CAUSAL LAW: a causal law that specifies a causal relationship of immediate practical importance in the light of some human need, goal, or interest.

PRE-ANALYTIC NOTION: an implicit understanding of a term that is not sufficient to insure fully correct use.

PREMISE: a proposition in an argument that the arguer offers as evidence for the conclusion.

PREMISED ANALOGY: a property asserted in the premises of an analogical argument to be common to all the individuals or classes involved.

PRINCIPLE OF INDUCTION: see INDUCTION, PRINCIPLE OF.

PROBABLE ARGUMENT: see NON-DEDUCTIVE ARGUMENT.

PROBABLE IMPLICATION: One proposition or set of propositions probably implies a second if and only if it gives reasonably good but less than conclusive evidence for the second.

PROPERTY CONSTANT: a capital letter of the alphabet 'A' through 'W' used to replace categorematic terms in propositional abbreviations.

PROPERTY NAME: a property term used to identify a subject of discourse.

PROPERTY TERM: a term used to stand for some trait or activity of individuals or classes.

PROPERTY VARIABLE: the Greek letters 'ϕ' and 'ψ' (*phi* and *psi*) used to replace categorematic terms in symbolizing the logical form of propositions.

PROPOSITION: the cognitive meaning, or assertive content, of a sentence.

PROPOSITIONAL ABBREVIATION: a formula used to symbolize a proposition.

PROPOSITIONAL CONSTANT: a capital letter of the alphabet 'A' through 'W' used to symbolize a proposition.

PROPOSITIONAL FORM: (1) the pattern of a class of propositions that may be symbolized with the aid of none but logical constants and logical variables; (2) a symbolic formula expressing a propositional form in sense 1.

PROPOSITIONAL VARIABLE: a lower-case letter of the alphabet 'p' through 'w' used in symbolizing propositional forms.

QUALITATIVE LAW: a law of nature saying that every instance of one property is an instance of a second property.

QUANTITATIVE LAW: a general term for statistical laws and laws of functional dependence.

RANDOM SAMPLE: a sample of a given class chosen unselectively, or without consideration for the significance or insignificance of the subclasses to which members of the sample belong. (See SIGNIFICANT SUBCLASS.)

REAL DEFINITION: (1) *a reportive definition (as opposed to a stipulative definition)*; (2) *a judicative definition (as opposed to a nominative definition)*; (3) *a judicative definition whose definiens cites "the essence" of the definiendum in some ill-defined metaphysical sense of that term.*

RECOMMENDATORY DEFINITION: a definition offered with the intent of securing the adoption of a certain cognitive meaning for a term.

RELATA: entities between which a relation holds. (The singular of 'relata' is 'relatum.')

RELATION: a designatum of a relational term.

RELATIONAL PROPOSITION: a proposition expressed by a sentence containing a relational term.

RELATIONAL TERM: a property term whose cognitive meaning is not clearly intelligible unless one assumes or presupposes the existence of more than one entity. (For example, 'is married to' or 'lies between.')

REPORTIVE DEFINITION: a definition offered in order to acquaint someone with the conventional cognitive meaning or meanings of a term.

REPRESENTATIVE SAMPLE: a sample of a given class chosen selectively so as to include members from significant subclasses.

RULE OF INFERENCE: see VALID RULE OF INFERENCE.

RULE OF REPLACEMENT: see ELEMENTARY RULE OF REPLACEMENT.

SECOND-ORDER COMPONENT: (1) a component of a truth-functional compound proposition that is directly relevant to the determination of the truth value of a first-order component but only indirectly relevant to the determination of the truth value of the proposition as a whole; (2) a sentence expressing a second-order component in sense 1.

SELF-CONTRADICTION: (1) a false proposition whose falsity can be fully determined from a knowledge of its logical form alone; (2) *either a self-contradiction in sense 1 or a definitional falsehood.* (See DEFINITIONAL PROPOSITION.)

SIGN: A phenomenon whose occurrence permits us to make a reasonable inference concerning the existence or nature of some second phenomenon.

SIGNIFICANT SUBCLASS: If 'C' stands for the class named by the subject of the conclusion of some argument from a fair sample and if 'E' stands for the phenomenon the conclusion says is universally related to C, then one subclass of C is more significant than a second if accumulated knowledge gives us reason to believe that the properties of the first are more relevant to E than the properties of the second.

SIMPLIFICATION: (1) an elementary valid rule of inference based on the following principle: if a conjunction is given, we are authorized to infer any of its conjuncts; (2) an elementary valid argument form exemplifying this rule of inference. For example,

$$\frac{p \cdot q}{p} \qquad \frac{p \cdot q}{q} \qquad \frac{p \cdot q \cdot r}{p} \qquad \frac{p \cdot q \cdot r}{q}$$

SINGULAR MORAL JUDGMENT: a moral judgment whose subject is a singular name.

SINGULAR NAME: a verbal token used to refer to a single individual, either real or imaginary. (This term is also used loosely to refer to verbal types whose tokens are conventionally used as singular names.)

SINGULAR PROPOSITION: a proposition expressed by a sentence whose subject is a singular name.

SORITES: a series of syllogisms in which the conclusion of the first is a premise of the second; the conclusion of the second, a premise of the third (if there is one); etc.

SOUNDNESS: An argument is sound when (1) it is clearly expressed, (2) its premises give evidence for the conclusion, and (3) there is reason to believe that the premises are true.

SPECIES: see SUBCLASS.

SPECIFIC DIFFERENCE: a defining property of a class term that distinguishes the members of the class term's denotation from the members of some more comprehensive class.

SPECIFICITY: (1) A class term is specific relative to a second if and only if it has all of the defining properties of the second and in addition one or more other defining properties. (2) A property term is specific relative to a second if and only if its corresponding class term is specific relative to the corresponding class term of the second. (3) A definition is specific relative to a second if and only if it provides an analysis of the definiens of the second. (Specificity is contrasted with generality.)

STANDARD LOGICAL OPERATOR: (1) a syncategorematic term used in symbolizing a proposition expressed in standard sentence form; (2) a symbol used to replace a logical operator in sense 1 in propositional abbreviations and propositional forms.

STANDARD SENTENCE FORMS: a relatively small set of sentences in ordinary language that clearly exhibit certain logical features of the propositions they express and that are conventionally used to facilitate the analysis and evaluation of arguments in which these propositions occur.

STATISTICAL CORRELATION: a particular proposition stating that a certain percentage of members in some closed class has a given property.

STATISTICAL LAW: a quantitative law of nature stating that every complex phenomenon of a given kind has a certain percentage of components with some property that distinguishes them from the other components.

STEREOTYPED THINKING: (1) a tendency to characterize an individual or a class in terms of a limited number of properties and to ignore other properties that are important to an understanding of the individual or class in its uniqueness or specificity; (2) *a tendency to ascribe to all members of a class properties that are believed to characterize most members.*

STIPULATIVE DEFINITION: a definition announcing a personal or group resolve to use a term with a certain cognitive meaning.

STRICT INTENSION: the set of a class term's defining properties considered collectively.

STRONG DISJUNCTION: see EXCLUSIVE DISJUNCTION.

SUBCLASS: One class is a subclass relative to a second if and only if it has all of the defining properties of the second and in addition one or more defining properties, called 'specific differences,' that distinguish its members from other members of the second. (The class with respect to which a subclass is a subclass is called in logic a 'genus.' The term 'species' when used in logic is a synonym for 'subclass.')

SUBTYPE: a class of tokens of an ambiguous term-type corresponding to one of this term's strict intensions.

SUFFICIENT CONDITION: (1) One phenomenon is a sufficient condition of a second if the presence of the first is a reliable sign of the presence of the second. (2) One class of phenomena is a sufficient condition of a second if the presence of a member of the first is a reliable sign of the presence of a member of the second.

SYLLOGISM: an argument consisting of exactly two premises and containing exactly three categorematic terms.

SYMBOLIC LOGIC: one or more of several logical systems devised by a number of philosophers and mathematicians in the nineteenth and twentieth centuries which differ from traditional Aristotelian logic by their extensive use of special symbols and by their usefulness in analyzing arguments that are not syllogisms.

SYMMETRICAL TERM: A relational term is symmetrical if and only if the knowledge that it may be correctly attributed to one of the relata permits us to infer that it may also be attributed to the others.

SYNCATEGOREMATIC TERM: a term that is not a categorematic term. (See CATEGOREMATIC TERM.)

SYNONYMOUS DEFINITION: a reportive definition whose definiens and definiendum are non-explicative synonyms. (Synonymous definitions are contrasted with connotative definitions, whose definiens are explicative synonyms of the definienda.)

SYNONYMY: Two terms are synonymous if and only if both have the same cognitive meaning.

SYSTEMATIC CLASSIFICATION: A classification is systematic if and only if the subclasses cited are mutually exclusive, that is, if no individual is a member of more than one of the subclasses.

TAUTOLOGY: (1) a true proposition whose truth can be fully determined from a knowledge of its logical form alone; (2) *a tautology in sense 1 that is also truth-functional;* (3) *a tautology in sense 1 or a true definitional proposition;* (4) the elementary rules of replacement

$$(1) \quad p \leftrightarrow (p \vee p)$$
$$(2) \quad p \leftrightarrow (p \cdot p)$$

TELEOLOGICAL LAW OF NATURE: a law of nature used to explain a phenomenon by showing that it contributes to some purpose or end.

TERM: a linguistic unit of less than sentence length with cognitive meaning.

TERMINAL DEFINITION: a judicative definition introduced to incorporate the results of inquiry into language.

THEORETICAL DEFINITION: a definition that contains a theoretical term.

THEORETICAL LAW: a law of nature expressed with the aid of a theoretical term.

THEORETICAL TERM: a term that stands for something that is not immediately or directly experienced but which is believed to be useful in explaining something that is immediately or directly experienced.

THEORY: *(1) an hypothesis; (2) an explanation of some phenomenon in theoretical terms; (3) a complex set of related propositions used to explain a large number of phenomena.*

TOKEN AMBIGUITY: A verbal token is ambiguous if and only if it is a member of an ambiguous verbal type and·the context of its utterance does not make clear which of the type's conventional meanings is intended.

TOTAL INTENSION: the defining properties, meaning criteria, and contingent properties of a class term considered collectively.

TRANSITIVE TERM: A relational term is transitive if and only if, when we know that X is related to Y and that Y is related to Z by virtue of the property designated, we can infer that X stands in the same relationship to Z.

TRANSPOSITION: the elementary rule of replacement

$$(p \rightarrow q) \leftrightarrow (-q \rightarrow -p)$$

TRUTH FUNCTION: (1) A compound proposition is a truth function if and only if its truth value can be wholly determined from a knowledge of the truth value of its components. (2) An argument is a truth-function if and only if its validity or invalidity can be wholly determined from a knowledge of the truth values of its non-compound components.

TRUTH TABLE: a diagram that gives an exhaustive list of the possible combinations of truth values for a given set of propositions. Truth tables are used (1) to define logical operators, (2) to determine whether a given truth-functional compound proposition is tautologous, self-contradictory, or factual, and (3) to determine whether truth-functional compound arguments are valid or invalid.

TRUTH-FUNCTIONAL COMPOUND: (1) a compound proposition whose truth value can be wholly determined from a knowledge of the truth value of its components; (2) a compound sentence that expresses a truth-functional compound in sense 1.

TRUTH-FUNCTIONAL VALIDITY: An argument is truth-functionally valid if and only if its validity follows wholly from truth-functional relationships among its non-compound components. An argument is truth-functionally invalid if and only if it is not valid by virtue of truth-functional relationships among its non-compound components. (Any argument that is truth-functionally valid is valid without qualification; but an argument that is truth-functionally invalid may nonetheless be valid by virtue of logical features characterizing its non-compound components.)

TYPE AMBIGUITY: A verbal type is ambiguous if and only if it has two or more conventional cognitive meanings.

ULTIMATE MORAL PRINCIPLE: a moral judgment that is more general than a moral rule and normally functions as a definition of a key moral concept.

UNIVERSAL GENERALIZATION: A valid rule of inference used in proving the validity of arguments whose validity does not depend entirely upon truth-functional relationships among their non-compound components. The rule authorizes the inference that what is true of any arbitrarily selected individual is true of all individuals.

UNIVERSAL PROPOSITION: a proposition expressed by a universal sentence.

UNIVERSAL QUANTIFIER: one of the logical constants '(x),' '(y),' or '(z).' (The chief use of universal quantifiers is to replace the logical operators 'all' and 'no' in symbolizing universal propositions expressed in standard sentence form.)

UNIVERSAL SENTENCE: a sentence whose subject is a class term and which says that all individuals in the denotation of its subject term possess or lack a given property. (When in standard sentence form a universal sentence begins with the standard logical operators 'all' or 'no.')

UNIVERSAL SPECIFICATION: a valid rule of inference used in proving the validity of arguments whose validity does not depend entirely on truth-functional relationships among their non-compound components. The rule has three applications. It authorizes the inference (1) that whatever is true of all individuals is true of any one named individual, (2) that what is true of all individuals is true of any arbitrarily selected individual, and (3) that what is true of all individuals is true of at least one individual.

USER AMBIGUITY: (1) A class term or a singular name is characterized by user ambiguity if and only if it is employed by different classes of users with two or more different strict intensions in similar contexts. (2) A property term is characterized by user ambiguity if and only if its corresponding class term is so characterized.

UTILITARIAN PRINCIPLE: an ultimate moral principle according to which one ought always to act so as to promote the greatest happiness of the greatest number.

VAGUENESS: (1) A class term is vague if and only if it denotes a range of phenomena without exact boundaries. (2) A property term is vague if and only if its corresponding class term is vague. (3) A singular name is vague if and only if it refers to a complex entity whose spatio-temporal span can not be precisely delimited or whose components can not be readily determined. (4) A sentence is vague if and only if it contains a vague class term, property term, or singular name. (See also VAGUENESS OF FAMILY RESEMBLANCE and LINEAR VAGUENESS.)

VAGUENESS OF FAMILY RESEMBLANCE: (1) A class term exhibits vagueness of family resemblance if and only if (a) at least one of its defining properties is a disjunctive property whose components are meaning criteria, (b) candidates for inclusion in its denotation may be arranged serially according to the number of component meaning criteria they possess, and (c) there is no rule of usage specifying how many of these components must be present. (2) A property term exhibits vagueness of family resemblance if and only if its corresponding class term does.

VALID RULE OF INFERENCE: a rule of inference corresponding to a valid argument form which authorizes an inference from propositions with the logical features symbolized by the premises of the argument form to a proposition with the logical features symbolized by the conclusion of the argument form. (See also ELEMENTARY VALID RULE OF INFERENCE.)

VALIDITY: (1) An argument is valid if and only if it is alleged to be deductive and its logical form is such that it is impossible for the conjunction of the premises to be true and the conclusion false. (2) An argument form is valid if there is no argument of that form with true premises and a false conclusion. (3) *An argument is valid if and only if it is an instance of a valid argument form (whether it is alleged to be deductive or not).* (In popular discourse 'validity' is often used as a synonym for 'soundness.')

VARIABLES: (1) properties related to one another by laws of functional dependence; (2) gross conditions or possible explanations of some phenomenon; (3) logical variables.

VERBAL TOKEN: a member of a verbal type.

VERBAL TYPE: a class of verbal tokens. For example,

chair
chair
chair

are three members of the same verbal type.

WEAK DISJUNCTION: see INCLUSIVE DISJUNCTION.

WORKING DEFINITION: a judicative definition introduced to prepare the way for inquiry.

Index

Abbott, Lawrence, 145
Abel, I. W., 96
Abele, von, Rudolph, 368
Abstractness, 49–50, 51, 154–56
Abusive ad hominem, 186–87
Ad hominem
  abusive, 186–87
  circumstantial, 185
Addition (rule of inference), 210, 212, 214
Affirming the consequent, 203–04
  fallacy of, 181
Alston, William P., 122
Ambiguity
  defining ambiguous terms, 106
  of class terms, 41–43
  of property terms, 50
  of sentences, 91
  of singular names, 51
  preliminary characterization of, 7–9, 14–15
  subtypes of ambiguous terms, 43
  ways of avoiding, 156–57
Amphiboly, 91
Analogical arguments, 274–79
  similarity to hypothetical confirmatory arguments, 298–99
  in ethics, 364–65
Analogical bases, 275
Analogical models, 277
Analogical subjects, 275
Antecedents (of conditional propositions), 60

Approximate laws of functional dependence, 331–32
Approximate laws of nature, 259–261
Ardrey, Robert, 141–42, 193–94, 307–08, 339–40
Arendt, Hannah, 160
Arguing beside the point, fallacy of, 185–86
Arguing in a circle, fallacy of, 189
Argument forms, 171, 172, 180, 205. *See also* Elementary valid argument forms
Argumentative discourse, 173–74
Arguments
  analogical, 274–79; similarity to hypothetical confirmatory arguments, 298–99; in ethics, 364–65
  by elimination, 293, 301–05
  by subsumption, 292, 293–97, 302, 317–19
  complete explanatory, 317–18
  corresponding conditionals of, 171–72, 204
  deductive: definition of, 175–79; testing for validity of, 201–24, 231–46
  explanatory, 317–19
  from analogical models, 277–79
  from fair samples, 266–71
  from statistical correlations, 271–74

Emotive meaning (cont.)
and persuasive definitions, 132–34
of sentences, 93, 94
of terms, 18–19
Emotivism, 356–58
Empty classes, 26
Engels, Friedrich, 144
Equivocation, fallacy of, 187–88
Evocative meaning, 93, 94
Exclusive disjunctions, 60, 112
Existential generalization, 235–37
Existential import, 70–71, 72
Existential propositions, 71–72
Existential quantifier, 69
Existential specification, 235, 237–38
Experimental groups, 272–74
Experimental definitions, 137–38
Explanatory arguments, 317–19
Explicanda, 297–98
Explicative definitions, 115
Explicative synonyms, 109
symbolizing in arguments, 242–43
Exportation (rule of replacement), 217
Extension. *See* Denotation
Eysenck, H. J., 125–26, 313–14

Factual propositions, 87, 291–92, 352
Fair samples. *See* Arguments from fair samples
Fallacies, 179–92
black and white, 190–92
formal, 181–83
informal, 181, 183–92
linguistic, 183, 187–92
of affirming the consequent, 181
of arguing beside the point, 185–86
of arguing in a circle, 189
of begging the question, 189
of composition, 188–89
of denying the antecedent, 181–82
of division, 188
of equivocation, 187–88
of false conversion, 182–83
of false precision, 190
of illegitimate appeal to authority, 187
of neglected aspect, 184
of relevance, 183–87
of wishful thinking, 185
False conversion, fallacy of, 182–83

False precision, fallacy of, 190
First-order components (of truth-functional compounds), 62
Fiske, Edward B., 376–77
Formal fallacies, 181–83
Formal propositions, 77, 78–89
Fraser, James George, 122
Functional dependence, laws of, 258, 330–32
Functional laws, 321

Galdston, Iago, 285
Galilei, Galileo, 259, 294–95, 322–24, 326, 331
General definitions, 114–15
General laws, 257–29
Generality, 45–47, 50, 51, 154–56
Genetic laws, 320
Goodman, Paul, 97
Gregory, Dick, 18
Gross conditions, 261

Harrington, Michael, 144–47
Herodotus, 309–12
Hilgard, Ernest R., 121, 123, 151
Hospers, John, 367–68
Hubben, William, 161
Hunt, H. L., 150, 164–65
Huxley, Aldous, 347
Huxley, T. H., 197–98
Hyman, Herbert, 284–85
Hypothetical confirmatory arguments, 292–93, 297–301
Hypothetical disconfirmatory arguments, 302–03
Hypothetical implication (rule of inference), 213
Hypotheses, 291–92

Illegitimate appeal to authority, fallacy of, 187
Implicit premises, 174
Implicitly relational terms, 23, 157
Inclusive disjunctions, 60
Incomplete explanatory arguments, 318–19
Incomplete strict intension, 106–07
Individual constants, 72
Individual variables, 69
Induction, principle of, 266
Inference, 173–74. *See also* Elementary valid argument forms